A Comprehensive Guide to
SPORTS SKILLS TESTS
AND MEASUREMENT

A Comprehensive Guide to
SPORTS SKILLS TESTS
AND MEASUREMENT

By

D. RAY COLLINS, Ed.D.

Professor and Chairman
Division of Health Technology and Physical Education
J. Sargeant Reynolds Community College
Richmond, Virginia

and

PATRICK B. HODGES, Ph.D.

Associate Professor and Chairman
Department of Physical Education and Athletics
Sinclair Community College
Dayton, Ohio

CHARLES C THOMAS · PUBLISHER
Springfield · Illinois · U.S.A.

Published and Distributed Throughout the World by

CHARLES C THOMAS • PUBLISHER

Bannerstone House

301-327 East Lawrence Avenue, Springfield, Illinois, U.S.A.

© *1978, by* CHARLES C THOMAS • PUBLISHER

ISBN 0-398-03745-0

Library of Congress Catalog Card Number: 77-12924

Library of Congress Cataloging in Publication Data

Collins, D. Ray.
  A comprehensive guide to sports skills tests and measurement.

  Bibliography: p.
  1. Athletic ability. I. Hodges, Patrick B., joint
author. II. Title.
GV436.C58   796'.07   77-12924
ISBN 0-398-03745-0

Printed in the United States of America

C-1

To Our Wives, Phyllis and Sue

Foreword

EVALUATION IS AN ESSENTIAL feature of the teaching profession. It is only through evaluation that the teacher can determine the extent to which the program's objectives are being met. Evaluation is a broad concept, involving a variety of sources of information concerning the student and the program. Obviously, the intelligent utilization and interpretation of tests and measurements are integral components of the evaluation process.

Numerous tests and measurements are available to physical education teachers for various purposes such as for grading, classification, diagnosis, assessment of status and progress, and for research. Unfortunately, many teachers fail to avail themselves of these valuable sources of information through complacency, lethargy, or ignorance. In fact, over the years some of the harshest criticism of physical education has centered around inadequate and/or unsound methods of evaluation.

A major objective of physical education is the development of neuromuscular skills. Included in this objective is the acquisition of sports skills. It is imperative then that the truly professional teacher select and utilize valid means by which to assess progress in meeting this objective. Sports skills tests can be effectively employed as a part of the evaluation process. Quite a number of sports skills tests have been developed and reported in theses, dissertations, various journals, and measurement and evaluation textbooks. A volume that is solely devoted to a compilation of sports skills tests, such as this work by Drs. Collins and Hodges, should be of immense value to the physical education teacher. As was mentioned earlier, reasons often cited for failure to employ tests and measurements include ignorance as to the existence of resources and lethargy with regard to the search for them. Moreover, the authors have endeavored to further assist the reader in decision making by providing a review of criteria for test selection, plus help-

vii

ful administrative considerations and comments concerning each test's salient features.

Sports skills tests can be used to good advantage as teaching aids, not only in assessing pupil progress but also in serving as drills to practice basic skills, and as a means to maximally utilize available space and teaching stations. Furthermore, sports skills tests can be employed productively in athletics as well as physical education.

It is believed that *A Comprehensive Guide to Sports Skills Tests and Measurement* represents a significant contribution to the literature and should aid in a more thorough and effective evaluation of sports performance.

JACK K. NELSON
Louisiana State University
Baton Rouge, Louisiana

Preface

IN OVER TWENTY YEARS of combined teaching and administrative experience in physical education, we have noted that instructors of activity courses make too little use of the many excellent sports skills tests in existence. Lack of accessibility is thought to be one of the reasons why instructors do not use them more commonly. Prior to this publication, a comprehensive compilation of scientifically assessed sports skills tests has not been available to physical education instructors for ready reference in test selection. As a result, only the most resourceful and ambitious physical educators have tended to delve into sources such as measurement textbooks, master's theses, doctoral dissertations, and research periodicals in an effort to locate tests that merit utilization. It is our hope that this reference guide will not only fill the long-standing void in the professional literature but will also find ready acceptance and use among public school and college physical education instructors.

Skills tests for twenty-six sports are found in the book. The order of test presentation for each sport is chronological except in some of the cases where modifications follow an original test. A few tests herein have not been fully authenticated in value, but certain unique features they possess justify their inclusion. Also, some tests may appear questionable in value but are considered to be the best available for particular sports and give basis for further test development or revision. A total of 103 sports skills tests appear in the book along with 83 illustrations and 127 tables.

An instructor's professional development is also served by this text. There are limitless opportunities for the enterprising physical educator to either revise existing skills tests or develop new ones. Throughout the book we have cited the most urgent needs for scientific research in skills tests development and revision.

Each chapter's bibliographical entry transcends the number of actual tests presented there. Our objective was to include references for all sports skills tests ever constructed, both authenticated and unauthenticated. To the best of our knowledge, this is the most complete reference listing on sports skills tests and measurement.

D. RAY COLLINS
PATRICK B. HODGES

Acknowledgments

WE ARE DEEPLY INDEBTED to Dr. Joseph Lisowski, English professor at J. Sargeant Reynolds Community College, for his constructive criticism of the writing style reflected in this textbook. Appreciation for the development of the many illustrations located throughout the text is extended to Sandra Preston and John Edwards. A special recognition goes to Pearline Harmon, reference librarian at J. Sargeant Reynolds Community College, and secretaries Lois Harden and Linda Utley of that institution for the cooperative attitude they displayed in fulfilling an extensive number of interlibrary loan requests. Gratitude is also expressed to the authors of the many sources from which the tests were derived and to those authors and publishers who permitted tables and illustrations to be reproduced.

Contents

A Comprehensive Guide to
SPORTS SKILLS TESTS
AND MEASUREMENT

Chapter 1

Introduction

HISTORICAL OVERVIEW

A LTHOUGH REFERRED TO as general motor ability tests, the Athletic Badge Tests of 1913 are generally recognized as the first sports skills tests ever devised. Developed by the Playground and Recreation Association of America, the tests included items from baseball, basketball, tennis, and volleyball.[5] Shortly thereafter, a succession of similar tests were constructed. Reilly's[18] test of 1916 consisted of baseball, basketball, golf, and tennis items. In 1918, Hetherington developed a decathlon of athletic events.[5]

Construction of sports skills tests accelerated after 1920 during a time when physical education was shifting toward a greater emphasis in that phase of instruction. Brace's[6] basketball test of 1924 is credited as the initial sports skills test battery for the field of physical education. Other notable examples of skills tests that were completed in the 1920s include two for the sport of tennis. An experimental study by Beall[4] in 1925 was conducted to determine a suitable test battery for the sport, and another battery was introduced in 1926 by Anderson.[1]

Sports skills testing became more sophisticated in the 1930s with the advent of tests developed by scientific procedures. Many quality tests have been developed in the last forty years; the majority of them are presented in this textbook.

Recognition of the need to standardize skills tests on a national level prompted the Research Council of the former American Association for Health, Physical Education and Recreation to initiate in 1959 what was called the *Sports Skills Test Project,* under the chairmanship of Frank D. Sills.[16] Since that time, test manuals have been developed for football (1965), basketball and softball for boys and girls (1966), archery for both sexes (1967), and volleyball for males and females (1969). The original goal

3

was to construct manuals for at least fifteen sports activities. Notwithstanding the absence of new manuals in recent years, interest in the project still remains as reflected by the comprehensive critique of existing tests which was completed in 1976 under the direction of the Measurement and Evaluation Council of the American Alliance for Health, Physical Education and Recreation.[16] Reference is made to certain aspects of the Sports Skills Test Project elsewhere in the book.

Promotion of the national sports skills standards could have influenced independent investigators because the period of the 1960s is regarded as the most prolific decade in the better than half-century history of skills tests investigation.

APPLICATION OF SPORTS SKILLS TESTS

There are at least nine reasons for using skills tests. A discussion of each follows.

MEASUREMENT OF ACHIEVEMENT: The primary purpose of skills tests is to measure student progress or level of achievement. Assessment of a course's content and methodology is largely dependent upon test results.

- GRADING OR MARKING: Students may be evaluated on the basis of their skills tests performance. A portion of the student's course grade is usually the result of the level of progress or achievement he or she demonstrates on skills tests.

~ CLASSIFICATION: Administering skills tests early in a class allows the instructor to immediately group the students instead of observing their performance for a few class periods and then dividing them into ability groups. Intramural teams could also be equated this way.

MOTIVATION: A number of students respond positively to a challenge. They often try harder to excel on a skills test than performing against their peers in class. Used properly, skills tests can serve as excellent motivators for student improvement and progress.

PRACTICE: Relating to the motivation purpose, some students practice test items in order to improve test scores. Monitoring of individual progress through self-testing is often the single greatest contributor to success in sports skills achievement. Coaches may require players to practice an item or items in a particular test, especially those clearly demonstrating face validity.

DIAGNOSIS: Skill development is one of the basic foundations of physical education. Thus, the ability to diagnose the performance level of students is paramount as a qualification for teaching physical education. Skills tests can assist the instructor in detecting weaknesses in student performance.

TEACHING AIDS: In some cases, the nature of instruction for a particular sport prohibits a ready check of student progress in skill development. Periodic use of skills tests may reveal areas of instruction needing increased emphasis.

INTERPRETIVE TOOL: One of the ways the physical education program is interpreted to the administration, parents, and the public is through the use of skills tests. This is especially effective at the public school level.[13]

COMPETITION: Since the competitive element is inherent in the structure of skills tests, they show potential as successful intramural and rainy day activities.[13]

SCIENTIFIC AUTHENTICITY

Several criteria must be met for a test of sports skills to be considered scientifically authentic. A test should be easy to administer and score plus lend itself to administration in a reasonable amount of time. Preparation time for testing should be minimal, and the necessary equipment and supplies should be standard for the particular sport or reasonably accessible. More importantly, a test should be valid, reliable, and objective. Further elaboration on the latter three criteria follows.

Validity

Each skills test purports to measure a subject's degree of proficiency in one or more skills. When a test actually measures the skill or skills for which it is designed, it is a valid one.

Validation of sports skills tests is achieved by determining the relationship between a test and an established criterion that equates well with the quality being measured by the test. Most common of the test criteria in sports skills measurement are subjective ratings of experts and tournament rankings. Consequently, a student's test performance is supposed to relate well to the experts' rating of his ability or his standing in tournament competition.

Face validity in the strictest sense is the most acceptable type of validity. An example of this kind of validity is when a test requirement is the same as a particular skill required in a certain sport. It is not uncommon to see face validity claimed for test items that only approximate required game skills. In these cases, the face validity claim becomes much less defensible. Pure face validity is difficult to attain because the test environment and the game setting seldom resemble, and certain extraneous factors present under game conditions cannot be controlled in a testing situation. Nevertheless, properly validated tests seem to consistently and accurately discriminate among the various ability levels of a test group.

A less common criterion measure in sports skills measurement is the use of an established test which allegedly measures essentially the same quality for which a new test is designed. A weakness of this criterion is that the test validation fails to reveal which of the tests is the most valid measure of the quality each proposes to measure.

Statistical procedures commonly utilized in test validation include the Pearson Product-Moment coefficient of correlation *(r)*, multiple correlation *(R)*, and rank-order correlation *(Rho)*. Each is discussed later in the chapter along with other measurement terms.

In determining which tests demonstrated sufficient validity value for inclusion in this text, the authors adhered to the correlation coefficient standards espoused by Garrett[11] which are presented below. A minimum validity coefficient of .40 was selected.

r from .00 to ± .20 denotes indifferent or negligible relationship

r from ± .20 to ± .40 denotes low correlation, present but slight

r from ± .40 to ± .70 denotes substantial or marked relationship

r from ± .70 to ± 1.00 denotes high to very high relationship

Reliability

A reliable test is expected to produce similar or identical results
when administered a second time to the same subjects under the
same test conditions. The tester should be aware that a reliable
test is not necessarily a valid one because measurement of a quality other than the test is intended to measure may produce consistent results from test subjects. On the other hand, a valid test
administered by a competent tester invariably shows a high level
of reliability.

In sports skills measurement, reliability coefficients are obtained
by the test-retest, split-half, and odd-even methods. The test-retest
method is preferable and most often used. This means that a test
is given twice in its entirety and the results compared to determine
their degree of relationship. In the split-half procedure, results of
one half of a test are compared with the other. The odd-even
method for obtaining reliability merely compares the degree of
consistency in performance between odd- and even-numbered
items.

As a focal point, the authors followed the guidelines used in the
aforementioned Sports Skills Test Project of the American Alliance for Health, Physical Education and Recreation when selecting the minimum reliability coefficient that a test must have demonstrated for inclusion in this text. In the project, the minimum
reliability coefficient for test items scored on the basis of distance
was .80, while a minimum coefficient of .70 was recommended for
skills scored on the basis of accuracy and form. Tests included in
this text demonstrate a reliability coefficient of at least .75.

Objectivity

How objective a test is depends upon the degree of consistency
that two or more testers demonstrate in its scoring. Tests of high
objectivity invariably show high reliability because a tester quite
naturally administers and scores the same test twice with greater

uniformity than two different individuals. Clarke[7] states that a highly reliable test may fail to contain an acceptable objectivity value in cases whereby two testers vary in interpretation of test procedures.

Objectivity takes on added significance in situations whereby instructors compare test results with local peers or national norms. Comparison of unlike variables with like criteria is futile and misleading at best. The old adage "Compare apples with apples" applies here.

Generally accepted objectivity standards are presented below.[7]

.95-.99 very high, found among best tests

.90-.94 high; acceptable

.80-.89 fairly adequate for individual measurement

.70-.79 adequate for group measurement, but not satisfactory for individual measurement

.60-.69 useful for group averages and school surveys, but entirely inadequate for individual measurement

Few sports skills tests have been investigated for objectivity determination. Whatever the reason, it stands to reason that more emphasis is placed on the use of local norms than those constructed on a national basis.

To a large extent, local norms are based on data gathered by the same instructor. Therefore, acceptable test reliability is paramount. On the other hand, lack of objectivity coefficients is another reason why the tester is cautioned to not rely too heavily on national norms utilization.

MEASUREMENT TERMS

In addition to the measurement terms discussed earlier in this chapter, other terms commonly used in this textbook deserve elaboration.

PEARSON PRODUCT-MOMENT COEFFICIENT OF CORRELATION *(r):* Commonly used to determine validity and reliability estimates of sports skills tests, this statistical procedure measures the relationship between two variables. For example, the degree to which ability in controlling a wall volley in tennis measures playing ability in that sport can be estimated with this procedure. The degree of relationship is based on a ±1.0 maximum. Of the scientifically documented tests found in this text, the vast majority were done so by the Pearson Product-Moment procedure. Reference is sometimes made to correlation coefficients without identifying the procedure. In those cases, the Pearson *r* was the correlation procedure utilized.

RANK-ORDER CORRELATION COEFFICIENT *(Rho):* Like the Pearson *r* procedure, the rank-order method for determining correlation coefficients measures the amount of relationship between two elements. However, the *Rho* method is less exact than the product-moment method because only the rank of scores is considered as opposed to the variance within the scores. Therefore, *Rho* is a more crude measure and less desirable correlation procedure than the Pearson *r*. It is particularly applicable in situations where the number of cases is thirty or less.

MULTIPLE CORRELATION *(R):* Frequently in the development of sports skills test batteries, this procedure is used. Multiple factors are related to only one which determines how much a single item in a test battery relates to the others in combination.

STANDARD DEVIATION *(s):* In educational measurement, a common measure of variability in test scores is known as a standard deviation. Once the mean or average is determined for a set of scores, the tester needs to know how much each score deviates from the mean for evaluation purposes. The standard deviation represents segments of a particular distribution of scores. Six standard deviations are found in a normal distribution with three above the mean and three below. The middle two standard deviations contain approximately 68 percent of the scores.

T-SCALE: Used to develop norms and make raw scores for a group more conducive to meaningful comparison, the T-scale converts those scores to normalized standard scores or T-scores. A T-score reflects the distance a raw score lies above or below the mean. With a mean of fifty and a standard deviation of ten, the T-scale extends five deviations to each side of the mean. Scores seldom range from more than a maximum of eighty-five and minimum of fifteen.

PERCENTILES: Also used to present test score norms, this standard score provides to the student a meaningful interpretation of his score position among peers completing a test. For example, a percentile rank of seventy indicates that 70 percent of individuals completing the particular test scored less than that amount and 30 percent scored better. The percentile method of determining variability cannot handle extreme scores as well as the T-scale and is based on the false assumption that distance is uniform between scores.

SPEARMAN-BROWN PROPHECY FORMULA: In utilizing the split-half and odd-even methods for determining test reliability, the resulting coefficient pertains to only half the test. Using the data collected this way, this statistical procedure allows one to estimate the reliability value of the entire test.

Computation details for the various statistical procedures that are used in sports skills measurement extend beyond the scope of this text. For a fuller understanding of the above terms and others of less frequent mention in the book, the reader is referred to any basic statistics or tests and measurements text.

SHORTCOMINGS OF EXISTING SPORTS SKILLS TESTS

Presentation of material in this text is slanted toward its basic premise, that sports skills tests available today are not being utilized at a rate commensurate to their potential value. In the ongoing debate among physical educators as to how extensive these tests should be used, opponents often point out that several sports activities possess a scoring system that naturally provides objective measurement. The implication is that scores in such sports as golf and archery, as well as round-robin tournament results in tennis supersede the effectiveness of skills tests. On the other hand, the gathering of data for student and skills course evaluation by this approach is often impractical and receives low marks in satisfying the criterion of administrative feasibility. For example, few schools own or even have access to a golf course, which suggests that skills tests should be used in the absence of this facility. Even if one were available, the time-consuming game does not readily lend itself to instruction or evaluation.

Not only have physical education instructors failed to make

proper use of the many fine tests of sports skill, but experts in measurement have not shown due concern to the improvement of this very basic instructional component of the physical education curriculum. Reference to sample tests and their value are commonly made in tests and measurements books for physical education. However, those tests are routinely presented with no reference made to their potential or obvious shortcomings. Critical analyses of the sports skills measurement area are infrequently included along with the presentation of tests. The literature is far too skimpy in its treatment of a subject so important and germane to a fundamental purpose of physical education.

Attention to the limitations and problems associated with sports skills measurement is given by Johnson and Nelson.[13] These authors often refer to the central theme of their work, that is, that strong emphasis should be placed upon the tester's ability to properly administer a test. Said another way, this implies that the test is no better than the tester. The reader is reminded that a well-constructed test can become worthless when administered by an incompetent tester.

Basically, the above mentioned authors emphasize the futility that is involved when a test constructor is too expansive in his attempt to increase the objectivity and reliability of a particular test while at the same time completely or measurably forfeiting its validity value. They cite examples of tests in which the influence of a second person is eliminated, yet in actual game competition, that individual may significantly influence the performer's execution of the skill. For example, elimination of the pitcher in baseball or softball in favor of a batting tee may require execution of a skill that is markedly unrelated to that of hitting a pitched ball. This is not to say that employment of a second person to simulate the required game skill is without its problems. Test reliability can be affected, for example, if the pitcher's throws are inconsistent, causing the hitter to become impatient and hit balls he would ordinarily let go by. To sum up this point, the tester should guard against the sacrifice of one standard of scientific authenticity at the expense of another.

Recognizing the value of national norms and the interest they engender among teachers and students, Johnson and Nelson also stress the need for local norms construction and utilization in order to insure test relevancy for the particular situation. Those authors further warn the user of sports skills tests not to grade the student solely on the basis of test performance. They contend that test score results should be combined with a careful subjective evaluation of the student's skill performance to arrive at a course grade that is most representative of the student's actual ability level in a given sport.

By far the most comprehensive critique of sports skills measurement the authors were able to locate was done by West.[23] Considerable insight into ways that current and future tests may be improved upon are provided. Recommendations for avoiding recurrence of the common errors believed to be found in many of the available tests were grouped into four general areas.

The first suggestion by West is that potentially good tests should be refined in quality through careful analysis prior to further test proliferation. In other words, it is felt that a sufficient number of promising tests exist and that an attempt to perfect these tests is more plausible than to develop new ones. One way in which a test might be strengthened has to do with the scoring of near misses in badminton short serve tests or other sports for which this potential scoring item has application. West correctly argues that many of the near misses in a badminton serve are really quality serves because they are played by the receiver due to his inability to judge whether the serves would land on or beyond the short service line.

Second, West calls for a reexamination of the validation process for sports skills tests. Use of round-robin tournament results as a criterion measure for a specific skill is questioned, and utilization of ratings of form for the same purpose also is suspect since quality performers often execute skills in an unorthodox manner. A need for creativity in selection of criterion measures is cited. Use of multiple criterion measures is proposed as an improvement over the present approach to test validation. Additionally, the importance of selecting relevant criterion measures in test construction is noted.

Third, West criticizes those tests that measure accuracy exclusively when the actual sport skill requires both accuracy and velocity for successful performance. She reminds the tester that a skills test requirement of accuracy only when velocity should also be required may very well be measuring something different than what the test purports to measure.

Next, the shortcomings in test construction pertaining to reliability are analyzed. In scoring, the tester is urged to use the average score of multiple trials instead of the best score since reliability is enhanced when all trials are considered. Allowing students to repeat test items in situations where violations occur is condemned. The importance of administering tests on separate days to obtain reliability coefficients is stressed along with a suggested day-to-day variation recording of student performance to aid the tester in selecting appropriate testing schedules.

Finally, West calls for a cooperative spirit between general and sports skills measurement experts. In summary, the critic feels that a sufficient amount of relevant material should be available to the potential tester when selecting a test. Information about the day-to-day variation in student performance as well as trial-to-trial variation of both sexes and various age groups should be available. Also, norms should be available, and validity coefficients should have been carefully selected. How the test relates to other similar tests would also be helpful to the potential user.

REFERENCES

1. Anderson, Lou E.: *Tennis for Women.* New York, B&N, 1926.
2. Barrow, Harold M. and McGee, Rosemary: *A Practical Approach to Measurement in Physical Education,* 2nd ed. Philadelphia, Lea & Febiger, 1971.
3. Baumgartner, Ted A. and Jackson, Andrew S.: *Measurement for Evaluation in Physical Education.* Boston, HM, 1975.
4. Beall, Elizabeth: Essential Qualities in Certain Aspects of Physical Education with Ways of Measuring and Developing the Same. Master's thesis, Berkeley, University of California, 1925.
5. Bovard, John F.; Cozens, Frederick W.; and Hagman, E. Patricia: *Tests and Measurements in Physical Education,* 3rd ed. Philadelphia, Saunders, 1949.

6. Brace, David K.: Testing basketball technique. *American Physical Education Review, 29:*159-165, 1924.
7. Clarke, H. Harrison: *Application of Measurement to Health and Physical Education,* 5th ed. Englewood Cliffs, P-H, 1976.
8. Downie, N. M. and Heath, R. W.: *Basic Statistical Methods,* 2nd ed. New York, Har-Row, 1965.
9. Eckert, Helen M.: *Practical Measurement of Physical Performance.* Philadelphia, Lea & Febiger, 1974.
10. Franks, B. Don and Deutsch, Helga: *Evaluating Performance in Physical Education.* New York, Acad Pr, 1973.
11. Garrett, Henry E.: *Statistics in Psychology and Education,* 6th ed. New York, McKay, 1966.
12. Haskins, Mary Jane: *Evaluation in Physical Education.* Dubuque, Iowa, Brown Bk, 1971.
13. Johnson, Barry L. and Nelson, Jack K.: *Practical Measurements for Evaluation in Physical Education,* 2nd ed. Minneapolis, Burgess, 1974.
14. Mathews, Donald K.: *Measurement in Physical Education,* 4th ed. Philadelphia, Saunders, 1973.
15. Meyers, Carlton R.: *Measurement in Physical Education,* 2nd ed. New York, Ronald, 1974.
16. Morris, Harold H.: A Critique of the AAHPER Skill Test Series. Paper read before the Measurement and Evaluation Council at the Annual Convention of the American Alliance for Health, Physical Education and Recreation, Seattle, March 25, 1977.
17. Neilson, N. P. and Jensen, Clayne R.: *Measurement and Statistics in Physical Education.* Belmont, Calif., Wadsworth Pub, 1972.
18. Reilly, Frederick J.: *New Rational Athletics for Boys and Girls.* Boston, Heath, 1916.
19. Safrit, Margaret J.: *Evaluation in Physical Education.* Englewood Cliffs, P-H, 1973.
20. Scott, M. Gladys and French, Esther: *Measurement and Evaluation in Physical Education.* Dubuque, Iowa, Brown Bk, 1959.
21. Stroup, Francis: *Measurement in Physical Education.* New York, Ronald, 1957.
22. Weber, Jerome C. and Lamb, David R.: *Statistics and Research in Physical Education.* St. Louis, Mosby, 1970.
23. West, Charlotte: Paper read before the Measurement and Evaluation Council at the Annual Convention of the American Alliance for Health, Physical Education and Recreation, Seattle, March 25, 1977.

Chapter 2

Archery

INTRODUCTION

A RCHERY IS ONE of those sports that does not require the construction of skills tests to measure student achievement because the most valid and objective indication of ability level is naturally provided in its scoring system. Since shooting accuracy is considered the chief criterion of achievement in archery and the score itself best reflects the person's ability level, achievement scales from the more common units of competition (rounds) have been developed in lieu of skills tests to measure student progress. Two of these scales are presented in this chapter.

Although conducive to objective measurement, the sport of archery is not without its problems in the evaluation of achievement. The validity and reliability of testing can be affected by certain factors which influence student achievement. This is especially a problem when the factors are uncontrollable. For example, natural elements such as extreme temperature and wind conditions may greatly affect one's performance. Inconsistency in the quality of equipment utilized may present a problem when scores are compared to national norms. Also, the amount and nature of practice prior to testing should be standardized whenever possible.

These factors illustrate some of the shortcomings of using national norms or achievement scales but give emphasis to the need for test standardization at the local level.

HYDE ARCHERY TEST[7]

Also cited as Hyde-Columbia Round, Hyde Archery Standards, Hyde Achievement Scale in Archery, Hyde Archery Achievement Scale, and Hyde's Archery Scales.

Date: 1937.

Purpose: To evaluate achievement in archery by college wom-

15

en, utilizing the Columbia Round at distances of 50, 40, and 30 yards.

EDUCATIONAL APPLICATION: College women.

Administrative Feasibility

TIME: A student should complete at least one distance (four ends of six arrows) per session. Three sixty-minute class periods should allow ample time to administer the test to an archery class of ten to twenty students.

PERSONNEL: An experienced instructor to administer and supervise the test. Students may serve as scorers.

TRAINING INVOLVED: It is recommended that a student shoot a minimum of 120 arrows at each of the three distances prior to taking the test. This recommendation does not include the recommended practice immediately prior to taking the test. Only one practice end per distance is permitted at that time.

EQUIPMENT AND SUPPLIES
a. Standard 48-inch target face–one per target.
b. Standard bows–one for every two students.
c. Matched arrows–six per student.
d. Targets–at least four per class.

Accessories: Arm guards, gloves, finger tabs, and quivers. Field marking and record keeping materials are also necessary.

Facilities and Space: A level or near level area of sufficient size to allow a minimum of ten students to assume a shooting stance at each of three lines at distances of 50, 40, and 30 yards from the targets. The center of the gold in each target should be located 4 feet from the ground.

Directions

A total of seventy-two arrows are shot in ends of six arrows each. One practice end is permitted, and twenty-four arrows are shot at each of the three distances. The student is not required to complete the whole test in one class period but must finish at least one of the distance requirements (twenty-four arrows) in each session.

SCORING METHOD AND NORMS: The values used in standard

target archery scoring are: gold, 9; red, 7; blue, 5; black, 3; white, 1; outside the white or missing the target, 0. An arrow striking two colors is assigned the score of higher value. If an arrow passes completely through the target face or bounces off the target, five points are given. Although seven points are commonly given in the above two instances, the five-point value is retained in the Hyde Test because the rule change to seven points was made after its development.

Scales were constructed by utilizing the data accumulated from over 1,400 student scores in twenty-seven colleges in sixteen states (Table I). One scale may be used to evaluate the first round score of students having a limited amount of practice (maximum of 120 arrows at each distance), and another shows the best round score after more extensive shooting experience is attained. This scale is recommended for use at the end of an archery class to assess student achievement. Another scale is based on scores made at distances of 30, 40, and 50 yards. This scale may be used at any time during the practice period, but caution is given to the user to expect beginners to fall relatively low on the scale since it was based on final round scores.

The scales below show total scores with corresponding scale values (Table I). A scale score of 50 reflects an average performance on the test. The scale values are helpful in the comparison of local norms to those collected on a national level.

Willgoose[20] suggests that the following scale score ranges estimate the quality of performance in the Hyde Test: Scale score 0–20, very poor; 21–40, poor; 41–60, fair or average; 61–80, good; and 81–100, excellent.

Scientific Authenticity

VALIDITY: Using the composite score of three distances as the criterion, validity coefficients obtained were .82 for beginners and .96 for advanced archers at the 50-yard distance; .91 for beginners and .95 for advanced archers at 40 yards; and .89 and .93 for the respective ability levels while shooting at 30 yards.

The group designated as advanced archers were thirty-five women who participated in the 1931 National Archery Tourna-

TABLE I

HYDE ACHIEVEMENT SCALES IN ARCHERY FOR COLLEGE WOMEN*

Scale Score	First Columbia Total Score	Total Score	Final Columbia Round (Target Score)		
			50 Yards	40 Yards	30 Yards
100	436	466	150	176	194
99	430	460	148	174	192
98	424	455	146	171	190
97	418	449	143	169	187
96	412	443	141	167	185
95	406	438	139	164	183
94	400	432	137	162	181
93	394	426	135	160	179
92	388	420	132	157	176
91	382	415	130	155	174
90	376	409	128	153	172
89	370	403	126	150	170
88	364	398	124	148	168
87	358	392	121	146	165
86	352	386	119	143	163
85	346	381	117	141	161
84	340	375	115	139	159
83	334	369	113	136	157
82	328	363	110	134	154
81	322	358	108	132	152
80	316	352	106	129	150
79	310	346	104	127	148
78	304	341	102	125	146
77	298	335	99	122	143
76	292	329	97	120	141
75	286	324	95	118	139
74	280	318	93	115	137
73	274	312	91	113	135
72	268	306	88	111	132
71	262	301	86	108	130
70	256	295	84	106	128
69	250	289	82	104	126
68	244	284	80	101	124
67	238	278	77	99	121
66	232	272	75	97	119
65	226	267	73	94	117
64	220	261	71	92	115
63	214	255	69	90	113
62	208	249	66	87	110
61	202	244	64	85	108
60	196	238	62	83	106

TABLE I (continued)

Scale Score	First Columbia Total Score	Total Score	Final Columbia Round (Target Score)		
			50 Yards	40 Yards	30 Yards
59	190	232	60	80	104
58	184	227	58	78	102
57	178	221	55	76	99
56	172	215	53	73	97
55	166	210	51	71	95
54	160	204	49	69	93
53	154	198	47	66	91
52	148	192	44	64	88
51	142	187	42	62	86
50	136	181	50	59	84
49	133	178	39	58	82
48	131	174		57	80
47	128	171	38	56	79
46	125	167	37	55	77
45	122	164	36	53	75
44	120	160	35	52	74
43	117	157		51	72
42	114	153	34	50	70
41	111	150	33	49	69
40	109	146	32	47	67
39	106	143	31	46	65
38	103	139		45	64
37	100	136	30	44	62
36	98	132	29	43	60
35	95	129	28	42	59
34	92	125	27	40	57
33	89	122		39	55
32	87	118	26	38	54
31	84	115	25	37	52
30	81	111	24	36	50
29	78	108	23	34	49
28	76	104		33	47
27	73	101	22	32	45
26	70	97	21	31	44
25	67	94	20	30	42
24	65	90	19	28	40
23	62	87		27	39
22	59	83	18	26	37
21	56	80	17	25	35
20	54	76	16	24	34
19	51	73	15	23	32
18	48	69		21	30

TABLE I (continued)

Scale Score	First Columbia Total Score	Total Score	Final Columbia Round (Target Score)		
			50 Yards	40 Yards	30 Yards
17	45	66	14.	20	29
16	43	62	13	19	27
15	40	59	12	18	25
14	37	55	11	17	24
13	34	52		15	22
12	32	48	10	14	20
11	29	45	9	13	19
10	26	41	8	12	17
9	23	38	7	11	15
8	21	34		9	14
7	18	31	6	8	12
6	15	27	5	7	10
5	12	24	4	6	9
4	10	20	3	5	7
3	7	17		4	5
2	4	13	2	2	4
1	1	10	1	1	2

*Based on scores of over 1400 college students. Scales arranged by Frederick W. Cozens.

From E. I. Hyde: An achievement scale in archery, *Research Quarterly,* 8:108-116, 1937. Courtesy of AAHPER.

ment. The beginners were seventy-five college freshmen and sophomore women.

RELIABILITY: The literature review failed to reveal any studies which presented reliability coefficients for the Hyde Test.

CRITERION MEASURE: Composite score of twelve ends or seventy-two arrows shot at a total of three distances.

Additional Comments

The wide recognition of the Hyde Archery Test would have been further promoted through the years had it and appropriate modifications been scientifically authenticated for both sexes from junior high through college. This gap presents an excellent opportunity for interested physical educators to make a professional contribution to the literature pertaining to sports skills tests. The popularity of archery should increase now that the sport is included in the Olympic Games competition. An increase in course offerings in a particular sport usually results at a rate parallel to its increase in popularity.

AAHPER ARCHERY TEST[2]

Also cited as AAHPER Archery Skills Test.
Date: 1967.
Purpose: To measure achievement in archery and to serve as a practice test for improvement of skill.
EDUCATIONAL APPLICATION: Junior high and secondary school boys and girls (twelve to eighteen years of age).

Administrative Feasibility

TIME: Archery classes of fifteen to twenty students should easily complete the shooting required at one distance in one class session. No more than two class periods is required for girls and a maximum of three for boys.

PERSONNEL: One instructor to administer and supervise while the students serve as scorers.

TRAINING INVOLVED: Four practice arrows are permitted at each distance.

EQUIPMENT AND SUPPLIES

a. Standard 48-inch face for targets.
b. Bows ranging from fifteen to forty pounds in pull according to age and ability of student.
c. Matched arrows (eight to ten per person) 24 to 28 inches in length with particular length fitted to bow and archer.
Accessories: Arm guards, finger tabs, gloves, quivers, field marking and scorekeeping materials.
Facilities and Space: A level or near level range of sufficient size to test ten to fifteen archers simultaneously at a distance of 10, 20, and 30 yards. For testing indoors, a standard-sized gymnasium with appropriate backstops should suffice.

Directions

It is recommended that no more than four archers shoot at any one target. Twelve arrows consisting of two ends of six arrows each are shot at distances of 10, 20, and 30 yards for boys, with the 30-yard distance eliminated for girls. The 10-yard distance must be completed before moving to the 20-yard distance, etc. Any students not scoring at least ten points at one distance may not advance to the next distance mark.

SCORING METHOD AND NORMS: The standard target archery scoring values are used: gold, 9; red, 7; blue, 5; black, 3; white, 1;

TABLE II

PERCENTILE SCORES FOR AAHPER ARCHERY TEST (BOYS)*

		Boys			
Age	12–13	14	15	16	17–18
Yards	10 20 30 Tot.	10 20 30 Tot.	10 20 30 Tot.	10 20 30 Tot.	10 20 30 Tot.
100	91 70 45 195	96 75 50 210	100 90 81 270	100 100 95 270	100 95 85 270
95	83 53 28 156	88 61 34 179	97 77 50 215	99 78 56 220	98 78 64 222
90	78 44 24 138	80 48 28 160	94 70 41 195	97 71 47 205	96 72 53 206
85	73 38 22 128	78 45 24 150	90 66 35 187	96 67 43 197	93 67 47 197
80	70 34 18 122	75 41 21 146	88 63 31 177	91 63 40 189	90 63 42 190
75	67 31 16 112	72 38 18 143	84 58 28 167	90 59 36 181	88 59 39 184
70	64 28 14 103	70 36 16 139	80 54 25 158	88 56 32 173	86 55 37 176
65	61 26 12 98	68 33 15 136	78 51 22 149	86 54 30 163	84 52 35 166
60	59 24 11 93	67 30 13 130	76 47 20 140	84 51 28 160	82 49 31 158
55	57 23 9 87	65 28 11 124	73 42 17 130	80 48 25 154	79 46 28 151
50	54 22 8 81	63 26 10 119	69 39 15 120	79 46 23 148	77 43 26 144
45	50 20 7 74	60 24 8 114	65 36 14 114	77 43 22 142	74 40 24 136
40	48 18 6 67	57 22 7 110	62 34 13 107	75 41 20 136	71 37 21 130
35	45 16 4 60	55 20 5 106	59 31 12 100	72 39 18 129	68 34 20 125
30	42 14 0 54	52 18 4 98	55 28 11 94	70 36 16 123	63 32 17 119
25	38 12 0 47	45 16 0 87	51 24 10 87	67 33 13 117	59 29 16 112
20	34 10 0 38	40 14 0 77	48 21 9 79	61 28 11 110	55 25 11 109
15	31 8 0 28	36 12 0 69	43 18 7 70	51 25 9 103	48 20 9 96
10	26 6 0 21	31 10 0 61	36 15 6 62	50 20 6 80	40 17 6 86
5	16 3 0 15	25 6 0 43	25 9 2 43	40 14 2 61	27 11 3 65
0	0 0 0 0	0 0 0 0	0 0 0 0	0 0 0 0	0 0 0 0

The first vertical label reads "Percentile Scores" (for rows 85 through 60) and again "Percentile Scores" (for rows 30 through 5).

*Based on scores of over 600 students for each age group (10–18).

From AAHPER: *Skills Test Manual: Archery for Boys and Girls,* 1967, D. K. Brace, test consultant. Courtesy of AAHPER, Washington, D.C.

outside the white or missing the target, 0. An arrow striking two colors is assigned the score of higher value. Seven points are scored for an arrow passing completely through or rebounding off the target.

The total score is accumulated by adding the totals made at each distance. The best possible score at each distance is 108 points; therefore, the maximum total for girls is 216 points, and 324 points is the greatest possible for boys.

National norms for the AAHPER Archery Skills Test are presented in Tables II and III.

TABLE III

PERCENTILE SCORES FOR AAHPER ARCHERY TEST (GIRLS)*

		Girls														
Age		12-13			14			15			16			17-18		
Yards		10	20	Tot.	10	20	Tot.	10	20	Tot.	10	20	Tot.	10	20	Tot.
100		85	60	129	89	70	159	96	81	160	100	91	161	100	95	180
95		69	40	100	74	47	109	82	55	130	87	58	134	87	71	149
90		60	29	89	68	38	99	75	47	112	80	50	115	80	60	129
85		50	22	81	63	35	89	70	43	103	73	44	107	73	52	123
80		46	19	69	58	32	84	66	39	96	67	40	100	69	47	116
75		41	17	64	54	28	79	63	34	89	64	36	96	66	42	109
70		38	15	60	50	25	75	60	32	85	60	32	91	62	40	104
65		35	13	55	48	23	70	56	29	80	56	29	87	58	36	100
60		34	12	50	46	21	66	53	27	77	53	27	80	55	32	95
55		32	10	46	43	20	62	51	25	73	49	25	76	52	29	91
50		30	9	42	41	18	58	49	23	70	46	22	72	48	26	85
45		27	7	38	38	16	54	46	22	66	43	20	67	46	24	78
40		24	6	35	35	14	50	43	20	62	41	18	63	42	21	73
35		22	1	32	33	13	17	40	19	59	38	16	60	40	19	68
30		19	0	28	30	10	45	37	16	55	33	14	56	38	18	64
25		16	0	25	28	8	42	34	13	51	31	12	52	35	16	60
20		14	0	22	25	7	40	31	11	45	29	10	47	31	14	53
15		12	0	17	22	0	34	27	8	40	25	8	41	28	12	45
10		10	0	12	19	0	28	21	6	33	21	6	36	24	9	38
5		6	0	5	12	0	22	13	0	25	16	0	26	19	0	30
0		0	0	0	0	0	0	0	0	0	0	0	0	0	0	0

*Based on scores of over 600 students for each age group (10-18).

From AAHPER: *Skills Test Manual: Archery for Boys and Girls,* 1967, D. K. Brace, test consultant. Courtesy of AAHPER, Washington, D.C.

Scientific Authenticity

VALIDITY: Face validity is accepted.

RELIABILITY: A reliability coefficient of .70 was set as the minimum requirement for tests of accuracy in the AAHPER Sports Skills Tests.

Additional Comments

The chief strength of the AAHPER Archery Skills Test is the availability of national norms that were derived from testing over 600 students of each sex. It is recommended that the 10-yard distance be eliminated and distances greater than 40 yards added for older children.[15]

REFERENCES

1. American Association for Health, Physical Education and Recreation: *Measurement and Evaluation of Materials in Health, Physical Education and Recreation.* Washington, AAHPER, 1950.
2. ———: *Skills Test Manual: Archery for Boys and Girls.* Brace, David K. (Test Consultant). Washington, AAHPER, 1967.
3. Bohn, Robert W.: An Achievement Test in Archery. Master's thesis, Madison, University of Wisconsin, 1962.
4. Clarke, H. Harrison: *Application of Measurement to Health and Physical Education.* 5th ed. Englewood Cliffs, P-H, 1976.
5. Glassow, Ruth B. and Broer, Marion R.: *Measuring Achievement in Physical Education.* Philadelphia, Saunders, 1938.
6. Haskins, Mary Jane: *Evaluation in Physical Education.* Dubuque, Iowa, Brown Bk, 1971.
7. Hyde, Edith I.: An achievement scale in archery. *Research Quarterly, 8:*108-116, 1937.
8. ———: The measurement of achievement in archery. *Journal of Educational Research, 27:*673-686, 1934.
9. ———: National research study in archery. *Research Quarterly, 7:* 64-73, 1936.
10. Johnson, Barry L. and Nelson, Jack K.: *Practical Measurements for Evaluation in Physical Education,* 2nd ed. Minneapolis, Burgess, 1974.
11. Larson, Leonard A. and Yocom, Rachael Dunaven: *Measurement and Evaluation in Physical, Health and Recreation Education.* St. Louis, Mosby, 1951.
12. Mathews, Donald K.: *Measurement in Physical Education,* 4th ed. Philadelphia, Saunders, 1973.

13. Meyers, Carlton R.: *Measurement in Physical Education,* 2nd ed. New York, Ronald, 1974.

14. Montoye, Henry J. (Ed.): *An Introduction to Measurement in Physical Education,* vol. III. Indianapolis, Phi Epsilon Kappa Fraternity, 1970.

15. Morris, Harold H.: A Critique of the AAHPER Skill Test Series. Paper read before the Measurement and Evaluation Council at the Annual Convention of the American Alliance for Health, Physical Education and Recreation, Seattle, March 25, 1977.

16. Neilson, N. P. and Jensen, Clayne R.: *Measurement and Statistics in Physical Education.* Belmont, Calif., Wadsworth Pub, 1972.

17. Reichart, Natalie: School archery standards. *Journal of Health and Physical Education, 14:*81, 124, 1943.

18. Scott, M. Gladys and French, Esther: *Measurement and Evaluation in Physical Education.* Dubuque, Iowa, Brown Bk, 1959.

19. Weiss, Raymond A. and Phillips, Marjorie: *Administration of Tests in Physical Education.* St. Louis, Mosby, 1954.

20. Willgoose, Carl E.: *Evaluation in Health Education and Physical Education.* New York, McGraw, 1961.

Badminton

INTRODUCTION

THE SPORT OF BADMINTON has proven to be a fertile subject area for skills tests investigators as evidenced by the extensive number surveyed by the authors. Campbell[7] is credited with devising the first scientifically documented badminton skills test in 1938. In the past decade, as many skills tests have been developed as existed beforehand.

Inasmuch as several of the authenticated badminton tests are similar in design, only a representative sampling is presented in this chapter. Collectively, they include all the skills common to badminton and are recognized as authentic tests, according to feasibility criteria for test construction.

FRENCH SHORT SERVE TEST[33]

Date: 1941.

Purpose: To measure the ability of accurately serving the shuttlecock with a low and short placement; to measure badminton playing ability when combined with the French Clear Test.

Description

A rope is stretched 20 inches directly above and parallel to the net. Using the intersection of the short service line and the center service line as a midpoint, a series of 2-inch lines in the form of arcs are placed in the right service court at distances of 22, 30, 38, and 46 inches from the midpoint, with each measurement including the width of the 2-inch line. It is recommended that the lines be coded in color.

EDUCATIONAL APPLICATION: Designed for college men and women; appropriate for any lower grade level that has developed the basic fundamental techniques associated with the serve.

Administrative Feasibility

TIME: A class of twenty students can be tested in one sixty-minute period.

26

PERSONNEL: One individual to score and record.

TRAINING INVOLVED: Practice serves are not necessary since twenty serves are allowed the subject. Students should demonstrate a reasonable level of skill on the serve prior to being tested.

EQUIPMENT AND SUPPLIES: Badminton racquet, shuttlecock, badminton net, clothesline rope the length of regulation net.

Accessories: Scoring materials and paint or tape.

Facilities and Space: Regulation badminton court.

Directions

The subject being tested may stand anywhere in the right service area diagonally opposite the target. The scorer should stand in the center of the left service court on the opposite court side of the server. It is important that the scorer stand facing the target for proper position in scoring the landing of the shuttlecock and determining whether or not it goes between the net and rope.

The subject serves twenty legal serves at the target (Fig. 1).

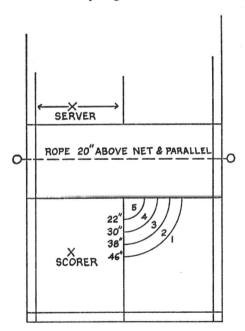

Figure 1. Court markings for French Short Serve Test. From M. G. Scott et al.: Achievement examinations in badminton, *Research Quarterly, 12*:242-253, 1941. Courtesy of AAHPER.

Each serve that passes between the badminton net and the rope adds to the point total, providing the shuttlecock falls somewhere in the proper service court area for doubles play. Illegal serves may be repeated since they are technically considered fouls.

SCORING METHOD AND NORMS: A score shall be awarded to any legal serve that passes between the net and the rope and lands in the proper service court for doubles play. Points are awarded based on placement of the shuttlecock. The low, short serve is obviously the most desired. The scoring areas are 5, 4, 3, 2, and 1, with the number decreasing as one moves away from the midpoint. Should the shuttlecock land on a line dividing two scoring areas, the subject receives the score of higher value; otherwise, points are awarded according to the area the shuttlecock lands in the target. The total score of twenty trials represents the final score.

TABLE IV

NORMS FOR FRENCH SHORT SERVE TEST

T-Score	Short Serve*	Short Serve†	T-Score
80	68	86	80
75	66	79	75
70	59	73	70
65	53	66	65
60	44	59	60
55	37	52	55
50	29	46	50
45	22	39	45
40	13	32	40
35	8	26	35
30	4	19	30
25	1	12	25
20	0	6	20

*Based on performance of 385 college women after a 25-lesson beginning course in badminton.
† Based on performance of 46 college women after a 30-lesson beginning course in badminton.

From M. G. Scott et al.: Achievement examinations in badminton, *Research Quarterly, 12:*242-253, 1941. Courtesy of AAHPER.

Scientific Authenticity

VALIDITY: From test scores of twenty-nine physical education majors, a validity coefficient of .66 was determined when correlated with the final standings of a ladder tournament.

RELIABILITY: A reliability coefficient of .88 was computed. The odd-even method of obtaining reliability was utilized, and the coefficients were stepped up by the application of the Spearman-Brown Prophecy Formula.

CRITERION MEASURE: Ladder tournament rankings.

Additional Comments

To assist the tester in drawing the arcs, it is suggested that a string at least 48 inches in length be marked at 22, 30, 36, and 48-inch intervals. It is further suggested that tape be used for the floor marking rather than paint. Tape is easily color coded once located on the floor.

Dividing the twenty serves into two sets of ten, possibly having ten serves taken from each service court, is another suggestion.

The French Short Serve Test was originally included in a battery of six tests. It and the French Clear Test proved superior to the others, according to validity coefficient values. When a multiple correlation was used to combine the two test scores, the resulting validity coefficient was .85. Both tests should be administered to measure general badminton playing ability. In using the test combination, the formula used to insure proper weighting is 1.0 serve and 1.2 clear.

FRENCH CLEAR TEST[33]

Date: 1941.

Purpose: To measure the ability to accurately place a clear shot; to measure general badminton playing ability when combined with the French Short Serve Test.

Description

A line is marked on the floor 2 feet in front of and parallel to the rear service line in the doubles game. Another line on the same side of the net should be placed 2 feet behind and parallel to the rear service line in the singles game. The measurements should be taken from the center of the appropriate lines. Both lines should be extended the width of the court to the sideline for doubles play. It is recommended that the lines be color coded for scoring ease. Figure 2 should help clarify the floor markings. A rope is stretched across the width of the court at a height of 8 feet and a distance of 14 feet from and parallel to the net on the target side.

A 2-inch square should be drawn in each of the service courts on the side of the net opposite the target. The center of each square should be 11 feet from the net and 3 feet from the center line. The measurements should be made from the center of the appropriate line.

EDUCATIONAL APPLICATION: Secondary school and college males and females.

Administrative Feasibility

TIME: A class of twenty students can be tested in one sixty-minute period.

PERSONNEL: The instructor or a skilled student may act as server with another student serving as a scorer-recorder.

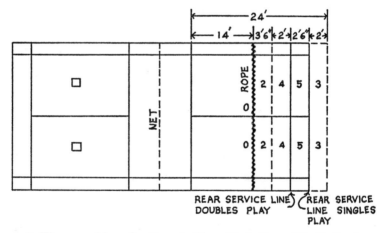

Figure 2. Floor markings for French Clear Test. From M. G. Scott et al.: Achievement examinations in badminton, *Research Quarterly, 12:*242-253, 1941. Courtesy of AAHPER.

TABLE V

NORMS FOR FRENCH CLEAR TEST*

T-Score	Clear
80	94
75	90
70	86
65	79
60	72
55	64
50	54
45	44
40	32
35	20
30	8
25	2
20	0

* Based on scores of 429 college freshman
and sophomore women.

From M. G. Scott et al.: Achievement examinations in badminton, *Research Quarterly, 12*:242-253, 1941. Courtesy of AAHPER.

TRAINING INVOLVED: Two practice trials per student are suggested on the testing date.

EQUIPMENT AND SUPPLIES: Badminton racquets, shuttlecocks, badminton net, additional set of standards, rope the width of court.

Accessories: Scoring and floor marking materials.

Facilities and Space: Regulation badminton court.

Directions

The subject assumes a position between the two squares located on the side of the net opposite the target. The server, who should demonstrate a minimum of intermediate badminton skill, stands at the intersection of the short service line and center line on the same side of the court with the target. Then the server serves the shuttlecock across the net so that it carries at least even with the two squares. Should the server not serve the shuttlecock far enough or outside the two squares, the subject should not play it.

Only shuttlecocks played by the subject count as official trials, and each subject takes twenty clear shot trials. The subject is allowed complete freedom of movement once the shuttlecock has been served. Any carried or slung clear shot may be repeated.

SCORING METHOD AND NORMS: Points are scored on any clear shot hit, providing the subject is standing in the proper area and the shuttlecock clears the rope and lands in the target area. The score is based on the total points accumulated in twenty trial clear shots. The target is marked for scoring as shown in Figure 2. Shuttlecocks landing on a line dividing scoring areas are assigned the higher point value.

Scientific Authenticity

VALIDITY: In a check of the test's validity, a correlation coefficient of .60 was computed. The test subjects were twenty-nine physical education majors.

RELIABILITY: The reliability was determined by using the odd-even method, with the coefficient stepped up by the Spearman-Brown Formula. A .96 relationship resulted.

CRITERION MEASURE: Tournament ranking.

Additional Comments

Two subjects can be tested simultaneously by simply dividing the court in half with the center line utilized. Each subject should stand in the middle of the short service line in his respective service court and no closer to the net than the short service line. It is suggested that the twenty trials be divided into two sets of ten and alternate service courts be used for each ten hits.

One possible disadvantage of the test might be the idea of having the shuttlecock put into play with a serve. This puts a great deal of responsibility on the server. It is essential that the server be a skilled server and as consistent as possible. The authors recommend that the same server be utilized throughout the test if at all possible for reliability purposes. The validity value of the test might be improved upon with additional study. As discussed earlier, the validity value increased considerably in the French study when the Short Serve Test was given in combination with the French Clear Test.

McDonald[26] developed a high clear test which involved both a measure of height and distance. She used thirteen feet as the ideal height and twenty feet as the ideal distance that a shuttlecock should be hit for the clear shot. One hundred and nineteen college students served as test subjects. The test showed satisfactory validity but questionable reliability.

FRENCH-STALTER BADMINTON SKILL TESTS[14]

Date: 1949.

Purpose: To measure general badminton playing ability and to assess individual, basic badminton skills.

Description

The French-Stalter Badminton Skill Tests comprise a battery of five different skills tests. This series of tests is a follow-up to the French Short Serve and French Clear Tests. French and Stalter wanted to develop a comprehensive battery to measure badminton skill, so they constructed three new tests dealing with footwork, wrist action, and smashing ability to include with the two authentic tests previously constructed. Added to the short serve and clear items were the wrist-volley, shuttle, and smash tests. Only the last three are discussed here since the first two were presented earlier in this chapter.

Wrist-Volley: Floor markings include a 1½-inch wide line that is 6 feet from and parallel to the base of the wall. The width of the line is included as part of the 6-foot distance.

Smash: The tester should begin by marking a 1½-inch wide line on the floor 4 feet, 4 inches behind and parallel to the short service line (SSL) as shown in Figure 3. A line of the same width is also marked 4 feet, 4 inches in front of and parallel to the long service line for doubles (LSLD). The back of the target is represented by the long service line for singles (LSLS). Those lines should be color coded for scoring ease and accuracy. Target areas are numbered 5, 4, 3, 2, and 1 in descending order from the badminton net to the long service line for singles play.

A rope is stretched across the width of the court on the target side from one sideline to the other for doubles play. Two standards hold the rope taut and are positioned 2 feet from and parallel to the net at a height of 7 feet from the floor.

EDUCATIONAL APPLICATION: Originally developed for college women but can be used for both males and females in high school and college.

Administrative Feasibility

TIME: Two to four sixty-minute class periods to test twenty students, depending upon the number of test items administered.

PERSONNEL: One or two individuals, again depending on the number of tests used in the battery.

TRAINING INVOLVED: A standardized five-minute practice period is recommended for the wrist-volley item and two practice trials are suggested for the smash test.

EQUIPMENT AND SUPPLIES: Badminton racquets, shuttlecocks, stop watch, badminton net, and additional set of standards necessary for administration of entire test battery.

Accessories: Scoring and floor marking materials, plus a rope at least 25 feet long.

Facilities and Space: A regulation badminton court is needed for the shuttle and smash tests. A smooth wall at least 15 × 15 feet in size and unobstructed floor space of equal dimensions are required for the wrist-volley item.

Directions

WRIST-VOLLEY: The subject assumes a server's position behind the restraining line, facing the wall with a badminton racquet and shuttlecock in hand. When ready, an audible command to begin is given, and the subject immediately performs a legal serve against the wall. The shuttlecock is continually volleyed against the wall with any desired stroke; in the meantime the subject makes every effort to stay behind the restraining line. Should the shuttlecock come to rest anywhere on the floor area at any time during one of the four thirty-second trials, the subject should retrieve it and immediately assume a position behind the restraining line, then put the shuttlecock back into play with a legal serve.

The subject is allowed to move anywhere on the floor area, but points are only scored when the restraining line is not violated. Rest periods should be allowed between trials.

SHUTTLE: The subject gets ready for the test by standing with a racquet in hand and facing the net. When the audible command to begin is given, he or she commences to run as rapidly as possible back and forth between the sidelines of the singles court, certain to cross over the center line on each trip. The subject may use either a sliding step or a crossover step. The main concern is not the step used, but that the subject keep his body in a favorable position to return the shuttlecock. It is recommended that the scorer stand between the short service line and the net, facing the subject. Four fifteen-second trials are administered to each subject.

SMASH: The server assumes a position behind the short service line on the target side of the net (Fig. 3). Shuttlecocks should be

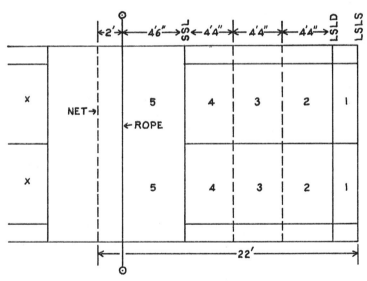

Figure 3. Floor markings for smash test. From E. French and E. Stalter: Study of skill tests in badminton for college women, *Research Quarterly,* 20:257-272, 1949. Courtesy of AAHPER.

served with enough force to clear the rope, net, and the short service line on the side opposite the target, and the serve should have enough height so the subject can properly execute an overhead smash shot. If the serve should hit the rope, net, or not be long or high enough, it constitutes a fault and is served again.

While being tested the subject stands behind the short service line opposite the target side of the net. The subject receives twenty serves and tries on each to hit a smash shot between the net and the rope, aiming for the area of highest value. The subject should only attempt to hit the good serves. Should the shuttlecock be smashed into the server on the opposite side of the net, the scorer estimates the target area it would have hit, and those points are assigned. A smash hit into the top of the net which falls over to the target side is legitimate.

SCORING METHOD AND NORMS

Wrist-Volley: A point is scored for each legal hit or volley against the wall during the four thirty-second trial periods. Any initial serve used to put the shuttlecock into play does not count as a legal hit. The subject's score is the sum total of legal hits for the four thirty-second trials.

Shuttle: One point is scored each time the subject goes from one side boundary line to the other. A trip across and back counts two points. The score of each fifteen-second trial is the total number of crossings made. Four trials are permitted, and the final total score is the total point accumulation on all four trials.

Smash: Each legitimate smash shot is assigned the point value earned. Shuttlecocks landing on a line dividing target areas are assigned the points associated with the area of higher value. Points are given based on where the shuttlecock initially hits and not where it eventually comes to rest. The scorer records all twenty trials, and a subject's final score is the cumulative total of those trials.

Scientific Authenticity

VALIDITY: In correlating test scores with the criterion, a coefficient of .78 was obtained for the wrist-volley item.

TABLE VI

NORMS FOR WRIST-VOLLEY TEST*

T-Score	Volley
75	148
73	138
71	128
69	114
65	108
63	106
61	102
59	98
57	92
55	88
53	84
51	82
49	80
45	72
40	62
35	54
30	48

*Based on scores of 91 college freshman
and sophomore women.

From E. French and E. Stalter: Study of skill tests in badminton for college women, *Research Quarterly, 20:*257-272, 1949. Courtesy of AAHPER.

TABLE VII

ACHIEVEMENT SCALES FOR FRENCH-STALTER BADMINTON SKILL TESTS

Rating	Serve	Clear	Wrist Volley	Smash	Shuttle
Superior	57 & up	88 & up	98 & up	89 & up	38 & up
Good	42 - 56	70 - 87	77 - 97	75 - 88	35 - 37
Average	27 - 41	51 - 69	55 - 76	60 - 74	31 - 34
Poor	12 - 26	33 - 50	34 - 54	45 - 59	28 - 30
Inferior	11 & below	32 & below	33 & below	44 & below	27 & below

From E. French and E. Stalter: Study of skill tests in badminton for college women, *Research Quarterly, 20:*257-272, 1949. Courtesy of AAHPER.

RELIABILITY: For the wrist-volley item, a .83 reliability coefficient was determined by the odd-even method and was stepped up by the Spearman-Brown Formula. Fifty-nine physical education majors served as subjects.

CRITERION MEASURE: Judges' ratings.

Multiple correlation coefficients for validity and weightings are shown below for the various possible test item combinations for the five-test battery:

Two-item test battery:

    a. 2.5 (wrist-volley) + 1.0 (short serve) = .87

    b. 1.0 (short serve) + 1.2 (clear) = .85

    c. 2.0 (wrist-volley) + 1.0 (clear) = .84

Three-item test battery:

    a. 2.0 (wrist-volley) + 1.0 (clear) + 1.0 (short serve) = .91

    b. Shuttle + 0.3 (clear) + 0.19 (wrist-volley) = .68

Four-item test battery:

    a. Shuttle + 0.19 (wrist-volley) + 0.12 (short serve) + 0.11 (clear) = .70

Additional Comments

The wrist-volley item seems to adequately measure that particular skill, even for evaluation purposes. Other test items should be used only as part of one of the possible batteries, regardless of the purpose.

To speed up the administration of the smash item, it is recommended that two subjects be tested simultaneously on one court. Also, the twenty trials can be divided into two sets of ten each with the two subjects exchanging sides of the court after completing ten trials. Additionally for the smash test, it is important that the servers are qualified and retain their assignment throughout the test to insure maximum consistency in test conditions.

Providing the tester an option of three different scientifically documented test batteries to use, the French-Stalter Badminton Skill Tests demonstrate a uniqueness that is not shown in many other sports skills test batteries. Determination of the multiple correlation coefficients and value weightings made this possible.

Variables such as skills stressed, available equipment and supplies, number of students, amount of time available, and desired test difficulty may all be considered before a particular battery is selected for utilization.

LOCKHART-MCPHERSON BADMINTON TEST[22]

Also cited as Lockhart-McPherson Badminton Wall Volley Test and the Lockhart-McPherson Badminton Volleying Test.

Date: 1949.

Purpose: To determine badminton playing ability.

Description

A 1-foot net line is marked on the wall 5 feet above and parallel to the floor. A starting line is marked on the floor 6½ feet from and parallel to the base of the wall. A restraining line is also marked on the floor that is only 3 feet from the base of the wall and parallel to the starting line.

EDUCATIONAL APPLICATION: Test originally developed for college women, but Mathews[25] later adapted it for college men. The test is also reportedly applicable to junior and senior high school males and females.[1]

Administrative Feasibility

TIME: One class of twenty students can easily take the test in a sixty-minute period.

PERSONNEL: One individual to time, score and record.

TRAINING INVOLVED: Each student is allowed a fifteen-second practice session immediately before being tested.

EQUIPMENT AND SUPPLIES. Badminton racquet, indoor shuttle cock, stop watch.

Accessories: Scoring materials.

Facilities and Space: A smooth wall that is at least 10 × 10 feet and floor space of equal dimensions.

Directions

When ready, the subject assumes a service position behind the starting line and on the starting command, she executes a legal badminton serve against the front wall. The shuttlecock is then

TABLE VIII

NORMS FOR LOCKHART-MCPHERSON BADMINTON TEST*

T-Score	Volley Test Sum of Three Trials
75	145
70	131
65	114
60	101
55	87
50	73
45	64
40	52
35	45
30	38
25	32

*Based on performance of 178 college women.

From A. Lockhart and F. A. McPherson: The development of a test of badminton playing ability, *Research Quarterly, 20:*402-405, 1949. Courtesy of AAHPER.

volleyed as many times as possible during the thirty-second time period, with the subject staying behind the restraining line. A legal hit, which counts one point, occurs anytime the subject hits the shuttlecock on or above the net line while remaining anywhere behind the restraining line. The subject may continue to hit the shuttlecock even if the net line or the restraining line has been

TABLE IX

ACHIEVEMENT SCALE FOR COLLEGE WOMEN

Rating	Test Score Sum of Three Trials
Superior	126 & up
Good	90 – 125
Average	62 – 89
Poor	40 – 61
Inferior	39 & below

From A. Lockhart and F. A. McPherson: The development of a test of badminton playing ability, *Research Quarterly, 20:*402-405, 1949. Courtesy of AAHPER.

violated, but no points are scored. Should the shuttlecock come to rest at any time during any one of the thirty-second trial periods, the subject needs only to promptly retrieve the shuttlecock, assume a service position behind the starting line, and quickly put the shuttlecock into play again with a legal serve against the wall.

Any wood shot, carry, or double hit counts as a legal hit providing the subject remains behind the restraining line and the shuttlecock hits on or above the net line.

SCORING METHOD AND NORMS: The subject's score is the sum total of legal hits in each of the three thirty-second trials.

A legal hit or point is not counted when the subject puts the shuttlecock into play with a serve while standing behind the starting line.

Scientific Authenticity

VALIDITY: An *r* or .71 was obtained when ratings of three experienced judges were correlated with actual test scores of sixty-eight girls. A .60 coefficient was determined for the relationship between round-robin tournament results of twenty-seven girls and their test scores.

Furthermore, an *r* of .90 was found for the relationship between three judges' ratings and the percentage of games won by each of the twenty-seven girls in the round-robin tournament.

RELIABILITY: The .90 reliability coefficient was determined by the test-retest method utilized on a three-day testing period. Fifty girls participated as test subjects.

CRITERION MEASURE: Judges' ratings and tournament rankings.

Additional Comments

Repeated positive results have been found in studies of the test's validity value. Additionally, high marks are given the test for reliability, time of administration, plus ease of administration and scoring. It has no discernible limitations.

MILLER WALL VOLLEY TEST[27]

Date: 1951.

Purpose: To measure the ability to hit the clear shot and to determine general badminton playing ability.

Description

In analyzing one of the United States Amateur Badminton Championship Tournaments, Miller discovered that the clear shot was used more often than any other shot in both singles and doubles play. Based on this knowledge, she proceeded to develop a rather uncomplicated wall volley test that is easily administered.

A 1-inch line, 7½ feet above and parallel to the floor, is marked on the wall. The floor marking simply consists of a restraining line located 10 feet back from the base of the wall, with a suggested safety line located 3 inches behind the restraining line.

EDUCATIONAL APPLICATION: College men and women.

Administrative Feasibility

TIME: One class of twenty students can easily take the test in a sixty-minute period.

PERSONNEL: One individual to time, score, and record.

TRAINING INVOLVED: Each subject is permitted a one-minute practice period immediately before the test begins.

EQUIPMENT AND SUPPLIES: Badminton racquet, outdoor shuttlecock with sponge ends, stop watch.

Accessories: Scoring materials plus those for floor and wall markings.

Facilities and Space: A smooth wall at least 10 × 15 feet and floor space of equal dimensions.

Directions

While standing behind the restraining line, the subject serves the shuttlecock in a legal manner against the wall and rallies for thirty seconds with clear shots. Any type of stroke may be used during the testing. The subject should try to volley the shuttlecock against the wall as many times as possible within each of three thirty-second time periods. To count as a legal hit or one point, the subject must stay behind the restraining line, and the shuttlecock must hit on or above the high wall line.

A carry or double hit is legal providing the subject does not violate either the restraining or wall line. Although the subject may move anywhere on the court, points are only tallied when he remains within the boundaries. Should the shuttlecock come to rest at any time during one of the thirty-second trial periods, the subject need only retrieve the shuttlecock, immediately assume a proper position behind the restraining line, and again put the shuttlecock into play with a legal serve. Intervening rest periods come between test trials.

SCORING METHOD: The subject's score is the sum total of legal hits in the three thirty-second trials.

When 115 college men were used as subjects, the resulting range of test scores was 20 to 118. The mean for this group was 76, and the sigma was 22.

In another study, scores of 100 university women ranged from 9 to 113 with a mean of 42 and a sigma of 20.

Scientific Authenticity

VALIDITY: A validity coefficient of .83 was determined by correlating the actual test scores with the results of a round-robin tournament in which twenty subjects played 380 single games.

RELIABILITY: A reliability coefficient of .94 was determined by use of the test-retest method during a testing period of one week. One hundred college girls with varied skill levels were the original test subjects.

CRITERION MEASURE: Round-robin tournament rankings.

Additional Comments

The tester is cautioned that the type of wall surface used can make a difference in subject scores. Therefore, it and the type of shuttlecock used should be consistent throughout a test administration for a class whenever possible. If any type shuttlecock other than an outdoor, sponge-tipped kind is used, the rebound from the wall varies significantly. Because of these variables, establishment of local norms should be done with consistency shown in the type of wall surface and shuttlecock used.

It is further suggested that during the three thirty-second trials, a person should be placed in charge of providing the subject with helpful information such as saying *"back"* whenever the subject consistently steps on or over the restraining line.

Miller[28] modified this test by simply changing the restraining line distance to 8 feet. The Modified Miller Wall Volley Test, as it is known, was developed for use in a research study which compared the effects of training sessions of diverse time periods on the skill and knowledge achievement of high school girls. The highest reliability coefficient found among student scores in one of the types of training sessions was .93. It was assumed that the test modification also possessed an acceptable degree of validity.

SCOTT-FOX LONG SERVE TEST[35]

Also cited as Scott-Fox Serve Test.

Date: 1959.

Purpose: To measure the ability to serve high and to the backcourt.

Description

The floor markings for this test are identical to those described for the French Short Serve Test, except for the location of the target. With the intersection of the long service line and the left side boundary line for singles utilized as a midpoint, a series of arcs are drawn in the left service court at distances of 22, 30, 38, and 46 inches from the midpoint. The measurements include the width of the 2-inch line. Each arc should be extended to the outside boundary of the long service line and the sideline (Fig. 4). The 2-inch wide lines can be made of tape or washable paint and should be color coded for scoring ease.

Using an additional set of standards, a rope is stretched across the court 14 feet from and parallel to the net at a height of 8 feet. Incidentally, the rope location for this test is identical to that required in the French Clear Test.

EDUCATIONAL APPLICATION: Originally developed for college women but is also appropriate for men at that level as well as for both sexes at the high school level.

Administrative Feasibility

TIME: A class of twenty students can take the test in one sixty-minute period.

PERSONNEL: One scorer-recorder.

TRAINING INVOLVED: Practice is unnecessary since twenty trials are completed by the subject.

EQUIPMENT AND SUPPLIES: Badminton racquets, shuttlecocks, badminton net, two sets of standards, and a rope 20 feet or more in length.

Accessories: Scoring and floor marking materials.

Facilities and Space: Regulation badminton court.

Directions

The subject (X) takes a position in the service court diagonally across from the target and may stand at any desired spot providing it is in the proper service court (Fig. 4). The subject then performs twenty legal serves over the net and rope to the target area. The target is marked in point values of 5, 4, 3, 2, and 1, in decreasing order from the midpoint. Illegal serves may be repeated.

SCORING METHOD AND NORMS: Points are scored when the subject serves a legal serve from the proper service court and the shuttlecock clears the net and rope and lands in the target area. Should a shuttlecock land on a line dividing two target areas, the higher value is awarded. The final score is the sum total of points for the twenty trials.

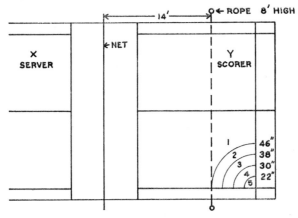

Figure 4. Court markings and rope location for Scott-Fox Long Serve Test. From M. G. Scott and E. French: *Measurement and Evaluation in Physical Education.* Dubuque, Iowa, Brown, 1959. With permission of M. G. Scott.

TABLE X

NORMS FOR SCOTT–FOX LONG SERVE TEST*

Long Serve	T-Score
35	75
34	68
33	67
32	65
27	60
22	55
18	50
13	44
9	40
5	34
2	31
1	24

*Based on scores of 91 college freshman and sophomore women.

From M. G. Scott and E. French: *Measurement and Evaluation in Physical Education.* Dubuque, Iowa, Brown, 1959. With permission of M. G. Scott.

The scorer (Y) should stand on the same side as the target between the rope and the end boundary line and face the target.

Scientific Authenticity

VALIDITY: A validity coefficient of .54 was determined by correlating the scores of forty-five college women with subjective ratings made by three judges during actual competition.

RELIABILITY: A .77 reliability coefficient was derived by use of the odd-even method and stepped up by the Spearman-Brown Formula. Again, the test subjects were forty-five college women.

CRITERION MEASURE: Judges' ratings.

Additional Comments

The arcs called for in the floor markings can easily be drawn by use of a string at least 46 inches long with marks placed at 22, 30, 38, and 46-inch intervals. It is suggested that tape be used instead of washable paint for the 2-inch wide floor lines. Coloring of the tape should be done after it is applied to the floor.

To boost the test's value in time of administration, both the right and left service court on one side of the net could be marked off to enable the testing of two subjects at once. Furthermore, the subjects could change sides of the service court after ten serves.

The Scott-Fox Long Serve Test has been included as part of various test batteries. In a study whereby subjective ratings of judges during tournament play was used as the criterion,[35] resulting multiple correlation coefficients and weightings were:

5.0 (wrist-volley) + 3.0 (clear) + 1.0 (long serve) $R = .88$

5.0 (wrist-volley) + 1.0 (long serve) $R = .83$

3.0 (clear) + 1.0 (long serve) $R = .71$

Davis[10] felt that the Scott-Fox Long Serve Test and the French Short Serve Test (see p. 26) should be combined to properly serve as an indicator of serving ability, since under game conditions a player must serve to both sides of the court and use both the short and long serves. Court markings in the Davis Test are similar to those found in the above mentioned tests, but the serving procedure differs significantly. Initially serving ten consecutive serves from the right service court while alternating between the short and long serve, the subject then moves to the left service court and repeats the procedure.

Sixty-one freshmen and sophomore college males who were enrolled in beginning badminton classes served as subjects. The relationship between their serving scores and the instructor's ratings resulted in a correlation coefficient of .70.

POOLE BADMINTON TEST[31]

Date: 1970.

Purpose: To measure performance in basic badminton skills.

Description

Tests for the smash, long serve, forehand clear, and backhand clear comprise the battery developed by Poole and Nelson.

Smash: The additional floor markings on a regulation badminton court include two spots (X) that are located in the center of both the left and right service courts and 13 feet from the net (Fig. 5). This permits two subjects to be tested at once. The target area on the opposite side of the net consists of a 4-foot,

4-inch area marked off on both the left and right service courts. The target area extends from the sideline for singles to a line that is parallel to and 4 feet, 4 inches from the singles sideline. Beginning at the short service line, the target ends at the back boundary and long service line for singles.

Long Serve: Besides those floor markings already on a regulation badminton court, four parallel lines are constructed in the back part of the designated service court along with a 15 × 15-inch square (Fig. 6). The first of the four lines is 2 inches behind and parallel to the back boundary line (BBL). The second line is 14 inches in front of the back boundary line and parallel to it. This places the long service line for doubles (DLSL) 16 inches from the second line, also in a parallel manner. The third line is 16 inches closer and parallel to the net, with the fourth line 16 inches from and parallel to the third line. This represents a five-point target area.

The previously mentioned square is located 11 feet from the net on the target side in the middle of the appropriate service court.

Forehand Clear: Additional floor markings include two parallel lines and two 15 × 15-inch squares (Fig. 7). The first line is constructed between the short service line (SSL) and the doubles long service line (DLSL) and parallel to them. The second line is located 6 inches beyond the back boundary line (BBL).

One square (0) is situated in the middle of the center line and 11 feet from the net on the target side. The other square (X) is constructed at the intersection of the doubles long service line and the center line.

Backhand Clear: Same as forehand clear test.

EDUCATIONAL APPLICATION: High school and college men and women for all items with the smash also considered applicable to junior high school students.

Administrative Feasibility

TIME: Twenty students can be tested in two to four sixty-minute class periods, depending upon the number of test stations available.

PERSONNEL: Only a scorer is needed for the smash test when

the Badminton Set-up Machine* is used; otherwise, a server is also necessary. For the long serve, forehand clear, and backhand clear tests, a scorer-recorder plus an assistant are required.

TRAINING INVOLVED: Students should demonstrate a reasonable level of skill mastery before being evaluated on the various battery items. Seven trials on the smash test item represent the extent of recommended uniformity in immediate pretest practice.

EQUIPMENT AND SUPPLIES: Badminton racquets, shuttlecock, and option of using Badminton Set-up Machine.

Accessories: Scoring and floor marking materials.

Facilities and Space: Regulation badminton court.

Directions

SMASH: The subject or subjects being tested should stand on the aforementioned spot while facing the net. The original test was designed so the subject would stand below the dropping point of the Badminton Set-up Machine and smash the shuttlecocks emitted from the machine. If the Johnson Badminton Set-up Machine is not available, it is recommended that the tester follow the same procedure as described for the smash test in the French-Stalter Badminton Skill Tests battery (see pp. 35-36).

That test utilized a server that stood behind the short service line on the target side of the net and served high, well-placed serves to the subject. The subject smashed the served shuttlecocks that were of sufficient height and depth. If the serve was not high or deep enough, the subject was instructed not to attempt a shot.

In the Poole-Nelson Test, subjects are required to smash the shuttlecock ten consecutive times into the designated target area. Any trial that is lacking reasonable speed or force must be repeated. If a repeated trial is also judged as insufficient, the trial is counted as zero.

LONG SERVE: The test subject stands in the service court diagonally opposite the target area anywhere behind the short service line. He proceeds to serve twelve consecutive, high, deep serves

---

* The Badminton Set-up Machine, Model A-7, Patent Pending 1972, by Barry L. Johnson, Texas A & I University at Corpus Christi, Texas.

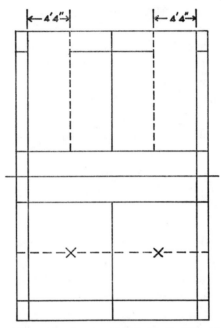

Figure 5. Floor markings for Poole Smash Test. From B. L. Johnson and J. K. Nelson: *Practical Measurements for Evaluation in Physical Education*, 1974. Courtesy of Burgess Publishing Company, Minneapolis.

over the opponent to the target area. A successful serve is one that has cleared the "opponent's" racquet and lands in the target area. The "opponent" is a student assistant who stands in the square and has a badminton racquet extended above his head. To be considered legal, the served shuttlecock must pass over the extended racquet, or the assistant gives an audible signal *"low."* The scorer-recorder should stand at point Z (Fig. 6).

FOREHAND CLEAR: Standing with his right foot in the square and holding the badminton racquet face in an upward direction, the subject tosses the shuttlecock high into the air and proceeds to hit twelve consecutive overhead forehand clear shots. A left-handed subject should place his left foot in the square and keep it in contact with the floor until the shuttlecock is struck. The shuttlecock should clear the net and the "opponent's" racquet

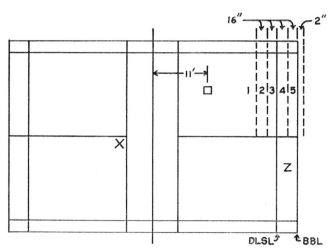

Figure 6. Floor markings for Poole Long Serve Test. From B. L. Johnson and J. K. Nelson: *Practical Measurements for Evaluation in Physical Education,* 1974. Courtesy of Burgess Publishing Company, Minneapolis.

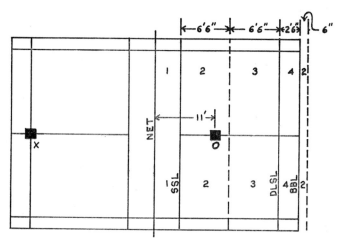

Figure 7. Floor markings for Poole Forehand and Backhand Clear Tests. From B. L. Johnson and J. K. Nelson: *Practical Measurements for Evaluation in Physical Education,* 1974. Courtesy of Burgess Publishing Company, Minneapolis.

plus land in the target area. The assistant serving as the opponent gives an audible signal *"low"* if the shuttlecock does not pass over the extended racquet.

BACKHAND CLEAR: Same as the forehand clear item except that the test subject stands with his left foot in the X square. The shuttlecock should be placed on the forehand side of the racquet and tossed into the air. This is followed by the subject's execution of a backhand clear shot deep into the opponent's court.

SCORING METHOD AND NORMS

Smash: Each subject is given ten test trials, and the final score is the number of times the smashed shuttlecock lands in the appropriate target area. A maximum score is ten points. Percentile scores of fifty college men and fifty-two college women are shown in Table XI.

Long Serve: Each subject completes twelve test trials or serves. The score of the best ten of twelve serves is counted and totaled.

TABLE XI

SMASH TEST SCORING SCALE*

Percentile	Boys	Girls	Percentile
100th	10	10	100th
95th	7	8	95th
90th	6	7	90th
80th	5	6	80th
70th	4	5	70th
60th	4	5	60th
50th	3	4	50th
40th	2	4	40th
30th	2	3	30th
20th	1	2	20th
10th	1	1	10th
0	0	0	0

*Based on scores of 50 college men and 52 college women as reported by Bill Parker, NLU, Monroe, La., 1973.

From B. L. Johnson and J. K. Nelson: *Practical Measurements for Evaluation in Physical Education,* 1974. Courtesy of Burgess Publishing Company, Minneapolis.

TABLE XII

LONG SERVE SCORING SCALE*

Preliminary Skill Test	Performance Level	Final Skill Test
26 & Above	Good	30 & Above
17 - 25	Fair	20 - 29
0 - 16	Poor	0 - 19

*Based on scores of a limited number of beginner course students.

From B. L. Johnson and J. K. Nelson: *Practical Measurements for Evaluation in Physical Education,* 1974. Courtesy of Burgess Publishing Company, Minneapolis.

A perfect score equals fifty points. A shuttlecock landing on a line that divides the target zone is assigned the higher point value. One point is subtracted from the assigned target value for any trial when the serve does not go above the extended racquet of the "opponent." Only legal serves are scored.

Forehand Clear: Twelve forehand clear shots are performed by the subject. The point value of the zone in which the shuttlecock lands is recorded. The final score is the total points for the best ten out of twelve forehand clear shots. A perfect score is forty points.

TABLE XIII

FOREHAND CLEAR SCORING SCALE*

Preliminary Skill Test	Performance Level	Final Skill Test
20 & Above	Good	24 & Above
13 - 19	Fair	16 - 23
0 - 12	Poor	0 - 15

*Based on scores of a limited number of beginner course students.

From B. L. Johnson and J. K. Nelson: *Practical Measurements for Evaluation in Physical Education,* 1974. Courtesy of Burgess Publishing Company, Minneapolis.

TABLE XIV

BACKHAND CLEAR SCORING SCALE*

Preliminary Skill Test	Performance Level	Final Skill Test
16 & Above	Good	22 & Above
9 - 15	Fair	11 - 21
0 - 8	Poor	0 - 10

*Based on scores of a limited number of beginner course students.

From B. L. Johnson and J. K. Nelson: *Practical Measurements for Evaluation in Physical Education,* 1974. Courtesy of Burgess Publishing Company, Minneapolis.

Any shuttlecock landing on a line that divides a target zone is assigned the higher point value, and one point is subtracted from each trial if the shuttlecock does not clear the extended racquet of the "opponent." Only legal serves are scored.

Backhand Clear: This test is the same as the Poole Forehand Clear Test with the exception of the scoring scale (Table XIV). The backhand shot is a more difficult shot to properly execute than the forehand clear, so the scores are naturally lower.

Scoring scales for the smash, long serve, forehand clear, and backhand clear are presented in Tables XI through XIV. The scales were based on the scores of a limited number of beginning badminton players.

Scientific Authenticity

VALIDITY: Face validity was accepted for the smash test. Validity coefficients of .51, .70, and .57 were determined for the long serve, forehand clear, and backhand clear tests, respectively.

RELIABILITY: Utilizing the scores of 102 college men and women, a coefficient of .77 was determined for the smash item. In a test-retest approach for obtaining reliability, coefficients of .81, .90, and .78 were found for the long serve, forehand clear, and backhand clear tests, respectively.

OBJECTIVITY: An objectivity coefficient of .94 was computed

for the smash item with an experienced and unexperienced scorer participating.

CRITERION MEASURE: Tournament results.

Additional Comments

Even though the Badminton Set-up Machine is a relatively inexpensive training and testing device, its lack of general availability necessitates the training of an experienced badminton player to serve the shuttlecock to the subject during the smash test. Therefore, norms and scoring scales should be developed at the local level. This is recommended for the other three items also because testers sometimes vary in their approach to testing, plus it neutralizes the need to standardize the height of the individuals serving as "opponents" in those tests. The tester should be certain that each student in a class is tested on the items while utilizing the same "opponent" or one of equal height. Poole's innovative idea of using the student assistants as "opponents" makes the setting of the tests more gamelike. If for some reason an assistant is not used for the long serve test, it is recommended that a 9-foot high rope be placed parallel to the net and 11 feet away.

To insure proper test reliability, the subjects should be well trained in the art of tossing up a shuttlecock to initiate the two clear test items. Beginning badminton players should be able to quickly learn this skill.

Poole and Nelson found that the number of recommended trials for the three test items could be reduced without sacrificing test reliability. Using the best six of eight trials as opposed to ten of twelve in administering the long serve, forehand clear, and backhand clear, correlation of the two scoring systems yielded coefficients of .95, .96, and .94 for the items in the order presented above.

REFERENCES

1. Barrow, Harold M. and McGee, Rosemary: *A Practical Approach to Measurement in Physical Education.* Philadelphia, Lea & Febiger, 1964.
2. ——— and ———: *A Practical Approach to Measurement in Physical Education,* 2nd ed. Philadelphia, Lea & Febiger, 1971.

3. Beverlein, Mary Ann: A Skill Test for the Drop Shot in Badminton. Master's thesis, Carbondale, Southern Illinois University, 1970.

4. Bobrich, Melsa: Reliability of an Evaluative Tool Used to Measure Badminton Skill. Master's thesis, Chicago, George Williams College, 1972.

5. Boldrick, Evelyn L.: The Measurement of Fundamental Skills in Badminton. Master's thesis, Wellesley, Mass., Wellesley College, 1945.

6. Brumbach, Wayne B.: Badminton Skills and Fitness Tests. Unpublished study. Eugene, University of Oregon, 1967.

7. Campbell, Virginia M.: Development of Achievement Tests in Badminton. Master's thesis. Austin, University of Texas, 1938.

8. Clarke, H. Harrison: *Application of Measurement to Health and Physical Education,* 5th ed. Englewood Cliffs, P-H, 1976.

9. Davis, Barbara: The Relationship of Certain Skill Tests to Playing Ability in Badminton. Master's thesis, Wellesley, Mass, Wellesley College, 1946.

10. Davis, Phyllis R.: The Development of a Combined Short and Long Badminton Service Skill Test. Master's thesis, Knoxville, University of Tennessee, 1968.

11. Dexter, Genevie: *Teacher's Guide to Physical Education for Girls in High School.* Sacramento, Calif., State Department of Education, 1949.

12. Edgren, Harry D. and Robinson, G. G.: *Group Instruction in Tennis and Badminton.* New York, B&N, 1939.

13. ——— and ———: *Individual Skill Tests in Physical Activities.* Chicago, the authors, 1937.

14. French, Esther and Stalter, Evelyn: Study of skill tests in badminton for college women. *Research Quarterly, 20:257-272,* 1949.

15. Greiner, Marilyn Rose: Construction of a Short Serve Test for Beginning Badminton Players. Master's thesis, Madison, University of Wisconsin, 1964.

16. Hale, Patricia Ann: Construction of a Long Serve Test for Beginning Badminton Players. Master's thesis, Madison, University of Wisconsin, 1970.

17. Haskins, Mary Jane: *Evaluation in Physical Education.* Dubuque, Iowa, Brown Bk, 1971.

18. Hicks, Joanna V.: The Construction and Evaluation of a Battery of Five Badminton Skill Tests. Doctoral dissertation, Denton, Texas Women's University, 1967.

19. Johnson, Barry L. and Nelson, Jack K.: *Practical Measurements for Evaluation in Physical Education,* 2nd ed. Minneapolis, Burgess, 1974.

20. Johnson, Rose Marie: Determination of the Validity and Reliability of

the Badminton Placement Test. Master's thesis, Eugene, University of Oregon, 1967.

21. Kowert, Eugene A.: Construction of a Badminton Ability Test for Men. Master's thesis, Iowa City, University of Iowa, 1968.

22. Lockhart, Aileene and McPherson, Francis A.: The development of a test of badminton playing ability. *Research Quarterly, 20:*402-405, 1949.

23. Lucey, Mildred A.: A Study of the Components of Wrist Action as they Relate to Speed of Learning and the Degree of Proficiency Attained in Badminton. Doctoral dissertation, New York, New York University, 1952.

24. Mathews, Donald K.: *Measurement in Physical Education,* 4th ed. Philadelphia, Saunders, 1973.

25. ———: Unpublished study in *Measurement in Physical Education,* 4th ed. Philadelphia, Saunders, 1973.

26. McDonald, E. Dawn: The Development of a Skill Test for the Badminton High Clear. Master's thesis, Carbondale, Southern Illinois University, 1968.

27. Miller, Francis A.: A badminton wall volley test. *Research Quarterly, 22:*208-213, 1951.

28. Miller, Susan E.: The Relative Effectiveness of High School Badminton Instruction When Given in Two Short Units and One Continuous Unit Involving the Same Total Time. Master's thesis, Seattle, University of Washington, 1964.

29. Montoye, Henry J. (Ed.): *An Introduction to Measurement in Physical Education,* vol. III. Indianapolis, Phi Epsilon Kappa Fraternity, 1970.

30. Neilson, N. P. and Jensen, Clayne R.: *Measurement and Statistics in Physical Education.* Belmont, Calif., Wadsworth Pub, 1972.

31. Poole, James and Nelson, Jack K.: Construction of a badminton skills test battery. Unpublished study. In Johnson, Barry L. and Nelson, Jack K.: *Practical Measurements for Evaluation in Physical Education,* 2nd ed. Minneapolis, Burgess, 1974.

32. Scott, James H.: A Study in the Evaluation of Playing Ability in the Game of Badminton. Master's thesis, Columbus, The Ohio State University, 1941.

33. Scott, M. Gladys; Carpenter, Aileen; French, Esther; and Kuhl, Louise: Achievement examinations in badminton. *Research Quarterly, 12:* 242-253, 1941.

34. Scott, M. Gladys and French, Esther: *Better Teaching Through Testing.* New York, B&N, 1945.

35. ——— and ———: *Measurement and Evaluation in Physical Education.* Dubuque, Iowa, Brown Bk, 1959.

36. Washington, Jean: Construction of a Wall Volley Test for the Badminton Short Serve and the Effect of Wall Practice on Court Performance. Master's thesis, Denton, North Texas State University, 1968.
37. Weiss, Raymond A. and Phillips, Marjorie: *Administration of Tests in Physical Education.* St. Louis, Mosby, 1954.
38. Willgoose, Carl: *Evaluation in Health Education and Physical Education.* New York, McGraw, 1961.
39. Williams, Glenna R.: A Study of Badminton Skills. Master's thesis, Denton, Texas State College for Women, 1945.

Chapter 4

Baseball

INTRODUCTION

A NUMBER OF skills tests have been developed in the sport of
baseball, but few were scientifically authenticated when constructed. This is a probable explanation why only a few useful
tests are presented in measurement textbooks that were written in
the last quarter century. The limited presentation of baseball tests
is also attributed to the uncommon practice of including baseball
in the sports activities curriculum, especially at the secondary and
college levels. As a result, the emphasis on skills tests construction in baseball is insignificant compared to the work that has
been done in some of the sports more commonly found in the
physical education curriculum.

Several factors influence the limited use of baseball in the curriculum of American schools and universities. The sport closely
relates to softball which is routinely offered in physical education
programs. Very little carry-over value is exhibited in baseball
which is less true of softball. Aside from professional baseball,
few opportunities exist for a person to play organized baseball
beyond the college years. More playing space is required for baseball than softball which makes softball a more logical choice to be
inserted into the curriculum.

The baseball skills tests that do exist and are presented in this
chapter are helpful tools to Little League coaches for classification purposes and public school physical education teachers for
the measurement of achievement.

KELSON BASEBALL CLASSIFICATION PLAN[6]

Also cited as Boys' Baseball Classification Plan and Kelson
Test.

Date: 1953.

Purpose: To classify boys for baseball participation at the elementary school and Little League levels. The test could also be

used to measure individual and team progress during a season or term of study.

EDUCATIONAL APPLICATION: The test was devised for boys, eight to twelve in age; however, it has potential for implementation at higher age and ability levels.

Administrative Feasibility

TIME: The test is very worthwhile with regard to time of administration. Several students can be tested in one class session.

PERSONNEL: One person is needed at the restraining line to check for violations and a scorer should be located every 25 feet within an area marked off from 50 to 200 feet. Two instructors or coaches would be ideal for the test administration, but one individual of that nature with a few student assistants (at least two) should suffice.

TRAINING INVOLVED: Since the baseball throw for distance alone is a valid index for baseball ability, training would be minimal. A routine warm-up period prior to throwing the ball constitutes the extent of any necessary training for the subject.

EQUIPMENT AND SUPPLIES: Little League baseballs.

Accessories: Field marking and scoring materials, plus a tape measure.

Facilities and Space: Level or near level field at least 250 feet in length and 50 feet in width.

Directions

The throwing area is marked off from 50 to 200 feet with lines every 5 feet apart. A scorer should be stationed every 25 feet from beginning to end of the throwing area. Since the throws of most students tend to cluster in a predictable range of the throwing area, the test can be adequately administered with fewer scorers than recommended.

In determining the ability to throw for distance, three trial throws are recorded in feet by the scorers. The subjects are permitted to run prior to throwing the ball as long as they do not cross the restraining line.

SCORING METHOD AND NORMS: The best throw of the three trials is selected as the official score.

TABLE XV
BASEBALL CLASSIFICATION INDEX FOR BOYS*

Ability Level	Distance of Throw
Superior	177 feet & over
Above Average	145 - 176 feet
Average	113 - 144 feet
Below Average	80 - 112 feet
Inferior	79 feet & under

*Based on scores of 151 boys, ages 8-12.

From R. E. Kelson: Baseball classification plan for boys, *Research Quarterly,* *24:*304-307, 1953. Courtesy of AAHPER.

Sixty-four boys, ages eight to twelve, participated in the original study. Eighty-seven additional boys were tested for the distance throw within a year of the original study for the expansion of the developed norms. The classification plan shown in Table XV was devised from the distance throwing scores of the previously mentioned 151 subjects.

Scientific Authenticity

VALIDITY: A correlation coefficient of .85 was obtained between the throw for distance test and a composite criterion composed of seasonal batting averages and judges' ratings on four other baseball skills.

RELIABILITY: Not reported.

CRITERION MEASURE: A composite score of baseball skills which included batting averages and the evaluation of twelve judges in throwing for accuracy and distance, catching fly balls, and fielding ground balls. Inferior to superior ability was rated from one to five points on all skills except batting. Each subject was then scored from one to five for batting ability. To correspond the batting score with the ability scores, the score given for an individual batting average was multiplied by twelve. The batting averages in the lower 10 percent of the distribution were assigned one point with the next higher 20 percent given two points. The middle 40 percent was assigned a rating of three with the next higher 20 percent given four points. The highest 10 percent of the distribution was assigned five points.

Additional Comments

Of all the well-constructed sports skills tests in existence today, few can match the Kelson Classification Plan in meeting the feasibility criteria for testing. Easy in its administration, economical in time of administration, and valid in the determination of baseball ability, the test has demonstrated its value as a worthwhile testing instrument for baseball skill.

Another advantage of the Kelson Test is its potential for adaptation. The test could possibly adapt well to the sport of softball and also to other age and ability levels. The latter adaptation could be made by simply using regulation baseballs instead of the Little League models.

The norms for the Kelson Test should be updated for the level it was originally designed for and also expanded to other age and ability levels.

The use of this test for classification purposes seems to have definite advantages over its use in the measurement of achievement. Since baseball throwing for distance seems to be more a result of nature than nurture, its use as an exclusive determinant of achievement is questionable. However, it should not be discarded for grading purposes because the acquired skill a student brings with him to any skills class is commonly assigned more value in grading than improvement.

HOOKS BASEBALL TEST BATTERY[5]

Date: 1959.

Purpose: The original study was designed to determine the relative importance of various structural and strength measures in predicting success in the performance of common baseball skills. The test battery used by Hooks in the above mentioned study merits consideration for use by coaches and physical education instructors.

Description

The Hooks Test Battery includes tests for skill in hitting, running, throwing, and fielding.

EDUCATIONAL APPLICATION: Original study used college men, but battery is adaptable to high school boys.

Administrative Feasibility

TIME: Specific items in the test battery lend themselves well to economy of time in testing; however, to use the whole battery would require at least one forty-minute class period per test item.

PERSONNEL: More than one instructor would be ideal for judging hitting ability while one instructor with student assistants should suffice for the other test items.

TRAINING INVOLVED: Brief warm-up drills routinely used in baseball, instituted on a uniform basis.

EQUIPMENT AND SUPPLIES: Automatic pitching machine plus balls, bats, gloves, etc. and stop watch.

Accessories: Line marking and scoring materials, plus a rope at least 8 to 10 feet in length.

Facilities and Space: Regulation baseball field for hitting and throwing tests that serves well for the administration of the other tests.

Directions

HITTING: The student stands in the batter's box and hits balls pitched by an automatic pitching machine until told to stop. Three experts judged the subject's hitting ability in Hooks' study; however, one or more instructors may rate an individual's hitting ability by standing behind and to the side facing the batter. Hooks' rating form may be used or the instructor may choose to develop his own.

RUNNING: Utilizing a start commonly recommended for stealing bases and one in which the student feels comfortable, the time recorded to the nearest tenth-second in running from home plate to second base is the criterion for running ability. The student leaves the batter's box on the command *"Go"* and is required to touch first and second base.

THROWING: As described in Kelson's Classification Plan for Boys on page 59, the baseball throw for distance is used to test throwing ability.

FIELDING: Three tests are used in measuring fielding skill, a ball toss test, a ball pick-up test, and a test to determine the ability to catch fly balls. The ball toss test begins with the subject stationed directly underneath a rope extended horizontally at a height of 10 feet. On a command to start, the subject tosses the ball over the rope and catches it on the opposite side. This is continued for a period of thirty seconds.

To initiate the ball pick-up test, the tester assumes a position at the highest point of a 90-degree angle with sides extended 8½ feet. The subject takes a crouched position between the two lines and faces the tester. On the command to start, the tester rolls a baseball down one side of the angle for the subject to catch and return. The tester then rolls the ball down the other line of the angle for the subject to field and toss back. The subject returns the ball as many times as possible in thirty seconds.

The test of catching fly balls begins with the subject standing on a line 60 yards from the tester. Eight successive fly balls are hit to the subject. The subject is instructed to catch the balls on the fly and toss them to a student assistant. The subject should disregard any ground balls hit to him.

SCORING METHOD: Hitting ability is scored by adding the sum of the instructor's objective ratings or the total assigned by an individual instructor. Running ability is scored by recording the best running time of two trials.

The score for throwing is the best of three throws measured to the nearest yard. This test differs from the Kelson Classification Plan as that test is scored by measuring the throws to the nearest foot.

Fielding skill is assigned a score by adding the total of the three fielding tests. The score for the ball toss test is the number of times the subject tosses the ball over the rope in a thirty-second time period. The ball pick-up test score reflects the number of times the subject returns the ball to the tester in thirty seconds. The fly ball catching score is the number of balls caught on the fly.

Scientific Authenticity

VALIDITY: The major purpose of Hooks' study was not to validate the skills he used to represent baseball ability; therefore, those skills were not correlated with a criterion for baseball playing ability. All the tests show a degree of acceptable face validity, possibly with the exception of the fielding tests, excluding the catching fly balls item.

RELIABILITY: The coefficients were computed by correlating the scores of fifty-six college freshmen on separate tests for each item. The correlation coefficients were as follows: hitting, .96; running, .83; throwing, .96; and fielding, .93.

Additional Comments

The value of this test could possibly be significantly increased if the test requirements were validated. The apparent face validity of the items should be confirmed.

At first glance the reliability of the ball pick-up test and the test of catching fly balls may seem questionable due to the seemingly strong chance for error in consistency on the part of the tester. However, the high reliability coefficients obtained by Hooks demonstrated a high degree of consistency in the student's test-retest performance on the five baseball skill items.

REFERENCES

1. Clarke, H. Harrison: *Application of Measurement to Health and Physical Education*, 5th ed. Englewood Cliffs, P-H, 1976.
2. Cobb, John W., Jr.: The Determination of the Merits of Selected Items for the Construction of a Baseball Skill Test for Boys of Little League Age. Doctoral dissertation, Bloomington, Indiana University, 1958.
3. Fry, John Benjamin: The Relationship Between a Baseball Skill Test and Actual Playing in Game Situations. Master's thesis, University Park, Pennsylvania State University, 1958.
4. Glassow, Ruth B. and Broer, Marion R.: *Measuring Achievement in Physical Education*. Philadelphia, Saunders, 1938.
5. Hooks, G. Eugene: Prediction of baseball ability through an analysis of measures of strength and structure. *Research Quarterly, 30:*38-43, 1959.
6. Kelson, Robert E.: Baseball classification plan for boys. *Research Quarterly, 24:*304-307, 1953.
7. McCloy, Charles Harold and Young, Norma Dorothy: *Tests and Measurements in Health and Physical Education,* 3rd ed. New York, Appleton, 1954.

8. Mathews, Donald K.: *Measurement in Physical Education,* 4th ed. Philadelphia, Saunders, 1973.
9. Meyers, Carlton R.: *Measurement in Physical Education,* 2nd ed. New York, Ronald, 1974.
10. Sheehan, F. E.: Baseball Achievement Scales for Elementary and Junior High School Boys. Master's thesis, Madison, University of Wisconsin, 1954.
11. Wardlaw, Charles D.: *Fundamentals of Baseball.* New York, Scribner, 1924.
12. Willgoose, Carl E.: *Evaluation in Health Education and Physical Education.* New York, McGraw, 1961.

Chapter 5

Basketball

INTRODUCTION

THE SPORT OF BASKETBALL is rich in the quantity of developed skills tests, but the quality of many tests is unsubstantiated by scientific evidence. Perhaps more skills tests have been devised in basketball than any other physical education activity. Although many are used for the purpose of evaluating achievement in skills classes, this is not their major use. Coaches use them as an aid in team selection since a number of the tests are designed to measure basketball potential. Physical education instructors more commonly use them for classifying their students into ability levels and for measurement of student progress.

The tests presented in this chapter are limited primarily to those with value for the measurement of student achievement and classification of students according to ability levels. Some of them are reputed to show value as determinants of potential basketball ability.

JOHNSON BASKETBALL TEST[40]

Also cited as the Johnson Basketball Ability Test, Johnson Test of Basketball Ability, and Johnson Basketball Battery.

Date: 1934.

Purpose: To measure basic shooting, dribbling, and throwing skills in boys' basketball.

Description

The ability test is composed of a field goal test item, basketball throw for accuracy, and dribbling item.

EDUCATIONAL APPLICATION: High school boys.

Administrative Feasibility

TIME: One forty-minute class period for fifteen to twenty students in a mass testing situation.

PERSONNEL: Instructor and trained assistants to serve as timers and scorers.

TRAINING INVOLVED: One practice trial per test item.

EQUIPMENT AND SUPPLIES: Three basketballs and four chairs.

Accessories: Materials to construct the wall target in the throw for accuracy test; scoring materials and stop watch.

Facilities and Space: Gymnasium with unobstructed wall space.

Directions

FIELD GOAL SPEED: Holding a basketball and standing at a position of his choice, the subject shoots lay-ups as rapidly as possible for thirty seconds.

THROW FOR ACCURACY: The subject completes ten trials at a target with dimensions as described in Figure 8. Either a hook or baseball type throw is recommended.

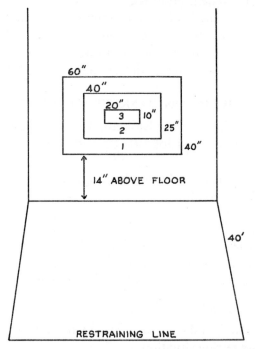

Figure 8. Target for basketball throw for accuracy test.

TABLE XVI

NORMS FOR THE JOHNSON BASKETBALL TEST

T-Score	Throw for Accuracy*			Field Goal Speed Test			Dribble Test			T-Score
	7th Grade	8th Grade	9th Grade	7th Grade	8th Grade	9th Grade	7th Grade	8th Grade	9th Grade	
85	25	23	25	14	19	22	24	26	26	85
80	23	21	23	13	18	21	23	25	26	80
75	21	19	20	12	16	19	22	24	25	75
70	19	16	18	10	14	17	21	23	24	70
65	16	14	16	9	13	15	20	22	22	65
60	14	12	14	7	11	12	19	20	21	60
55	11	10	11	6	9	10	18	19	20	55
50	9	8	9	5	7	8	17	18	19	50
45	7	5	7	4	6	6	16	17	18	45
40	4	3	4	2	4	4	15	16	17	40
35	2	1	2	1	2	2	14	15	16	35
30							13	14	15	30
25							12	13	14	25
20							11	12	13	20
15							10	11	12	15

*35-foot restraining line for 7th grade boys; 42-foot restraining line for 8th and 9th grade boys.

From Jacobson, Theodore Vernon: An Evaluation of Performance in Certain Physical Ability Tests Administered to Selected Secondary School Boys. Master's thesis, Seattle, University of Washington, 1960.

DRIBBLE: On the starting signal, the subject leaves the starting line by dribbling to the left of the first chair and then to the right of the next chair. This pattern of direction is continued for thirty seconds (Fig. 9).

SCORING METHOD AND NORMS: The number of shots made in thirty seconds is the score for the field goal speed test. The score for the dribbling item is the number of chairs passed in thirty seconds. Using a 3-2-1 scoring method from inner to outer rectangles, the total number of points represents the score for the throw for accuracy item.

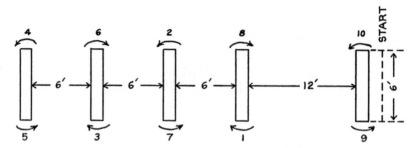

Figure 9. Layout for dribbling test.

TABLE XVII

GRADE RANGES FOR THE JOHNSON BASKETBALL ABILITY TEST

Event	(Based on the Raw Scores) Grade	7th Grade	8th Grade	9th Grade
Basketball Throw (In points)	A	18 & over	16 & over	18 & over
	B	13 - 17	11 - 15	13 - 17
	C	7 - 12	6 - 10	7 - 12
	D	1 - 6	1 - 5	1 - 6
	E	0	0	0
Basketball Shooting (Baskets made)	A	10 & over	14 & over	16 & over
	B	7 - 9	10 - 13	12 - 15
	C	4 - 6	6 - 9	7 - 11
	D	1 - 3	2 - 5	2 - 6
	E	0	1 & under	1 & under
Basketball Dribbling (In points)	A	21 & over	23 & over	24 & over
	B	19 - 20	20 - 22	21 - 23
	C	16 - 18	18 - 19	18 - 20
	D	14 - 15	15 - 17	16 - 17
	E	13 & under	14 & under	15 & under
Total Test (Total points)	A	46 & over	48 & over	53 & over
	B	37 - 45	39 - 47	43 - 52
	C	27 - 36	29 - 38	32 - 42
	D	18 - 26	20 - 28	22 - 31
	E	17 & under	19 & under	21 & under

From Jacobson, Theodore Vernon: An Evaluation of Performance in Certain Physical Ability Tests Administered to Selected Secondary School Boys. Master's thesis, Seattle, University of Washington, 1960.

Scientific Authenticity

VALIDITY: One hundred and eighty boys were divided into groups referred to as "good" or "poor." The "good" group contained fifty boys and the "poor" group had a total of 130. The individual test items ranged from .65 to .79 in validity values.

RELIABILITY: A range of .73 to .80 for the individual items.

CRITERION MEASURE: Success in winning a berth on a basketball squad.

Additional Comments

This well-constructed test originated from a potential battery of nineteen items. Aside from the Johnson Basketball Ability Test, a potential ability test was also derived from the nineteen items.

Norms for the Johnson Test have been established for grades seven through twelve. Therefore, it is important to remember that test conditions should be standardized for the particular grade level. For example, Jacobson[38] used a 35-foot restraining line in the throw for accuracy test when testing seventh grade boys and a 42-foot line for assessing the eighth and ninth grade boys. The original test for high school boys called for a 40-foot restraining line.

Test administrators should also be aware of the potential difference in test scores on the field goal speed item if a net is not used. Norms based on shots made in a netless goal might reflect greater achievement due to the time factor difference.

YOUNG-MOSER BASKETBALL ABILITY TEST[71]

Also cited as Young-Moser Basketball Test.
Date: 1934.
Purpose: To measure basketball playing ability of females.

Description

Originally published as a five-item test, only three are presented here due to the low reliability values shown for the other two items. The wall speed test measures speed of passing with the

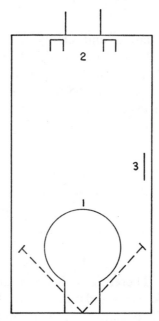

Figure 10. Floor plan for Young-Moser Test. From G. Young and H. Moser: A short battery of tests to measure playing ability in women's basketball, *Research Quarterly, 5:*3-23, 1934. Courtesy of AAHPER.

moving target item assessing passing accuracy. The bounce and shoot test measures shooting accuracy.

Notwithstanding the dimensions shown in Figures 11 and 12, a layout description of the space planning for the bounce and shoot, moving target, and wall speed pass tests is warranted and presented above.

Bounce and Shoot: As shown in Figure 11, a perpendicular is dropped from the center of the backboard to the floor. A semicircle with a radius of 15 feet is drawn with the above mentioned point as the center. Other necessary drawings include two radii that form a right angle with each other and a 45-degree angle with the diameter of the semicircle. Also, straight lines are drawn a foot long where the radii and circumferences intersect.

Moving Target

The target is suspended so that its lower edge is three feet and nine inches from the floor. The point from which it hangs is eleven feet from the floor. The six-inch rope attached to the ring is fastened to the rods that brace the backboard of the basket, at the place where they intersect. (Adjustments must be made for different types of backboard construction.) A line ten feet from the target is drawn on the floor from which the throws are made (a perpendicular is dropped from the target as it hangs straight, the place where the perpendicular touches the floor is marked, and the ten feet are measured from that point). Two lines, five feet apart, are drawn on the wall behind the target so that the midpoint between them lies directly behind a perpendicular dropped from the center of the target (Fig. 12).[71]

EDUCATIONAL APPLICATION: High school girls and college women.

Administrative Feasibility

TIME: In a mass testing setup, one sixty-minute period for fifteen to twenty students.

PERSONNEL: A scorer for each test and a timer for the wall speed pass item. The two assistants assigned to swing the target in the moving target test should show thorough familiarity with that assignment prior to testing.

TRAINING INVOLVED: The students should be permitted to practice each test item prior to being tested for score.

EQUIPMENT AND SUPPLIES: At least three basketballs and a stop watch.

Accessories: Materials for scoring and construction of target which is made of 1-inch board and is 18 inches square.

Facilities and Space: Gymnasium with flat-surfaced wall.

Directions

BOUNCE AND SHOOT: The shooting accuracy test is initiated with the student facing the basket on the right-hand side and holding the ball. The ball is bounced toward the basket and a lay-up is shot. The same action is repeated on the left side, and the sides are alternated thereafter. Ten trials are allowed.

MOVING TARGET: Standing behind the line with ball in hands, the subject waits for two student assistants to initiate the test for passing accuracy. The students stand on each side of the target with one holding the target at a position whereby the lower inside edge of the target is 6 feet from the floor at release. The target is

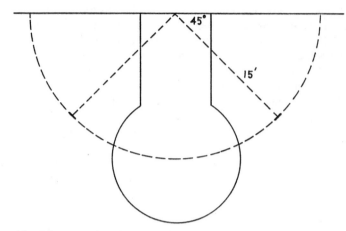

Figure 11. Diagram for bounce and shoot test. From G. Young and H. Moser: A short battery of tests to measure playing ability in women's basketball, *Research Quarterly,* 5:3-23, 1934. Courtesy of AAHPER.

held with the palms flat and is released by simply releasing the grasp. The second student catches the target and repeats the procedure in like manner. Release time for the target is not announced, but the subject is given time to get ready. Any type of

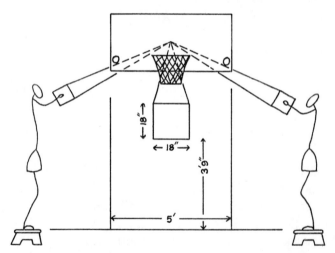

Figure 12. Test layout for moving target item. From G. Young and H. Moser: A short battery of tests to measure playing ability in women's basketball, *Research Quarterly,* 5:3-23, 1934. Courtesy of AAHPER.

pass may be used with ten opportunities given. The subject attempts to hit the swinging target as it passes through the 5-foot area marked on the wall.

WALL SPEED PASS: To measure the speed of passing, the subject stands behind a 6-foot restraining line while facing the wall and holding a basketball. At the sound of a whistle, the subject throws the ball against the wall, catches the rebound, and continues this procedure until the thirty-second trial is completed. The type of stance and pass used is the student's choice, but she must always keep both feet behind the line preceding each pass. Two trials are given.

SCORING METHOD

Bounce and Shoot: Number of successful baskets. An ability score for the three items may be calculated in situations whereby raw scores are converted to T-scores. The T-scores are added and the sum divided by three.

Moving Target: Number of times the ball strikes any part of the target as it passes through the 5-foot area.

Wall Speed Pass: Number of hits made in thirty-second time period. Total score is the sum score of two trials.

Scientific Authenticity

VALIDITY: A correlation coefficient of .86 was found between the judgment criterion and test scores of the original five items.

RELIABILITY: Three items range from .89 to .90.

CRITERION MEASURE: Judges' ratings of playing performance in a game situation.

Additional Comments

The three items presented show merit as tests of specific skill and could have value as part of a more comprehensive battery. The battery lends itself well to time and ease of administration since student assistants can be utilized both extensively and effectively.

WISCONSIN BASKETBALL TEST[31]

Also cited as Glassow et al. Basketball Test.
Date: 1938.

Purpose: To measure basketball playing ability of college women for grading purposes.

Description

Bounce and Shoot: As shown in Figure 13, an 18-foot dotted line is drawn at a 45-degree angle on each side of the basket. The lines originate from a spot directly below the center of the backboard. Perpendicular to the 18-foot lines are 24-inch lines. One foot behind and 30 inches to the outside of the 18-foot lines, additional 18-inch lines are drawn. A chair with a ball is placed at each of these areas.

Zone Toss: A zone 6 feet, 4 inches wide is marked on the floor. An inside dotted line, 6 inches from each boundary line, is included. Jump standards bisect the zone and are placed parallel to the boundary lines at 10 feet apart with a rope strung between them. The height of the rope is 7 feet, 1 inch from the floor.

Wall Speed: A line is drawn 6 feet from and parallel to the wall.

EDUCATIONAL APPLICATION: College women.

Administrative Feasibility

TIME: Utilizing a rotational plan, a class of thirty students divided into four stations could be tested in two forty-minute class periods.

PERSONNEL: The bounce and shoot test requires a timer, scorer, and two ball catchers. The zone toss test and wall speed item each require a timer and scorer.

TRAINING INVOLVED: The students should be thoroughly familiarized with the test items prior to testing.

EQUIPMENT AND SUPPLIES: Four basketballs, two stop watches, two chairs, two jump standards, and one 12-foot rope.

Accessories: Floor marking and target materials, plus those for scoring.

Facilities and Space: Gymnasium with at least one flat-surfaced wall.

Directions

BOUNCE AND SHOOT: Standing at the 24-inch line on the B side of the basket, the subject when signaled to begin picks up the ball from the chair, bounces, shoots, recovers the rebound, and passes the ball back to the catcher at B (Fig. 13). The subject runs immediately to A, picks up the ball from the chair and repeats the aforementioned action. This action is continued, alternating five times on each side. Each of the ten repetitions must begin from behind the 24-inch line on the appropriate side.

In addition to regular timing and scoring, the timer notes and records the fouls while the scorer keeps an account of the number of shots and notifies the timer on the ninth shot taken.

Fouls include traveling, double bounces, and failure to begin from behind the 24-inch line.

Zone Toss: The subject holds the ball, faces the zone, and on the timer's signal, tosses the ball over the rope and retrieves it on the other side. Ten tosses are completed on an alternate basis. Each toss should be made from outside the zone boundaries, but a penalty is not assessed unless the subject's foot crosses the 6-inch line.

Fouls include tossing the ball under the rope, or crossing the 6-inch line before the ball is tossed.

Wall Speed Pass: See Young-Moser Basketball Ability Test on pages 71-75.

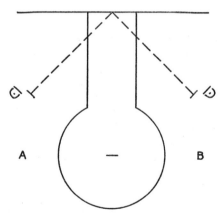

Figure 13. Specifications for bounce and shoot test. From Glassow, Ruth B.; Colvin, Valerie; and Schwarz, M. Marguerite: Studies in measuring basketball playing ability of college women, *Research Quarterly, 9:*60-68, 1938.

SCORING METHOD

Bounce and Shoot: The time and accuracy scores are combined for each trial. The best two of three trials for score are suggested by the test constructors, but only one trial of ten shots is recommended when time is a factor. One second is added to the time score for each foul made. The time score is measured to the nearest tenth-second.

The accuracy score is the total number of points made in ten shots at the basket. Two points are counted for each basket made, one for hitting the rim but missing the basket, and zero for missing both the basket and the rim.

The time and accuracy scores are converted to T-scores which are added. This sum divided by two is the final score.

Zone Toss: The sum of two trials is recommended for the final score. The developers of the test suggested that the best four trials of six be used, but this arrangement detracts from its feasibility in time of administration.

Time to the nearest tenth-second is measured for the ten tosses. A second is added for each foul.

Wall Speed: The sum score of the two trials is official. The number of hits in thirty seconds constitutes a trial.

Scientific Authenticity

VALIDITY: With fifty-four college women providing the data, the investigators experimented with five test items. The three items selected showed a multiple R of .66 which was as valid as the five-test combination.

RELIABILITY: Test-retest reliability values ranged from .74 to .82 on the three tests as computed from the test scores of fifty-one physical education majors.

CRITERION MEASURE: Judges' ratings of playing ability.

Additional Comments

Montoye[55] referred to the common criticism given to the bounce and shoot item, i.e. the variability of the time and accuracy elements. For example, one element could suffer as a result of an intense concentration on the other. He suggests that someone should experiment with a revision of the test which would include a constant time variable in the bounce and shoot item.

Lambert[44] revised the bounce and shoot item of the Wisconsin Test by omitting the fouls of traveling with the ball, double bounce, and failure to start from behind the 24-inch line. Twenty-five women varsity basketball players were tested on the revised version, and some significant findings resulted. The revision was shown to be statistically reliable, valid, and administratively feasible. Also, a combination of twice time plus accuracy was determined to be the most valid and reliable method for scoring the bounce and shoot test item for either the original or revised version.

DYER-SCHURIG-APGAR BASKETBALL TEST[23]

Also cited as Dyer et al. Basketball Test.
Date: 1939.
Purpose: To measure basketball playing ability of college women and high school girls.

Description

The four-item test resulted from a fundamental skills analysis which placed basketball skills into general categories of ball handling, shooting, and jumping. Several skills test items were experimented with before Dyer and her associates settled upon the four represented in this test. They felt that the four items comprehensively measure motor ability in basketball.

EDUCATIONAL APPLICATION: College women, junior and senior high girls.

Administrative Feasibility

TIME: Two forty-minute class periods for a class of fifteen to twenty students.

PERSONNEL: One examiner per test item with two trained assistants for the moving target test. The Edgren Ball Handling Test may require the use of both a timer and scorer.

TRAINING INVOLVED: The test designers mentioned the need for practice trials only in the case of the free jump and reach item; one trial is permitted.

EQUIPMENT AND SUPPLIES: Four basketballs, three chairs, and one stop watch represent the necessary equipment to administer the test battery items simultaneously.

Accessories: Rope, boards, paper, harness snaps, rings, strips of wood, and chalk or tape as specified in the test directions; scoring materials.

Facilities and Space: Gymnasium with unobstructed wall space.

Directions

MOVING TARGET: A chalk line is drawn 10 feet from and parallel to the plane of target movement. Two lines, 5 feet apart, are drawn on the wall behind the target, so that the center of the target lies midway between them when it is in a motionless state.

The target is 18 inches square and constructed of 1-inch boards with a reinforcement of 1×4 material; the weight is approximately 4 pounds. The target is suspended by ropes from a height of 11 feet above the floor; the lower edge is 3 feet, 9 inches above the floor. Harness snaps are used in attaching the ropes to the corners at the top of the target and to the point of suspension. The target may be suspended from the back of the basketball backboard, or from any object of proper height (see Fig. 12 in this Chapter).

An assistant prepares the target for motion by pulling it to the side at a position 6 feet from the floor. The target is held with the palms of the hands and released by simply parting the hands. If the assistant pushes the target, the trial should be repeated. The assistant on the other side repeats the action and the target is released alternately from right to left.

The subject holds the ball behind the 10-foot restraining line and passes the ball at the target as it swings through the 5-foot area. The subject receives no warning when the target is released, and the assistant must be certain that the subject is ready before releasing the target. Ten passes are made by each subject.

EDGREN[25] BALL HANDLING: Standing behind the 8-foot restraining line in area A as illustrated in Figure 14, the subject passes the ball against the wall at an angle whereby the ball will rebound in area B. The student runs across the 6-foot area to recover the pass. This action is repeated as rapidly as possible until ten legal passes are recovered. A fumbled or lost ball must be re-

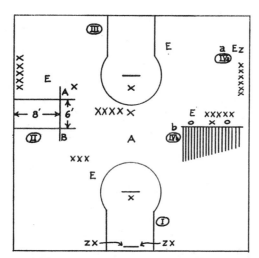

Figure 14. Floor plan for Dyer-Schurig-Apgar Basketball Test. From J. T. Dyer et al.: A basketball motor ability test for college women and secondary school girls, *Research Quarterly*, 10:128-147, 1939. Courtesy of AAHPER.

covered and thrown from the proper area, and any ball recovered in the 6-foot area must be dribbled to the proper area before passing again. At least one foot must be outside the 6-foot area on all passes. One foot may be in the air during passes but not touching the floor inside the 6-foot area. Violations in procedure require that the test item be repeated after a rest period. Each subject performs two test trials with intervening rest periods.

BOUNCE AND SHOOT: The subject assumes a position behind the center of the free throw line, then bounces the ball out of the free throw circle, and attempts a basket. Alternating right and left, ten trials are performed. Another student should recover the ball for the subject being tested. A trial is repeated if the subject's feet are not outside the circle or if a dribbling violation occurs.

FREE JUMP AND REACH: A reach scale must be constructed on large size brown paper. The paper is designed in graduated half-inches from 70 to 90 inches and attached to a clear wall space so that the bottom of the scale is 70 inches from the floor.

For use as a jump target, twenty-four strips of wood are attached to a board that is attached to the wall and hung level with the floor. The strips are graduated in length from 1 to 24 inches. They are numbered from one to twenty-four and allowed to hang free from the board. The target is hung by some convenient method in such a way that the shortest strip is unreachable by the tallest girl when jumping. The exact distance from the floor to only one strip needs to be determined as the distance of the other strips can be calculated from that measurement.

The subject faces the reach scale and with her preferred hand reaches as high as possible to place the palm flat on the scale. Undue stretching is not permitted. The middle finger location is recorded to the nearest half-inch to represent the subject's reach height. The examiner should stand on a chair to read the distance, since his eyes should be level with or above the particular reach height.

After the reach height is taken, the subject proceeds to the jump target station and stands beneath the target. From a stationary jump and again with the preferred hand, she jumps and reaches toward one of the strips, attempting to cause it to swing. The height of the highest strip the subject is able to move is recorded as the jump height. The subject is informed of her score for reinforcement in case she miscalculates her jumping ability which results in several jumps having to be made. She should be allowed to rest until the others finish the test, then her jumping ability is retested by starting at a height close to her previously higher jump.

SCORING METHOD

Moving Target: The number of successful target hits in ten trials.

Edgren Ball Handling: The elapsed time from the starting signal until the tenth throw hits the hands of the subject in area A. The better performance of two trials is recorded.

Bounce and Shoot: Two points for each successful basket and one for hitting the rim but not entering. Sum of points made in ten trials is official score.

Free Jump and Reach: The difference between the reach and jump height measured to the nearest half-inch is recorded.

Scientific Authenticity

VALIDITY: Test scores were accumulated from the performance of students enrolled in two colleges, one high school, and one junior high school. Validity coefficients were computed to determine the relationship between the test scores of each school group and each of three performance criteria. These relationships ranged from .76 to .91.

RELIABILITY: The whole test battery was administered on a test-retest basis to two of the school groups. Coefficients of .89 and .90 were obtained with thirty-nine and thirty-five students participating in the respective groups.

CRITERION MEASURE: Three criteria were used; the examiner's rank order list of the students by playing ability was developed for each group of students. An expert judgment criterion was utilized for two groups while an examiner rating of game play performance was completed for one group.

Additional Comments

The Dyer-Schurig-Apgar Basketball Test was one of the earlier tests for women and girls to be scientifically authenticated. It also was the first test designed to comprehensively measure basketball skill of females.

KNOX BASKETBALL TEST[41]

Date: 1947.

Purpose: To measure basketball ability.

Description

The four item test includes a speed dribble test item to test dribbling ability; a speed pass to assess passing ability; a dribble-shoot item that tests a combination of ability to dribble and shoot; a penny-cup test which is designed to measure reaction time. The original intent of the test was for classification purposes, but it seems to have merit as a tool for measurement of achievement. Therefore, it may show value for grading student progress.

EDUCATIONAL APPLICATION: High school boys.

Administrative Feasibility

TIME: Two sixty-minute class periods for fifteen students in a rotational test plan.

PERSONNEL: A timer and scorer for each test; the instructor should give the verbal commands in the penny-cup item.

TRAINING INVOLVED: Some uniform practice should be allowed for each of the test items.

EQUIPMENT AND SUPPLIES: The equipment needed for the entire battery includes ten chairs; three regulation basketballs; four stop watches; and three tin cups. Coffee cans are suggested, one painted blue, one red, and one white.

Accessories: Scoring materials plus an ample supply of tape and pennies for tests utilizing those items.

Facilities and Space: A regular gymnasium with unobstructed wall space.

Directions

SPEED DRIBBLE: Standing in back of the restraining line with hands on knees, the subject begins on the starting command by picking up the ball and dribbling in the direction shown in Figure 15. Time is recorded from the starting signal until the subject crosses the finish line.

SPEED PASS: The subject stands behind a line which is marked parallel to the wall and 5 feet away. Using a chest pass, the subject passes the ball against the wall fifteen times as fast as possible.

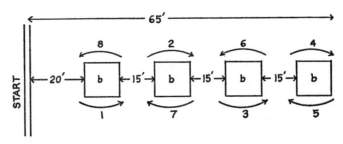

Figure 15. Diagram for speed dribble test. From R. D. Knox: Basketball ability tests, *Scholastic Coach,* 17:45-48, 1947. Courtesy of *Scholastic Coach.*

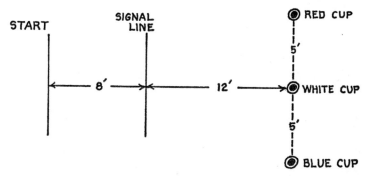

Figure 16. Floor markings for penny-cup test. From R. D. Knox: Basketball ability tests, *Scholastic Coach,* 17:45-48, 1947. Courtesy of *Scholastic Coach.*

Time is recorded from the starting signal until the ball hits the wall the fifteenth time. The test is repeated if any rebound requires the student to take more than one step for recovery.

DRIBBLE-SHOOT: Utilizing the speed dribble testing procedure with three chairs, the subject must make a basket before the return dribble. More than one shot may be required. The subject chooses the type of shot, but the one-handed lay-up is recommended.

PENNY-CUP: The test is initiated with the subject standing on the starting line with his back to the cups and a penny in one hand. On the command to start, the subject turns, runs, and when crossing the signal line, the test administrator gives him a direction signal. The subject proceeds in the direction of the cup corresponding to the signal and places the penny in that cup. A verbal command of *"red," "white,"* or *"blue"* indicates the desired direction. The elapsed time between the starting signal and the sound of the penny falling into the cup is recorded. The test should be given privately to each individual to insure consistency in test conditions. Four trials are given.

SCORING METHOD

Speed Dribble: The number of expired seconds from the starting signal until the subject crosses the finish line.

Speed Pass: The number of seconds from the starting command until the ball hits the wall the fifteenth time.

Dribble-Shoot: The number of seconds taken in completing the test.

Penny-Cup Test: The total number of seconds required to perform the four test trials.

Scientific Authenticity

VALIDITY: The test was validated on the basis of the number of boys selected to high school basketball teams. There was 80 percent agreement between the test scores and squad membership with 81 percent agreement on the ability to make the starting team. Two hundred and sixty boys served as subjects in the test validation.

The validity value of the Knox Test was further substantiated in a study at the University of Florida where a biserial correlation of .96 was found between the test scores and subjects who were selected to squads and those who were not selected to squads.[10]

RELIABILITY: A reliability coefficient of .88 was derived for the test battery by use of the test-retest method with fifty boys participating. The individual items ranged from a .58 coefficient of correlation on the dribble-shoot item to a .90 relationship for the penny-cup test.

CRITERION MEASURE: Success in making a ten-man squad and winning a starting berth on a high school basketball team.

Additional Comments

The results of the Knox Test are impressive; the ten best total scores in each school represented in the study were made by the ten boys who were varsity players, and the five best scores were made by members of the first team. Furthermore, Knox predicted sixty-one of sixty-eight squad members and twenty-nine of thirty-six first team members. However, investigators who have studied the Knox Test are not in agreement on its value as a classifier for competition.[10, 32, 48, 60] Conclusions from study results ranged from a rating of "high regard" to "little value demonstrated."

KOSKI BASKETBALL CLASSIFICATION TEST[48]

Date: 1950.

Purpose: To classify students into ability groups as measured by dribbling and field goal shooting skills; to serve as an aid in evaluation of student ability.

Description

The test consists of two items that are commonly included in basketball skills tests, field goal shooting and dribbling.

The dribbling test item requires twelve folding chairs for use as obstacles. The chairs are placed in two rows of six each with the rows 6 feet apart. The 6-foot distance is measured from the outside leg of one chair to the outside leg of its counterpart. The distance between two chairs is 8 feet, as measured from the front leg of one chair to the front leg of the chair directly behind it. The starting point is centered in the middle of the distance between pairs of chairs and located 6 feet from the first pair (Fig. 17).

EDUCATIONAL APPLICATION: Designed for college men but appropriate for college women and high school students of both sexes.

Administrative Feasibility

TIME: If two testers are available, a class of twenty students could be tested in one forty-minute class session.

PERSONNEL: The instructor of a class should probably serve as scorer for the dribbling test because its degree of difficulty in scoring is greater than the field goal shooting test. Student assistants may serve as timer and scorer for the shooting test.

TRAINING INVOLVED: Uniform practice on the two test items should be allowed for the students to gain familiarity with the test.

EQUIPMENT AND SUPPLIES: A basketball and stop watch for each test and twelve folding chairs for the dribbling test.

Accessories: Line marking materials for the dribbling test. Ordinarily these lines would not be necessary but are advantageous as time savers when a student inadvertently bumps a chair, causing an inconsistency in distance between two chairs. Strips of tape or chalk marks should suffice as distance markers. Scoring materials should be available.

Facilities and Space: A basketball court with a regulation goal.

Directions

DRIBBLING: The subject holds a basketball while assuming a position behind the starting line. On the starting signal, the subject dribbles around the first obstacle on his right and continues in the manner outlined in Figure 17. The time period for the test is thirty seconds. When the subject is beside or beyond a chair, it is considered a completed obstacle. A subject that completes the twelve obstacles in less than thirty seconds should continue on as shown in the test diagram.

FIELD GOAL SHOOTING: The student takes a position in front of the basket while holding a basketball. On the starting signal, the first shot is taken and rebounded. Succeeding shots may be taken anywhere on the floor. This action is continuous for thirty seconds.

SCORING METHOD: The number of obstacles the subject passes is the final score in the dribbling test. The number of goals made in thirty seconds constitutes the official shooting test score.

Scientific Authenticity

VALIDITY: Coefficients of correlation were .87 for the dribbling test and .78 for the field goal item. The two-item battery showed a *r* of .93.

RELIABILITY: Coefficients of .85 for the dribbling test and .78 for the field goal test using the test-retest method with seventy-one male college freshmen participating. The two-item battery coefficient was .88.

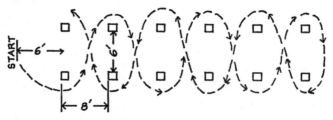

Figure 17. Floor plan for dribbling test.

CRITERION MEASURE: Subjective ratings of physical education instructors.

Additional Comments

Koski's original intent was to develop a four-item test battery, but two items were eliminated due to low reliability values. The reliability value of the two items finally included in the test, especially that of the field goal test, could probably be strengthened if multiple trials were given instead of only one trial. However, Koski's findings substantiated the scientific authenticity of the two test items included. Authentic basketball skills tests commonly include dribbling and thirty-second field goal tests either identical or related to those in the Koski Test.

LEILICH BASKETBALL TEST FOR WOMEN[47]

Also cited as Leilich Test and Leilich Basketball Test.
Date: 1952.
Purpose: To measure basketball skill achievement of females.

Description

The specific skills that represent general basketball ability are included in this three-item battery. The bounce and shoot test measures agility and ball handling ability plus speed and accuracy of shooting. Shooting accuracy is more directly assessed in the half-minute shooting test, and the push pass test measures speed and accuracy of passing. These items were selected by Leilich to represent general basketball skill after extensive factor analysis experimentation.

EDUCATIONAL APPLICATION: Secondary school girls and college women.

Administrative Feasibility

TIME: Two forty-minute class periods for a class of fifteen to twenty students.

PERSONNEL: Each test requires one timer and one scorer.

TRAINING INVOLVED: One practice trial for the bounce and shoot test. Warm-up time for the half-minute shooting test should be minimal since the better score of two trials is recorded.

EQUIPMENT AND SUPPLIES: Two basketballs, one regulation basketball goal, and one stop watch. Two chairs are needed for the bounce and shoot test.

Accessories: Chalk or tape for the court and wall markings; scoring materials.

Facilities and Space: Basketball court with some unobstructed wall space.

Directions

BOUNCE AND SHOOT: The starting signal allows the student to pick up the basketball from chair A, take one bounce, move toward the basket, and shoot (Fig. 18). The subject rebounds and passes the ball to the student assistant standing behind chair A. Proceeding in rapid fashion to chair B, the student repeats the procedure on an alternate basis until ten shots are attempted.

The student must always start behind the restraining line and may bounce the ball only once. Traveling violations are disallowed.

HALF-MINUTE SHOOTING: Standing near the basket and holding a basketball, the subject on the starting signal begins shooting and continues for thirty seconds from any position on the floor.

PUSH PASS: Using a two-hand push pass, the subject begins the test behind the 10-foot restraining line and passes the ball at the target (Fig. 19). The procedure is repeated as often as possible

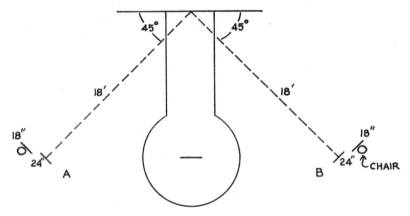

Figure 18. Floor plan for bounce and shoot test.

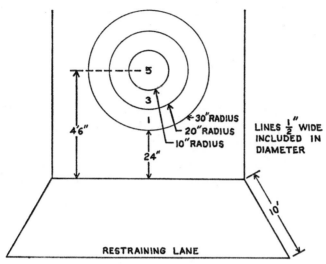

Figure 19. Target for push pass test.

TABLE XVIII

T-SCORES FOR LEILICH BASKETBALL TEST*

T-Score	½-Minute Shooting	½-Minute Shooting†	Bounce and Shoot Accuracy	Speed	Push Pass	T-Score
80	20	15			137	80
75	18	14		41	130	75
70	16	12		46	123	70
65	14	9	19	52	117	65
60	13	8	17	58	110	60
55	11	6	15	64	103	55
50	9	5	13	70	96	50
45	7	4	11	76	90	45
40	6		9	82	83	40
35	4	3	7	88	76	35
30	2	2	5	94	70	30
25	1		3	100	63	25
20		1	1	106	56	20

*Based on scores of 1,812 women physical education majors.
†Based on scores of 307 freshman and sophomore college students.

From Miller, Wilma K.: Achievement levels in basketball skills for women physical education majors. *Research Quarterly, 25:*450-455, 1954. Also from Scott, M. Gladys and French, Esther: *Measurement and Evaluation in Physical Education.* Dubuque, Iowa, Brown Bk, 1959.

for thirty seconds. Both feet must remain behind the restraining line on the pass release. The student may then move forward for retrieval of the ball.

SCORING METHOD AND NORMS

Bounce and Shoot: The best score in three trials is recorded. The score reflects both speed and accuracy. The total number of points accumulated from the shots is the accuracy score utilizing the following tally system: two points per basket, one for hitting the rim but missing the basket, and no points for missing both the rim and basket. The total number of seconds utilized in taking the test is the speed score.

TABLE XIX

PERCENTILE SCORES FOR LEILICH BASKETBALL TEST

Percentile	½-Minute Shooting	Bounce and Shoot Speed	Bounce and Shoot Accuracy	Push Pass	Percentile
100	18	50	20	125	100
95	14	56		115	95
90	13	58	17	110	90
85	12	60		108	85
80			16	105	80
75	11	61		104	75
70		63	15	103	70
65	10	64		101	65
60		66	14	100	60
55	9	67		99	55
50		68	13	97	50
45	8	70		95	45
40		71	12	94	40
35	7	72	11	92	35
30		74	10	91	30
25	6	76		89	25
20		79	9	86	20
15	5	81	8	83	15
10	4	86	6	79	10
5	3	89	4	73	5
1	1			44	1

From W. K. Miller: Achievement levels in basketball skills for women physical education majors, *Research Quarterly, 25:*450-455, 1954. Courtesy of AAHPER.

TABLE XX

CLASSIFICATION OF RAW SCORES ON LEILICH TEST

Classification	½-Minute Shooting	B & S Speed	B & S Accuracy	Push Pass
Superior	16 & above	47 & below	21 & above	122 & above
Good	12 – 15	48 – 61	16 – 20	106–121
Average	7 – 11	62 – 77	10 – 15	89 – 105
Fair	3 – 6	78 – 91	6 – 9	72 – 88
Poor	2 & below	92 & above	5 & below	71 & below
	N 1812	N 1645	N 1645	N 1646
	M 9.11	M 69.69	M 12.95	M 96.66
	SD 3.50	SD 12.00	SD 4.12	SD 13.47

From W. K. Miller: Achievement levels in basketball skills for women physical education majors, *Research Quarterly, 25:*450-455, 1954. Courtesy of **AAHPER**.

Half-Minute Shooting: The number of baskets a subject makes in thirty seconds is the official score with the better of two trials counted.

Push Pass: The total points made in a thirty-second period with the better of two trials recorded is the score. A ball striking a part of two circles is given the score of higher value.

An outstanding contribution was made by Miller[53] in her development of achievement levels for the Leilich Test. The T-scores and percentile ranks (see pp. 91-92) were developed from the performance scores of 1,812 women physical education majors in fifty-nine collegiate institutions.

Scientific Authenticity

VALIDITY: Content or face validity accepted.
RELIABILITY: Not reported.

Additional Comments

The highly regarded Leilich Test merits an examination for scientific authentication and should be evaluated although it appears to be a valid test. A test of such wide recognition should not go unsubstantiated in scientific authentication.

STROUP BASKETBALL TEST[64]

Date: 1955.

Purpose: To measure basketball playing ability of college men and high school boys.

Description

The three-item battery includes tests for shooting, passing, and dribbling skills.

EDUCATIONAL APPLICATION: College men and high school boys.

Administrative Feasibility

TIME: Two sixty-minute class periods. If an adequate number of testing stations and trained assistants are available, only one period is necessary.

PERSONNEL: Instructor and two trained assistants per testing station.

TRAINING INVOLVED: A brief warm-up should be permitted immediately prior to testing. One practice trial is given for the dribbling test.

EQUIPMENT AND SUPPLIES: A regulation basketball goal, three basketballs, seven Indian clubs or substitute markers, and three stop watches.

Accessories: Tape for the wall marking in the passing test item; scoring materials.

Facilities and Space: A gymnasium with some unobstructed wall space.

Directions

GOAL SHOOTING: On a starting signal, the student may be standing at any position on the court. He shoots as many baskets as possible in one minute, retrieving the ball himself after each shot.

WALL PASSING: At the command to start, the subject while standing behind a 6-foot restraining line begins passing the ball against the wall and continues as many times as possible in one minute.

DRIBBLING: Seven Indian clubs are placed in a line 15 feet

apart for a 90-foot distance with the subject stationed at a starting line 15 feet from the first club. On the command to begin, the subject dribbles the ball in zigzag fashion through the clubs. Dribbling is initiated from left to right and the end club must be circled each time. Dribbling continues for one minute.

Scoring Method and Norms

Goal Shooting: One point for each basket made in a one-minute time period.

TABLE XXI

STROUP BASKETBALL TEST SCALE SCORES*

Shooting	Passing	Dribbling	Scale Score	Shooting	Passing	Dribbling	Scale Score
6	53	27	51	24	78	42	76
7	55		52				77
8	56	28	53	25	79	43	78
9	57	29	54	26	80		79
	59	30	55	27	81	44	80
10	60	31	56		82		81
11	61		57	28		45	82
12	62	32	58	29	83		83
13	64	33	59		84	46	84
14	65	34	60	30	85		85
	66		61		86	47	86
15		35	62	31	87		87
16	67		63	32	88	48	88
	68	36	64		89	49	89
17	69		65	33	90	50	90
	70	37	66	34	91		91
18			67	35	93	51	92
19	71	38	68	36	94		83
	72		69	37	95	52	94
20	73	39	70		97		95
21			71	38	98	53	96
	74	40	72	39	99		97
22	75		73	40	100	54	98
23	76	41	74	41	102	55	99
	77		75	42	103	56	100

*Based on performance of 121 college men.

From F. Stroup: Game results as a criterion for validating basketball skill test, *Research Quarterly, 26:*353-357, 1955. Courtesy of AAHPER.

Wall Passing: The number of legal passes made in one minute. A pass is disallowed if the subject steps over the restraining line as he passes or if he bats the ball instead of catching it.

Dribbling: The number of clubs the subject passes properly within the one-minute time span. A club must be passed on the proper side to count. Also, no point is given if a club is knocked over.

Scientific Authenticity

VALIDITY: The test was validated on the performance of 121 college students. Test scores revealed a correlation coefficient of .83 with student opinion of basketball ability. The test was also validated by a comparison of game scores and average test scores of the competing teams. In a series of forty-one ten-minute games, the teams with higher skill score average won approximately 84 percent of games played in intraclass competition.

RELIABILITY: Not reported.

CRITERION MEASURE: Scores made by competing teams and student opinion of playing ability.

Additional Comments

The directions for the Stroup Test failed to mention whether or not multiple trials are recommended for the test items. Multiple trials should promote a maximum reliability value because the influence of a learning effect is always a possibility when limited practice and only one trial are permitted in skills tests administration.

CUNNINGHAM BASKETBALL TEST[21]

Date: 1964.

Purpose: To measure basketball playing ability of high school girls.

Description

The three-item basketball test battery includes the run and pass, dribbling, and ball handling tests. The run and pass test measures running ability, including both speed and endurance. The dribbling test assesses body control and dribbling ability while the ball handling item not only measures ball handling skill but ability to change direction. This test is a modification of the Edgren Ball Handling Test,[25] a well-known basketball skills test item.

EDUCATIONAL APPLICATION: High school girls.

Administrative Feasibility

TIME: Assuming only one instructor is available, at least two sixty-minute class periods are necessary to administer the test battery to a class of fifteen to twenty students.

PERSONNEL: The instructor and students serving as scorers. The instructor should serve as the timer for the ball handling and dribbling test items.

TRAINING INVOLVED: One practice trial is permitted for the dribbling and ball handling items, but no practice is allowed for the run and pass test.

EQUIPMENT AND SUPPLIES: The run and pass item requires two regulation basketballs plus two chairs with each having a small box (6 inches in depth) attached to the seat. A basketball is placed in each box. A stop watch is also needed.

The dribbling test item requires only one regulation basketball and one stop watch. The Modified Edgren Ball Handling Test necessitates the availability of one regulation basketball and one stop watch. The same basketball should be used by all the subjects in both the dribbling and ball handling tests to promote consistency in test conditions.

Accessories: Line marking tape that is functional in visibility and wear; scoring materials.

Facilities and Space: A regulation basketball court and a wall free of obstructions.

Directions

RUN AND PASS: A line 4 feet long and 15 feet from each end of the gymnasium is constructed, with a chair placed opposite each of the 4-foot lines. Each chair faces the same side wall and has a box attached to the center of the seat.

With the subject standing behind one of the 4-foot lines, the test is initiated with a *"Ready, Go"* command. Running forward to the opposite chair, the subject picks up and throws the ball to

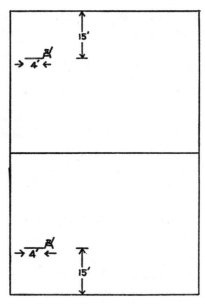

Figure 20. Floor markings for run and pass test.

the end wall, then catches the ball and places it back into the box. The subject immediately proceeds to the chair on the other end, repeating the test item for ninety seconds. The instructor calls the time every fifteen seconds and blows the whistle at the end of ninety seconds. At the sound of the whistle the subject stops and remains in position until the score is announced. Only one trial is allowed.

Details of the test should be thoroughly explained with at least one demonstration conducted.

DRIBBLING: The unobstructed wall space should be at least 16 feet long and 7 feet high with 10 feet of free floor space facing the wall. Four 12-inch radius circles are placed as shown in Figure 21. A student is stationed in each of circles II and III during the testing of a third student. The subject in circle II faces circle IV and the one in circle III faces circle I. The test is initiated with the subject standing in circle I and holding the basketball. At the command of *"Ready, Go"* the subject dribbles the ball according to the route outlined by arrows in Figure 21. The ball is

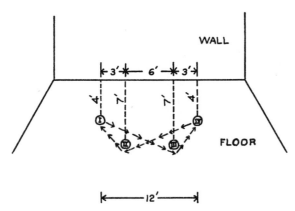

Figure 21. Floor and wall markings for dribble test.

passed to the wall and the return bounce caught at circles IV and I. This sequence is repeated as many times as possible within a thirty-second time span.

A traveling violation between catches of the ball results in forfeiture of that score. Three trials are permitted. The test item should be explained and demonstrated by the instructor prior to testing the subjects.

BALL HANDLING: The wall and floor area space used in the dribbling test suffices for the Modified Edgren Ball Handling item. The parallel lines shown on the wall in Figure 22 start at 18 inches from the floor, and the two lines that are perpendicular to the line parallel to the wall are located 15 inches to the outside of the wall lines.

The numbers in Figure 22 represent the following:

I. On floor–starting zone for first and succeeding odd-numbered throws.

I. On wall–target for odd-numbered throws.

II. On floor–starting zone for second and succeeding even-numbered throws.

II. On wall–target for even-numbered throws.

The test is initiated with the subject standing in area I and holding the basketball. On the *"Ready, Go"* command the subject throws the ball to area I on the wall and then proceeds to corner

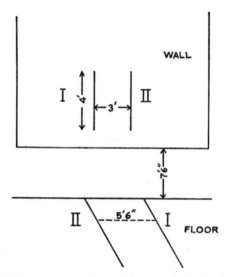

Figure 22. Floor and wall markings for ball handling test.

II to catch the return. The same action is taken at area II with the subject continuing in this sequence as rapidly as possible for a thirty-second time span. Three trials are allowed.

The subject is not permitted to cross the 7½-foot line during the entire test, and throws must be made while in the proper area. Throws may not hit the 3-foot neutral zone on the wall. There is no penalty for traveling and any type of pass is permitted. Also, there is no restriction on the number of times the ball may bounce on the floor between the rebound and catch.

Scoring Method and Norms: The score for the run and pass test is the number of times the ball is placed in the box plus one-fourth point for crossing the center line, one-half point for having the ball in the hands before the throw, and three-fourths point if the ball has been thrown but not returned to the box when the time period ends.

The score per trial on the dribbling test is the total number of catches minus any traveling violations, plus one-half point if even or more with the subject standing in the far circle when the time period ends. The official score is the total of three trials.

For the ball handling test, the number of successful hits made

TABLE XXII

T-SCALE FOR CUNNINGHAM BASKETBALL TEST*

T-Score	Run and Pass N = 132	Dribbling N = 137	Modified Edgren N = 131	T-Score
75	111	77	61	75
70	109	75	58	70
65	105	70	52	65
60	100	65	48	60
55	96	60	45	55
50	92	54	43	50
45	88	50	40	45
40	84	42	35	40
35	82	36	32	35
30	78	30	27	30
25	73	18	23	25

*Based on performance of high school girls.

From Cunningham, Phyllis: Measuring Basketball Playing Ability of High School Girls. Doctoral dissertation, Iowa City, University of Iowa, 1964.

on the proper wall area within the allotted time period constitutes the score on each trial. The test score is the total for three trials.

The total score for comparison purposes is attained by adding the T-score total of the three tests and computing the average T-score.

Scientific Authenticity

VALIDITY
  Run and Pass—.46
  Dribbling—.46
  Ball Handling—.60
RELIABILITY
  Run and Pass—.71
  Dribbling—.89
  Ball Handling—.94

The above validity and reliability coefficients were derived by correlating the Cunningham Test scores with judges' ability ratings of 108 high school girls.

CRITERION MEASURE: Judges' ratings.

Additional Comments

The addition of a shooting item, which commonly exhibits a high level of validity, would strengthen the Cunningham Test. The run and pass test must be administered on a regulation size basketball court if comparison of norms is to be meaningful. Local norms may be obtained on a floor less than regulation size but, if the norms are used for comparison of individual or group performance, etc., the floor area used must be consistent in size for all tests administered.

The Cunningham Test might be of greater value when administered in part as a supplement to a test that demonstrates higher validity.

AAHPER BASKETBALL SKILL TEST[2, 3]

Also cited as AAHPER Basketball Test.

Date: 1966.

Purpose: To measure general basketball ability, to stimulate motivation, and promote improvement.

Description

The AAHPER Test consists of nine practice-type items which may be used to measure basketball ability or to motivate the student toward self-improvement in certain basketball skills.

EDUCATIONAL APPLICATION: Boys and girls, grades five through twelve.

Administrative Feasibility

TIME: Test does not lend itself well to mass testing due to the large number of skill items represented. Some of the items could serve well as supplements to other established tests.

PERSONNEL: Dependent upon number of items to be administered. A requirement beyond one instructor and a reasonable number of trained assistants would not satisfy the ease of administration criterion.

TRAINING INVOLVED: One practice trial per test item immediately prior to testing. General practice during nonschool hours should be encouraged.

EQUIPMENT AND SUPPLIES: A few standard basketballs and

two goals comprise the major equipment needs. Other needs include six chairs and a stop watch or a wrist watch with a sweep-second hand.

Accessories: Materials to make required targets and tape or chalk for floor and wall markings; scoring materials.

Facilities and Space: A regulation gymnasium floor with unobstructed wall space.

Directions and Scoring Method with Norms

FRONT SHOT: From a marked spot just behind the free throw line and outside the circle to the left side, the subject takes fifteen shots with two points scored for each basket made and one for hitting the rim. Balls striking the backboard prior to hitting the rim do not count, and the fifteen shots must be taken in five-shot series with the subject leaving the area at each interval. Any shooting method is allowed.

SIDE SHOT: Ten corner shots are taken on each side of the basket behind a line 20 feet from the basket for boys and 15 for girls. Any type shot is permitted with two points scored for hits and one point for balls hitting the rim. A ball may hit the backboard prior to striking the rim and still count.

FOUL SHOT: Five shots are taken on four separate occasions with one point scored for each basket made. The subject must leave the free throw line after each series. Any shooting style is permitted.

UNDER BASKET SHOT: For thirty seconds, lay-ups are shot as rapidly as possible. The subject chooses the type of shot and recovery to be used. The better of two trials is recorded as the score.

SPEED PASS: Standing behind a line drawn 9 feet from the wall, on the starting signal the subject passes the ball against the wall as fast as possible until ten passes have hit the wall. Passes must be made behind the line with the student recovering the passes. The elapsed time from the moment the first pass hits the wall until the tenth ball strikes the wall is recorded to the nearest tenth-second. Two trials are given.

JUMP AND REACH: Also known as the vertical jump, the test item is completed with the subject holding a piece of chalk ¾ inch in length to make a mark while standing and one while jumping.

One side faces the wall while the marks are made, and two trials are permitted. The better of two trials to the nearest inch constitutes the score.

OVERARM PASS FOR ACCURACY: A wall target consisting of three concentric circles of 18, 38, and 58 inches in diameter with the lower edge 3 feet above the floor is utilized in this test. The subject completes ten single overarm passes from behind the passing line (35 feet from the wall for boys and 20 feet for girls). Score values of 3, 2, and 1 are assigned to hits in the inner, middle, and outer circles, respectively. The higher score is recorded for a ball hitting a line.

PUSH PASS FOR ACCURACY: From a line 25 feet from the wall for boys and 15 for girls, the subject completes ten two-hand push or chest passes at the target used in the overarm pass test. The scoring method is the same as that used in the overarm pass test.

DRIBBLE: Six chairs are placed in a straight line with the first chair 5 feet from the starting line and the other five chairs set

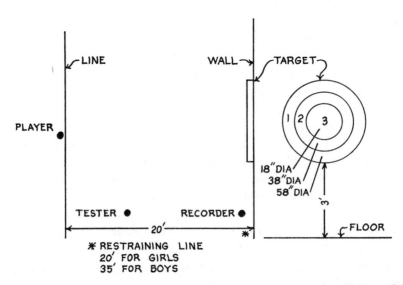

Figure 23. Overarm pass for accuracy test target. From AAHPER: *Skills Test Manuals: Softball for Boys and Girls,* D. K. Brace, test consultant, 1966. Courtesy of AAHPER, Washington, D. C.

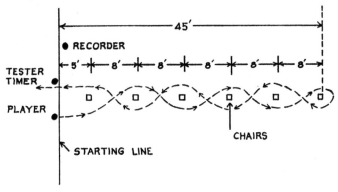

Figure 24. Floor plan for dribble test. From AAHPER: *Skills Test Manuals: Softball for Boys and Girls*, D. K. Brace, test consultant, 1966. Courtesy of AAHPER, Washington, D. C.

Tables XXIII through XL are percentile scores for AAHPER Basketball Test, based on scores of over 600 students for each sex and age group (10 to 18). From AAHPER: *Skills Test Manual: Basketball for Boys*, 1966 and *Skills Test Manual: Basketball for Girls*, 1966. Courtesy of AAHPER, Washington, D.C.

TABLE XXIII

FRONT SHOT (BOYS)
Test Scores in Points

Percentile	10	11	12	13	14	15	16	17-18	Percentile
100th	23	26	27	27	27	29	29	30	100th
95th	17	17	18	21	22	22	22	24	95th
90th	15	16	18	19	20	21	21	22	90th
85th	13	15	17	18	20	20	20	21	85th
80th	12	14	16	17	19	20	20	20	80th
75th	11	13	15	16	18	19	19	19	75th
70th	10	12	14	16	17	18	18	18	70th
65th	9	12	14	15	17	17	17	18	65th
60th	9	11	13	15	16	17	17	17	60th
55th	8	10	12	14	16	16	16	17	55th
50th	7	9	11	14	15	16	16	16	50th
45th	7	9	11	13	15	15	15	16	45th
40th	6	8	10	12	14	15	15	15	40th
35th	5	7	9	12	13	14	14	14	35th
30th	4	6	9	11	12	14	14	14	30th
25th	4	6	8	10	12	13	13	13	25th
20th	3	5	7	10	11	12	12	12	20th
15th	2	4	6	8	10	11	11	11	15th
10th	1	2	5	7	9	10	10	10	10th
5th	0	1	3	5	7	7	8	8	5th
0	0	0	0	0	0	3	3	3	0

TABLE XXIV

FRONT SHOT (GIRLS)
Test Scores in Points

Percentile	Age							Percentile
	10-11	12	13	14	15	16	17-18	
100th	21	21	30	30	30	30	30	100th
95th	14	15	17	18	18	18	18	95th
90th	12	13	15	16	16	17	17	90th
85th	11	12	14	15	15	15	16	85th
80th	10	11	13	14	14	14	15	80th
75th	9	10	12	13	13	14	14	75th
70th	8	9	11	12	13	13	13	70th
65th	7	9	10	11	12	12	13	65th
60th	6	8	9	10	11	12	12	60th
55th	6	8	9	9	10	11	11	55th
50th	5	7	8	9	9	10	11	50th
45th	4	6	7	8	9	9	10	45th
40th	3	6	6	8	8	9	9	40th
35th	3	5	6	7	7	8	9	35th
30th	2	4	6	6	7	8	8	30th
25th	1	4	5	5	6	7	7	25th
20th	1	3	4	4	5	6	6	20th
15th	1	2	3	3	4	5	5	15th
10th	0	1	2	2	3	4	4	10th
5th	0	0	1	1	2	2	3	5th
0	0	0	0	0	0	0	0	0

TABLE XXV

SIDE SHOT (BOYS)
Test Scores in Points

Percentile	Age 10	11	12	13	14	15	16	17-18	Percentile
100th	27	29	32	33	35	35	35	36	100th
95th	17	18	21	25	26	26	26	26	95th
90th	14	16	20	21	24	24	25	25	90th
85th	13	14	17	20	22	22	22	24	85th
80th	11	13	17	19	21	21	21	22	80th
75th	9	12	15	17	20	20	20	21	75th
70th	8	11	14	16	19	19	19	21	70th
65th	7	10	13	15	18	18	18	20	65th
60th	6	9	12	14	17	17	17	19	60th
55th	5	8	12	14	16	16	16	18	55th
50th	5	7	11	13	16	16	16	18	50th
45th	4	6	10	12	15	15	15	17	45th
40th	3	5	9	11	15	15	15	16	40th
35th	3	5	8	10	14	14	14	15	35th
30th	2	4	7	9	13	13	13	14	30th
25th	1	3	6	8	12	12	12	13	25th
20th	1	2	5	7	11	11	11	12	20th
15th	0	2	4	6	10	10	10	11	15th
10th	0	2	3	5	7	7	9	9	10th
5th	0	2	2	3	5	5	7	7	5th
0	0	0	0	1	1	2	2	2	0

TABLE XXVI

SIDE SHOT (GIRLS)
Test Scores in Points

| Percentile | Age | | | | | | | Percentile |
	10-11	12	13	14	15	16	17-18	
100th	25	26	29	30	31	31	32	100th
95th	16	16	19	21	22	23	22	95th
90th	13	15	17	18	20	20	20	90th
85th	12	13	15	17	18	18	18	85th
80th	11	12	14	16	17	17	17	80th
75th	9	11	13	15	16	16	16	75th
70th	8	10	12	14	15	15	15	70th
65th	7	9	11	13	14	14	14	65th
60th	6	8	11	12	13	13	13	60th
55th	5	7	10	12	12	12	12	55th
50th	4	6	9	11	12	12	12	50th
45th	4	6	8	10	11	11	11	45th
40th	3	5	7	9	10	10	10	40th
35th	2	4	6	8	9	9	9	35th
30th	1	3	6	8	8	8	8	30th
25th	1	3	5	7	7	7	7	25th
20th	0	2	4	6	6	6	6	20th
15th	0	1	3	5	5	5	5	15th
10th	0	0	1	3	3	3	3	10th
5th	0	0	0	1	2	1	1	5th
0	0	0	0	0	0	0	0	0

TABLE XXVII

FOUL SHOT (BOYS)
Test Scores in Number of Baskets Made

Percentile	10	11	12	13	14	15	16	17-18	Percentile
100th	13	16	17	20	20	20	20	20	100th
95th	7	8	10	12	13	16	16	16	95th
90th	5	7	8	10	11	13	13	13	90th
85th	4	6	7	9	10	12	12	12	85th
80th	4	5	7	8	10	11	11	11	80th
75th	3	5	6	7	9	10	10	10	75th
70th	3	4	6	7	8	9	9	9	70th
65th	3	4	5	6	8	8	8	9	65th
60th	2	3	5	6	7	8	8	8	60th
55th	2	3	4	5	7	8	8	8	55th
50th	2	3	4	5	6	8	8	8	50th
45th	2	3	4	5	6	7	7	7	45th
40th	1	2	3	4	5	7	7	7	40th
35th	1	2	3	4	5	6	6	6	35th
30th	1	1	3	3	4	5	5	5	30th
25th	0	1	2	3	4	5	5	5	25th
20th	0	1	2	2	4	4	4	4	20th
15th	0	1	1	2	3	4	4	4	15th
10th	0	0	1	1	2	3	3	3	10th
5th	0	0	0	1	2	2	2	2	5th
0	0	0	0	0	0	0	0	0	0

TABLE XXVIII

FOUL SHOT (GIRLS)
Test Scores in Number of Baskets Made

Percentile	Age							Percentile
	10-11	12	13	14	15	16	17-18	
100th	20	20	20	20	20	20	20	100th
95th	7	8	9	9	9	10	10	95th
90th	5	6	7	7	8	9	9	90th
85th	4	5	6	6	7	8	8	85th
80th	4	5	5	5	6	7	7	80th
75th	3	4	5	5	6	6	6	75th
70th	3	4	4	4	5	6	6	70th
65th	2	3	4	4	5	5	5	65th
60th	2	3	3	3	4	5	5	60th
55th	2	2	3	3	4	4	5	55th
50th	1	2	3	3	4	4	4	50th
45th	1	2	2	3	3	4	4	45th
40th	1	2	2	2	3	3	4	40th
35th	0	1	2	2	3	3	3	35th
30th	0	1	1	2	2	3	3	30th
25th	0	1	1	2	2	2	3	25th
20th	0	1	1	1	2	2	2	20th
15th	0	0	1	1	1	1	2	15th
10th	0	0	0	1	1	1	2	10th
5th	0	0	0	0	0	0	1	5th
0	0	0	0	0	0	0	0	0

TABLE XXIX

UNDER BASKET SHOT (BOYS)
Test Scores in Number of Baskets Made

	Age								
Percentile	10	11	12	13	14	15	16	17-18	Percentile
100th	14	23	23	23	23	29	33	34	100th
95th	10	11	13	15	16	18	19	20	95th
90th	9	10	11	13	15	17	17	18	90th
85th	7	9	10	12	14	16	17	17	85th
80th	7	8	10	12	14	15	15	16	80th
75th	6	8	9	11	13	15	15	15	75th
70th	6	7	9	10	12	14	14	15	70th
65th	6	6	8	10	12	13	14	14	65th
60th	6	6	8	10	12	13	14	14	60th
55th	5	6	7	9	11	13	13	14	55th
50th	5	6	7	8	10	11	12	13	50th
45th	4	5	7	8	10	11	12	12	45th
40th	4	5	5	6	9	10	11	11	40th
35th	4	4	5	6	9	9	10	11	35th
30th	3	4	5	6	8	9	9	10	30th
25th	3	4	4	5	8	8	9	10	25th
20th	3	3	4	5	7	8	8	9	20th
15th	2	3	4	5	6	7	7	8	15th
10th	2	2	3	3	4	6	6	7	10th
5th	1	1	2	2	3	4	5	6	5th
0	0	1	1	1	1	1	1	1	0

TABLE XXX

UNDER BASKET SHOT (GIRLS)
Test Scores in Number of Baskets Made

Percentile	Age							Percentile
	10-11	12	13	14	15	16	17-18	
100th	15	15	16	16	18	19	20	100th
95th	8	10	10	11	11	13	13	95th
90th	7	8	8	10	10	11	11	90th
85th	6	7	8	9	9	10	10	85th
80th	5	7	7	8	8	9	9	80th
75th	5	6	7	8	8	8	8	75th
70th	5	6	7	7	7	8	8	70th
65th	5	5	6	7	7	7	7	65th
60th	4	5	6	6	6	7	7	60th
55th	4	5	6	6	6	6	6	55th
50th	4	4	5	6	6	6	6	50th
45th	4	4	5	5	5	5	5	45th
40th	3	4	5	5	5	5	5	40th
35th	3	4	4	5	5	5	5	35th
30th	3	3	4	4	4	4	4	30th
25th	2	3	4	4	4	4	4	25th
20th	2	3	3	4	4	4	4	20th
15th	2	2	3	3	3	3	3	15th
10th	1	2	2	3	3	3	3	10th
5th	1	1	1	2	2	2	2	5th
0	0	0	0	1	1	1	1	0

TABLE XXXI

SPEED PASS (BOYS)
Test Scores in Seconds and Tenths

Percentile	Age								Percentile
	10	11	12	13	14	15	16	17-18	
100th	10.0	8.5	5.5	5.5	5.5	4.5	4.5	4.5	100th
95th	11.6	10.5	8.5	7.8	7.6	7.4	7.3	6.8	95th
90th	11.6	11.2	9.7	8.3	8.0	7.8	7.7	7.2	90th
85th	12.2	11.6	10.1	8.8	8.3	8.0	7.9	7.5	85th
80th	12.5	11.9	10.4	9.3	8.6	8.3	8.1	7.8	80th
75th	12.8	12.2	10.7	9.8	8.9	8.5	8.4	8.0	75th
70th	13.1	12.4	11.1	10.0	9.0	8.7	8.6	8.2	70th
65th	13.3	12.7	11.4	10.3	9.2	8.9	8.7	8.3	65th
60th	13.6	12.9	11.7	10.6	9.4	9.1	8.9	8.6	60th
55th	13.9	13.2	11.7	10.8	9.6	9.3	9.1	8.8	55th
50th	14.2	13.4	12.2	11.1	9.9	9.4	9.2	9.0	50th
45th	16.6	13.7	12.5	11.4	10.2	9.6	9.4	9.2	45th
40th	14.9	14.0	12.7	11.8	10.4	10.0	9.6	9.4	40th
35th	15.2	14.3	13.0	12.2	10.6	10.2	9.9	9.6	35th
30th	15.6	14.6	13.3	12.6	11.0	10.5	10.2	9.9	30th
25th	16.0	14.9	13.6	13.0	11.3	10.9	10.5	10.2	25th
20th	16.5	15.3	14.2	13.4	11.7	11.3	11.1	10.5	20th
15th	17.3	15.7	14.9	14.2	12.2	12.0	11.6	11.1	15th
10th	18.1	16.3	15.5	15.1	13.0	12.8	12.5	11.9	10th
5th	19.3	17.5	16.9	16.6	14.4	14.1	14.0	13.4	5th
0	26.0	26.5	25.0	21.4	20.4	20.4	20.3	20.0	0

TABLE XXXII

SPEED PASS (GIRLS)
Test Scores in Seconds and Tenths

Percentile	Age 10-11	12	13	14	15	16	17-18	Percentile
100th	7.5	7.5	7.5	7.5	7.5	6.5	6.5	100th
95th	11.9	10.5	10.4	10.0	9.5	9.5	9.5	95th
90th	12.6	11.1	11.1	10.7	10.2	10.1	10.0	90th
85th	12.9	11.7	11.7	11.1	10.7	10.6	10.4	85th
80th	13.2	12.0	12.0	11.5	11.0	10.9	10.7	80th
75th	13.5	12.4	12.4	11.8	11.3	11.2	11.0	75th
70th	13.9	12.8	12.7	12.1	11.6	11.5	11.3	70th
65th	14.2	13.1	13.0	12.4	11.9	11.8	11.6	65th
60th	14.5	13.4	13.2	12.7	12.2	12.1	11.9	60th
55th	14.9	13.7	13.5	13.0	12.5	12.4	12.2	55th
50th	15.3	14.0	13.8	13.4	12.8	12.7	12.5	50th
45th	15.6	14.4	14.2	13.7	13.1	13.0	12.8	45th
40th	15.9	14.8	14.5	14.0	13.5	13.4	13.1	40th
35th	16.3	15.1	14.9	14.4	13.9	13.6	13.4	35th
30th	16.7	15.5	15.3	14.8	14.3	14.1	13.8	30th
25th	17.2	16.1	15.8	15.1	14.8	14.5	14.4	25th
20th	17.7	16.8	16.4	15.5	15.3	15.1	15.0	20th
15th	18.3	17.6	17.1	16.2	16.1	15.7	15.7	15th
10th	19.1	18.4	18.2	17.3	17.0	16.6	16.6	10th
5th	20.3	21.1	20.0	19.2	18.6	18.0	17.9	5th
0	25.5	25.4	25.4	25.4	25.4	25.4	24.4	0

TABLE XXXIII

JUMP AND REACH (BOYS)
Test Scores in Inches

					Age				
Percentile	10	11	12	13	14	15	16	17-18	Percentile
100th	18	22	25	29	29	31	31	34	100th
95th	14	16	18	20	22	24	24	26	95th
90th	13	15	17	19	21	22	23	25	90th
85th	13	14	16	18	21	21	22	24	85th
80th	12	14	16	17	20	21	21	24	80th
75th	12	13	15	17	19	20	21	23	75th
70th	12	13	15	17	19	20	21	23	70th
65th	11	12	14	16	18	19	20	22	65th
60th	11	12	14	16	18	19	20	22	60th
55th	11	12	13	15	17	18	19	21	55th
50th	10	11	13	15	17	18	19	20	50th
45th	10	11	13	14	16	17	18	20	45th
40th	10	11	13	14	16	17	18	19	40th
35th	10	10	12	14	15	17	18	19	35th
30th	9	10	12	13	15	16	17	18	30th
25th	9	10	11	13	14	16	17	18	25th
20th	9	9	10	11	13	14	15	16	20th
15th	8	9	10	11	13	14	14	15	15th
10th	8	8	10	11	13	13	14	15	10th
5th	6	7	9	9	12	12	13	14	5th
0	4	4	5	5	7	7	8	13	0

TABLE XXXIV

JUMP AND REACH (GIRLS)
Test Scores in Inches

	Age							
Percentile	10-11	12	13	14	15	16	17-18	Percentile
100th	18	21	24	24	25	25	25	100th
95th	15	16	17	18	18	18	18	95th
90th	14	15	16	16	17	17	17	90th
85th	13	14	15	15	16	16	16	85th
80th	12	14	15	15	16	16	16	80th
75th	12	13	14	14	15	15	15	75th
70th	11	13	14	14	15	15	15	70th
65th	11	13	13	14	14	14	14	65th
60th	11	12	13	13	14	14	14	60th
55th	10	12	12	13	14	14	14	55th
50th	10	12	12	13	13	13	13	50th
45th	10	11	12	12	13	13	13	45th
40th	10	11	11	12	13	13	13	40th
35th	9	11	11	12	12	12	12	35th
30th	9	10	11	11	12	12	12	30th
25th	9	10	10	11	11	11	12	25th
20th	9	9	10	10	11	11	11	20th
15th	8	9	9	10	10	10	11	15th
10th	8	9	9	9	10	10	10	10th
5th	7	8	8	9	9	9	9	5th
0	5	5	5	5	7	7	7	0

TABLE XXXV

OVERARM PASS FOR ACCURACY (BOYS)
Test Scores in Points

| Percentile | Age | | | | | | | | Percentile |
	10	11	12	13	14	15	16	17–18	
100th	18	27	27	27	29	31	31	31	100th
95th	14	18	20	20	22	24	24	25	95th
90th	13	15	18	19	21	22	22	23	90th
85th	11	14	17	18	20	21	21	22	85th
80th	10	12	16	17	19	20	20	21	80th
75th	8	11	15	16	18	19	19	20	75th
70th	7	11	14	16	18	19	19	19	70th
65th	6	10	13	15	17	17	18	18	65th
60th	6	9	12	15	17	17	17	17	60th
55th	5	8	12	14	16	17	17	17	55th
50th	4	7	11	13	16	16	16	16	50th
45th	3	6	10	12	15	15	15	15	45th
40th	2	5	10	12	14	15	15	15	40th
35th	2	4	9	11	14	14	14	14	35th
30th	1	3	8	10	13	13	13	13	30th
25th	0	2	7	9	12	12	12	12	25th
20th	0	2	6	9	10	11	11	11	20th
15th	0	1	5	8	10	10	11	11	15th
10th	0	1	3	6	9	9	9	9	10th
5th	0	0	2	4	7	7	8	8	5th
0	0	0	0	0	0	0	0	0	0

TABLE XXXVI

OVERARM PASS FOR ACCURACY (GIRLS)
Test Scores in Points

Percentile	Age							Percentile
	10-11	12	13	14	15	16	17-18	
100th	27	29	30	30	30	30	30	100th
95th	23	24	25	25	26	26	26	95th
90th	22	23	24	24	25	25	25	90th
85th	21	22	23	23	24	24	24	85th
80th	19	21	22	22	23	23	23	80th
75th	18	20	21	21	22	22	22	75th
70th	17	19	20	20	22	22	22	70th
65th	16	18	19	20	21	21	21	65th
60th	14	17	18	19	20	21	20	60th
55th	13	16	18	18	20	20	19	55th
50th	12	15	17	18	19	19	19	50th
45th	11	15	17	17	18	18	18	45th
40th	10	14	15	16	17	17	17	40th
35th	8	13	14	15	17	17	15	35th
30th	7	12	13	15	16	16	14	30th
25th	5	11	12	14	15	15	13	25th
20th	4	9	11	13	13	14	11	20th
15th	2	7	9	11	12	12	10	15th
10th	0	4	7	9	9	9	8	10th
5th	0	1	4	6	6	6	5	5th
0	0	0	0	0	0	0	0	0

TABLE XXXVII

PUSH PASS FOR ACCURACY (BOYS)
Test Scores in Points

Percentile	Age							Percentile
	11	12	13	14	15	16	17-18	
100th	29	29	29	29	29	30	30	100th
95th	19	22	24	25	27	27	29	95th
90th	17	20	22	24	25	26	28	90th
85th	14	18	21	23	24	25	28	85th
80th	12	16	20	21	23	24	27	80th
75th	11	14	19	21	23	23	27	75th
70th	9	13	18	20	22	23	26	70th
65th	8	12	17	19	21	22	26	65th
60th	7	11	16	18	21	21	26	60th
55th	5	10	15	18	20	21	25	55th
50th	4	9	13	17	19	20	24	50th
45th	3	8	13	16	19	19	24	45th
40th	2	7	12	15	18	18	23	40th
35th	1	5	11	14	17	18	23	35th
30th	1	4	10	14	16	17	22	30th
25th	1	3	9	12	15	16	21	25th
20th	1	2	7	11	14	15	20	20th
15th	0	2	5	10	13	14	18	15th
10th	0	1	2	8	11	12	17	10th
5th	0	1	1	4	6	9	14	5th
0	0	0	1	1	2	4	5	0

TABLE XXXVIII

PUSH PASS FOR ACCURACY (GIRLS)
Test Scores in Points

Percentile	Age							Percentile
	10-11	12	13	14	15	16	17-18	
100th	29	30	30	30	30	30	30	100th
95th	26	27	28	28	29	29	29	95th
90th	24	26	27	28	28	28	28	90th
85th	23	25	26	27	27	27	27	85th
80th	22	24	25	26	27	27	27	80th
75th	21	23	24	25	26	26	26	75th
70th	21	22	24	25	25	26	26	70th
65th	20	22	23	24	25	25	25	65th
60th	19	21	22	23	24	25	25	60th
55th	18	20	22	23	24	24	24	55th
50th	17	19	21	22	23	24	24	50th
45th	16	19	21	22	23	23	23	45th
40th	15	18	20	21	22	22	23	40th
35th	13	17	19	20	22	22	22	35th
30th	12	16	18	19	21	21	21	30th
25th	10	14	17	18	20	20	20	25th
20th	8	12	15	17	19	19	19	20th
15th	7	10	13	15	18	17	17	15th
10th	4	8	11	13	16	12	13	10th
5th	2	4	7	10	12	8	9	5th
0	0	0	0	0	0	0	0	0

TABLE XXXIX

DRIBBLING (BOYS)
Tests Scores in Seconds and Tenths

Percentile	Age								Percentile
	10	11	12	13	14	15	16	17-18	
100th	12.0	10.5	6.5	6.5	6.5	5.5	5.5	5.5	100th
95th	13.0	12.0	10.3	9.8	9.7	9.5	9.5	8.8	95th
90th	13.7	12.8	11.3	10.4	10.1	9.8	9.8	9.5	90th
85th	14.1	13.0	11.7	10.8	10.7	10.1	10.0	9.9	85th
80th	14.6	13.3	12.1	11.2	10.9	10.3	10.3	10.3	80th
75th	14.8	13.6	12.3	11.6	11.1	10.6	10.5	10.5	75th
70th	15.1	13.9	12.6	11.9	11.3	10.9	10.8	10.8	70th
65th	15.3	14.1	12.9	12.2	11.5	11.1	11.0	11.0	65th
60th	15.5	14.4	13.2	12.4	11.8	11.4	11.3	11.2	60th
55th	15.8	14.7	13.4	12.7	12.0	11.7	11.5	11.5	55th
50th	16.0	15.0	13.7	13.0	12.3	12.0	11.8	11.7	50th
45th	16.3	15.3	14.1	13.3	12.6	12.3	12.1	11.8	45th
40th	16.5	15.6	14.4	13.6	12.9	12.6	12.3	12.0	40th
35th	16.9	16.0	14.7	13.9	13.2	12.9	12.6	12.3	35th
30th	17.2	16.3	15.0	14.2	13.6	13.2	12.9	12.6	30th
25th	17.6	16.8	15.3	14.4	13.9	13.5	13.2	13.0	25th
20th	18.0	17.2	15.8	14.9	14.3	14.0	13.4	13.3	20th
15th	18.4	17.9	16.5	15.3	14.8	14.5	13.8	13.7	15th
10th	19.4	18.8	17.3	16.1	15.6	15.2	14.2	14.2	10th
5th	21.4	20.4	18.7	18.3	17.4	16.5	14.7	14.6	5th
0	26.0	26.5	26.5	23.0	22.0	22.0	21.6	21.5	0

TABLE XL

DRIBBLING (GIRLS)
Test Scores in Seconds and Tenths

Percentile	10-11	12	13	14	15	16	17-18	Percentile
100th	9.5	9.5	9.5	9.5	9.5	8.5	7.5	100th
95th	13.7	12.0	11.7	11.7	11.7	10.9	10.8	95th
90th	14.5	12.9	12.8	12.6	12.3	11.7	11.7	90th
85th	14.9	13.5	13.3	13.0	12.8	12.1	12.0	85th
80th	15.2	14.0	13.7	13.4	13.1	12.5	12.4	80th
75th	15.6	14.3	14.0	13.7	13.4	12.7	12.7	75th
70th	15.9	14.6	14.4	14.0	13.6	13.0	13.0	70th
65th	16.2	14.9	14.7	14.3	13.8	13.2	13.2	65th
60th	16.5	15.2	14.9	14.5	14.0	13.5	13.4	60th
55th	16.8	15.5	15.1	14.8	14.2	13.7	13.6	55th
50th	17.1	15.8	15.4	15.0	14.5	14.0	14.0	50th
45th	17.5	16.2	15.7	15.2	14.7	14.3	14.3	45th
40th	17.8	16.5	16.1	15.5	15.0	14.6	14.5	40th
35th	18.2	16.9	16.4	15.8	15.3	14.9	14.7	35th
30th	18.5	17.3	16.7	16.2	15.6	15.2	15.0	30th
25th	19.0	17.7	17.1	16.5	16.0	15.5	15.2	25th
20th	19.5	18.2	17.5	17.0	16.3	16.0	15.5	20th
15th	20.4	18.7	18.0	17.5	16.9	16.5	16.3	15th
10th	21.1	20.5	18.2	17.8	17.2	17.1	17.0	10th
5th	22.4	21.2	20.6	19.8	18.9	18.4	18.0	5th
0	29.0	24.5	24.5	24.5	24.5	24.5	24.5	0

8 feet apart. On the starting signal, the subject dribbles to the right of the first chair and left of the second, following this sequence to the end of the line of chairs and back to the starting line. Either hand may be used in dribbling with violations disallowed. The subject must dribble at least once as a chair is passed. The elapsed time to the nearest tenth-second from the starting line to the finish line is recorded. Two trials are permitted.

Scientific Authenticity

VALIDITY: Face validity is claimed.

RELIABILITY: In the AAHPER Skills Tests, a reliability coefficient of at least .80 is required for all items except those which measure accuracy or form. For those two items, the minimum is .70.

Additional Comments

The use of the AAHPER Test for measuring student progress or classifying students for competition is discouraged until the individual items are scientifically authenticated in validity and reliability. The test also fails the ease of administration criterion due to the large number of items that require administration. The test is presented here because its items show potentiality for acceptable validity and reliability values, especially potential for validation as face validity is commonly accepted for the test battery. As a comprehensive measure of basketball ability, the test should include a defensive item which admittedly could present some difficulty in design.

The AAHPER Basketball Test receives its highest marks when used for player practice purposes. A student can evaluate his or her improvement by practicing the items and comparing scores with the established norms.

LSU LONG AND SHORT TEST[57]

Date: 1967.

Purpose: To measure the combined ability of shooting and dribbling a basketball.

Description

The single-item test measures the combined skills of shooting and dribbling, which is basic to measurement of basketball ability.

EDUCATIONAL APPLICATION: Junior high to college males and females.

Administrative Feasibility

TIME: One sixty-minute class period for a class of twenty to thirty students.

PERSONNEL: One timer and one scorer.

TRAINING INVOLVED: Some practice should be permitted. However, the test measures a very basic basketball skill; therefore, practice time need not be extensive.

EQUIPMENT AND SUPPLIES: A basketball and one stop watch.

Accessories: In addition to scoring materials, a piece of string of sufficient length to construct the restraining arc for the long shot, plus chalk to mark the restraining arc.

Facilities and Space: A regulation basketball facility.

Directions

The student stands with the ball in back of the restraining line or arc which is developed by stretching a string from directly under the basket to the top of the free throw circle, then making an arc with chalk from the top of the circle to the end line on each side of the basket. On the starting signal, the subject shoots from behind the restraining line, then rushes in to recover the rebound, and takes a shot close to the basket. He then returns to the restraining line for the long shot and repeats the action until one minute expires. Dribbling is required at all times between shots. The long shot must be taken behind the restraining line, and the short shot may be taken from any position on the floor. Two trials are administered with a rest period between the trials.

SCORING METHOD AND NORMS: Successful long shots count two points with a made short shot counting one point. The total points accumulated in the two trials is the official score.

Scientific Authenticity

VALIDITY: Face validity is accepted for the test.

RELIABILITY: Not reported.

TABLE XLI

LSU LONG AND SHORT TEST SCORING SCALE*

College Men	Performance Level
19 & Above	Excellent
15 - 18	Good
6 - 14	Average
2 - 5	Poor
0 - 1	Very Poor

*Based on scores of 100 college men as reported by Mike Recio, NLU, Monroe, La., 1972.

From B. L. Johnson and J. K. Nelson: *Practical Measurements for Evaluation in Physical Education,* 1974. Courtesy of Burgess Publishing Company, Minneapolis.

Additional Comments

The test is an improvement upon many other established tests because its performance requirement better simulates the combined shooting and ball handling skills of actual game situations. Furthermore, the test would serve well as the principal test item in a battery. The reliability value of the test should be determined to confirm its usefulness. The norms presented are limited to the performance scores of college men.

LSU BASKETBALL PASSING TEST[57]

Date: 1967.
Purpose: To measure the abilities of passing and pass receiving.

Description

The test is restricted to the measurement of skill in passing and pass receiving.

EDUCATIONAL APPLICATION: Upper elementary, junior high, senior high school, and college males and females.

Administrative Feasibility

TIME: One forty-minute class period for a class of twenty to thirty students.

PERSONNEL: One timer and one scorer.

TRAINING INVOLVED: The performance requirement in this test dictates some orientation to the subject prior to testing. Practice should be allowed until test familiarization is evident on the part of the subject.

EQUIPMENT AND SUPPLIES: One basketball and stop watch.

Accessories: Tape or other materials for wall and floor markings; plus scoring materials.

Facilities and Space: An unobstructed, smooth wall surface of sufficient size to satisfy test area dimensions.

Directions

In a test area with dimensions as illustrated in Figure 25, the test is initiated with the subject holding the ball and standing behind the restraining line on the far left side. On the starting signal,

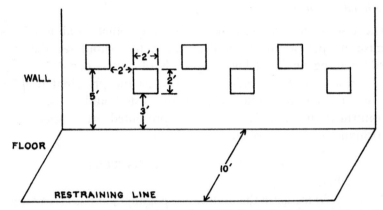

Figure 25. Floor and wall markings for LSU Basketball Passing Test. From B. L. Johnson and J. K. Nelson: *Practical Measurements for Evaluation in Physical Education,* 1974. Courtesy of Burgess Publishing Company, Minneapolis.

the student passes the ball to the first target, receives the rebound, repeats the action at the second target and continues this pattern on to the far right target. The subject starts moving to the left again by passing a second time to the far right target. The subject must move continuously and not pass at a target twice in succession, excluding the end targets. He must pass from behind the restraining line but may receive the return in front of the line.

Two trials are permitted. If the ball eludes the subject, a second trial is administered. Only one repetition is allowed.

TABLE XLII

LSU BASKETBALL PASSING TEST SCORING SCALE

College Men	Performance Level
47 & Above	Excellent
43 - 46	Good
37 - 42	Average
33 - 36	Poor
0 - 32	Very Poor

From B. L. Johnson and J. K. Nelson: *Practical Measurements for Evaluation in Physical Education,* 1974. Courtesy of Burgess Publishing Company, Minneapolis.

SCORING METHOD AND NORMS: The time is recorded from the instant that the first pass hits the wall until thirty seconds elapse. A point is given for each target that is hit. If any part of the target is struck, this constitutes a legal hit. The official score is derived by adding the total number of points for the two trials.

Scientific Authenticity

VALIDITY: The test appears to possess face validity.
RELIABILITY: Not reported.

Additional Comments

Although the test seems to contain face validity, its value should be substantiated by scientific authentication.

The designer of the LSU Basketball Passing Test suggests that the dimensions of the test area be modified when used at lower grade levels. It is recommended that the bottoms of the low and high targets be located 2 and 4 feet, respectively, and the restraining line placed 7 feet from the wall when testing upper elementary and junior high school age students.

PIMPA MODIFICATION OF BUNN BASKETBALL TEST[59]

Date: 1968.
Purpose: To measure basketball ability of high school boys and college men.

Description

The Pimpa Modification of the Bunn Basketball Test[12] is used to classify students for instruction and competition. The two-item battery correlated highly with Bunn's six-item test battery for both skilled and unskilled players, making it more functional with regard to time and efficiency of administration. The alternate lay-up test measures the amount of time taken in completing ten successful alternating lay-up shots. The penny-cup test item measures the subject's level of agility and reaction time.

EDUCATIONAL APPLICATION: Junior and senior high boys and college men.

Administrative Feasibility

TIME: Provided an adequate number of testing stations and stop watches are available, a class of fifteen to twenty students can be tested in one sixty-minute class period.

PERSONNEL: Two instructors are preferable to maximize the use of time. Student assistants are also needed to serve as timers. One instructor could possibly administer the tests with the help of student assistants.

TRAINING INVOLVED: A few practice shots by each student are the extent of necessary practice for the alternate lay-up test. Practice for the penny-cup test item is unnecessary due to the nature of the test item.

EQUIPMENT AND SUPPLIES: One basketball and goal plus a stop watch or sweep-hand wrist watch for the lay-up item. Three tin cups and several pennies for each testing area in addition to a stop watch for the penny-cup item. Red, white, and blue tape or paint is put on the cups.

Accessories: Scoring materials.

Facilities and Space: The alternate lay-up test requires a facility with a regulation basketball goal and free of obstacles within a reasonable distance from the basket. An unobstructed floor space at least 30 feet in length and 10 feet in width is needed for the penny-cup test.

Directions

ALTERNATE LAY-UP: Starting on his choice of the side to the basket and a verbal command of *"Go,"* the subject completes ten successful alternate lay-ups as quickly as possible. The shots are alternated regardless of the circumstances that prevail during the shooting of the ten lay-ups.

PENNY-CUP: The test begins with the subject standing on the starting line with his back to the cups and holding a penny in his hand. With a person stationed behind each cup, preferably an instructor, the student commences on the *"Go"* signal and runs to the cup to which a direction signal has been given and drops in a penny. The signal is either *"red,"* *"white,"* or *"blue."* A timer is assigned for each of the three colors. The timer for the particular

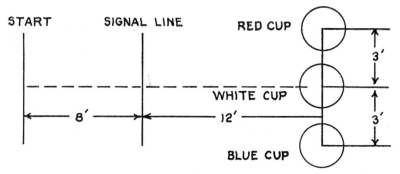

Figure 26. Floor plan for penny-cup test.

color measures the time that elapses between the starting signal and the sound of the penny falling into the cup. The time taken to return and prepare for the next trial is not recorded. The process is repeated four times in random order.

SCORING METHOD: The alternate lay-up test is scored by recording the amount of time required to make ten alternate lay-ups.

The score for the penny-cup test is the sum of times required in the four trials.

Scientific Authenticity

VALIDITY: A correlation coefficient of .88 was obtained between the scores of fifty skilled subjects on the six-item Bunn Test and the two-item Pimpa Modification. The relationship of scores on the two tests for fifty unskilled subjects was .95.

RELIABILITY: Not given.

CRITERION MEASURE: Bunn's Basketball Skill Test was used by Pimpa as the criterion. He found that the alternate lay-up and the penny-cup tests appear comprehensive enough to measure general basketball skill.

Additional Comments

The Pimpa Modification of the Bunn Basketball Test appears to have merit as a test for classification purposes. The test's high relationship with Bunn's rather comprehensive measure of basketball skill substantiates its value as an adequate test of basketball skill, assuming the six-item Bunn Test demonstrates content or face validity.

HARRISON BASKETBALL ABILITY TEST[34]

Date: 1969.

Purpose: To measure basketball playing ability.

Description

The four-item test battery measures player proficiency in the basic skills of shooting, passing, dribbling, and rebounding. The comprehensive test is well suited for grading and classification purposes.

EDUCATIONAL APPLICATION: Junior and senior high school boys.

Administrative Feasibility

TIME: Two sixty-minute class periods for a class of twenty students in a multiple-station test design.

PERSONNEL: One scorer and one timer for each test item.

TRAINING INVOLVED: The test source did not suggest a need for practice trials.

EQUIPMENT AND SUPPLIES: Four basketballs, four stop watches, five chairs or hurdles.

Accessories: Marking tape to construct the restraining line for the speed pass test item; scoring materials.

Facilities and Space: A basketball facility with unobstructed wall space.

Directions

FIELD GOAL TEST: The subject assumes a position of his choice close to the basket while holding a basketball. On the starting signal, he attempts to make as many baskets as possible in thirty seconds. The type of shot used is the subject's choice. Two trials are given.

SPEED PASS TEST: On the starting signal, the subject passes the ball against the wall while standing behind an 8-foot restraining line. This action is continued for thirty seconds. The ball must be passed and received from behind the restraining line. The student may use any type of pass he chooses. Two trials are allowed.

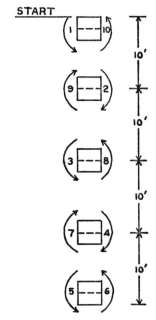

Figure 27. Diagram of dribbling test.

DRIBBLE TEST: Following the dribbling route shown in Figure 27, the subject when instructed to begin dribbles the ball for thirty seconds. Two trials are permitted.

REBOUND TEST: The subject stands near the backboard while holding a basketball. On the signal to start, the subject tosses the ball against the backboard and catches the ball in the air to return it to the backboard. This action is continued for thirty seconds. The subject may catch the ball and return to the floor before making the next toss if he is unable to perform the test item as recommended. Two trials are given.

SCORING METHOD AND NORMS

Field Goal Test: One point is recorded for each successful basket. The better of the two trials is the subject's official score.

Speed Pass Test: One point is scored each time the ball hits the wall with the better of the two test trials recorded as the official score.

TABLE XLIII

T-SCALES FOR THE HARRISON BASKETBALL TEST

T-Scale	Goal Shooting				Speed Pass				Dribble				Rebounding			
	7th	8th	9th	10th	7th	8th	9th	10th	7th	8th	9th	10th	7th	8th	9th	10th
76					37	38	39	42	39	37	40	36	27	29	34	
75																
74																
73		17	18	18	35			41	38						33	32
72	14				34				37	36	39		26		32	
71					33	37			36						31	
70							40					35	25	28	30	31
69											38				29	30
68		16	17	17		36	38	39	35					27		
67	13				32					35		34	24	26		
66				16	31	35		38	34		37				28	29
65	12	15	16											25		
64		14		15			37	37	33				23		27	
63			15	14	30	34				34	36	33				28
62		13					36	36	32						26	
61	11				29	33				33				24		
60				13			35	35				32				27
59			14		28				31	32	35		22			
58		12				32	34								25	26
57	10							34				31		23		
56		11	13			31	33		30	31	34		21			25
55				12	27						33	30			24	
54	9	10				30		33						22		
53			12						29	30	32		20		23	24
52				11			32				31	29				
51	8	9	11					32							22	
50					26	29			28	29		28	19			23
49			10	10			31				30			21		
48									27	28		27			21	
47		8	9	9		28	30	31					18	20		22
46					25					27	29	26				
45	6						29				28		17			21
44			8	8		27		30	26			25		19	20	
43					24		28				27		16			20
42		7						29		26						
41				7					25			24	15		19	
40			7		23	26	27				26			18		19
39		6						28				23	14			
38	4			6					24	25	25			17	18	18
37			6		22	25	26					22	13			
36				5				27	23		24		12	16	17	
35		5			21		25		22			21				17
34			5		20	24				24			11	15	16	
33		4		4		24	26				23	20	10			
32	3				19				21		22	19				

TABLE XLIII (continued)

T-Scale	Goal Shooting				Speed Pass				Dribble				Rebounding			
	7th	8th	9th	10th	7th	8th	9th	10th	7th	8th	9th	10th	7th	8th	9th	10th
31					18					23						16
30			4	3		23	23		20	22	21		9	14		
29										19		18	8			
28	2	3	3		17				18	21	20		7		15	
27					16	22	22		17		17		6	13	14	
26							21		16		14		5			
25							20	25			11					
24	1		2	2	15		19		15	20	9	17	4	12		15

Dribble Test: A point is scored each time the midpoint of a chair or hurdle is reached. The better score of the two trials is the official score.

Rebound Test: One point is given for each time the ball hits the backboard. The better of the two trials is recorded.

Scientific Authenticity

VALIDITY: A validity coefficient of .89 was obtained between the test battery scores and mean ratings of three criteria consisting of a previously validated battery, a peer rating, and a jury rating. The scores of twenty-three high school varsity basketball players were used in the test battery validation.

RELIABILITY: Reliability coefficients of the test battery ranged from .91 to .97 for the five subject categories. The twenty-four students in grade seven produced the .91 coefficient of correlation while the .97 relationship was derived from the test scores of twenty-four students in grade ten.

CRITERION MEASURE: Combined criteria of a previously validated test battery, a peer rating, and a jury rating.

Additional Comments

The Harrison Basketball Ability Test is one of the more comprehensive basketball skill tests as all major skill areas are represented. This, in addition to its impressive validity and reliability values, indicates that the test was well-constructed.

The validity and reliability values are particularly impressive since practice trials were disallowed immediately prior to test item administration. Perhaps the practice of counting the better of two trials as the official one for each of the four test items compensated for any effect the lack of practice may have had upon the test's scientific authentication.

REFERENCES

1. American Association for Health, Physical Education and Recreation: *Measurement and Evaluation of Materials in Health, Physical Education and Recreation.* Washington, AAHPER, 1950.
2. ———: *Skills Test Manual: Basketball for Boys.* Brace, David K. (Test Consultant). Washington, AAHPER, 1966.
3. ———: *Skills Test Manual: Basketball for Girls.* Brace, David K. (Test Consultant). Washington, AAHPER, 1966.
4. Anderson, Lou E.: *Basketball for Women.* New York, Macmillan, 1929.
5. Barrow, Harold M.: Basketball skill test. *Physical Educator, 16:*26-27, 1959.
6. ——— and McGee, Rosemary: *A Practical Approach to Measurement in Physical Education,* 2nd ed. Philadelphia, Lea & Febiger, 1971.
7. Baumgartner, Ted A. and Jackson, Andrew S.: *Measurement for Evaluation in Physical Education.* Boston, HM, 1975.
8. Bliss, J. G.: *Basketball.* Philadelphia, Lea & Febiger, 1929.
9. Bovard, John F. and Cozens, Frederick W.: *Tests and Measurements in Physical Education,* 2nd ed. Philadelphia, Saunders, 1938.
10. Boyd, Clifford A.; MacCachren, James R.; and Waglow, I. F.: Predictive ability of a selected basketball test. *Research Quarterly, 26:* 364, 1955.
11. Broderick, Robert J.: A Speed, Endurance, Accuracy, (S.E.A.) Test for Assessing the Basketball Playing Performance Levels of High School Boys. Specialist in Education, Ann Arbor, University of Michigan, 1968.
12. Bunn, John: *Basketball Methods.* New York, Macmillan, 1959.
13. Burr, Wendell Pomeroy: The Development of a Classification Test of Basketball Ability. Master's thesis, Springfield, Mass., Springfield College, 1948.
14. Campbell, W. R. and Tucker, N. M.: *An Introduction to Tests and Measurements in Physical Education.* London, Bell & Sons, 1967.
15. Catlin, Oscar J., Jr.: An individual skills test for basketball. *The NAIA Coach, 1:*6-7, 1966.
16. Chambers, D. E.: Testing for basketball ability. *Scholastic Coach, 22:* 36, 1952.
17. Clarke, H. Harrison: *Application of Measurement to Health and Physical Education,* 4th ed. Englewood Cliffs, P-H, 1967.
18. ———: *Application of Measurement to Health and Physical Education,* 5th ed. Englewood Cliffs, P-H, 1976.

19. Cubberly, Hazel J. and Cozens, Frederick W.: The measurement of achievement in basketball. *Spalding's Athletic Library*. New York, Am Sports, 1936.

20. Culp, Perry: Basketball ability tests. *Scholastic Coach, 12:*11, 1943.

21. Cunningham, Phyllis: Measuring Basketball Playing Ability of High School Girls. Doctoral dissertation, Iowa City, University of Iowa, 1964.

22. Davis, C. A.: An Experiment in Measuring Ability and Progress in Basketball Skills. Master's thesis, Springfield, Mass., Springfield College, 1932.

23. Dyer, Joanna T.; Schurig, Jennie C.; and Apgar, Sara L.: A basketball motor ability test for college women and secondary school girls. *Research Quarterly, 10:*128-147, 1939.

24. Eckert, Helen M.: *Practical Measurement of Physical Performance.* Philadelphia, Lea & Febiger, 1974.

25. Edgren, Harry D.: An experiment in the testing ability and progress in basketball. *Research Quarterly, 3:*159-171, 1932.

26. Franks, B. Don and Deutsch, Helga: *Evaluating Performance in Physical Education.* New York, Acad Pr, 1973.

27. Fraser, D. C.: Motor Ability Tests in Basketball. Master's thesis, Springfield, Mass., Springfield College, 1934.

28. Friermood, Harold T.: Basketball progress tests adapted to class use. *Journal of Health and Physical Education, 5:*45-47, 1934.

29. Frymir, Alice W.: *Basketball for Women.* New York, B&N, 1928.

30. Glassow, Ruth B. and Broer, Marion R.: *Measuring Achievement in Physical Education.* Philadelphia, Saunders, 1938.

31. Glassow, Ruth B.; Colvin, Valerie; and Schwarz, M. Marguerite: Studies in measuring basketball playing ability of college women. *Research Quarterly, 9:*60-68, 1938.

32. Glines, Don and Peterson, Kay: Unpublished study. In Clarke, H. Harrison: *Application of Measurement to Health and Physical Education,* 4th ed. Englewood Cliffs, P-H, 1967.

33. Grandstaff, Gena: Grandstaff-Murphy Basketball Skills Test for High School Girls. Master's thesis, Chadron, Nebraska, Chadron State College, 1969.

34. Harrison, Edward Roy: A Test to Measure Basketball Ability for Boys. Master's thesis, Gainesville, University of Florida, 1969.

35. Haskins, Mary Jane: *Evaluation in Physical Education.* Dubuque, Iowa, Brown Bk, 1971.

36. Hill, Leo James: Determining Basketball Ability Through the Use of Basketball Skill Tests. Master's thesis, Pullman, State College of Washington, 1956.

37. Hughes, Lawrence, Jr.: Comparison of the Validation of Six Selected

Basketball Ability Tests. Master's thesis, University Park, Pennsylvania State University, 1957.

38. Jacobson, Theodore Vernon: An Evaluation of Performance in Certain Physical Ability Tests Administered to Selected Secondary School Boys. Master's thesis, Seattle, University of Washington, 1960.

39. Johnson, Barry L. and Nelson, Jack K.: *Practical Measurements for Evaluation in Physical Education,* 2nd ed. Minneapolis, Burgess, 1974.

40. Johnson, L. William: Objective Test in Basketball for High School Boys. Master's thesis, Iowa City, State University of Iowa, 1934.

41. Knox, Robert D.: Basketball ability tests. *Scholastic Coach, 17:*45-48, 1947.

42. ————: An Experiment to Determine the Relationship Between Performance in Skill Tests and Success in Playing Basketball. Master's thesis, Eugene, University of Oregon, 1937.

43. Koski, W. Arthur: A Basketball Classification Test. Master's thesis, Ann Arbor, University of Michigan, 1950.

44. Lambert, Ann Thomas: A Basketball Skill Test for College Women. Master's thesis, Greensboro, University of North Carolina, 1969.

45. Larson, Leonard A. and Yocom, Rachael Dunaven: *Measurement and Evaluation in Physical, Health and Recreation Education.* St. Louis, Mosby, 1951.

46. Lehsten, Nelson: A measurement of basketball skills in high school boys. *Physical Educator, 5:*103-105, 1948.

47. Leilich, Avis R.: The Primary Components of Selected Basketball Tests for College Women. Doctoral dissertation, Bloomington, Indiana University, 1952.

48. Loose, W. A.: A Study to Determine the Validity of the Knox Basketball Test. Master's thesis, Pullman, Washington State University, 1961.

49. Mathews, Donald K.: *Measurement in Physical Education,* 4th ed. Philadelphia, Saunders, 1973.

50. Matthews, Leslie E.: A Battery of Basketball Skills Tests for High School Boys. Master's thesis, Eugene, University of Oregon, 1963.

51. McCloy, Charles Harold and Young, Norma Dorothy: *Tests and Measurements in Health and Physical Education,* 3rd ed. New York, Appleton, 1954.

52. Meyers, Carlton R.: *Measurement in Physical Education,* 2nd ed. New York, Ronald, 1974.

53. Miller, Wilma K.: Achievement levels in basketball skills for women physical education majors. *Research Quarterly, 25:*450-455, 1954.

54. Money, C. V.: Tests for evaluating the abilities of basketball players. *Athletic Journal, 14:*18-19, 1933.

55. Montoye, Henry J. (Ed.): *An Introduction to Measurement in Physical*

Education, vol. III. Indianapolis, Phi Epsilon Kappa Fraternity, 1970.

56. Neilson, N. P. and Jensen, Clayne R.: *Measurement and Statistics in Physical Education.* Belmont, Calif., Wadsworth Pub, 1972.

57. Nelson, Jack K.: The measurement of shooting and passing skills in basketball. Unpublished study. In Johnson, Barry L. and Nelson, Jack K.: *Practical Measurements for Evaluation in Physical Education,* 2nd ed. Minneapolis, Burgess, 1974.

58. Peters, Gerald V.: The Reliability and Validity of Selected Shooting Tests in Basketball. Master's thesis, Ann Arbor, University of Michigan, 1964.

59. Pimpa, Udom: A Study to Determine the Relationship Between Bunn's Basketball Skill Test and the Writer's Modified Version of That Test. Master's thesis, Springfield, Mass., Springfield College, 1968.

60. Randall, Charles Ross, Jr.: Determining the Validity of the Knox Basketball Test. Master's thesis, Pullman, Washington State University, 1958.

61. Schwartz, Helen: Knowledge and achievement tests in girls' basketball on the senior high school level. *Research Quarterly, 8:*143, 1937.

62. Scott, M. Gladys and French, Esther: *Measurement and Evaluation in Physical Education.* Dubuque, Iowa, Brown Bk, 1959.

63. Sobo, Don D.: A Comparison of the Performance of Basketball Teams of High School Age Selected by Test Results and by the Judgement of the Coach. Master's thesis, DeKalb, Northern Illinois University, 1960.

64. Stroup, Francis: Game results as a criterion for validating basketball skill test. *Research Quarterly, 26:*353-357, 1955.

65. ———: *Measurement in Physical Education.* New York, Ronald, 1957.

66. Stubbs, Helen Carol: An Explanatory Study of Girl's Basketball Relative to the Measurement of Ball Handling Ability. Master's thesis, Knoxville, University of Tennessee, 1968.

67. Thornes, M. Ann Brown: An Analysis of a Basketball Shooting Test and Its Relationship to Other Basketball Skill Tests. Master's thesis, Madison, University of Wisconsin, 1963.

68. Walter, Ronald J.: A Comparison Between Two Selected Evaluative Techniques for Measuring Basketball Skill. Master's thesis, Macomb, Western Illinois University, 1968.

69. Weiss, Raymond A. and Phillips, Marjorie: *Administration of Tests in Physical Education.* St. Louis, Mosby, 1954.

70. Wilbur, Carol D.: Construction of a simple skills test. *DGWS Basketball Guide (1959-1960).* Washington, AAHPER, 1959.

71. Young, Genevieve and Moser, Helen: A short battery of tests to measure playing ability in women's basketball. *Research Quarterly, 5:*3-23, 1934.

Chapter 6

Bowling

INTRODUCTION

S KILLS TESTS PER SE are not necessary for bowling since the game in itself represents objective measurement. Furthermore, the instructional approach commonly used in bowling allows for constant evaluation of student progress. As a result, the primary emphasis in the evaluation of bowling skill has been the development of achievement scales or norms. Bowling norms are especially valuable for score comparison purposes because of the high level of consistency shown in test conditions.

The literature reveals three studies of bowling norms. Each is presented in this chapter. Some of the format topics used throughout this text to describe sports skills tests are not used in presenting the bowling norms; many are not applicable.

PHILLIPS-SUMMERS BOWLING NORMS[13]

Also cited as Phillips and Summers Bowling Achievement Scales.

Date: 1950.

Purpose: To measure bowling achievement in college women of various ability levels.

Description

The Phillips-Summers Bowling Norms classify beginning bowling students into eight levels of ability. The ability levels range from 50–59.5 for the first level to 120–129.5 for the higher level. Student progress may be measured at the end of ten, fifteen, twenty, and twenty-five lines.

EDUCATIONAL APPLICATION: College women.

Administrative Feasibility

TIME: A half-semester or two-thirds of a quarter term would be required for a class of fifteen to twenty students to bowl twenty-five lines.

138

PERSONNEL: One bowling instructor and students serving as scorers.

TRAINING INVOLVED: Five lines are bowled to obtain an average for classifying the student according to ability.

EQUIPMENT AND SUPPLIES: One bowling ball per student.

Accessories: Scoring materials.

Facilities and Space: Bowling alley.

Directions and Scoring Method with Norms

The student bowls five lines for an average. The average classifies the student according to her beginning level of bowling ability. Assessment of the student's progress is made at the completion of ten, fifteen, twenty, and twenty-five lines. The student's bowling average at each progress assessment is compared to the established norms.

The norm values are expressed in both quantitative and qualitative terms with ranges of bowling averages categorized as superior, good, average, poor, and inferior (Table XLIV). The performance ratings were determined by the number of standard deviation units a score departs from the mean. Each performance rating and its range of deviation from the mean are as follows:

Superior–1.8 standard deviations above mean.

Good–Between 0.6 and 1.8 standard deviations above mean.

Average–Between 0.6 standard deviations below and 0.6 standard deviations above mean.

Poor–Between 0.6 and 1.8 standard deviations below mean.

Inferior–1.8 standard deviations below mean.

To determine the amount of progress made by a student, an average of her bowling score is taken at the end of five lines and checked with the performance rating that corresponds with the average. The same procedure is taken for the average of the first ten lines bowled. Thereafter, only the particular line interval is averaged. For example, lines eleven through fifteen are averaged as are intervals of sixteen to twenty and twenty to twenty-five.

The Phillips-Summers Bowling Norms were developed from the scores of 3,634 women students from twenty-two colleges.

TABLE XLIV

PHILLIPS-SUMMERS BOWLING NORMS*

Level of Ability, 50-59.9

Rating	Lines 1-10	Lines 11-15	Lines 16-20	Lines 21-25
Superior	75 & up	102 & up	109 & up	113 & up
Good	69 - 74	89 - 101	96 - 108	99 - 112
Average	61 - 68	75 - 88	81 - 95	84 - 98
Poor	55 - 60	62 - 74	67 - 80	70 - 83
Inferior	54 & below	61 & below	66 & below	69 & below
N	99	64	59	40
M	64.5	81.4	87.8	90.1
S.D.	5.1	10.7	11.5	11.7

Level of Ability, 60-69.9

Rating	Lines 1-10	Lines 11-15	Lines 16-20	Lines 21-25
Superior	85 & up	109 & up	114 & up	115 & up
Good	78 - 84	96 - 108	100 - 113	102 - 114
Average	70 - 77	81 - 95	85 - 99	88 - 101
Poor	63 - 69	68 - 80	71 - 84	76 - 87
Inferior	62 & below	67 & below	70 & below	75 & below
N	322	206	151	114
M	73.5	88.0	92.2	94.8
S.D.	6.0	11.3	11.6	10.7

Level of Ability, 70-79.9

Rating	Lines 1-10	Lines 11-15	Lines 16-20	Lines 21-25
Superior	93 & up	117 & up	118 & up	124 & up
Good	86 - 92	101 - 116	103 - 117	109 - 123
Average	78 - 85	85 - 100	88 - 102	92 - 108
Poor	71 - 77	70 - 84	74 - 87	76 - 91
Inferior	70 & below	69 & below	73 & below	75 & below
N	611	378	280	213
M	81.3	92.7	95.2	99.7
S.D.	5.7	12.7	12.0	13.1

Level of Ability, 80-89.9

Rating	Lines 1-10	Lines 11-15	Lines 16-20	Lines 21-25
Superior	101 & up	119 & up	120 & up	125 & up
Good	94 - 100	106 - 118	106 - 119	111 - 124
Average	86 - 93	91 - 105	91 - 105	96 - 110
Poor	79 - 85	78 - 90	77 - 90	82 - 95
Inferior	78 & below	77 & below	76 & below	81 & below
N	818	492	337	249
M	89.3	97.8	98.2	102.8
S.D.	5.8	11.1	11.6	11.7

TABLE XLIV (continued)

Level of Ability, 90-99.9

Rating	Lines 1-10	Lines 11-15	Lines 16-20	Lines 21-25
Superior	110 & up	126 & up	127 & up	131 & up
Good	102 - 109	111 - 125	112 - 126	116 - 130
Average	93 - 101	96 - 110	97 - 111	100 - 115
Poor	86 - 92	82 - 95	82 - 96	86 - 99
Inferior	85 & below	81 & below	81 & below	85 & below
N	797	502	342	255
M	97.2	103.4	104.2	107.8
S.D.	6.5	11.8	12.1	12.2

Level of Ability, 100-109.9

Rating	Lines 1-10	Lines 11-15	Lines 16-20	Lines 21-25
Superior	117 & up	130 & up	134 & up	134 & up
Good	110 - 116	117 - 129	119 - 133	120 - 133
Average	102 - 109	103 - 116	104 - 118	105 - 119
Poor	95 - 101	89 - 102	90 - 103	91 - 104
Inferior	94 & below	88 & below	89 & below	90 & below
N	552	369	247	200
M	105.6	109.1	111.1	112.1
S.D.	6.0	11.0	11.9	11.6

Level of Ability, 110-119.9

Rating	Lines 1-10	Lines 11-15	Lines 16-20	Lines 21-25
Superior	125 & up	135 & up	139 & up	139 & up
Good	118 - 124	122 - 134	125 - 138	124 - 138
Average	110 - 117	107 - 121	110 - 124	109 - 123
Poor	103 - 109	94 - 106	96 - 109	95 - 108
Inferior	102 & below	93 & below	95 & below	94 & below
N	310	209	153	119
M	113.6	114.1	116.8	116.3
S.D.	5.8	11.2	11.8	11.8

Level of Ability, 120-129.9

Rating	Lines 1-10	Lines 11-15	Lines 16-20	Lines 21-25
Superior	135 & up	145 & up	146 & up	150 & up
Good	127 - 134	132 - 144	133 - 145	135 - 149
Average	118 - 126	117 - 131	120 - 132	118 - 134
Poor	110 - 117	104 - 116	107 - 119	103 - 117
Inferior	109 & below	103 & below	106 & below	102 & below
N	125	93	60	50
M	122.4	124.0	126.0	126.0
S.D.	6.6	11.0	10.4	12.8

*Based on scores of 3,634 college women.

From M. Phillips and D. Summers: Bowling norms and learning curves for college women, *Research Quarterly, 21*:377-385, 1950. Courtesy of AAHPER.

Additional Comments

A key feature of the Phillips-Summers Bowling Norms is the demonstrated value the scale provides as a motivator for improvement in bowling performance. Its design removes some of the pressure of peer competition and promotes a concentration on self-improvement. The norms seem to illustrate a well-conceived method of evaluating bowling skill at the beginner level.

MARTIN BOWLING NORMS[5]

Date: 1960.

Purpose: To measure bowling achievement of college students of different skill levels.

Description and Scoring Method with Norms

Each student without prior bowling experience is automatically placed in the beginner level of ability. Other students in the class bowl five lines for average which places them in one of three ability groups:

	Men	*Women*
Beginning	120 or under	98 or under
Intermediate	121 to 145	99 to 119
Advanced	146 and over	120 and over

TABLE XLV

MARTIN BOWLING NORMS*

	Scores					
	Beginning		Intermediate		Advanced	
Rating	Men	Women	Men	Women	Men	Women
Superior	127 & above	113 & above	150 & above	125 & above	162 & above	None
Good	116 - 126	101 - 112	140 - 149	120 - 124	157 - 161	
Average	107 - 115	93 - 100	126 - 139	115 - 119	152 - 156	
Poor	96 - 106	81 - 92	115 - 125	110 - 114	147 - 151	
Inferior	95 & below	80 & below	114 & below	109 & below	146 & below	
N	162	292	155	58	37	
Range	86 - 132	70 - 123	107 - 155	101 - 135	143 - 174	
M	111.26	97.31	134.42	117.11	154.46	
SD	8.22	8.18	7.33	4.02	4.41	

*Based on scores of 704 college students.

From J. L. Martin: Bowling norms for college men and women, *Research Quarterly, 31:*113-116, 1960. Courtesy of AAHPER.

After a student completes twenty-six lines of bowling (omitting the first five lines), his or her average is computed. The student's rate of improvement is determined by checking the performance rating that coincides with his or her final average (Table XLV). The performance ratings are categorized as superior, good, average, poor, and inferior.

The Martin Bowling Norms were derived from the bowling averages of 704 freshmen and sophomore male and female college students enrolled in bowling classes. The averages were accumulated over a period of three years.

EDUCATIONAL APPLICATION: College men and women.

Administrative Feasibility

TIME: About one-half semester or two-thirds of a quarter term for a class of fifteen to twenty students meeting twice weekly.

PERSONNEL: An instructor with students serving as scorers.

EQUIPMENT AND SUPPLIES: One bowling ball per student.

Accessories: Scoring materials.

Facilities and Space: Bowling alley.

Additional Comments

The set of norms shows value as a motivator for student improvement in bowling performance. The inclusion of both sexes in the development of the norms is a notable advantage of the Martin Norms since college bowling classes are commonly co-educational in design and reality.

MARTIN-KEOGH BOWLING NORMS[6]

Date: 1964.

Purpose: To measure bowling achievement of college students of different skill levels.

Description and Scoring Method with Norms

The average of the first two games bowled after the practice period and the average of the final two games at the end of the instructional term constitute the basis for the norms. The norms are categorized as superior, good, average, poor, and inferior.

These norms were based upon scores made by 320 men and women students who enrolled for bowling classes on an elective

TABLE XLVI

MARTIN-KEOGH BOWLING NORMS*

	Scores							
	Nonexperienced				Experienced			
	Men		Women		Men		Women	
Item	Initial	Final	Initial	Final	Initial	Final	Initial	Final
Superior†	133	157	117	131	181	182	148	152
Good	122–132	146–156	103–116	122–130	162–180	167–181	135–147	140–151
Average	99–121	122–145	76–102	103–121	125–161	138–166	110–134	117–139
Poor	88–98	110–121	62–75	95–102	106–124	123–137	97–109	105–116
Inferior‡	87	109	61	94	105	122	96	104
N	38	38	67	67	139	139	76	76
Range	57–147	104–182	61–122	77–147	100–222	100–221	83–180	82–172
M	110.3	133.1	89.0	112.2	143.4	151.7	121.9	128.7
SD	17.9	19.3	22.6	14.6	30.7	23.3	19.7	18.3

*Based on scores of 320 college students.

†and above.

‡and below.

From J. L. Martin and J. Keogh: Bowling norms for college students in elective physical education classes, *Research Quarterly, 35:*325-327, 1964. Courtesy of AAHPER.

basis. As reflected in Table XLVI, the means and standard deviations of the scores for nonexperienced men students were 110.3 and 17.9, 113.1 and 19.3. For the experienced men students, the values were 143.4 and 30.7, 151.7 and 23.3. The nonexperienced women students showed values of 89.0 and 22.6, 112.2 and 14.6; for experienced women students, values of 121.9 and 19.7, 128.7 and 18.3 were achieved.

EDUCATIONAL APPLICATION: College men and women.

Administrative Feasibility

TIME: The amount of time required for each student in a class of fifteen to twenty students to bowl a minimum of twenty-six games, based on the assumption that the class meets twice weekly.

PERSONNEL: An instructor with students serving as scorers.

TRAINING INVOLVED: Prior to the recording of scores for those students classified as inexperienced, four to six class periods of instruction are recommended. The inexperienced classification includes students who have bowled less than ten games and have received no formal instruction. The students who possess more experience than the above description also participate in four to six class periods of instruction before bowling the games to be included in a final average.

EQUIPMENT AND SUPPLIES: One bowling ball per student.

Accessories: Scoring materials.

Facilities and Space: Bowling alley.

Additional Comments

It is important to remember that the Martin and Keogh Norms were collected from college bowling classes consisting of students who completed the courses for elective credit. This is especially notable since in this study the initial averages of the nonexperienced men and women students were twenty-two and fifteen points greater than for those groups of the same classification in the Martin Norms study. The higher averages are probably a result of greater motivation and interest shown by the students taking bowling for elective credit as opposed to those students completing the course simply to complete a required credit.

REFERENCES

1. Baumgartner, Ted A. and Jackson, Andrew S.: *Measurement for Evaluation in Physical Education.* Boston, HM, 1975.
2. Clarke, H. Harrison: *Application of Measurement to Health and Physical Education,* 4th ed. Englewood Cliffs, P-H, 1967.
3. Johnson, Barry L. and Nelson, Jack K.: *Practical Measurements for Evaluation in Physical Education,* 2nd ed. Minneapolis, Burgess, 1974.
4. Johnson, Norma Jean: Tests of Achievement in Bowling for Beginning Girl Bowlers. Master's thesis, Boulder, University of Colorado, 1962.
5. Martin, Joan L.: Bowling norms for college men and women. *Research Quarterly, 31:*113-116, 1960.
6. Martin, Joan L. and Keogh, Jack: Bowling norms for college students in elective physical education classes. *Research Quarterly, 35:*325-327, 1964.
7. Mathews, Donald K.: *Measurement in Physical Education,* 4th ed. Philadelphia, Saunders, 1973.
8. McCloy, Charles Harold and Young, Norma Dorothy: *Tests and Mea-*

surements in Health and Physical Education, 3rd ed. New York, Appleton, 1954.

9. Meyers, Carlton R.: *Measurement in Physical Education,* 2nd ed. New York, Ronald, 1974.

10. Montoye, Henry J. (Ed.): *An Introduction to Measurement in Physical Education,* vol. III. Indianapolis, Phi Epsilon Kappa Fraternity, 1970.

11. Neilson, N. P. and Jensen, Clayne R.: *Measurement and Statistics in Physical Education.* Belmont, Calif., Wadsworth Pub, 1972.

12. Olson, Janice and Liba, Marie R.: A device for evaluating spot bowling ability. *Research Quarterly, 38:*193-201, 1967.

13. Phillips, Marjorie and Summers, Dean: Bowling norms and learning curves for college women. *Research Quarterly, 21:*377-385, 1950.

14. Scott, M. Gladys and French, Esther: *Measurement and Evaluation in Physical Education.* Dubuque, Iowa, Brown Bk, 1959.

15. Weiss, Raymond A. and Phillips, Marjorie. *Administration of Tests in Physical Education.* St. Louis, Mosby, 1954.

16. Willgoose, Carl E.: *Evaluation in Health Education and Physical Education.* New York, McGraw, 1961.

Chapter 7

Canoeing

INTRODUCTION

CANOEING AND OTHER related activities have shown a popularity gain in recent years largely because of the prevalent "back to nature" trend. It is probably only a matter of time until the educational institutions begin to offer these courses with greater regularity, and once that happens, skills test development will most likely be a natural outcome. Of course, canoeing will probably never reach the popularity level of some sports in the physical education curriculum because it exemplifies a course offering which requires a special type of teaching environment, namely a large body of water that may be unavailable.

Instructors of canoeing are advised to consider the sport's only apparent scientifically documented skills test.[1]

CRITZ CANOEING TEST[1]

Date: 1948.

Purpose: To determine the general ability to handle a canoe.

Description

The subject paddles a canoe as fast as possible in a figure-eight path around two buoys set 525 feet apart.

EDUCATIONAL APPLICATION: Originally used to evaluate college women, but it is applicable to any canoeist, regardless of sex or educational level.

Administrative Feasibility

TIME: Two sixty-minute class periods for a class of twenty students.

PERSONNEL: One person to serve as both timer and scorer.

TRAINING INVOLVED: Prior to being tested for score, the student should demonstrate proper familiarity with the skills required in the test item.

147

EQUIPMENT AND SUPPLIES: Canoes, two buoys, paddles, and stop watch.

Accessories: Scoring materials.

Facilities and Space: A body of water at least 550 feet in length.

Directions

In preparation for the test, the tester places the two buoys as prescribed above. The subject takes a position at the stern of the boat with a paddle in hand. Assuming a position at the bow of the canoe, the tester does not paddle but merely rides along to keep the canoe on a more even keel.

The subject assumes a rowing position behind the buoy selected as the starting point. On an audible command, she paddles the canoe as rapidly as possible to the other buoy, circles it, and paddles back to the starting point. It is recommended that the canoe be put in motion far enough behind the starting point so that it is moving when that buoy is reached. The subject may start out paddling on either the port or starboard side of the canoe, but she must remain in that position for the entire test. Whatever side the subject chooses in passing the buoy at the half-way point of the test course, she must follow the figure-eight path around the buoys.

SCORING METHOD AND NORMS: As the bow of the boat passes the first buoy or starting point, the timer begins recording the time and continues until the course is completed when the bow of the boat passes the same buoy where the test was initiated. The elapsed time is the official score.

TABLE XLVII

ACHIEVEMENT SCALE FOR CRITZ CANOE TEST

Excellent	– 4 min. to 5 min. & 29 sec.
Good	– 5 min. & 30 sec. to 6 min. & 59 sec.
Average	– 7 min. to 8 min. & 29 sec.
Fair	– 8 min. & 30 sec. to 9 min. & 59 sec.
Poor	– 10 min. or slower

Scientific Authenticity

VALIDITY: A validity value of .64 was determined by correlating the T-scores on the test times with judges' ratings. Each of 104 college women was rated on stroking form and general ability to handle a canoe.

RELIABILITY: On successive days with similar wind and current conditions, twenty-three college women were tested to determine the reliability of the test. The resulting coefficient was .92.

CRITERION MEASURE: Judges' ratings.

Additional Comments

The Critz Canoeing Test was well-conceived by test feasibility standards. However, a possible limitation is the amount of time required to administer the test. Giving the test to one student at a time takes a minimum of two sixty-minute class periods for a class of twenty students. To reduce the test administration time, two subjects may be tested simultaneously by staggering the starts. As one subject makes the turn around the second buoy, another subject could begin with this testing method continuing until all the students are tested.

Critz indicated that any modification of the test course distance should be restricted to an increase in its length. A shorter course would not allow the lesser skilled canoeist to stray far from the course, thus causing a cluster effect or grouping of scores. This would naturally affect the validity of the test.

Each tester is encouraged to develop his or her own set of achievement scales, based on the test population, course condition, and canoe design.

REFERENCES

1. Critz, Mary E.: An Objective Test for Beginning Canoeists. Master's thesis, Iowa City, State University of Iowa, 1948.
2. Scott, M. Gladys and French, Esther: *Measurement and Evaluation in Physical Education*. Dubuque, Iowa, Brown Bk, 1959.

Chapter 8

Diving

INTRODUCTION

T HE BENNETT TEST[1] is the only scientifically documented skills test the authors were able to locate. The literature review indicated that many of the testers prefer to utilize the *Official Collegiate-Scholastic Swimming Guide,*[6] and simply adapt its judging and scoring procedures in diving to their own situation.

Foster[2] conducted an interesting study involving a part method of judging divers. His part method consisted of having each judge rate only one part of a dive, with each dive being divided into three different parts. Each dive was divided into the approach and take-off, height and mechanics of the dive, alignment and entry.

Foster concluded that the part method gave very close relative rankings, higher total scores, and a greater range of scores.

BENNETT DIVING TEST[1]

Date: 1942.

Purpose: To determine the diving ability of beginning divers.

Description

Originally developed to test the diving skill of beginners, the fifty-item test requires each subject to complete as many dives as possible for score and may be used to test diving skill beyond the beginner level.

EDUCATIONAL APPLICATION: Elementary, secondary, and college males and females.

Administrative Feasibility

TIME: A class of twenty students can probably be tested in two sixty-minute class periods.

PERSONNEL: A scorer-recorder.

TRAINING INVOLVED: The test should be administered toward

150

the end of a beginners' class to assure that each student has developed some competency in basic skills such as the approach and take-off.

EQUIPMENT AND SUPPLIES: Diving boards of 1 and 3 meters.

Accessories: Score cards.

Facilities and Space: Swimming pool with diving area.

Directions

Progressing from the simple to the more difficult dives, with the more difficult dives being divided into parts, each subject starts with the first dive and moves through the list as far as possible. A diver may progress to the next dive, however, without either trying or successfully completing the previous dive. None of the dives are weighted since the progressive steps are considered approximately equal and the value of each dive in points is the same.

Certain terms need to be clearly defined for the students, since the successful completion of each dive is dependent to a large degree on their understanding of the following definitions:

1. Headfirst: implies the hands, head, hips, knees, and feet enter the water in consecutive order. Anything short of a "belly flop" is classified as a headfirst entry.
2. Belly flop: occurs when the hands, head, hips, knees, and feet enter the water simultaneously or nearly so.
3. Straight headfirst: means a near perfect vertical headfirst dive with the feet entering the same or nearly the same opening in the water as the head. The body should be straight with no bend.
4. Feetfirst: implies the feet, knees, hips, shoulders, and head enter the water in consecutive order.
5. Straight feetfirst: means a near perfect vertical feetfirst entry with the head entering the same opening in the water as the feet. There should be no body bend and the hands should be touching the sides of the body.

TEST ITEMS

1. Standing dive from pool edge: enter straight headfirst.
2. Standing dive from pool edge with return to surface: enter

straight headfirst, keeping hands and arms in same relative position until return to surface.

3. Standing dive from pool edge to bottom of pool: enter straight headfirst and touch the bottom at an 11-foot depth.

4. Sitting tuck position with fall into the water from the 1-meter board: remain completely tucked (hands grasping shins and forehead on knees which are drawn up to chest) until under the water. Any starting position.

5. Standing dive from board: enter straight headfirst.

6. Standing feetfirst dive: body must be in the straight feetfirst position in air and at entry. Jump from board, do not step.

7. Forward approach: must include at least three steps and a hurdle, landing on both feet. Accompanying arm motion must be smooth; no pauses in entire approach. Toes must be pointed to the board during the hurdle before landing on the end of the board.

8. Running feetfirst dive: combine requirements of numbers seven and six.

9. Springing the board: rise from the board at least 6 inches with five consecutive jumps, using the arms to help in gaining height.

10. Rocking chair: sit on the end of the board facing the water, and by rocking backward with feet over head, gain enough momentum to rock forward headfirst into the water. Enter headfirst.

11. Springing the board with a double tuck position: same as number nine except that a tuck position must be assumed when in the air. Knees must be bent when hands touch shins in tuck position. Do four consecutive tucks.

12. Running front tuck dive: enter straight headfirst after assuming a tuck position in the air (knees bent, hands on shins).

13. Forward dive over pole hip high: enter straight headfirst, clearing the pole.

14. Elementary front jackknife dive (standing): bend enough at the hips to have the hands below the knees (though not necessarily touching the legs) at the time of the bend. Enter headfirst.

15. Running jackknife dive: enter straight headfirst. Keep knees together and straight after leaving the board. Wrists below knees at time of jackknife bend.

16. Advanced jackknife dive: same as number fifteen except that diver must actually touch ankles or top of arch and must enter water within 6 feet of the end of the board.

17. Elementary back jackknife dive: (taken to the side of the board) enter headfirst with the head entering the water behind the starting point. Must have some bend at hips.

18. Back jackknife dive: same as number seventeen except that the dive is taken straight back from the end of the board.

19. Advanced back jackknife dive: same as number eighteen except that there must be a straight headfirst entry and knees must be kept together and straight after leaving the board.

20. Back approach: must include at least three steps, correct direction of turn (free leg swings out over the water, not over the board), and no hesitations.

21. Back spring to the water feetfirst: use arms in the spring-up from the board; jump, do not step, from the board, and enter the water straight feetfirst.

22. Back spring to the board: from the back stance, spring upward from the board (using arms smoothly to assist) with knees straight and toes pointed to the board. Toes must be at least 6 inches above the board when in the air. Return to the board.

23. Back bend: from the back stance position, bend backward and enter the water headfirst.

24. Elementary back dive: same as number twenty three, but hold straight headfirst position in air and at entry.

25. Back dive: same as number twenty-four but use some preparatory spring with smooth use of arms.

26. Advanced back dive: same as number twenty-five, but done in two parts–(1) keep the head up, eyes forward, as body is rising from the board, then (2) head is thrown back when the crest of the height is reached. Enter straight headfirst within 6 feet of the board (no twist). Toes pointed throughout the dive.

27. Standing forward dive with an arch: when in the air look distinctly forward and up. Look down just before entering straight headfirst. Lead with hands throughout the dive.
28. Butterfly dive: same as number twenty-seven, either running or standing, but with hands on hips when in the air. Enter straight headfirst.
29. Running swan dive: must have the body arched in the air. No body bends, arms above shoulder height and extended to sides, head up. The regular position of the swan dive in the air must be attained even if only for a moment. Enter headfirst.
30. Advanced running swan dive: same as number twenty-nine, entering straight headfirst.
31. Running forward half twist, feetfirst: turn at least 180 degrees and enter straight feetfirst.
32. Quarter twist: assume a distinct swan position in the air, followed by a turn on the long axis of the body of at least 90 degrees. (Shoulders determine degree of turn.) Enter headfirst.
33. Half twist: same as number thirty-one, but turn at least 180 degrees.
34. Jackknife with a quarter twist: assume a distinct jackknife position in the air, followed by a turn of at least 90 degrees. Enter headfirst.
35. Elementary jackknife with a half twist: same as number thirty-three but turn at least 180 degrees.
36. Neck stand: lie with back to board and head at the "water" end of the board. Bring the feet up over the head, aim them toward the water, and enter the water feetfirst. Hands must be at sides at time of feetfirst entry.
37. Handstand dive: enter straight headfirst. Entire body must clear the board.
38. Handstand feetfirst dive: enter feetfirst, after assuming the handstand position on board and holding on until feet complete the arc and point toward the water.
39. Rocking chair (3-meter board): enter headfirst.
40. Neck stand (3-meter board): enter feetfirst, see number thirty-six.
41. Forward fall dive (3-meter board): from an erect forward

standing position with arms extended over head, fall forward, entering the water headfirst. Remain perfectly still throughout the fall.

42. Backward fall dive (3-meter board): same as number forty-one except that the fall is taken from a backward standing position.

43. Tuck and roll with a spring from edge of pool (a forward somersault in the air from the edge of the pool, turning in the tuck position): turn at least far enough forward so that the head clears the water and the back strikes the water first.

44. Forward somersault (1-meter board): turn a forward somersault in the air so that the feet hit the water first.

45. Backward somersault: turn a backward somersault in the air so that the feet hit the water first.

46. Half gainer: only requirement is to enter headfirst.

47. Full gainer: only requirement is to enter feetfirst.

48. Back half twist: from the back stance position, make a half twist, entering the water straight headfirst. Do not twist until after leaving the board.

49. Forward 1½ somersault: only requirement is to enter headfirst.

50. Perform any of the standard dives (including also the handstand dive and the handstand feetfirst dive) from the 3-meter board. No requirements as to form except that the dive is recognizable to the judges and has a headfirst or feetfirst entry depending on the dive selected. If, for instance, a jackknife dive is done with very little bend at the hips, it would not be evident to the judges whether it was intended to be a jackknife or a plain forward dive.

SCORING METHOD: Each dive attempted is assigned a score of either one or zero, depending only on the successful completion of the dive. The final score is the sum total of points accumulated on the fifty test items successfully completed.

Scientific Authenticity

The group of test subjects used in this study consisted of twenty-six college women who completed elementary diving classes.

VALIDITY: A validity coefficient of .94 was determined by comparing the results of this test with a rating of eight selected dives by three expert judges who used the official 10-point rating scale and degree of difficulty as discussed in the *Official Collegiate-Scholastic Swimming Guide* at the time of the test.

RELIABILITY: A reliability value of .95 was determined by the split-half method and stepped up by the Spearman-Brown Formula.

OBJECTIVITY: An objectivity value of .89 was determined by having three judges rate four divers simultaneously on forty-two dives each or a total of 168 dives. Two of the judges were experienced and together had an objectivity coefficient of .93.

CRITERION MEASURE: Judges' ratings.

Additional Comments

The Bennett Diving Test is a highly regarded, scientifically documented diving test that is simple enough for true beginners, yet diversified enough for the rapid learners or intermediate divers. This test is unlimited for a beginning class since all the standard dives may be attempted from the high board.

A legitimate concern might arise when the tester realizes that no distinction is made between the subjects that pass a test item on their first attempt and those who require additional attempts. The authors suggest that a limit be set either on the time or number of attempts required to complete a particular test item. Placing higher value on successful completion of a dive on the first attempt is another possibility.

In addition to its value as an evaluation tool, the Bennett Test has proven valuable as a teaching aid. It is useful in the classification of students by skill level, and its design allows the student a natural progression from simple to more difficult skills. Local norms should be developed by age group and ability level.

NCAA DIVING TEST GUIDE[6]

Date: 1976.

Purpose: To determine the diving ability of competitive divers.

Description

As indicated earlier, many physical educators who work as diving instructors or teach diving classes use the NCAA diving rules as a guide in evaluating their students. Depending on the competency of the tester and/or the skill level of the subjects to be tested, the official diving rules and regulations can be adapted to one's own individual situation.

EDUCATIONAL APPLICATION: High school and college males.

Administrative Feasibility

TIME: Officially, each diver is allowed between six and eleven dives depending on the number of contestants and/or teams. The time of administration varies depending on how the tester chooses to adapt the guide.

PERSONNEL: Officially, the number varies from six to twelve, but again this depends entirely on the changes made by the tester. In an official meet, a diving referee, a judging panel consisting of either 3, 5, 7, or 9 judges, an announcer, and a secretary are required.

TRAINING INVOLVED: According to the test's original purpose, each diver should possess advanced diving skill when tested.

EQUIPMENT AND SUPPLIES: Diving boards of 1 and 3 meters which are 16 feet long and 20 inches wide with the end projecting 6 feet beyond the end of the pool.

Accessories: Score cards.

Facilities and Space: Diving area that has a side clearance of at least 10 feet for the 1-meter board and 12 feet for the 3-meter board, with at least an 8-foot distance between the boards. The water depth should be 12 and 13 feet for the 1- and 3-meter boards, respectively.

Directions

The administration of this test will vary according to the different changes or adaptations made by each tester. There are five groups of dives that each diver may choose from in the selection process. This group includes the forward (9), back (7), reverse (7), inward (7), and twist (35) dives. The number of dives and attempts given to each subject will naturally vary depending on the tester.

SCORING METHOD AND NORMS: Each dive is assigned a degree of difficulty rating that varies from 1.2 to 3.0. This degree of

TABLE XLVIII

NCAA POINT SCALE FOR DIVERS

Very Good		8.5	9.0	9.5	10.0
Good		6.5	7.0	7.5	8.0
Satisfactory			5.0	5.5	6.0
Deficient	2.5	3.0	3.5	4.0	4.5
Unsatisfactory		0.5	1.0	1.5	2.0
Completely Failed				0

From National Collegiate Athletic Association: *Official Collegiate—Scholastic Swimming Guide,* 1976. Reprinted with the permission of the NCAA Publishing Service, Shawnee Mission, Kansas.

difficulty will even vary on the same dive depending on the height of the springboard (1- or 3-meter) used and the body position (straight, pike, tuck, and free) of the diver during the dive.

When evaluating a dive, the areas that the judge or tester should consider include the forward approach, take-off, technique, grace of the dive, and the water entry.

Points may be awarded based on a scale ranging from zero to ten, with half points being used.

If three or fewer judges are used, the scores from each judge are added and then multiplied by the degree of difficulty. When five or seven judges are utilized, the same procedure is followed with the exception of dropping the highest and lowest scores. If nine judges are used, the two highest and the two lowest scores are dropped, and the combined score of the remaining five judges is multiplied by $\frac{3}{5}$ plus the degree of difficulty of the dive.

The diver accumulating the highest point total on a predetermined number of dives is obviously the most highly skilled diver. It is the responsibility of each tester to construct his own evaluation scale concerning the total points accumulated. This should naturally be based on the age group involved.

Scientific Authenticity

Actual correlation coefficients are not available, but the degree of difficulty scale has been continually studied and revised since its initial development by the top judges, coaches, and divers in this sport. The point scale has also undergone a careful and accurate development process by the same qualified individuals.

It is the opinion of most experts that the scales used in the NCAA diving competition have a high degree of validity, reliability, and objectivity.

Additional Comments

It should again be emphasized that the aforementioned source of the NCAA is designed primarily for advanced levels of diving competition. It can be and has been adapted many times to lower levels of diving skills. Modification is the key underlying philosophy when using the diving guide for evaluation purposes. Changes may be made by the tester, such as varying the number of dives, the degree of difficulty associated with each dive, the type of dives to be attempted, the point scale, plus many other possible modifications.

REFERENCES

1. Bennett, LaVerne M.: A test of diving for use in beginning classes. *Research Quarterly, 13:*109-115, 1942.
2. Foster, John T.: Alternate Procedures for Judging and Scoring Competitive Diving. Master's thesis, Iowa City, State University of Iowa, 1956.
3. Meyers, Carlton R. and Blesh, T. Erwin: *Measurement in Physical Education.* New York, Ronald, 1962.
4. Meyers, Carlton R.: *Measurement in Physical Education,* 2nd ed. New York, Ronald, 1974.
5. Montoye, Henry J. (Ed.): *An Introduction to Measurement in Physical Education,* vol. III. Indianapolis, Phi Epsilon Kappa Fraternity, 1970.
6. National Collegiate Athletic Association: *Official Collegiate—Scholastic Swimming Guide.* Shawnee Mission, Kansas, NCAA, 1976 (periodically updated).

Chapter 9

Equitation

INTRODUCTION

E QUITATION OR HORSEBACK riding is an age-old art that dates
back to early civilizations. As expected, the techniques and
equipment associated with the equestrian art have been refined considerably through the years. Today, many of the nation's colleges
and universities offer equitation courses, yet the authors were able
to locate only one reputedly objective riding test.[1] A reason for
this might be that students are usually evaluated on the basis of
horsemanship, and this umbrella term encompasses general knowledge, skill both on and off the animal, and other related areas.
Also, subjective evaluations are common in a sport whereby form
is of primary importance in the evaluation process.

CRABTREE RIDING TEST[1]

Date: 1943.
Purpose: To judge riding performance in competition.

Description

The Crabtree Riding Test is an empirically based test that
consists of eight items.

EDUCATIONAL APPLICATION: Junior high, high school, and
college males and females.

Administrative Feasibility

TIME: One class of twenty students can take the test in two
sixty-minute periods.

PERSONNEL: One judge.

TRAINING INVOLVED: Recommended practice at the discretion
of the tester.

EQUIPMENT, SUPPLIES, AND OTHER PHYSICAL NEEDS:
Horse, riding equipment.

Accessories: Score card.

160

Facilities and Space: Riding area of sufficient size to properly administer each test item.

Directions

The subject prepares and mounts the horse, then begins to execute the following performance items:

Item	Points	Description
Mounting	3	Reins (1½); ease and coordination (1½)
Dismounting	3	Reins (1½); ease and coordination (1½)
Walk	5	Hands (1); circle (1); reverse (1); form (2)
Trot Collected	11	Change diagonals (2); figure-eight (2); circle (1); reverse (1); elbows (1); hands (1); legs (1); heels (1); rhythm (1)
Extended	3	Seat (1); hands (1); control (1)
Canter Collected	8	Right lead (1); left lead (1); figure-eight (2); seat (2); hands (2)
Extended	3	Seat (1); hands (1); control (1)
General Horsemanship	4	A general opinion item

SCORING METHOD: Points are scored for each of the eight test items based on the quality of the performance. Forty points is the maximum score.

Scientific Authenticity

The Crabtree Riding Test is empirically based; therefore, validity and reliability coefficients are not reported.

Additional Comments

In addition to its apparent value as a comprehensive test of riding ability, the Crabtree Riding Test serves well as a teaching and learning aid for the instructor and student. When students train for the test, they receive practice in all essential riding skills, and the test items provide a basic content checklist for the instructor in teaching the riding component of horsemanship.

REFERENCES

1. Crabtree, Helen K.: An objective test for riding. *Journal of Health and Physical Education, 15:*419, 1943.
2. Meyers, Carlton R.: *Measurement in Physical Education,* 2nd ed. New York, Ronald, 1974.
3. Willgoose, Carl E.: *Evaluation in Health Education and Physical Education.* New York, McGraw, 1961.

Chapter 10

Fencing

INTRODUCTION

FENCING IS ONE of the oldest sports known to man, yet it is not a popular activity in the majority of American high school and college instructional programs. Most authorities seem to agree, however, that the sport has of late been experiencing a popularity increase. Consequently, the need for an objective means of evaluating fencing skills is now greater than ever. There is an abundance of literature available on fencing, yet very little has been done with the skills testing aspect, and most of the existing skills tests are subjective in nature.

Most of the available tests today were developed in the last twenty years. Moreover, the better ones tend to come from that time period.

SCHUTZ FENCING TEST[18]

Date: 1940.

Purpose: To measure selected fundamental elements of fencing.

Description

One of the items originally included in the Schutz Test, the lunge for speed and accuracy, yielded a rather low validity value and, therefore, is not discussed here. The remaining item, speed in footwork and lunge, requires the subject to advance and lunge at a wall target, then recover and retreat back to a restraining line. This action continues until the foil touches the target the third time.

A thick target pad made of a soft, yielding material is hung on a wall at an appropriate height for the test administration. No additional wall or target markings are required. A short restraining line is placed on a smooth floor surface exactly 15 feet from the wall or target.

EDUCATIONAL LEVEL: College women.

163

Administrative Feasibility

TIME: Twenty subjects can be tested in one sixty-minute class period.

PERSONNEL: A timer-recorder.

TRAINING INVOLVED: Prior class instruction adequately prepares the subject for the speed in footwork and lunge item. No practice trials are necessary immediately before testing.

EQUIPMENT AND SUPPLIES: Fencing foils, stop watch, target.

Accessories: Score card.

Facilities and Space: Smooth floor surface with a minimum length of 20 feet.

Directions

The subject assumes an on-guard position behind the restraining line. On an audible signal, she advances as many times as needed toward the target before the lunge. The lunge is followed by a recovery and retreat. Once the restraining line has been crossed, the subject immediately starts the next advance. The "call" (two taps with the front foot) must be given each time the subject retreats behind the starting line before beginning the next advance. This insures balance. The subject continues the advance, lunge, recovery, and retreat pattern three consecutive times while the third lunge must be held with the foil on the target. The third lunge should be a balanced skill maneuver that is executed without the subject losing her balance in any way. If balance is lost, the test must be repeated.

Two legal test trials are allowed. Any type of jumping action, crossing the feet, or other exhibitions of poor technique by the subject results in a retrial.

SCORING METHOD: Each score of the two trials represents the elapsed time between the starting signal and the instant the third foil touches the target. Times are recorded to the nearest tenth-second. The final score is the best time of the two trials.

Data presented in Table XLIX may be of value to the tester in constructing grading or achievement scales.

TABLE XLIX

SPEED IN FOOTWORK AND LUNGE TEST DATA

Interval	$\underline{f}$	$\underline{d}$	$\underline{fd}$	$\underline{fd}^2$
8.5- 8.9	2	6	12	72
9.0- 9.4	6	5	30	90
9.5- 9.9	8	4	32	128
10.0-10.4	17	3	51	153
10.5-10.9	13	2	26	52
11.0-11.4	27	1	27	27
11.5-11.9	8	0	0	0
12.0-12.4	22	-1	-22	22
12.5-12.9	7	-2	-14	28
13.0-13.4	18	-3	-54	162
13.5-13.9	6	-4	-24	96
14.0-14.4	6	-5	-30	150
14.5-14.9	3	-6	-18	108
15.0-15.4	2	-7	-14	98
15.5-15.9	3	-8	-24	192
16.0-16.4	2	-9	-18	162
Totals	150		40	1540

Scientific Authenticity

VALIDITY: Statistical data for this test were based on the scores of 150 college women enrolled in fencing classes. Student performances were rated as either good, average, or poor based on subjective ratings of experts. A validity coefficient was not reported, but apparently the test demonstrates face validity.

RELIABILITY: Utilizing the test-retest method, the students were tested on separate days but not more than two days apart. A reliability coefficient of .96 was determined.

CRITERION MEASURE: Expert judgment ratings.

Additional Comments

Additional study of the speed in footwork and lunge item of the Schutz Test is recommended to determine its potential as a valid measure of general fencing ability. Other fundamental fencing skills that correlate highly with each other may reveal a strong relationship with the easily administered item.

EMERY FENCING PERFORMANCE TEST[6]

Also cited as the Emery Rating Scale for Foil Fencing.
Date: 1960.
Purpose: To measure general fencing ability.

Description

The test is a seven-item rating scale for beginning fencers with each required skill assigned a numerical value of one to three points.

EDUCATIONAL APPLICATION: High school and college females.

Administrative Feasibility

TIME: One sixty-minute time period to test twenty students.

PERSONNEL: One judge.

TRAINING INVOLVED: The test should be administered near the end of the beginners' course so the students can have maximum exposure in performing the required skill items.

EQUIPMENT AND SUPPLIES: Fencing foils.

Accessories: Score cards.

Facilities and Space: Fencing area.

Directions

Subjects are tested one at a time. Each attempts to successfully complete the seven test items. Item evaluations by the judge are based on the quality of performance, not the time required to perform the particular skill.

TEST ITEMS

1. On-Guard
    A. Foil Arm
       (1) Elbow comfortable distance from waist
       (2) Pommel flat on wrist
       (3) Hand supinated
       (4) Point in line with opponent's eyes

B. Non-foil Arm
  (5) Upper arm parallel with floor
  (6) Forearm at right angles
  (7) Hand relaxed toward head
C. Upper Body
  (8) Hand supinated
  (9) Trunk erect, head toward opponent
  (10) Hips tucked under
D. Lower Extremities
  (11) Feet at right angles
  (12) Distance two foot lengths
  (13) Right foot toward opponent
  (14) Knees over insteps
  (15) Right knee toward opponent

2. Advance
  A. Lower Extremities
    (1) Right foot lift first, heel touches first
    (2) Left foot one movement
    (3) Both feet move close to floor, no sliding

3. Lunge
  A. Foil Arm
    (1) Extended shoulder high
    (2) Hand supinated
  B. Non-foil Arm
    (3) Arm straightened
    (4) Palm turned up
  C. Lower Extremities
    (5) Right foot forward, straight line toward opponent
    (6) Right knee over instep, toward opponent
    (7) Left foot flat on floor
    (8) Left knee and leg straight

4. Disengage
    (1) On-guard position
    (2) Foil arm extended
    (3) Drop foil arm around opponent's bell guard in same movement as arm extension

    (4) Lunge

    (5) Movement continuous and done with fingers

5. Parry-Lateral

    (1) On-guard position

    (2) Hand half-supination throughout

    (3) Middle of blade against middle of opponent's blade

    (4) Blade moved enough to cover line being attacked

    (5) Hand level, no change

6. Parry-Counter

    (1) On-guard position

    (2) Circle made by finger action

    (3) Small circle

    (4) Last three fingers

    (5) Counter parry quarte counterclockwise

    (6) Counter parry sixte clockwise

    (7) Hand level, no change

7. Riposte-Simple

    (1) On-guard position

    (2) Follows successful parry, no delay

    (3) Arm extended if needed

    (4) Lunge if needed

SCORING METHOD AND NORMS: Each subject receives either one, two, or three points for each of the seven skill items, depending upon the quality of performance. If the tester declares that no more than one part of a skill is lacking in quality, the student should be awarded three points. A score of twenty-one is maximum.

TABLE L

ACHIEVEMENT STANDARDS FOR EMERY
FENCING PERFORMANCE TEST

Raw Score	21	20	19	18	17	16	15	14	13
Letter Grade	A	B	B	C	C	C	D	D	F
T-score	74	68	62	56	48	44	38	32	26

From L. Emery: Criteria for rating selected skills of foil fencing. *DGWS Bowling-Fencing-Golf Guide (1960-1962)*, 1962. Courtesy of AAHPER, Washington, D.C.

Scientific Authenticity

VALIDITY: A coefficient of .80 was determined when judges' ratings were correlated with rating scale scores.

RELIABILITY: Not reported.

CRITERION MEASURE: Ratings by jury of experts.

Additional Comments

The value of the Emery Fencing Test should be further substantiated. A study of the test's reliability value is one obvious need. Of equal importance is the need to study the objectivity value of this particular fencing test. Consistency among judges in their performance evaluations is imperative if a test of this type is to demonstrate any significant worth.

BOWER FENCING TEST[3]

Date: 1961.

Purpose: To determine general foil fencing ability.

Description

In order to provide a comprehensive measure of general fencing ability, Bower included both offensive and defensive skill items in her test. Each subject attempts to attack a defender and also defend an attack in completing the test requirement.

EDUCATIONAL APPLICATION: College men and women.

Administrative Feasibility

TIME: Twenty students can be tested in sixty minutes.

PERSONNEL: One scorer-recorder.

TRAINING INVOLVED: A few minutes should be set aside in several class periods to prepare the students properly for the test's skills and scoring requirement.

EQUIPMENT AND SUPPLIES: Regular fencing attire including costume, gloves, jacket, and mask; fencing foil.

Accessories: Scoring and floor marking materials.

Facilities and Space: A fencing room or area with a smooth floor and a flat wall surface.

Directions

To prepare for the test, the defender takes an on-guard position with his rear foot against the wall. The attacker determines his lunging position by making a full lunge which reaches the defender and results in a slight bend of the foil blade. Once the correct attack distance is determined, the scorer draws a chalk line along the inner border of the attacker's rear foot. This line is the starting line and the attacker's back foot must remain behind this line before starting his attack. Another line is drawn five inches nearer the wall from the starting line and is designated as the foul line.

More than one test group may perform for score simultaneously. Each group contains an attacker, a defender, and a scorer. The attacker makes five attacks at his own pace with each attack beginning behind the starting line. He may choose any acceptable attack to use. At the conclusion of each attack, the rear foot must be on the floor behind the foul line.

The defender may use any parry or parries he so chooses. After five consecutive attacks, the subjects switch positions with five attacks then made by the new attacker. The scorer marks two different sets of chalk lines for each attacker.

SCORING METHOD: Standing slightly behind and one yard to the right of the attacker, the scorer decides whether or not a point is landed on the attack, or if there is a complete miss. He must also make sure the rear foot of the attacker remains behind the foul line. This assures a proper lunge attack.

One point is scored by the attacker for each disengage which lands on a valid target area. No points are scored on an incorrect attack, or an attack that lands off target and is not parried.

One point is scored by the defender for each successful counter parry. Should the defender parry the blade with a counter parry so the attack lands foul, it is considered a good parry and a point is awarded the defender. No points are scored for an incorrect parry. Also, a direct parry which stops the attack earns no score.

Scores should be called out after each attack to keep the fencers informed of their running scores. There is a total of ten possible points for each test, five on attack and five on defense.

Scientific Authenticity

VALIDITY: Fifty-one college students enrolled in two beginning coeducational foil fencing classes were the subjects for the Bower study. In comparing test results with round-robin tournament rankings, a validity coefficient of .80 was obtained.

RELIABILITY: Utilizing the test-retest method for obtaining reliability, a .82 coefficient of correlation resulted.

CRITERION MEASURE: Round-robin tournament rankings.

Additional Comments

The mass testing capability of the Bower Test adds greatly to its value as a feasible test of general foil fencing ability. Also, the test is unusually easy to administer. There is a plus connected with the practice requirement: The students are drilled in both basic offensive and defensive fencing skills which contributes to improvement in overall fencing ability. On the negative side, the extra practice time required in regular class sessions makes the test somewhat less attractive.

SAFRIT FENCING TEST[15]

Date: 1962.

Purpose: To measure the speed of the lunge recovery; to determine general fencing ability.

Description

The Safrit Fencing Test originally was designed to measure the speed of the lunge recovery along with appropriate form checks and an accuracy measure of the lunge by utilizing a wall target.

The latter item demonstrated a low reliability value and was not considered to be a practical test. Therefore, discussion of the Safrit Test is limited to the lunge recovery speed item.

EDUCATIONAL APPLICATION: College women.

Administrative Feasibility

TIME: One sixty-minute period for a class of twenty students.

PERSONNEL: One scorer and possibly a timer, depending upon the equipment used in testing.

TRAINING INVOLVED: Reasonable period of instructional time for students to gain familiarity with test requirements.

EQUIPMENT AND SUPPLIES: Automatic Performance Analyzer* (optional), fencing foils, stop watches measuring one-hundredth of a second.

Accessories: Scoring materials.

Facilities and Space: Proper floor space for lunging and a flat, smooth wall surface.

Directions

The subject stands far enough from the wall so that a lunge recovery can be executed with the tip of the foil touching the wall.

She assumes an on-guard position with the forward foot on a mat which is used with a rather elaborate piece of equipment called the "Automatic Performance Analyzer." This apparatus measures reaction time, movement time, or total time of a simple or complex movement. It was used in the original Safrit Fencing Test but is not an absolute necessity. Stop watches that measure one-hundredth of a second may also be used. A mat is not needed if stop watches are used.

Any time after an audible command, the subject may make a lunge against the wall. The clock starts when the forward foot of the subject is lifted off the mat or floor and stops after the lunge when the forward foot has recovered and is placed back on the mat so that the body weight is equally distributed over both feet. Subjects must be balanced before the clock is stopped. Five trials are given.

Form is also an important part of the test, so appropriate form checks are made by the tester. They include:
1. upward bend of the blade
2. foil arm extension
3. back knee extension
4. back and front foot position

SCORING METHOD: Two scores are recorded for each of five trials. A time score is recorded based on the elapsed time from the

---

* The Automatic Performance Analyzer, Model 631, by George J. Dekan, Dekan Athletic Equipment, Inc., Carol Stream, Illinois.

instant the forward foot is lifted until the forward foot has fully recovered and the subject is again in a balanced position. The score for each form check is five if the form is correct and zero if the form is not correct. With five form checks per trial, twenty-five points is maximum, and 125 are possible for all five trials.

Scientific Authenticity

Forty-three beginning fencers in three collegiate classes provided the test data in the Safrit study. None had any previous fencing experience.

VALIDITY: Face validity is apparent.

RELIABILITY: Coefficients ranging from .81 to .85 were obtained, depending upon the number of trials given and the amount of time allowed between trials.

Additional Comments

Reliability of the test should be confirmed with the use of stop watches because many schools either do not own or cannot purchase the Automatic Performance Analyzer. Although it is commonly believed that good reaction time is foremost in fencing skills, the test's validity value should be determined to substantiate the importance of that physical attribute in fencing performance.

KUHAJDA FENCING SKILL TEST[9]

Date: 1970.

Purpose: To measure the ability to riposte and lunge from the parry four position.

Description

Of six possible parries to choose from, the direct parry was selected for use in this test since it involves a shorter movement than the others and can be performed more quickly. From five different types of ripostes, the simple, direct type was chosen because it best measures speed and accuracy of the riposte.

A wall target is constructed which consists of ten concentric circles, with the center circle having a 2-inch diameter with each consecutive outer circle showing a diameter increase of 2 inches. The middle of the center circle is 45 inches above the base of the floor (Fig. 28).

A reference line is drawn on the floor perpendicular to the wall and directly under the center of the target. This line should extend back to the distant restraining line or 8 feet, 6 inches from the wall.

Three sets of restraining lines are placed on the floor. Each line should be 1 foot long and 6 inches on either side of the reference line. The distance the restraining lines should be from the wall are as follows:

Line	1st Line	2nd Line
Green	6'9"	7'8"
Red	7'2"	8'1"
Blue	7'7"	8'6"

Three pairs of colored *X*s are placed on the floor. Each pair matches the color of a corresponding restraining line, and each *X* is 7 inches on either side of the reference line and 17 inches in front of the first appropriately colored restraining line (Fig. 29).

The *X* markings are for the placement of the parrying targets or poles. These poles are 6 feet long and are tied together at the top so that a distance of 14 inches is maintained between the poles. If the green restraining line is used, the green *X*s should also be used.

EDUCATIONAL APPLICATION: Originally developed for college women but is appropriate for both sexes at the high school and college levels.

Administrative Feasibility

TIME: One class of twenty students can easily be tested in one sixty-minute period.

PERSONNEL: One scorer and one timer.

TRAINING INVOLVED: Regular class instruction provides adequate subject preparation for the test.

EQUIPMENT AND SUPPLIES: Fencing foils, two 6-foot bamboo poles, stop watches measured to one-hundredth of a second.

Accessories: Score sheets for timers and scorers.

Facilities and Space: A flat floor space for lunging purposes that measures 10 × 6 feet and a flat, smooth wall surface 4 feet wide and 6 feet high.

Directions

The tester should determine the appropriate restraining line to be used by each subject before the actual testing begins. This is done by simply instructing each subject to assume an on-guard position with his side to the wall. The fencing arm is then extended so that the tip of the foil touches the wall. Next, the subject extends the back leg into a full lunge position, making sure to keep the tip of the foil on the wall. The lunge distance is the distance from the wall to the side of the back foot nearer the wall. It might be helpful for the tester to know that the average lunge distance for the college women in the Kuhajda study was 8 feet, 1 inch. Tape should be placed on the foil 11½ inches from the bell guard. This designates the correct parrying portion of the foil for both the subject and tester. The subject assumes an on-guard position with the fencing arm in a guard position six with that

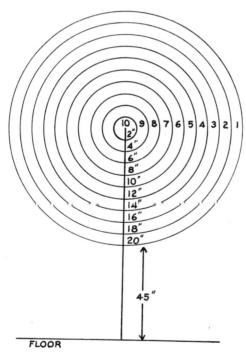

Figure 28. Wall target for Kuhajda Fencing Test.

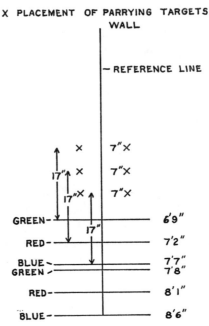

Figure 29. Floor markings for Kuhajda Fencing Test.

portion of the blade between the bell guard and the tape resting against the pole to his right side (opposite for left-handers).

The subject's back foot should be behind and parallel to the restraining line farthest from the wall. The heel of the front foot should be perpendicular to and on the corresponding restraining line nearer the wall.

When the subject hears a verbal signal to begin, a parry four is executed by touching the pole with that part of the blade between the bell guard and the tape. The parry four is followed by a riposte and lunge toward the wall target. Recovering to the original on-guard position the subject prepares to repeat the trial. Five trials are given.

SCORING METHOD: Two scores are recorded for each of the five trials. An accuracy score is tabulated based on the exact contact point of the foil on the target. The point total is determined by adding the points of each of the five trials. A contact point occurring on a line receives the higher of the two values. A time

TABLE LI

RELIABILITY COEFFICIENTS AND AVERAGES
FOR SEVEN VARIABLES IN KUHAJDA
FENCING TEST*

Variables	Averages	r for Group A	r for Group B
Mean Time	48.14 seconds	.96	.90
Mean Accuracy	7.66 points	.71	.66
Mean Velocity	2.06 in./sec.	.92	.90
Mean Accuracy Plus Mean Time	55.31	.95	.85
Mean Accuracy Times Mean Time	368.04	.90	.82
Mean Accuracy Plus Mean Velocity	9.72	.72	.65
Mean Accuracy Times Mean Velocity	15.67	.79	.77

*Based on scores of 38 college women.

score is also recorded and is based on the elapsed time from the moment the blade contacts the pole until the foil tip contacts the wall target. The time should be recorded to the nearest one-hundredth of a second. If the hand stops between two numbers, the slower time is recorded.

Scientific Authenticity

VALIDITY: Since the test measures the components of the riposte-lunge as defined by experts, content validity was claimed.

RELIABILITY: In the Kuhajda study, five trials were administered on each of two days to thirty-eight college women who were randomly divided into two groups of nineteen subjects (Table LI).

Reliability coefficients for the seven variables along with the average of each are shown in Table LI.

Additional Comments

In general the Kuhajda Test adequately meets all the feasibility criteria for quality tests with one exception. Construction time for the test target poles and floor markings appears extensive. Development of a more practical test layout would greatly strengthen the value of the Kuhajda Test, making it more attractive to the potential tester.

REFERENCES

1. Barrow, Harold M. and McGee, Rosemary: *A Practical Approach to Measurement in Physical Education,* 2nd ed. Philadelphia, Lea & Febiger, 1971.
2. Bernhard, Fredrica: Fencing altelier. *DGWS Bowling-Fencing-Golf Guide (1954-56).* Washington, AAHPER, 1956.
3. Bower, Muriel G.: A Test of General Fencing Ability. Master's thesis, Los Angeles, University of Southern California, 1961.
4. Busch, Roxanne E.: The Construction of a Fencing Test Using a Moving Target. Master's thesis, Greensboro, University of North Carolina, 1966.
5. Cooper, Cynthia K.: The Development of a Fencing Skill Test for Measuring Achievement of Beginning Collegiate Women Fencers in Using the Advance, Beat and Lunge. Master's thesis, Macomb, Western Illinois University, 1968.
6. Emery, L.: Criteria for rating selected skills of foil fencing. *DGWS Bowling-Fencing-Golf Guide (1960-62).* Washington, AAHPER, 1962.
7. Fein, Judith T.: Construction of Skill Tests for Beginning Collegiate Women Fencers. Master's thesis, Iowa City, University of Iowa, 1964.
8. Johnson, Doris V.: A Study to Devise Practice Drills for Basic Fencing Skills. Unpublished study, Madison, University of Wisconsin, 1952.
9. Kuhajda, Patricia F.: The Construction and Validation of a Skill Test for the Riposte-Lunge in Fencing. Master's thesis, Carbondale, Southern Illinois University, 1970.
10. Larson, Leonard A. and Yocom, Rachael Dunaven: *Measurement and Evaluation in Physical, Health and Recreation Education.* St. Louis, Mosby, 1951.
11. Lindsey, Ruth: Teaching devices. *DGWS Bowling-Fencing-Golf Guide (1958-60).* Washington, AAHPER, 1960.
12. Mastropaolo, Joseph A.: Analysis of the fundaments of fencing. *Research Quarterly, 30:*258-291, 1947.
13. Meyers, Carlton R.: *Measurement in Physical Education,* 2nd ed. New York, Ronald, 1974.
14. Montoye, Henry J. (Ed.): *An Introduction to Measurement in Physical Education,* vol. III. Indianapolis, Phi Epsilon Kappa Fraternity, 1970.
15. Safrit, Margaret J.: Construction of Skill Tests for Beginning Fencers. Master's thesis, Madison, University of Wisconsin, 1962.

16. ————: *Evaluation in Physical Education.* Englewood Cliffs, P-H, 1973.
17. Schmitter, Charles: Evaluating fencing classes. *DGWS Bowling-Fencing-Golf Guide (1958-60).* Washington, AAHPER, 1960.
18. Schutz, Helen J.: Construction of An Achievement Scale in Fencing for Women. Master's thesis, Seattle, University of Washington, 1940.
19. Swanson, Allys H.: Measuring Achievement in Selected Skills for Beginning Women Fencers. Master's thesis, Iowa City, University of Iowa, 1967.

Chapter 11

Field Hockey

INTRODUCTION

FOR A SPORT that has been played in America for only seventy-five years, field hockey today is regarded as the most popular outdoor team sport among females. Commonly found in high school and college physical education programs, the sport is one of the oldest for which skills tests have been formulated.

Skills tests construction for field hockey has not kept pace with the sport's popularity increase. Of the several tests available today, only a few are scientifically documented. Most were developed before 1950, but the authenticated ones emerged after that time.

SCHMITHALS-FRENCH FIELD HOCKEY TEST[18]

Also cited as Schmithals-French Achievement Test in Field Hockey.

Date: 1940.

Purpose: To measure achievement in field hockey skills; to aid in student classification for instructional purposes.

Description

The original test of six skills included the items of ball control, field and drive, goal shooting left, push pass, drive for distance, and combined goal. Ball control proved to be the best single item for measuring field hockey ability, and according to statistical evidence, the fielding and drive test and the goal shooting left item provide the best two-item combination for assessing achievement. Weightings of 1.0 for goal shooting left and 1.2 for the fielding and drive item are suggested when using this combination. The above items along with the ball control test comprise the best three-item battery.

Ball Control: A line 20 feet in length serves both as a starting and finishing line, and a 35-foot foul line extends downfield and bisects the starting line in a perpendicular manner. Constructed

30 feet from the starting line is a 10-foot line that is perpendicular to and bisects the foul line. Three 1-foot lines are marked perpendicular to and bisect the foul line or an imaginary extension of the foul line. The first of the three lines is placed 35 feet from the starting line or point A (Fig. 30). The other two lines, which bisect each other, are placed 45 feet from the starting line or point B. One high jump standard is placed at point A and one at point B, making sure that the middle of the base of each is directly over the previously described points.

Goal Shooting Left: A 6½-foot starting line is drawn along with a parallel line of the same length 15 feet away. The second line represents the end of the rectangle nearest the starting line. The rectangle measures 11 feet in length and 6½ in width. The midpoint (point A) of the far end of the rectangle has three lines radiating from a common point. A center line (C) which is 34 feet in length and perpendicular to the end of the rectangle opposite the starting line is constructed. A 12-foot line bisects the center line and is perpendicular to it at the end. A right and left line are also constructed. The two sidelines radiate at a 45-degree angle and are 36½ feet in length. They terminate in the middle of a 12-foot line that is placed at a 45-degree angle to the radiating lines. Refer to Figure 31 for additional clarification.

The target, which is 9 inches wide, 12 feet long and at least ½ inch thick, is positioned on one of the specified 12-foot lines with the numbers facing the starting line.

The length of the target is divided into eleven equal spaces. Each space should be colored with the alternate spaces starting from the end painted black and other remaining spaces staying a natural wood color. Numbers are painted on each of the eleven spaces as follows: 1-2-3-4-5-6-5-4-3-2-1. It is further suggested that a 3-inch wide board of 12 feet in length be nailed to the bottom so that 2½ inches extend beyond the back of the target. Ice picks or similar instruments may help anchor the target (Fig. 31).

Fielding and Drive: The goal line is drawn along with a 12-foot parallel line (foul) which lies 10 feet away. An imaginary line drawn from the midpoint (point B) of the goal line is perpendicular to and bisects the foul line. Ice picks or similar instruments are placed at the ends of the foul line. A 30-foot restraining line is marked off ten feet from and parallel to the foul line. The mid-point (point B) of the goal line also bisects the restraining line. A regulation striking circle is placed in front of the goal (Fig. 32).

EDUCATIONAL APPLICATION: High school and college females.

Administrative Feasibility

TIME: A class of twenty students can be tested in two sixty-minute periods.

PERSONNEL: Either one or two timer-recorders depending on the particular test or test battery used.

TRAINING INVOLVED: A practice trial is allowed for each item on the day of the test which should come toward the end of an instructional period when used for evaluation purposes.

EQUIPMENT AND SUPPLIES: Hockey sticks and balls, stop watch, regulation goal, high jump standards, target, and two ice picks. Selection from the above depends on the tests or test batteries used.

Accessories: Scoring and field marking materials.

Facilities and Space: A field hockey facility.

Directions

BALL CONTROL: The test is initiated with the subject standing behind the starting line while the ball rests on the starting line and to the left of the foul line. When an audible starting signal is

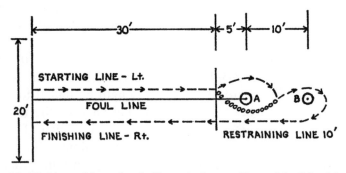

Figure 30. Field markings for ball control test. From M. Schmithals and E. French: Achievement tests in field hockey for college women, *Research Quarterly,* 11:84-92, 1940. Courtesy of AAHPER.

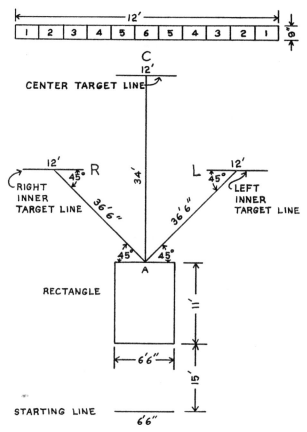

Figure 31. Target and field markings for goal shooting left test. From M. Schmithals and E. French: Achievement tests in field hockey for college women, *Research Quarterly*, 11:84-92, 1940. Courtesy of AAHPER.

given, the subject proceeds to dribble the ball as rapidly as possible to the restraining line while making sure to stay on the left side of and parallel to the foul line.

When the restraining line is reached, the ball should be sent to the right of the first obstacle (point A in Fig. 30), and the subject runs around the left side of the obstacle and recovers the ball. This move is comparable to the dodge in field hockey. The subject proceeds to dribble the ball under control around the left side of the second obstacle (point B), and heads back toward the finish line with a hard drive. This last move is comparable to a circular tackle, followed by the drive. If the drive is not hard enough to reach the finish line, the subject follows up on it and drives again. Six trials are given.

GOAL SHOOTING LEFT: Standing behind the starting line with the hockey ball directly on the starting line, the subject when signaled dribbles the ball as rapidly as possible to the rectangle. From within the confines of the rectangle, the subject drives the ball hard to the target. Ten test trials are administered.

FIELDING AND DRIVE: The subject stands behind the goal line with a hockey stick and the tester takes a position immediately behind the striking circle and in front of the goal. While holding a hockey ball and stop watch, the tester gives an audible signal, then proceeds to roll the hockey ball toward the goal at the speed of forty feet in 1.7 seconds. The ball is rolled as the starting signal is given. At the same time, the subject starts to run toward the rolling ball, attempts to field it before it reaches the foul line, taps

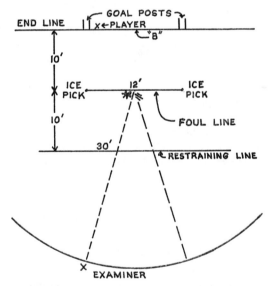

Figure 32. Field markings for fielding and drive test. From M. Schmithals and E. French: Achievement tests in field hockey for college women, *Research Quarterly, 11*:84-92, 1940. Courtesy of AAHPER.

it once, and quickly drives it out of the striking circle. The drive should occur between the restraining line and the foul line. Sixteen trials are given.

Scoring Method and Norms

Ball Control: The score for one trial is the amount of time taken to negotiate the course from the starting signal until the finish line is crossed, providing

1. the foul line is not crossed by either the subject or ball before the restraining line is passed;
2. the ball is not sent from the left side of the foul line when executing the dodge;
3. the subject does not make "sticks."

Should any of the above three circumstances occur, the trial does not count. The score for the entire test is the average of the six trials.

Goal Shooting Left: The score for one trial is the time that elapses from the starting signal until the ball strikes the target. The score for the test is the sum of the two best times made on the even trials and the two best times on the odd trials. This means that the best four trials may not be counted. All three target placements may be utilized by the tester. The final score is the sum of twelve shots.

The score counts when the ball bounces over the top of the target providing the time is stopped the second the ball clears the target.

A score of zero is recorded when

1. the ball is not driven from within the rectangle;
2. the driven ball fails to reach the target or goes wide;
3. "sticks" are made;
4. the subject hits the ball in such a way as to cause the ball to fly over the target without ever touching the ground.

When singly given, the test item has an accuracy score which is combined with the speed score for evaluation purposes. Only the speed score is used when the item is administered as part of a battery.

Fielding and Drive: The score for one trial is the elapsed time

TABLE LII

T-SCALE FOR SCHMITHALS-FRENCH
FIELD HOCKEY TEST

T-Score	Ball Control*	Ball Control†	Goal Shooting‡	Fielding and Drive†	T-Score
76	9.1- 9.5				76
75		9.6-10.0			75
74					74
73	9.6-10.0		19.4-19.6	4.1	73
72					72
71		10.1-10.5	19.7-21.4	4.3	71
70	10.1-10.5				70
69					69
68			21.5-21.7	4.4	68
67					67
66	10.6-11.0				66
65				4.5	65
64		10.6-11.0	21.8-22.0	4.6	64
63	11.1-11.5				63
62				4.7	62
61	11.6-12.0		22.1-22.3	4.8	61
60		11.1-11.5	22.4-22.6		60
59	12.1-12.5		22.7-22.9	4.9	59
58			23.0-23.2		58
57		11.6-12.0	23.3-23.8	5.0	57
56	12.6-13.0		23.9-24.1	5.1	56
55			24.2-25.0	5.2	55
54	13.1-13.5		25.1-25.3	5.4	54
53		12.1-12.5	25.4-25.6	5.6	53
52				5.8	52
51	13.6-14.0		25.7-25.9	5.9	51
50		12.6-13.0	26.0-26.5	6.0	50
49	14.1-14.5		26.6-26.8	6.1	49
48			26.9-27.1	6.2	48
47			27.2-27.4	6.4	47
46	14.6-15.0	13.1-13.5	27.5-28.0	6.5	46
45			28.1-28.3		45
44	15.1-15.5				44
43			28.4-28.6	6.6	43
42	15.6-16.0	13.6-14.0	28.7-28.9		42
41			29.0-29.5	6.7	41
40	16.1-16.5		29.6-29.8	6.9	40
39	16.6-17.0	14.1-14.5	29.0-30.7	7.2	39
38			30.8-31.0	7.3	38
37	17.1-17.5		31.1-31.9		37
36		14.6-15.0	32.0-32.8	7.4	36
35	17.6-18.0			7.6	35
34			32.1-33.1		34
33	18.1-18.5	15.1-15.5		7.7	33
32	18.6-19.0		33.2-33.4	8.0	32

TABLE LII (continued)

T-Score	Ball Control*	Ball Control†	Goal Shooting‡	Fielding and Drive‡	T-Score
31	19.1-19.5		33.5-33.7	9.0	31
30					30
29	19.6-20.0		33.8-34.3	9.2	29
28		15.6-16.0			28
27	20.1-20.5		34.4-34.6	10.7	27
26					26
25	20.6-21.0				25
24					24
23	21.1-25.5				23
22					22
21	25.6-26.0				21

*Scale constructed from data collected on 310 freshman and sophomore students.

†Scale constructed from data collected on 79 sophomore major students.

‡Scales constructed from data collected on 51 students.

From M. Schmithals and E. French: Achievement tests in field hockey for college women, *Research Quarterly, 11*:84-92, 1940. Courtesy of AAHPER.

from the second the ball is touched by the subject until the ball reaches the striking circle. To obtain the official score, the three best even- and odd-numbered trials are averaged.

Trials do not count when

1. the rolled ball does not pass between the ice picks;
2. the rolled ball does not have the desired speed;
3. the player makes "sticks."

The player does not receive a trial score if the ball

1. is advanced illegally;
2. passes the foul line before being touched by the subject;
3. is not driven out of the striking circle from within the specified boundaries.

Scientific Authenticity

Fifty-one women of college age provided the test data in the Schmithals-French study. Their performance was rated by three nationally recognized judges.

VALIDITY: Ball control, .44; goal shooting left, .44; fielding and drive, .48.

RELIABILITY: Ball control, .92; goal shooting left, .87; fielding and drive, .90.

CRITERION MEASURE: Judges' ratings.

Additional Comments

The goal shooting item is an excellent practice aid for the student. Its accuracy score is used to make the situation somewhat analogous to the actual game in that the player has to decide how much speed she can afford to sacrifice for the sake of accuracy.

Results of the Schmithals-French study reflected a high reliability value for the fielding and drive test. This is surprising since the speed of the ball roll which initiates the test requires a high rate of consistency. Testers should give ample practice time to the ball rolling assignment.

Although widely accepted through the years as a worthwhile skills test for field hockey, the Schmithals-French Test yielded item validity coefficients which are definitely too low for individual evaluative purposes. More confidence can be placed in the discriminatory value of the battery as a whole since a validity coefficient of .62 was derived in the aforementioned study for the three items combined.

FRIEDEL FIELD HOCKEY TEST[6]

Also cited as Pass Receiving, Fielding and Drive While Moving Test.

Date: 1956.

Purpose: To objectively measure general playing ability; to measure ability to control the ball in a variety of gamelike situations.

Description

The Friedel Field Hockey Test involves the subject fielding, controlling, and driving a rolled ball while on the move. A total of twenty trials is given, ten from the right and ten from the left. The score is the total number of seconds it takes to complete all twenty trials.

Test layout dimensions for a single testing station call for a rectangle that is 25 yards long and 10 yards wide. The starting line is simply the end line of the rectangle and is located 15 yards from a parallel restraining line.

A target, 2 yards in length and 1 yard in width, is located in the center of the restraining line. The target is placed on the starting line side of the restraining line. One-yard diagonal lines should be constructed at right angles to the target in the left and right corners of the starting line. This is the point from which the balls are rolled to the test subject (Fig. 33).

EDUCATIONAL APPLICATION: High school girls.

Administrative Feasibility

TIME: A class of twenty students can be tested in two sixty-minute periods.

PERSONNEL: One roller-timer.

TRAINING INVOLVED: Practice trials are allowed but less necessary for this test than most since good reliability is insured by the administration of twenty trials for each subject.

EQUIPMENT AND SUPPLIES: Hockey sticks, balls, stop watch.

Accessories: Scoring and field marking materials.

Facilities and Space: Level outdoor space of 30 × 15 yards for each testing station.

Directions

Standing behind the starting line with a field hockey stick in hand, the subject responds to an audible signal by proceeding to run forward to the area between the starting and restraining lines. She fields and controls the rolled ball which is rolled from either the left- or right-hand side. The rolled ball is aimed toward the target area and when the ball does not pass through the target area, it is rolled again. The subject should have the ball under control by the time the restraining line has been passed. The subject continues to dribble the ball toward the end line, crosses it, then turns and drives the ball back to the starting line 25 yards away. Should the driven ball not have enough momentum to reach the starting line, the subject follows the first drive with a second and proceeds until the ball crosses the starting line. The return

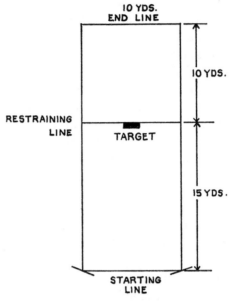

Figure 33. Field markings for Friedel Field Hockey Test.

TABLE LIII

T-SCORES FOR FRIEDEL AND SCHMITHALS-FRENCH
BALL CONTROL FIELD HOCKEY TESTS*

T-Score	Friedel Test (Total seconds in 20 trials)	Schmithals-French Test (Average seconds in 6 trials)	T-Score
80	193		80
75	209	11.0	75
70	224	12.3	70
65	239	13.6	65
60	255	14.9	60
55	270	16.2	55
50	285	17.5	50
45	301	18.8	45
40	316	20.1	40
35	331	21.4	35
30	347	22.6	30
25	361	23.9	25
20	376		20

*Based on scores of 68 high school girls.

drive or drives must stay within the 10-yard lane for the trial to count. A total of twenty trials is given, ten each on the left and right.

SCORING METHOD AND NORMS: The score for one trial is the time taken to negotiate the course from the starting signal until the ball crosses the starting line at the completion of the drive. Score for the entire test is the total time elapsed for the twenty trials.

T-scores for both the Friedel and Schmithals-French Ball Control Field Hockey Tests are presented in Table LIII since the latter was used in validating the Friedel Test. The T-scores for both tests are based on the performance of sixty-eight high school girls in regular physical education classes.[6]

Scientific Authenticity

VALIDITY: Coefficient of .87 in the Friedel study.

RELIABILITY: Coefficients of .90 and .77 on trials from the left and right sides, respectively.

CRITERION MEASURE: Performance on the Schmithals-French Ball Control Test.

Additional Comments

The validity value of the Friedel Test is somewhat suspect since that test was validated by the ball control item in the Schmithals-French Test which demonstrated questionable validity itself. Also, Friedel's test is time-consuming for one of the single-item variety. A multiple test station setup is recommended if qualified testing personnel are available.

The absence of need for special equipment and large outdoor space is an asset of this test. In addition to its use in evaluation, the test provides a useful service as a practice and teaching device.

STRAIT FIELD HOCKEY TEST[21]

Also cited as Strait Field Hockey Rating Scale and Dribble, Dodge, Drive, Receive, and Circular Tackle Test.

Date: 1960.

Purpose: To measure field hockey ability.

Description

The field markings include a 10-foot starting line with a stake (A) placed at the midpoint of the line (Fig. 34). Two 10-foot parallel sidelines are also constructed. Stake B is placed in the ground at 42 feet and directly across from stake A with line markings constructed similar to those surrounding stake A. A backboard (F) with minimum dimensions of 12 × 18 feet is located at a spot indicated by Figure 34. Four 1-foot squares (C, D, E, and F) are also part of the field markings.

EDUCATIONAL APPLICATION: College women.

Administrative Feasibility

TIME: Twenty students can be tested in two sixty-minute class periods.

PERSONNEL: A scorer-timer and one stick holder.

TRAINING INVOLVED: A practice trial per student.

EQUIPMENT AND SUPPLIES: Hockey sticks, balls, stop watch, and backboard.

Accessories: Scoring and field marking materials.

Facilities and Space: A grass field with minimum measurements of 52 × 62 feet.

Directions

The subject stands behind the starting line while holding a field hockey stick. Behind the starting line and in front of the subject, a ball is placed. On an audible signal, the subject dribbles the ball away from stake A toward square C (Fig. 34). A designated person (G) is standing at square C, holding a hockey stick. A legal dodge must be executed around the motionless assistant, and the ball is quickly recovered and driven to the backboard (F). The ball rebounding from the backboard is fielded and dribbled to stake B. A circular tackle is made around stake B, and the subject then repeats the same procedure as she heads back to stake A. This means the subject leaves stake B by dribbling the ball toward square D. A dodge is executed around square D and is followed by a drive, dribble, and ends with a circular turn

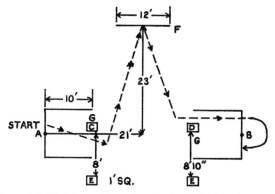

Figure 34. Field markings for Strait Field Hockey Test.

around stake A. The subject then begins the complete circuit again, and the watch is stopped when the subject passes stake A the second time. The assistant (G) must remember to stand on square C at the beginning of the test and quickly shift to square D in time for the subject's return trip. This shifting continues for the second half of each trial.

Should a driven ball miss the backboard by passing it, the subject proceeds to the nearest ball enclosure (E) for another ball and continues the test circuit. Assuming the driven ball fails to reach the backboard, the subject continues to play the same ball by driving it again. Her feet must stay in the lane boundaries during the dribble or the trial is repeated.

SCORING METHOD: The score for one trial is the time required to complete two continuous circuits beginning at stake A and ending when the subject dribbles past stake A for the second time. The final score is the best of three trials. A rest and recovery interval should be given to each subject between trials.

Scientific Authenticity

VALIDITY: In correlating test scores with judges' ratings, a coefficient of .76 was obtained. The judges used a five-point scale developed by Strait. This scale shows potential as an aid in evaluating individual progress or achievement. It has value for self-testing and motivation purposes.

Rating Scale

Excellent–5 points
1. Stick work is superior
2. Footwork is consistently controlled
3. Ball control is excellent
4. Passes are well timed and accurate
5. Very rarely fouls
6. Positions herself well
7. Cuts to receive passes
8. Takes advantage of nearly all opportunities

Good–4 points
1. Shows ability to make proper use of the stick
2. Feet are used to good advantage most of the time
3. Ball is usually under control
4. Passes are well timed and accurate
5. Rarely fouls
6. Positions herself well most of the time
7. Is able to see opportunities and take advantage of them
8. Cuts to receive passes

Average–3 points
1. Drives and fielding are good, but lacks fine control of the ball for consistent dodges and tackles
2. Full use is not made of the feet
3. When in possession of the ball, occasionally loses it because of poor control
4. Some passes are good, but others are not well timed or accurate
5. Fouls moderately often
6. Is not sure as to where her position should be many times
7. Misses some available opportunities
8. Does not consistently cut for passes

Low–2 points
1. Drives are not strong
2. When fielding, often misses the ball
3. Rarely tries dodges

4. Tackles unsuccessfully
5. Feet are sometimes in the way
6. Has small degree of ball control
7. Passes are poorly timed and not accurate
8. Fouls fairly often
9. Lacks good positioning
10. Usually fails to take advantage of opportunities
11. Is slow in getting to the ball

Poor–1 point

1. Lacks general control of the stick
2. Feet are in the way
3. Ball is rarely under control
4. Passes are poorly timed and are not well directed
5. Fouls often
6. Appears not to realize the benefits of good positioning
7. Rarely takes advantage of opportunities
8. Usually does not move to meet the ball
9. Lacks body control, in general

RELIABILITY: Utilizing the test-retest method, a .87 correlation coefficient was determined.

CRITERION MEASURE: Judges' ratings.

Additional Comments

Simulating a gamelike condition, this test naturally shows value as both a practice and testing device. Its validity value is also sufficient enough to measure individual achievement.

Sustained vigorous activity is necessary to complete the test requirement. The testor should guard against the fatigue factor as reliability in performance may be affected.

STEWART FIELD HOCKEY TEST[20]

Date: 1965.
Purpose: To measure general field hockey ability.

Description

Stewart developed a five-item test battery, three of which are included in the previously discussed Schmithals-French Test. In the ball control test, the distance between the high jump standards was lengthened from 10 to 15 feet.

A fourth item demonstrated an unacceptable reliability coefficient. The remaining item or backboard test is distinctive since it is administered indoors. Discussion of the Stewart Test is restricted to the backboard item for the above explained reasons.

Two square wall targets, 3 × 3 feet in size, are located 1 foot apart with their bottoms constructed even with the floor. An 11-foot restraining line is drawn 8 feet from and parallel to the wall. Another mark is made on the floor at 20 feet from the wall and parallel to the area between the two targets. This mark designates the spot where the extra balls are placed during the test administration.

EDUCATIONAL APPLICATION: College women.

Administrative Feasibility

TIME: A class of twenty students can be tested in one sixty-minute period.

PERSONNEL: One or two timer-recorders, depending on the test or test battery used.

TRAINING INVOLVED: One practice trial is recommended for the subject immediately before testing.

EQUIPMENT AND SUPPLIES: The equipment and supplies need varies depending upon the test or test battery used, but basically it is the same as that for the earlier presented Schmithals-French Field Hockey Test (see p. 180).

Accessories: Scoring, field, and wall marking materials.

Facilities and Space: Same as for the Schmithals-French Field Hockey Test plus indoor area with a wall space 15 feet long and 6 feet high and a 15 × 20-foot floor space.

Directions

Standing behind the restraining line with a hockey stick positioned to strike the hockey ball, the subject hits the ball into one of the two targets when signaled to begin. She continues to strike the rebounding ball back to the targets, making sure to remain behind the restraining line, and alternates targets with each shot.

When the left target is first struck, the right target should be hit with the second shot, and the alternation should be continued for each of the six trials. The targets should be continually alternated even if the ball does not strike the appropriate target.

A subject may go in front of the restraining line to retrieve a ball but must assume a position behind the restraining line again before putting the ball back into play. If the subject loses complete control of the ball, a second ball may be used from the extra ball location on the floor.

A hit does not count if either the ball fails to hit within the target lines or the subject strikes the ball in front of the restraining line. Flick shots are not allowed.

Stewart recommended that four subjects be grouped together at a testing station. This insures adequate rest between trials. All subjects should complete the first trial before the second trial begins.

SCORING METHOD: Each subject completes six thirty-second trials. The score for one trial is the total number of times the ball hits in the appropriate target with the final score constituting the sum of the best three trials. Although norms are not available, the mean for the backboard test in the Stewart study was 25.75 with a standard deviation of 5.32.

Scientific Authenticity

A total of 228 college women participated in the study.
VALIDITY: Not reported.
RELIABILITY: A .81 coefficient in a test-retest situation.
OBJECTIVITY: A .99 coefficient was obtained.

Additional Comments

Perry[16] investigated the reliability and validity values of a Stewart Test modification. The reliability coefficient was less than that derived for the original test, and the validity coefficient was not impressive.

Further experimentation with the validity value of the Stewart Test is needed. Results of Perry's study make it doubtful that the backboard test can legitimately be accepted as having face validity.

REFERENCES

1. Armfield, Helen: Some ideas for a hockey practice. *Sports Women, 5:* 12, 1928.
2. Barrow, Harold M. and McGee, Rosemary: *A Practical Approach to Measurement in Physical Education,* 2nd ed. Philadelphia, Lea & Febiger, 1971.
3. Clarke, H. Harrison: *Application of Measurement to Health and Physical Education,* 4th ed. Englewood Cliffs, P-H, 1967.
4. Cozens, Frederick W.; Cubberley, Hazel J.; and Neilson, N. P.: *Achievement Scales in Physical Education Activities for Secondary School Girls and College Women.* New York, B&N, 1937.
5. Cubberley, Hazel J.: *Field Hockey Analyzed.* New York, B&N, 1928.
6. Friedel, Jean E.: The Development of a Field Hockey Skill Test for High School Girls. Master's thesis, Normal, Illinois State University, 1956.
7. Hartley, Grace: Motivating the physical education program for high school girls. *American Physical Education Review, 3:*284, 344, 405, 1929.
8. Hillas, Marjorie and Knighton, Marian: *An Athletic Program for High School and College Women.* New York, B&N, 1929.
9. Howland, Amy: *National Physical Achievement Standards.* New York, National Recreation Association, 1936.
10. Illner, Julee A.: The Construction and Validation of a Skill Test for the Drive in Field Hockey. Master's thesis, Carbondale, Southern Illinois University, 1968.
11. Lucey, Mildred A.: A Study of Reliability in Relation to the Construction of Field Hockey Tests. Master's thesis, Madison, University of Wisconsin, 1934.
12. Maris, Elizabeth: Hockey from fourth grade through advanced high school. *Official Field Hockey Guide.* New York, Am Sports, 1932.
13. Meyers, Carlton R.: *Measurement in Physical Education,* 2nd ed. New York, Ronald, 1974.
14. Montoye, Henry J. (Ed.): *An Introduction to Measurement in Physical Education,* vol. III. Indianapolis, Phi Epsilon Kappa Fraternity, 1970.
15. Neilson, N. P. and Jensen, Clayne R.: *Measurement and Statistics in Physical Education.* Belmont, Calif., Wadsworth Pub, 1972.
16. Perry, E. L.: An Investigation of Field Hockey Skills Tests for College Women. Master's thesis, University Park, Pennsylvania State University, 1969.

17. Safrit, Margaret J.: *Evaluation in Physical Education.* Englewood Cliffs, P-H, 1973.
18. Schmithals, Margaret and French, Esther: Achievement tests in field hockey for college women. *Research Quarterly, 11*:84-92, 1940.
19. Scott, M. Gladys and French, Esther: *Measurement and Evaluation in Physical Education.* Dubuque, Iowa, Brown Bk, 1959.
20. Stewart, Harriet E.: A Test for Measuring Field Hockey Skill of College Women. Doctoral dissertation, Bloomington, Indiana University, 1965.
21. Strait, Clara J.: The Construction and Evaluation of a Field Hockey Skills Test. Master's thesis, Northampton, Mass., Smith College, 1960.
22. Weiss, Raymond A. and Phillips, Marjorie: *Administration of Tests in Physical Education.* St. Louis, Mosby, 1954.

Chapter 12

Figure Skating

INTRODUCTION

FIGURE SKATING is an activity that has been slow to develop in the United States, and few American universities include it as part of their educational curriculum. As a result, less than ten skills tests exist for figure skating and related activities. Those related activities refer to school or compulsory figures, free skating, pair skating, and ice dancing.

During the past ten years, however, the number of figure skating participants has grown tremendously. This naturally has resulted in the development of additional facilities, advanced techniques, and more publications, yet only a limited number of scientifically documented skills tests have resulted. Unfortunately, most of the tests developed to date are subjective.

Recknagel[9] reported that the United States Figure Skating Association has devised one of the better subjective tests for beginners in figure skating. It is called "The Preliminary Test" and is the first of a series of nine tests which the Standards and Tests Committee of the above mentioned association has authorized. Members of that group use the test series as a means of granting promotions, certificates, and awards.

The United States Skating Association requires the use of at least three official judges in a testing situation or competition. The performance mark (0–10) is multiplied by the degree of difficulty for the test score. The degree of difficulty is one (1) for all the items in the Preliminary Test.

The Preliminary Test could be modified for educational use, providing the tester has the necessary experience and training to act as a qualified judge.

CARRIERE SKATING TEST[2]

Date: 1969.
Purpose: To determine basic figure skating ability.

Description

The Carriere Skating Test contains forty items which are progressively more difficult and provides a comprehensive measure of basic figure skating skills.

EDUCATIONAL APPLICATION: College men and women.

Administrative Feasibility

TIME: A class of twenty students can be tested in two sixty-minute class periods.

PERSONNEL: One scorer-recorder.

TRAINING INVOLVED: The test should be administered late in the academic term to allow the student a maximum period of time to develop the basic skills in figure skating.

EQUIPMENT AND SUPPLIES: Skates.

Accessories: Score cards.

Facilities and Space: Ice rink or other similar skating area.

Directions

It is best to administer the test in a rink with regular ice hockey markings to insure uniformity. The ice markings should include the following:

1. Hockey blue line to goal line–60 feet
2. Face-off mark to other face-off mark–60 feet
3. Face-off circle diameter–20 feet
4. Face-off mark diameter–2 feet

The subjects should try to successfully execute as many of the forty test items as possible. The items do not have to be attempted or successfully completed in any particular order and may be attempted any number of times. All of the items are of equal value.

Certain terms and abbreviations need to be clarified before the testing begins since successful execution depends to a great extent on the subject's understanding of the terminology. The subjects and tester should refer to a book by Ogilvie[8] for more specific and technical information.

Abbreviations

R–right	F–forward	I–inside edge
L–left	B–backward	O–outside edge

Terms
1. Inside shoulder: shoulder toward inside of curve.
2. Employed skate: skate on ice.
3. Free skate: skate off ice.
4. Free arm: arm that is forward when the free leg is back.
5. Leading leg: when skating backwards, means the free leg is extended in back of the body.
6. Continuous axis: an imaginary line running the length of the rink.
7. Lobe: any step or sequence of steps on one side of the continuous axis.
8. Transverse axis: an imaginary line intersecting the continuous axis at a right angle.

TEST ITEMS

Forward
1. Skate 60 feet in any manner.
2. Stroke and parallel glide alternately for 60 feet; start with T push-off.
3. T push-off and cover 60 feet with three more strokes.
4. Take three strokes (R-L-R or L-R-L) and glide 30 feet on one skate with skating knee slightly bent (not straight) and head up.

Backward Sculling: Each sculling motion must start with feet less than 6 inches apart.
5. Scull with both feet for 60 feet in a straight line.
6. Scull around face-off circle with R scull and L glide. Repeat with L scull and R glide.
7. Scull straight with alternate feet for 60 feet; gliding skate must remain on red or blue line.
8. Scull straight with alternate feet and glide straight on either skate for 30 feet with skating knee slightly bent, back straight, arms down and out to the side.

Stops
9. Skate five strokes forward and execute three consecutive STOPS using either snowplow, T, or side parallel stops.

10. Skate forward from one face-off circle and stop on the other face-off mark.

Turns: Each turn must start from head and shoulders.

11. Forward to backward turn on two feet: skate four F strokes, parallel glide on both skates, half turn R and STOP. Repeat with half turn L.

12. Forward to backward three turn on both feet and backward to forward turn changing from one foot to the other around face-off circle. Preliminary strokes, parallel glide, clockwise (RFO and LFI), three turn to RBI and LBO, shift weight to left skate, and turn to RFO. Repeat counterclockwise.

Forward Curves

13. Four alternate, parallel glide half-circles (10-foot radius): push off on RFO from line; glide with feet parallel around half-circle and back to line; change at line to LFO and parallel glide; change again to RFO and LFO at line. Lean with body straight from ankles up.

14. Ten alternate single strokes along straight line: push off on RFO, curve back to line, shift to LFO (and back) four times.

15. Ten alternate single FI strokes along straight line: same as item fourteen but on single inside edges.

Backward Curves

16. Four alternate, backward, parallel glide half-circles (5-foot radius): like item thirteen but backward; push off on RBO from line, glide around half-circle with feet parallel, change at line to LBO and parallel glide; repeat. No toe scratches.

17. Ten alternate single BO strokes along straight line: push off on RBO and curve back to line, shift to LBO, etc.

18. Ten alternate single BI strokes along straight line: same as item seventeen but on single inside edges.

Forward Crossovers

19. Five forward crossovers around face-off circle, clockwise and counterclockwise (preliminary strokes permissible), STOP (no stepping).

20. T push off, complete circuit of face-off circle with four (or less) crossovers, clockwise or counterclockwise. Must show a bent skating knee, outward thrust with trailing skate, outside arm and shoulder forward, and inside arm back.

Advanced Turns

21. RFO three turn and LFO three turn: start with two or three preliminary strokes, turn from RBO to RBI and hold RBI for three seconds, then parallel glide, and STOP. Repeat with LBO to LBI turn. Movement must be straight or around face-off circle.
22. Four consecutive, alternate, small three turns in a straight line and STOP: T push off, RFO to RBI to LFO and LBI and repeat, STOP.
23. Controlled three turn, RFO to RBI or LFO to LFI: T push off, glide for three seconds on RFO preparing to turn with arms and shoulders, turn to RBI and glide for three seconds going back to line, and STOP. Skater must prepare for turn with arms and shoulders and come out strongly checked (free arm, shoulder, and hip back).
24. Forward inside open Mohawk: start with three or four preliminary strokes from LFO, glide for three seconds on RFI, change to LBI (inside R) and glide for three seconds, then parallel glide, skate backward to starting line, and STOP. May be done to opposite side.
25. Forward inside closed Mohawk: start like item twenty-four, RFI glide, L goes behind to LBI and glide three seconds, then parallel glide, three backward strokes, and STOP.

Advanced Stops

26. Forward T stop: skate three or four strokes, short glide, and STOP, alternate R and L braking skate behind at R angle and parallel to shoulders. No ankle dragging on inside edge of blade, arms held down and out to the side.
27. Parallel side stop (hockey stop): take ten to fifteen strokes with increasing speed, parallel glide, and STOP (hold position one second). Shoulders must face the direction of travel; skates are parallel and knees strongly bent.

Jumps

28. Three bunny hop jumps: executed consecutively or alternated with one or two strokes between each jump. Free leg thrown forward, landing on toe pick, then push from toe pick into that of skating foot blade, stroke, and STOP.

29. Waltz jump: start with preliminary strokes, glide on a FO, swing free leg forward and push up with skating foot, make half turn in air, land on opposite BO, glide, and STOP. Free arm forward and head facing the initial direction. The jump is done on a curve.

Spins

30. Three complete two-foot spins and STOP. Spin on the flat of the blades without traveling on ice.

Intermediate and Advanced

31. Five backward crossovers around face-off circle, clockwise and counterclockwise. When skating counterclockwise the left foot never loses contact with the ice and vice versa for clockwise (no toe scratch).

32. Six alternate sequences of progressive and chasse steps along the blue line with a count of six for each sequence (2-1-3) Curves should be equal size and about a third of a circle of ten-foot radius.

33. Six alternate FO swing rolls. Same as item thirty-two but the free leg is extended and swinging from the back to the front of the body. Free toe pointed down and turned slightly out.

34. Forward change of edges on one foot: a moving start or start from rest may be used to change from RFO edge to RFL. Curves should be equal sizes and change on blue or red line.

35. Shoot the duck: take as many preliminary strokes as desired before going into a sitting position with free leg extended in front, head up, back straight. Glide for five seconds and come back to initial upright position, stroke, and STOP.

36. Forward spiral: start off with preliminary strokes, glide on one foot, bring extended free leg up and behind. Head and free foot should be at least at the level with the upper part of

the seat. Arms are extended to the side of the body. Glide for five seconds; bring free foot on ice, stroke, and STOP.

37. Four alternate FI curves along an axis (blue or red line): push off from rest. Free shoulder and arm are held low and in leading position. Skating shoulder and arm are held back. The free foot is in front at the middle of the curve. Approaching the long axis shoulder square to the line of travel. Size of the curves same as item thirty-two.

38. Four alternate BO curves along axis (blue or red line): push off from rest. Free shoulder and arm in front, skating shoulder and arm in leading position. Body rotates; free leg is behind at the middle of the curve. Approaching the long axis, free side is in open position. Size of curves same as item thirty-two.

39. Full circle on one foot (outside edge): push off from rest position to a forward outside edge, complete the face-off circle circuit on one foot, and STOP.

40. Forward outside eight: push off on a right forward outside complete circle and stroke into the left forward outside edge crossing the transverse axis. Stay close to the marker in the ice (a range of one foot is allowed only). Diameter of circles: 15 feet.

SCORING METHOD: Each maneuver attempted is assigned a score of either one or zero, depending only upon the successful completion of that particular item. The final score is the sum total of points accumulated on the forty-item or point test.

It might help the tester to know that the number of test items successfully completed in the Carriere study ranged from ten to thirty-four. None of the subjects passed items thirty-nine or forty.

An item is failed for improper execution involving such mistakes as

1. falling or having to recover;
2. not covering distance in specified time;
3. not holding stop for three seconds;
4. using a toe pick (unless specifically allowed);
5. not changing feet on the line when specified.

Scientific Authenticity

The original test group consisted of forty-nine male and female college students from two ice skating classes. Seven students ultimately did not have their data included so the test group ended with forty-two subjects.

VALIDITY: The .90 validity value was determined by correlating the sum of three judges' ratings and the number of items passed.

RELIABILITY: The .97 reliability coefficient was determined by the split-half method and corrected by the Spearman-Brown Prophecy Formula.

OBJECTIVITY: The objectivity was determined by having the test originator, a student from the skating class, and a student assistant from another skating class judge three students when performing eleven randomly selected items.

CRITERION MEASURE: Judges' ratings.

Additional Comments

A questionnaire was given to the subjects at the end of the previously mentioned skating classes, and 82 percent thought the test helped motivate them to learn and progress at their own pace. This test is particularly valuable in the assessment of individual progress and achievement.

The test items show a degree of flexibility in range of difficulty enough to motivate the lesser experienced skaters and challenge the intermediate and advanced ones.

No distinction is made between the subjects that pass a test item on their first attempt and those that require additional attempts. When the test is used as an evaluation tool, the authors suggest that the tester limit the number of attempts per subject or set some type of time limit. This would naturally place a higher value on successful completion of a maneuver on the first try. It would also reduce the time involved in the testing process.

REFERENCES

1. Barrow, Harold M. and McGee, Rosemary: *A Practical Approach to Measurement in Physical Education,* 2nd ed. Philadelphia, Lea & Febiger, 1971.

2. Carriere, Diane L.: An Objective Figure Skating Test for Use in Beginning Classes. Master's thesis, Urbana, University of Illinois, 1969.

3. Kimpel, Douglas L.: Dialogue. *Skating, 43:*10-12, 1966.

4. Leaming, Thomas W.: A Measure of Endurance of Young Speed Skaters. Master's thesis, Urbana, University of Illinois, 1959.

5. Maroney, Mary: *Maroney Skating Ladder.* Ann Arbor, Michigan, Edwards Bros, 1965.

6. Moore, Kathleen F.: An Objective Evaluation System for Judging Free Skating Routines. Master's thesis, East Lansing, Michigan State University, 1967.

7. Meyers, Gertrude H.: Children's tests. *Skating, 23:*9, 1946.

8. Ogilvie, Robert S.: *Basic Ice Skating Skills.* New York, Lippincott, 1968.

9. Recknagel, Dorothy: A test for beginners in figure skating. *Journal of Health and Physical Education, 16:*91-92, 1945.

10. Safrit, Margaret J.: *Evaluation in Physical Education.* Englewood Cliffs, P-H, 1973.

11. Southward, Barbara: First lessons in figure skating. *Journal of Health, Physical Education and Recreation, 31:*31-32, 1960.

Chapter 13

Football

INTRODUCTION

IN THE SAME LENGTH of time, no other American sport has grown in popularity as much as football. The sport has literally become a cultural phenomenon in the last half-century, enjoying success at all organized levels.

Normally thought of in terms of tackle football, the type found in physical education programs is either flag or touch football. From elementary school to college, these are rather common and popular offerings in the physical education curriculum. However, the majority of football skills tests either pertain to tackle football or lack scientific documentation. Those that follow in this chapter have either been authenticated in value, or at least are widely accepted and used.

BORLESKE TOUCH FOOTBALL TEST[3]

Date: 1936.

Purpose: To measure basic skills and classify students for instruction and competition in touch football.

Description

Borleske constructed an eighteen-item test battery which was later reduced to five and then three items. Using a criterion of expert judgment, validity coefficients of .93 and .88 were derived for the five- and three-item batteries, respectively.

The larger battery modification included the forward pass for distance, punt for distance, run for time, catching forward pass, and pass defense zone items. Comprising the smaller battery are the forward pass for distance, punt for distance, and run for time tests. Each item in the smaller battery is included in the five-item battery, and a description of all five follows.

Forward Pass for Distance: No special field markings are needed if the test is administered on a regulation football field. Otherwise yard markers spaced at 5-yard intervals are used.

Punt for Distance: Field markings same as for the forward pass for distance item.

Run for Time: A 50-yard distance is marked off if a regulation football field is unavailable.

Catching Forward Pass: Regulation football field or an area designed as for the forward pass for distance test.

Pass Defense Zone: The field or testing area is marked off into four equal rectangles or quadrants. Each has a measurement of 42 × 36 feet (Fig. 35).

EDUCATIONAL APPLICATION: College men.

Administrative Feasibility

TIME: One class of twenty students can be tested in one or two sixty-minute class periods for the three-item battery, depending on the number of test stations available. Twenty students can complete the five-item battery in two or three sixty-minute class periods, depending again on how many test stations are available.

PERSONNEL: One to five scorers, depending on the particular test battery used and number of test stations utilized simultaneously. Student assistants also play an instrumental role in the test administration.

TRAINING INVOLVED: A warm-up of one minute is recommended for each student immediately prior to three of the test items. None is recommended for the catching forward pass and pass defense zone tests.

Considerable student practice in preparation for the catching forward pass test is recommended during class periods prior to the test date.

EQUIPMENT AND SUPPLIES: Footballs, stop watch, and field markers.

Accessories: Scoring materials.

Facilities and Space: Regulation football field or an outdoor field or playing area of similar size.

Directions

FORWARD PASS FOR DISTANCE: The subject receives the ball from center while standing at the end line and executes three forward passes for distance. The forward pass should be as straight as possible and at right angles to the end line. The subject remains behind the end line when executing the forward pass. He allows ample space behind the end line for proper execution of the pass without going over that line.

Borleske recommended that the subjects throw in pairs with one throwing and the other marking and retrieving the thrown ball. Each subject alternates throws with his partner. The subject is not required to throw the ball if the center pass is not a good one.

PUNT FOR DISTANCE: The administration of this test is similar to that of the forward pass for distance item except that the subject receives the ball seven yards behind the end line where the center snaps the ball. Subjects punt the ball within two seconds after receiving the center snap.

RUN FOR TIME: Subjects line up in a three-point stance five yards from the center. When the ball is snapped, the subject proceeds to sprint fifty yards. The 50-yard distance is measured from the point where the run initiated.

Only one trial is given to each subject. The trial is repeated when a bad center snap occurs. The ball may be carried by the subject in any desired manner.

CATCHING FORWARD PASS: Subjects run three different pass patterns and catch a forward pass. The running patterns vary, and it is important that the subject follow the designed pass route as closely as possible. Pass patterns are as follows:

a. Square-out pattern–subject goes 10 yards straight down the field from the center, cuts right at a 90-degree angle, and runs toward the sideline.

b. Post or flag pattern–subject goes 10 yards down the field from the center, cuts left at a 35-degree angle, and continues to run.

c. V pattern–subject goes 15 yards down the field at a 45-degree angle from the center, cuts right at another 45-degree angle, and continues the run across the field parallel to the end line.

The forward pass should be caught while the subject is running the pattern. Three "fair" trials are given for each subject. A "fair" trial is one in which the pass is thrown accurately enough for the subject to have a reasonable opportunity to catch the ball. A bad pass results in a retrial. If the subject can touch the ball with a reasonable effort, it counts as a fair trial.

Pass Defense Zone: The subject takes a position in one of the four quadrants (Fig. 35). A center (C) snaps the football to a passer (P) who is standing 10 yards to the rear. Three receivers (R) run predetermined pass patterns. Three pass plays are executed and each has either one, two, or three receivers running to the same quadrant as the defensive subject (X). The order of plays may be varied, but it is absolutely necessary that the number of eligible receivers vary for each of three plays. The passer and receivers should huddle before each play so patterns can be assigned.

The subject or defensive player should play a zone defense and when the pass is thrown, he attempts to either knock the ball away from the receiver or intercept it. More credit is naturally given for an interception.

A defender is penalized if defensive pass interference occurs.

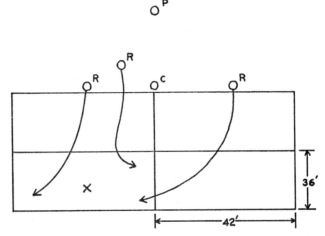

Figure 35. Field markings and participant positions in pass defense zone test.

Only one trial is allowed for each play unless a poor pass is thrown that neither the receiver nor defensive player can reach. The subject is cautioned to stay in the assigned quadrant and only defense receivers who enter that particular quadrant.

SCORING METHOD AND NORMS

Forward Pass for Distance: Each subject is allowed three trials, and the final score is the best of the three throws measured to the nearest yard.

Punt for Distance: Same as for the forward pass for distance test.

Run for Time: Each subject is allowed one trial, and the final score is the time elapsed from the instant the player receives the ball until the 50-yard line is crossed.

Catching Forward Pass: Subjects are allowed three "fair" trials when completing the pass patterns. Each pass caught and retained by the subject counts ten points with a perfect score being thirty points.

Pass Defense Zone: The subject completes one trial for each of the three plays. Should the receiver catch the pass and it is ruled a legal completion under football rules, no points are given to the subject. One-third of the total earned points are deducted from the score for each defensive pass interference that occurs.

Two points are awarded if the defensive player knocks down the ball when one receiver is in the quadrant, and four points are given if the ball is intercepted under that circumstance. Six points are awarded if the defensive player knocks down the ball with two receivers in the quadrant, and eight points are given if the ball is intercepted in the same situation. Ten points are awarded if the defensive player either knocks down or intercepts the pass with three receivers in the quadrant.

The maximum score a defensive player can achieve is twenty-two points.

Conversion of the raw scores to T-scores enables an instructor to classify students according to ability levels for the purpose of grading.

TABLE LIV

T-SCORES FOR BORLESKE TOUCH
FOOTBALL TEST*

T-Score	Forward Pass-Yds.	Punting-Yds.	Running-Sec.	Catching-Points	Pass Defense-Points
76					8.0-8.49
75	56-58	50.6-53.5			
74					
73	53-55		5.36-5.55		7.0-7.99
72					
71		47.6-50.5			6.5-6.99
70					6.0-6.49
69	50-52	44.6-47.5			5.5-5.99
68					5.0-5.49
67					4.5-4.99
66	47-49				
65			5.56-5.75		4.0-4.49
64					
63	44-46				
62		41.6-44.5			
61			5.76-5.95		
60				9.51-10.0	
59	41-43				
58					3.5-3.99
57					3.0-3.49
56		38.6-41.5	5.96-41.5		
55				7.01-9.50	2.5-2.99
54	38-40				
53					2.0-2.49
52			6.16-6.35		
51		35.6-38.5		6.51-7.00	
50	35-37				
49					1.5-1.99
48		32.6-35.5	6.36-6.55		
47					1.0-1.49
46	32-34			3.51-6.50	0.5-0.99
45		29.6-32.5			
44			6.56-6.75		
43				3.01-3.50	
42	29-31				
41			6.76-6.95		
40		26.6-29.5			0.0-0.49
39	26-28				
38		23.6-26.5	6.96-7.15	0.51-3.00	
37		20.6-23.5			
36	23-25				
35		17.6-20.5	7.16-7.35		
34	20-22			0.00-0.50	
33					
32			7.36-7.55		

TABLE LIV (continued)

T-Score	Forward Pass-Yds.	Punting- Yds.	Running- Sec.	Catching- Points	Pass Defense- Points
31	17-19				
30		14.6-17.5			
29					
28			7.56-8.95		
27	14-16	11.6-14.5			
26					
25	11-13	8.6-11.5			

*Based on scores of 87 college men.

TABLE LV

GRADING SCALE FOR BORLESKE TOUCH
FOOTBALL TEST

Classification	Points
Superior	314-over
Above Average	274-313
Average	232-273
Below Average	191-231
Inferior	190-below

Scientific Authenticity

The Borleske Touch Football Test was administered to five college physical education classes, consisting of eighty-seven men.

VALIDITY: Coefficients for specific items were not reported. However, the three-item and five-item battery validity coefficients are .88 and .93, respectively.

RELIABILITY: Not reported.

CRITERION MEASURE: Judges' ratings.

Additional Comments

The forward pass and punt for distance items plus the run for time test all are easy to administer with minimum equipment involved. These items are very conducive to a multistation testing plan.

In addition to the practice needed by the subject in preparation for the catching forward pass item, it is also imperative that the passer be consistent and accurate in throwing; otherwise, the fatigue factor may significantly affect results. Running pass patterns is time-consuming and can be tiring for the subject, even when receivers are alternated.

For the pass defense zone test, a center is needed who can snap the ball in a consistent and accurate manner. The same is true for the passer. Receivers should readily comprehend and master the assigned pass patterns.

The Borleske Test should be tested for reliability to further substantiate its seeming value.

JACOBSON-BORLESKE TOUCH FOOTBALL TEST[14]

Date: 1960.
Purpose: To measure general ability in touch football.

Description

Jacobson designed an instrument to objectively evaluate touch football skills of junior high school boys. The three-item test battery of the Borleske Touch Football Test was selected for investigation because it was the only test of demonstrated value constructed prior to 1960.

The investigator proceeded to administer the three-item test battery (forward pass for distance, punt for distance, and run for distance) to junior high boys' physical education classes. An average of fifty-five boys per class existed, and there were four classes of seventh, eighth, and ninth graders, for a total of twelve classes containing 660 subjects.

EDUCATIONAL APPLICATION: Junior high school boys.

Administrative Feasibility

Same as the previously discussed Borleske Test (p. 209).

Directions

The punt for distance and run for time tests are administered according to the directions of the Borleske Test, but directions for the forward pass for distance item differ somewhat from Borleske's original test. One to six passers are tested at once, and the subject throws three consecutive passes. Also, the center snap is

TABLE LVI

T-SCORES FOR JACOBSON-BORLESKE TOUCH FOOTBALL TEST*

| T-Score | Pass for Distance | | | Punt for Distance | | | Run for Speed | | | T-Score |
	7th Grade	8th Grade	9th Grade	7th Grade	8th Grade	9th Grade	7th Grade	8th Grade	9th Grade	
85	41	48	53	38	43	47				85
80	39	45	50	36	40	44	6.3	5.8	5.7	80
75	36	41	46	33	37	41	6.7	6.2	6.0	75
70	34	38	43	31	34	38	7.0	6.6	6.3	70
65	31	35	39	28	31	34	7.3	7.0	6.7	65
60	28	32	36	26	28	32	7.7	7.4	7.0	60
55	25	29	33	23	25	28	8.0	7.7	7.3	55
50	23	26	29	20	22	25	8.3	8.1	7.6	50
45	20	23	26	18	19	22	8.6	8.5	7.9	45
40	18	20	23	16	16	19	9.0	8.9	8.3	40
35	15	17	19	13	13	16	9.3	9.2	8.6	35
30	13	14	16	11	10	13	9.6	9.6	8.9	30
25	10	10	13	8	7	10	10.0	10.0	9.2	25
20	8	8	10	6		7	10.3	10.4	9.5	20
15	5	6					10.6	10.7	9.9	15

*Based on scores of 220 boys in each of the above grades.

TABLE LVII

GRADING SCALE FOR JACOBSON-BORLESKE TOUCH FOOTBALL TEST

Event	Grade	7th Grade	8th Grade	9th Grade
Pass for Distance	A	33 & over	38 & over	42 & over
(Measured in Yards)	B	27 – 32	30 – 37	34 – 41
	C	21 – 26	23 – 29	26 – 33
	D	15 – 20	15 – 22	18 – 25
	E	14 & under	14 & under	17 & under
Punt for Distance	A	30 & over	34 & over	37 & over
(Measured in Yards)	B	24 – 29	26 – 33	30 – 36
	C	18 – 23	19 – 25	22 – 29
	D	12 – 17	12 – 18	15 – 21
	E	11 & under	11 & under	14 & under
Running Speed	A	7.1 & under	6.7 & under	6.4 & under
(Measured in Seconds)	B	7.2 – 7.8	6.8 – 7.6	6.5 – 7.1
	C	7.9 – 8.7	7.7 – 8.5	7.2 – 7.9
	D	8.8 – 9.5	8.6 – 9.4	8.0 – 8.7
	E	9.6 & over	9.5 & over	8.8 & over
Total Test	A	195 & over	193 & over	195 & over
(Measured in T-Scores)	B	166 – 194	165 – 192	165 – 194
	C	137 – 165	137 – 164	136 – 164
	D	108 – 136	108 – 136	106 – 135
	E	107 & under	107 & under	105 & under

eliminated, and a trial may be repeated when the passer steps over the restraining line.

SCORING METHOD AND NORMS: Each of the three test items is scored as indicated in the Borleske Test.

Table LVI includes the T-scores for each of the three test items when applied to seventh, eighth, and ninth grade boys. The tester may wish to use the data found in Table LVII for classification or, possibly, grading purposes.

Scientific Authenticity

Scientific documentation data of the Borleske Test were accepted for this test since only minor modifications were made in the test items.

Additional Comments

Jacobson made a valuable contribution to skills testing literature by formulating the two sets of scales which should greatly aid instructors of touch football classes at the junior high level.

Like Borleske, Jacobson failed to document the reliability value of the three test items. This is an area that needs exploration.

AAHPER FOOTBALL SKILLS TESTS[1]

Date: 1965.

Purpose: To measure the fundamental skills associated with football.

Description

The AAHPER Football Skills Tests result from the Sports Skills Test Project sponsored by the American Alliance for Health, Physical Education and Recreation. Each of the ten tests is designed to measure a specific football skill. They are regarded as not only a tool for evaluation but also as a practice device for the purpose of player improvement.

This particular test can be used for either tackle, touch, or flag football, with the exception of the blocking item. Special test layout markings are restricted to those test items described below.

FORWARD PASS FOR DISTANCE: A restraining area is formed which consists of two parallel lines drawn 6 feet apart.

BLOCKING: A starting line is drawn, and a blocking bag is positioned 15 feet away. A second bag is located 15 feet directly to the right of bag one, and a third bag is stationed 15 feet from the second at a 45-degree angle toward the starting line.

FORWARD PASS FOR ACCURACY: Requirements for this item include a target, 8 × 11 feet in size. The target has three concentric circles of 2, 4, and 6 feet in diameter, from inside to outside. Circle lines should be coded with colors to promote scoring ease. The canvas target may be hung between the goal posts with the narrow end tied over the cross bar. The bottom of the outer circle is located 3 feet above the ground, and the canvas is stretched tight.

A restraining line is drawn 15 feet away from the target.

BALL CHANGING ZIGZAG RUN: Five chairs are placed 10 feet apart in a straight line with the first chair positioned 10 feet from the starting line. The chairs face away from the starting line.

CATCHING FORWARD PASS: Thirty feet and straight away from the starting line, an appropriate marker signifies the "turning point" for the subject to cut around as part of the test requirement. Directly to its right at 30 feet is a "receiving point," which should be some marker that in no way could possibly interfere with the subject in catching the ball.

PULL-OUT: A finish line is drawn 30 feet away and parallel to the scrimmage line.

EDUCATIONAL APPLICATION: Junior and senior high school boys.

Administrative Feasibility

TIME: A class of twenty students can be tested in approximately five sixty-minute class periods.

PERSONNEL: One scorer-timer per test station plus assistants wherever indicated in test directions.

TRAINING INVOLVED: One practice pass is recommended for each subject immediately before being tested on the forward pass for distance item. A warm-up is suggested in preparation for the 50-yard dash, and a practice trial is allowed for the blocking, forward pass for accuracy, football punt for distance, ball changing zigzag run, pull-out, kick-off, and dodging run items. A practice pass pattern for both the right and left direction is recommended for the catching forward pass test.

EQUIPMENT AND SUPPLIES: Footballs, stop watch, blocking bags, goal posts, 8 × 11-foot canvas target, chairs, kicking tee, and hurdles.

Accessories: Scoring and field marking materials, white handkerchief.

Facilities and Space: Regulation football field properly marked off, or a playing field of similar size.

Directions, Scoring Method and Norms

FORWARD PASS FOR DISTANCE: Each subject is given three trials to pass the ball as far as possible. The subject may take one or more running steps but must stay within the 6-foot restraining area and not step over the second restraining line or the goal line. A wire stake is used to mark the longest pass.

The score is the longest throw of three trials. The distance is measured to the last foot passed at right angles to the throwing line.

FIFTY-YARD DASH WITH FOOTBALL: The subject stands behind the starting line while holding a football. The starter gives the audible signal *"Go"* and drops a white handkerchief. This signals the timer to start the watch. The subject proceeds to sprint the 50-yard distance while carrying the ball.

Two trials are allowed with a rest period in between, and the score is the best of the two trials timed to the nearest tenth-second.

BLOCKING: The subject takes a position behind the starting line. When the audible signal *"Go"* is given, the watch is started and the subject proceeds to sprint to the first blocking bag.

Once the subject has cross-body blocked the first bag, he should quickly scramble to his feet and sprint toward the second bag and then the third, repeating the same action at each. Once all the bags have been properly cross-body blocked, the subject sprints over the starting line which terminates the trial.

Two test trials are given with an intervening rest period. Each of the three bags must be cross-body blocked to the ground which means a bump does not count. The score is the lowest time recorded for the two trials when measured to the nearest tenth-second.

FORWARD PASS FOR ACCURACY: Positioned behind the restraining line, the subject should take two or three running steps behind and parallel to the line, hesitate, and throw at the target. The subject may run to either the right or left, but the restraining line must not be crossed. The pass should have some "zip" on it or be of "good speed."

Ten test trials are given and the score is the total number of points accumulated on all ten trials. The target areas yield one, two, or three points, and a ball striking a dividing line receives the higher point value.

FOOTBALL PUNT FOR DISTANCE: Directions and scoring method same as for forward pass for distance item.

BALL CHANGING ZIGZAG RUN: The subject stands behind the starting line with a football under the right arm. Positioned to the right of the first chair and responding to the audible signal *"Go,"* he proceeds to sprint to the right side of the first chair. When the first chair is passed, the subject changes the ball to the left arm and runs to the left of the second chair. The subject continues to run between the chairs, changing the ball from one side to the other. The ball should always be kept under the outside arm, with the inside arm extended in an imaginary stiff-arm position. The fifth or end chair should be circled from right to left and the subject continues back through the chairs as before with the trial ending when he crosses the starting line.

The chairs should not be hit for any reason. Two test trials are administered with a rest period between them. The score is the best time in two trials which are timed to the nearest tenth-second.

CATCHING FORWARD PASS: The subject assumes a position immediately behind the scrimmage line and 9 feet to the right of center. When the audible signal *"Go"* is given, the center snaps the ball directly back to the passer while the subject proceeds to run to the designated "turning point." The subject cuts around the "turning point" to the right and runs to the "receiving point."

The passer should receive the center snap, take one step and pass the ball at head height and directly over the "passing point." The subject attempts to catch as many of the passes as possible.

Poorly thrown passes or passes not thrown over the "passing point" do not count as test trials.

Ten test trials on both the right and left side are given. The running pattern and procedure are the same for each side. The score is the sum of total passes caught from each side. One point is scored for each pass reception.

PULL-OUT: The test subject assumes a set position (three- or four-point stance) while facing straight ahead, and his hands are placed on a line running between the goal posts. The subject is located exactly half the distance between the two posts.

When the audible signal *"Go"* is given, the subject immediately pulls out or off of the line of scrimmage and proceeds to run behind and parallel to the line until reaching the right-hand goal post. The subject makes a sharp turn around the right goal post and sprints directly downfield to the finish line.

Each subject is allowed two test trials with a rest period between. Final score is the best of two trials timed to the nearest tenth-second.

KICK-OFF: Directions and scoring method are the same as for the first item above with two exceptions. First, there is no restraining area, so the approach run may be as long as the subject desires. Second, the ball is placed on the kicking tee with a slight backward tilt.

DODGING RUN: Holding a football and standing behind a point designated on the starting line to the right of the first hurdle, the subject responds to the audible signal *"Go"* by sprinting to the left of the second hurdle which is located 5 yards in front of the starting point. The subject continues to run around the right side of the third hurdle, which is located to the right of the second hurdle and 2 yards farther up the field. The fourth hurdle is passed on the left and is located to the left of the third hurdle which is also 2 yards farther up the field. Circling the fifth hurdle right to left, the subject continues to run between the hurdles while progressing back to the first hurdle. That hurdle is circled from right to left, and a repeat trip is made with the test trial ending when two complete round trips are completed. The fifth hurdle is located to the right of the fourth hurdle and again is two yards on up the field.

Two trial runs are given with a rest period scheduled between them. The tester should note that the subject is not required to switch the ball from side to side as the run is being made. If the ball is dropped, the run does not count. The final score is the best time recorded for the two trials which are timed to the nearest tenth-second.

TEN-ITEM BATTERY: Percentile scores of boys, ages ten to eighteen, are shown in Tables LVIII through LXVII. Subjects ranging from 600 to 900 in number were tested on each item.

Tables LVIII through LXVII are percentile scores for AAHPER Football Test, based on scores of over 600 boys in each age group (10 to 18). From AAHPER: *Skills Test Manual: Football*, D. K. Brace, test consultant, 1965. Courtesy of AAHPER, Washington, D.C.

TABLE LVIII

FORWARD PASS FOR DISTANCE
Test Scores in Feet

				Age					
Percentile	10	11	12	13	14	15	16	17-18	Percentile
100th	96	105	120	150	170	180	180	180	100th
95th	71	83	99	115	126	135	144	152	95th
90th	68	76	92	104	118	127	135	143	90th
85th	64	73	87	98	114	122	129	137	85th
80th	62	70	83	95	109	118	126	133	80th
75th	61	68	79	91	105	115	123	129	75th
70th	59	65	77	88	102	111	120	127	70th
65th	58	64	75	85	99	108	117	124	65th
60th	56	62	73	83	96	105	114	121	60th
55th	55	61	71	80	93	102	111	117	55th
50th	53	59	68	78	91	99	108	114	50th
45th	52	56	66	76	88	97	105	110	45th
40th	51	54	64	73	85	94	103	107	40th
35th	49	51	62	70	83	92	100	104	35th
30th	47	50	60	69	80	89	97	101	30th
25th	45	48	58	65	77	85	93	98	25th
20th	44	45	54	63	73	81	90	94	20th
15th	41	43	51	61	70	76	85	89	15th
10th	38	40	45	55	64	71	79	80	10th
5th	33	36	40	46	53	62	70	67	5th
0	14	25	10	10	10	20	30	20	0

TABLE LIX

FIFTY-YARD DASH WITH FOOTBALL
Test Scores in Seconds and Tenths

Percentile	Age 10	11	12	13	14	15	16	17-18	Percentile
100th	7.3	6.8	6.2	5.5	5.5	5.8	5.5	5.0	100th
95th	7.7	7.4	7.0	6.4	6.4	6.2	6.0	6.0	95th
90th	7.9	7.6	7.2	6.8	6.6	6.3	6.1	6.1	90th
85th	8.1	7.7	7.4	6.9	6.8	6.4	6.3	6.2	85th
80th	8.2	7.8	7.5	7.0	6.9	6.5	6.4	6.3	80th
75th	8.3	7.9	7.5	7.1	7.0	6.6	6.5	6.3	75th
70th	8.4	8.0	7.6	7.2	7.1	6.7	6.6	6.4	70th
65th	8.5	8.1	7.7	7.3	7.2	6.8	6.6	6.5	65th
60th	8.6	8.2	7.8	7.4	7.2	6.9	6.7	6.6	60th
55th	8.6	8.3	7.9	7.5	7.3	7.0	6.8	6.6	55th
50th	8.7	8.4	8.0	7.5	7.4	7.0	6.8	6.7	50th
45th	8.8	8.5	8.1	7.6	7.5	7.1	6.9	6.8	45th
40th	8.9	8.6	8.1	7.7	7.6	7.2	7.0	6.8	40th
35th	9.0	8.7	8.2	7.8	7.7	7.2	7.1	6.9	35th
30th	9.1	8.8	8.3	8.0	7.8	7.3	7.2	7.0	30th
25th	9.2	8.9	8.4	8.1	7.9	7.4	7.3	7.1	25th
20th	9.3	9.1	8.5	8.2	8.1	7.5	7.4	7.2	20th
15th	9.4	9.2	8.7	8.4	8.3	7.7	7.5	7.3	15th
10th	9.6	9.3	9.0	8.7	8.4	8.1	7.8	7.4	10th
5th	9.8	9.5	9.3	9.0	8.8	8.4	8.0	7.8	5th
0	10.6	11.0	12.0	12.0	12.0	11.0	10.0	10.0	0

TABLE LX

BLOCKING
Test Scores in Seconds and Tenths

Percentile	10	11	12	Age 13	14	15	16	17-18	Percentile
100th	6.9	5.0	5.5	5.0	5.0	5.0	5.0	5.0	100th
95th	7.5	6.6	6.6	5.9	5.8	6.0	5.9	5.5	95th
90th	7.7	7.1	7.3	6.5	6.2	6.2	6.1	5.7	90th
85th	7.9	7.5	7.6	6.7	6.6	6.3	6.3	5.8	85th
80th	8.1	8.0	7.7	6.9	6.8	6.5	6.5	6.0	80th
75th	8.3	8.3	7.9	7.2	7.0	6.7	6.7	6.2	75th
70th	8.5	8.6	8.1	7.4	7.1	6.9	7.0	6.3	70th
65th	8.9	9.1	8.4	7.6	7.3	7.0	7.2	6.5	65th
60th	9.3	9.5	8.6	7.7	7.5	7.2	7.4	6.7	60th
55th	9.6	9.7	8.8	7.9	7.7	7.4	7.6	7.0	55th
50th	9.8	9.9	9.0	8.1	7.8	7.5	7.8	7.2	50th
45th	10.1	10.2	9.2	8.3	8.0	7.8	8.0	7.4	45th
40th	10.5	10.4	9.4	8.4	8.1	7.9	8.3	7.6	40th
35th	10.7	10.6	9.6	8.6	8.3	8.2	8.6	7.8	35th
30th	11.0	10.9	9.7	8.9	8.5	8.3	8.8	8.0	30th
25th	11.3	11.1	9.9	9.1	8.7	8.5	9.1	8.2	25th
20th	11.6	11.3	10.2	9.4	9.0	8.8	9.5	8.5	20th
15th	12.0	11.6	10.5	9.8	9.2	9.0	9.0	9.0	15th
10th	12.8	12.0	10.9	10.2	9.5	9.4	10.6	9.4	10th
5th	14.4	13.1	11.6	11.2	10.3	10.4	10.7	10.8	5th
0	17.5	18.0	15.0	15.0	15.0	13.0	15.0	14.0	0

TABLE LXI

FORWARD PASS FOR ACCURACY
Test Scores in Points

	Age								
Percentile	10	11	12	13	14	15	16	17-18	Percentile
100th	18	26	26	28	26	26	28	28	100th
95th	14	19	20	21	21	20	21	22	95th
90th	11	16	18	19	19	19	20	21	90th
85th	10	15	17	18	18	18	18	19	85th
80th	9	13	16	17	17	17	17	18	80th
75th	8	12	15	16	16	16	16	18	75th
70th	8	11	14	15	15	15	15	17	70th
65th	6	10	13	14	14	14	15	16	65th
60th	5	9	12	13	13	13	14	15	60th
55th	4	8	11	13	13	13	13	15	55th
50th	3	7	11	12	12	12	13	14	50th
45th	2	6	10	11	11	11	12	13	45th
40th	2	5	9	11	10	11	12	12	40th
35th	1	5	8	10	9	9	11	12	35th
30th	0	4	7	9	8	9	10	11	30th
25th	0	3	6	8	8	8	9	10	25th
20th	0	2	5	7	7	7	8	9	20th
15th	0	1	4	5	5	6	7	8	15th
10th	0	0	3	4	4	5	6	7	10th
5th	0	0	1	2	2	3	4	5	5th
0	0	0	0	0	0	0	0	0	0

TABLE LXII

FOOTBALL PUNT FOR DISTANCE
Test Scores in Feet

| Percentile | Age | | | | | | | | Percentile |
	10	11	12	13	14	15	16	17-18	
100th	87	100	115	150	160	170	160	180	100th
95th	75	84	93	106	119	126	140	136	95th
90th	64	77	88	98	110	119	126	128	90th
85th	61	75	84	94	106	114	120	124	85th
80th	58	70	79	90	103	109	114	120	80th
75th	56	68	77	87	98	105	109	115	75th
70th	55	66	75	83	96	102	106	110	70th
65th	53	64	72	80	93	99	103	107	65th
60th	51	62	70	78	90	96	100	104	60th
55th	50	60	68	75	87	94	97	101	55th
50th	48	57	66	73	84	91	95	98	50th
45th	46	55	64	70	81	89	92	96	45th
40th	45	53	61	68	78	86	90	93	40th
35th	44	51	59	64	75	83	86	90	35th
30th	42	48	56	63	72	79	83	86	30th
25th	40	45	52	61	70	76	79	81	25th
20th	38	42	50	57	66	73	74	76	20th
15th	32	39	46	52	61	69	70	70	15th
10th	28	34	40	44	55	62	64	64	10th
5th	22	27	35	33	44	54	56	53	5th
0	11	9	10	10	10	10	10	10	0

TABLE LXIII

BALL CHANGING ZIGZAG RUN
Test Scores in Seconds and Tenths

Percentile	Age								Percentile
	10	11	12	13	14	15	16	17-18	
100th	7.2	7.4	7.0	6.0	6.5	6.0	6.0	6.0	100th
95th	9.9	7.7	7.8	8.0	8.7	7.7	7.7	8.4	95th
90th	10.1	8.1	8.2	8.4	9.0	8.0	8.0	8.7	90th
85th	10.3	8.6	8.5	8.7	9.2	8.3	8.4	8.8	85th
80th	10.5	9.0	8.7	8.8	9.4	8.5	8.6	8.9	80th
75th	10.7	9.3	8.8	9.0	9.5	8.6	8.7	9.0	75th
70th	10.9	9.6	9.0	9.2	9.6	8.7	8.8	9.1	70th
65th	11.1	9.8	9.1	9.3	9.7	8.8	8.9	9.2	65th
60th	11.2	10.0	9.3	9.5	9.8	8.9	9.0	9.3	60th
55th	11.4	10.1	9.5	9.6	9.9	9.0	9.1	9.4	55th
50th	11.5	10.3	9.6	9.7	10.0	9.1	9.3	9.6	50th
45th	11.6	10.5	9.8	9.8	10.1	9.2	9.4	9.7	45th
40th	11.8	10.6	10.0	10.0	10.2	9.4	9.5	9.8	40th
35th	11.9	10.9	10.1	10.2	10.4	9.5	9.7	9.9	35th
30th	12.2	11.1	10.3	10.3	10.5	9.6	9.9	10.1	30th
25th	12.5	11.3	10.5	10.3	10.7	9.9	10.1	10.3	25th
20th	12.8	11.6	10.8	10.8	10.9	10.1	10.3	10.5	20th
15th	13.3	12.1	11.1	11.1	11.2	10.3	10.6	10.9	15th
10th	13.8	12.9	11.5	11.4	11.5	10.6	11.2	11.4	10th
5th	15.8	14.2	12.3	12.1	12.0	11.5	12.2	12.1	5th
0	24.0	15.0	19.0	20.0	14.5	20.0	17.0	15.0	0

TABLE LXIV

CATCHING FORWARD PASS
Test Scores in Number Caught

Percentile	10	11	12	13	14	15	16	17-18	Percentile
100th	20	20	20	20	20	20	20	20	100th
95th	19	19	19	20	20	20	20	20	95th
90th	17	18	19	19	19	19	19	19	90th
85th	16	16	18	18	18	19	19	19	85th
80th	14	15	18	17	18	18	18	18	80th
75th	13	14	16	17	17	18	18	18	75th
70th	12	13	16	16	16	17	17	17	70th
65th	11	12	15	15	15	16	16	16	65th
60th	10	12	14	15	15	16	16	16	60th
55th	8	11	14	14	14	15	15	15	55th
50th	7	10	13	13	14	15	15	15	50th
45th	7	9	12	13	13	14	14	14	45th
40th	6	8	12	12	12	13	13	13	40th
35th	5	7	11	11	11	12	12	13	35th
30th	5	7	10	10	10	11	11	12	30th
25th	4	6	10	9	9	10	10	11	25th
20th	3	5	8	8	8	9	9	10	20th
15th	2	4	7	7	8	8	8	9	15th
10th	1	3	6	6	6	7	6	8	10th
5th	1	1	5	4	4	6	4	6	5th
0	0	0	0	0	0	0	0	0	0

TABLE LXV

PULL-OUT
Test Scores in Seconds and Tenths

Percentile	Age								Percentile
	10	11	12	13	14	15	16	17-18	
100th	2.5	2.2	2.2	2.4	2.2	2.0	2.0	1.8	100th
95th	2.9	2.5	2.8	2.8	2.7	2.5	2.5	2.6	95th
90th	3.2	2.7	3.0	2.9	2.8	2.6	2.6	2.7	90th
85th	3.3	2.8	3.0	3.0	2.9	2.7	2.7	2.8	85th
80th	3.4	2.9	3.1	3.0	3.0	2.8	2.9	2.8	80th
75th	3.5	2.9	3.1	3.1	3.0	3.0	2.9	2.9	75th
70th	3.5	3.0	3.2	3.1	3.0	3.0	3.0	2.9	70th
65th	3.6	3.1	3.3	3.2	3.1	3.0	3.0	3.0	65th
60th	3.6	3.2	3.3	3.2	3.1	3.1	3.1	3.0	60th
55th	3.7	3.3	3.4	3.3	3.2	3.1	3.1	3.1	55th
50th	3.8	3.4	3.4	3.3	3.2	3.2	3.2	3.1	50th
45th	3.8	3.5	3.5	3.4	3.3	3.2	3.2	3.1	45th
40th	3.9	3.6	3.5	3.4	3.3	3.3	3.3	3.2	40th
35th	3.9	3.7	3.6	3.5	3.4	3.3	3.3	3.2	35th
30th	4.0	3.8	3.7	3.5	3.4	3.4	3.3	3.2	30th
25th	4.0	3.9	3.8	3.6	3.5	3.5	3.4	3.3	25th
20th	4.1	4.0	3.9	3.7	3.5	3.6	3.5	3.4	20th
15th	4.2	4.1	3.9	3.8	3.6	3.7	3.7	3.5	15th
10th	4.3	4.2	4.1	3.9	3.7	3.9	3.9	3.6	10th
5th	4.4	4.4	4.2	4.0	4.0	4.1	4.3	3.9	5th
0	5.5	5.0	5.0	5.0	5.0	5.0	5.0	5.0	0

TABLE LXVI

KICK-OFF

Test Scores in Feet

| Percentile | | | | | Age | | | | Percentile |
	10	11	12	13	14	15	16	17-18	
100th	88	110	120	129	140	160	160	180	100th
95th	69	79	98	106	118	128	131	138	95th
90th	64	72	83	97	108	120	125	129	90th
85th	59	68	78	92	102	114	119	124	85th
80th	58	64	74	86	97	108	114	119	80th
75th	55	60	70	81	94	104	108	113	75th
70th	53	58	67	78	90	100	104	108	70th
65th	50	56	65	75	86	96	99	105	65th
60th	47	54	64	72	84	93	97	103	60th
55th	46	52	60	69	81	90	95	98	55th
50th	45	50	57	67	77	87	93	95	50th
45th	43	48	54	64	74	83	90	92	45th
40th	40	46	52	62	71	79	87	88	40th
35th	39	44	48	59	68	76	83	84	35th
30th	37	42	45	56	65	72	79	79	30th
25th	35	40	42	52	62	69	75	74	25th
20th	32	37	38	48	58	64	70	70	20th
15th	30	34	34	42	52	59	65	64	15th
10th	26	30	29	36	45	50	60	57	10th
5th	21	24	22	26	38	40	47	43	5th
0	5	10	0	0	0	10	10	10	0

TABLE LXVII

DODGING RUN
Test Scores in Seconds and Tenths

Percentile	Age 10	11	12	13	14	15	16	17-18	Percentile
100th	21.0	18.0	18.0	17.0	16.0	16.0	16.0	16.0	100th
95th	24.3	20.4	23.8	23.3	22.6	22.4	22.3	22.2	95th
90th	25.8	21.6	24.6	24.2	23.9	23.5	23.3	23.2	90th
85th	26.3	22.5	25.0	24.8	24.6	24.1	23.9	23.7	85th
80th	26.4	23.5	25.2	24.9	24.7	24.6	24.3	24.1	80th
75th	27.5	24.0	25.3	25.3	25.2	24.9	24.7	24.4	75th
70th	27.8	25.0	25.8	25.7	25.2	25.2	25.0	24.7	70th
65th	28.1	25.7	26.3	26.1	26.1	25.5	25.3	25.0	65th
60th	28.4	26.3	26.6	26.5	26.3	25.8	25.5	25.3	60th
55th	28.7	26.9	26.9	26.8	26.6	26.1	25.8	25.6	55th
50th	28.9	27.4	27.3	27.2	26.9	26.4	26.1	26.0	50th
45th	29.3	28.0	27.6	27.5	27.2	26.7	26.3	26.3	45th
40th	29.7	28.3	27.9	27.9	27.5	27.0	26.7	26.6	40th
35th	30.1	28.8	28.4	28.3	27.9	27.4	27.0	26.9	35th
30th	30.5	29.2	28.8	28.7	28.3	27.8	27.3	27.2	30th
25th	30.9	29.8	29.2	29.1	28.7	28.2	27.7	27.6	25th
20th	31.3	30.4	29.8	29.5	29.3	28.6	28.1	28.0	20th
15th	31.8	31.1	30.4	30.1	29.9	29.1	28.8	28.7	15th
10th	32.7	32.0	31.3	30.8	30.7	29.8	29.6	29.2	10th
5th	33.6	33.5	33.0	32.3	31.8	31.0	30.6	30.4	5th
0	40.0	40.0	41.0	40.0	36.0	36.0	36.0	36.0	0

Scientific Authenticity

VALIDITY: Face validity claimed for each item.

RELIABILITY: Reliability standards were established at a minimum level of .80 for the tests or events scored on the basis of distance, and not less than .70 for the tests measuring accuracy or form.

The test items were administered to students from schools located in several different cities throughout the United States. All had recently experienced a complete instructional unit on the test contents.

Additional Comments

The administrative feasibility of the AAHPER Football Test is questionable when used only as an evaluation tool. Learning drills could be developed for each item to periodically measure student progress.

The face validity assumption should be confirmed for the ball changing zigzag run, pull-out, and dodging run items because they only approximate actual football skill requirements. Other criticisms leveled at the AAHPER Football Test include its omission of a time limit in the punt for distance item, the scoring difficulty that the blocking test presents, and that the pass catching item is too time-consuming. Also, a ball snapping item should be included in the battery to make it a fully comprehensive measure of football ability.[21]

REFERENCES

1. American Association for Health, Physical Education and Recreation: *Skills Test Manual: Football.* Brace, David K. (Test Consultant). Washington, AAHPER, 1965.
2. Barrow, Harold M. and McGee, Rosemary: *A Practical Approach to Measurement in Physical Education,* 2nd ed. Philadelphia, Lea & Febiger, 1971.
3. Borleske, Stanley E.: A Study of Achievement of College Men in Touch Football. Master's thesis, Berkeley, University of California, 1936.
4. Brace, David K.: Validity of football achievement tests as measures of motor learning as a partial basis for the selection of players. *Research Quarterly, 14:*372, 1943.
5. Brechler, Paul W.: A Test to Determine Potential Ability in Football

(Backs and Ends). Master's thesis, Iowa City, University of Iowa, 1940.

6. Committee on Motor Ability Tests of the American Physical Education Association: Motor ability tests. *American Physical Education Review,* 1929.

7. Cormack, Herbert P.: A Test to Determine Potential Ability in Football (Linemen). Master's thesis, Iowa City, University of Iowa, 1940.

8. Cowell, C. C. and Ismail, A. H.: Validity of a football rating scale and its relationship to social integration and academic ability. *Research Quarterly, 33:*461-467, 1961.

9. Cozens, Frederick W.: *Achievement Scales in Physical Education Activities for College Men.* Philadelphia, Lea & Febiger, 1936.

10. ———: Ninth annual report of the committee on curriculum of the College Physical Education Association. *Research Quarterly, 8:*73-78, 1937.

11. Edwards, Reuben L.: A Method for Selecting Linemen for High School Football. Master's thesis, Salt Lake City, University of Utah, 1960.

12. Haskins, Mary Jane: *Evaluation in Physical Education.* Dubuque, Iowa, Brown Bk, 1971.

13. Hatley, Fred J.: A Battery of Functional Tests for the Prediction of Football Potentiality. Master's thesis, Iowa City, University of Iowa, 1942.

14. Jacobson, Theodore V.: An Evaluation of Performance in Certain Physical Ability Tests Administered to Selected Secondary School Boys. Master's thesis, Seattle, University of Washington, 1960.

15. Johnson, Barry L. and Nelson, Jack K.: *Practical Measurements for Evaluation in Physical Education,* 2nd ed. Minneapolis, Burgess, 1974.

16. Lee, Robert C.: A Battery of Tests to Predict Football Potential. Master's thesis, Salt Lake City, University of Utah, 1965.

17. Mathews, Donald K.: *Measurement in Physical Education,* 3rd ed. Philadelphia, Saunders, 1968.

18. McElroy, H. N.: A report on some experimentation with a skill test. *Research Quarterly, 9:*82-88, 1938.

19. McGauley, Thomas: A Scoring Device for Analyzing Individual Defensive Football Performance. Master's thesis. Brookings, South Dakota State College, 1959.

20. Meyers, Carlton R.: *Measurement in Physical Education,* 2nd ed. New York, Ronald, 1974.

21. Morris, Harold H.: A Critique of the AAHPER Skill Test Series. Paper read before the Measurement and Evaluation Council at the Annual Convention of the American Alliance for Health, Physical Education and Recreation, Seattle, March 25, 1977.

22. New York State Physical Education Standards Project: *Standards Manual for Football, Soccer, and Softball Skills, Boys, Grades 7-12,* Bulletin 3. Albany, New York State Education Department, 1951.

23. Wallrof, Paul J.: Methods for Rating Defensive Proficiency of High School Football Players. Master's thesis, Seattle, University of Washington, 1965.

24. Weiss, Raymond A. and Phillips, Marjorie: *Administration of Tests in Physical Education.* St. Louis, Mosby, 1954.

Chapter 14

Golf

INTRODUCTION

A LARGE NUMBER of skills tests have been developed for the game of golf. This seems somewhat ironic because objective measurement of a participant's ability level occurs each time the game is played. Even though the score provides a valid measure of golfing skill, having students play an actual round of golf for grading purposes is not absolutely necessary. A good indication of playing proficiency may be obtained by the use of available skills tests as they simulate game conditions well and generally possess a high degree of face validity.

Both indoor and outdoor tests exist for golf, with the outdoor variety generally more preferable when the necessary equipment and facilities are available. However, the time and space requirements for the indoor tests are usually less than those of outdoor tests. Examples of each type of test are found in this chapter.

CLEVETT GOLF TEST[7]

Date: 1931.

Purpose: To measure general golf putting ability.

Description

The empirically based, indoor test battery was designed to measure accuracy with the brassie, midiron, mashie, and putter. Since Clevett's test is not scientifically documented and only a very limited number of golf skills tests include putting, the test's putting item alone was selected for presentation. The practically designed test requires each subject to putt ten times to a target area located on a smooth carpet or similar surface, measuring 20 feet in length and 27 inches wide. The carpet is placed on a level, smooth floor area. It is divided into three equal 9-inch sections running the full length of the putting surface. Forty-eight scoring areas, each 9 inches square, are marked off on the carpet beginning 8 feet from the starting point with square ten or the imaginary hole located 15 feet from that point. Figure 36 gives additional clarification.

EDUCATIONAL APPLICATION: Males and females from junior high through college.

Administrative Feasibility

TIME: A class of twenty students can easily be tested in one sixty-minute period.

PERSONNEL: A scorer-recorder.

TRAINING INVOLVED: A uniform practice period should be allowed for each subject to adjust to the putting surface.

EQUIPMENT AND SUPPLIES: Putters, balls, smooth carpet or similar putting surface.

Accessories: Scoring materials.

Facilities and Space: Indoor area that is level and free of obstructions with minimum measurements of 25 feet by 30 inches.

Directions

The subject assumes a proper putting stance at the starting point and proceeds to putt ten consecutive balls for the imaginary hole 15 feet away.

SCORING METHOD: Each ball receives a numerical score based on the spot the ball comes to rest. The final score is the total number of points for all ten trials. Balls that come to rest on a line are given the higher point value.

Scientific Authenticity

No data available.

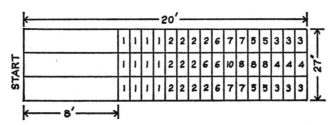

Figure 36. Carpet markings for putting test. From M. A. Clevett: An experiment in teaching methods of golf, *Research Quarterly,* 2:104-106, 1931. Courtesy of AAHPER.

Additional Comments

The Clevett Putting Test is a practical one that closely parallels the actual putting skill required in golf. The portability and accessibility features of the carpet make the test a functional one. It can be rolled up, stored, and used over and over without having to be marked again.

Synthetic grass or artificial turf could be used as the putting surface. The tester is reminded that norms construction should be specific to the type of putting surface used.

MCKEE GOLF TEST[16]

Date: 1950.

Purpose: To provide a diagnostic test as it relates to a full-swinging golf shot; to measure general golf ability.

EDUCATIONAL APPLICATION: College women.

Administrative Feasibility

TIME: Two sixty-minute periods for testing twenty students.

PERSONNEL: One time-recorder and two people to place stakes.

TRAINING INVOLVED: A few warm-up swings immediately prior to testing. Test should be given toward the end of a term for grading purposes, but may be used anytime for skill diagnosis.

EQUIPMENT AND SUPPLIES: Number 2- or 5-irons, at least eighty golf balls, 175-yard rope, strips of ribbon, 100-foot steel tape, stop watch, and four sets or eighty colored stakes.

Accessories: Scoring materials.

Facilities and Space: Open area such as a driving range or playfield that has a minimum space of 175 × 80 yards.

Description, Directions, and Scoring Method

This rather unique golf skills test determines the results of a full-swinging golf shot by calculating the range, velocity of the ball, angle of impact of the club head with the ball, and the angle of deviation to the right or left of the intended line of flight by utilizing trigonometric functions. Twenty shots are performed by each subject.

McKee experimented with both a hard and soft (cotton) ball

in her study. Only the hard ball test is presented here since the diagnostic value of the cotton ball test was greatly impaired due to the low validity coefficients found for the velocity, angle of impact, and angle of deviation.

A rope, 175 yards in length, is marked at 25-yard intervals with a colored strip of ribbon and every five yards (between the colored ribbons) with white ribbons. The rope is stretched out directly in front of the subject (A) to designate the intended line of flight (Fig. 37). Assuming a proper hitting position at the zero end of the rope, the subject proceeds to hit twenty full-swinging golf shots. Unless the ball is in the air for at least six-tenths of a second, it does not count as a trial.

As each trial is taken, a numbered colored stake (C) that corresponds with the same numbered test trial is placed in the ground at the point where the ball initially lands. It is recommended that the tester make four sets of different colored stakes, numbered one through twenty, so four subjects may be tested before taking time for measurements. This does not mean the subjects can be tested simultaneously, but that the time factor can be reduced.

A stop watch is used to determine the time each shot is airborne, that is, from the moment of impact until the ball first touches the ground.

The following measurements are recorded for each subject:
1. the time to the nearest tenth-second each ball was airborne;
2. the distance the ball traveled (B) along the intended line of flight, measured by the rope;
3. the distance the ball deviated from the intended line of flight as measured by the 100-foot steel tape which is placed at a right angle to the rope.

Using the recorded data and trigonometric functions, the tester can then determine the angle of deviation and the distance the ball actually traveled, or the range. Refer to Figure 37 for additional clarification.

In order to calculate the angle of impact, another right triangle is constructed using the range as one side of the triangle and the height to which the ball would have risen, had gravity played no part in the ball's flight, as the other side. The latter side of the

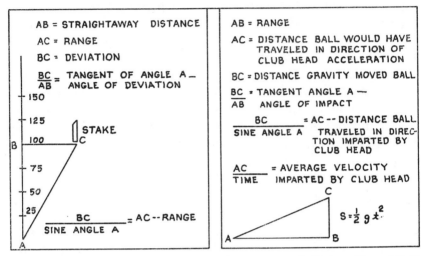

Figure 37. Construction of right triangle for McKee Golf Test. From M. E. McKee: A test for the full-swinging shot in golf, *Research Quarterly, 21:* 40-46, 1950. Courtesy of AAHPER.

triangle is found by using the formula $S = \frac{1}{2}gt^2$, where S is the distance through which gravity moved the ball; g is the acceleration of gravity, and t represents the time the ball is in the air. Again, by using trigonometric functions, the angle of impact is determined along with the distance that the ball could have traveled without the effect of gravity. This latter distance is the hypotenuse of the triangle. The hypotenuse divided by the time that the ball is in the air determines the average velocity of the ball as imparted by the club head. For further clarification, refer to Figure 37.

The calculations are based on the assumption that the ball did not slice or hook. However, at a distance of 300 feet, an additional 15 feet makes only a 1-degree error in the angle of impact calculation and a difference of 3 feet per second in the velocity. In summary, four measures calculated include range, velocity, angle of impact, and angle of deviation to the right or left of the intended line of flight.

Scientific Authenticity

Thirty college women and faculty members served as subjects.

TABLE LXVIII

RELIABILITY OF MCKEE HARD-BALL TEST*

Club	Range	Velocity	Angle of Impact	Angle of Deviation
2-iron	.92	.86	.81	.82
5-iron	.95	.89	.89	.60

*Derived from scores of 30 college women students and faculty.

The experience and skill level of the subjects varied greatly.

VALIDITY: Face validity was claimed.

RELIABILITY: The reliability of the McKee Hard-Ball Test was calculated from the average of the ten odd-numbered and the ten even-numbered trials (Table LXVIII).

No explanation was given for the marked difference in the coefficients between the number 2- and 5-irons on the angle of deviation item.

Additional Comments

The tester should not avoid utilization of the McKee Test because the scoring procedure may seem too complicated. Familiarity with trigonometric functions and other pertinent mathematical concepts would be helpful, but reference to basic mathematics texts or consultation with an instructor in that discipline should clarify any questions about specifics of the test's scoring procedure.

Although it is commonly believed that proficiency with the use of a 5-iron is a good indication of general golfing ability, the use of this test for that purpose is questionable. To obtain maximum benefit from its use, the McKee Test should probably be given as one component in a battery of golf skill items.

VANDERHOOF GOLF TEST[27]

Also cited as Vanderhoof Indoor Golf Test.

Date: 1956.

Purpose: To measure general golfing ability.

Description and Directions

The Vanderhoof Golf Test is designed for indoor use and utilizes a plastic golf ball. Originally, a subject's skill with a 2-wood, 5-iron, and 7-iron was measured by the test. All three involve the same area specifications, and the drive item (2-wood) proved to be the best single indicator of playing ability. The 5- and 7-iron items are very similar, with the latter showing less value as an instrument to measure general golfing ability according to results of the Vanderhoof study.

Should both the drive test and 5-iron item be given, the formula to be used is 1.3 drive + 1.0 five-iron. Only the drive test is discussed in this chapter since both the 7-iron and 5-iron tests are administered exactly as the drive test, except that no tee is used. The target area or gymnasium floor is marked off with three equal scoring areas that are each 20 feet in length. The subject stands at a designated tee area and attempts to drive each ball under a rope that is 8 feet high and located 14 feet from and parallel to the line from which the balls are being hit.

When the subject (X) is ready, he proceeds to drive fifteen consecutive balls from the practice tee toward the target area while aiming for the ten pin. Figure 38 further clarifies the test layout.

EDUCATIONAL APPLICATION: College women.

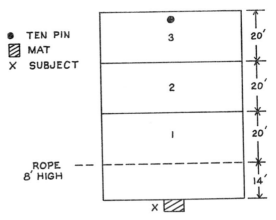

Figure 38. Scoring area for Vanderhoof Golf Test.

TABLE LXIX

NORMS FOR VANDERHOOF DRIVE TEST*

T-Score	Raw Score (Total of 15 trials)
75	45
70	41
65	38
60	33
55	28
50	24
45	19
40	13
35	9
30	7
25	4

*Based on scores of 110 college women.

Administrative Feasibility

TIME: Twenty students can be tested in one sixty-minute period.

PERSONNEL: One scorer-recorder.

TRAINING INVOLVED: Practice swings may be taken as needed, but only two or three practice balls may be hit during the warm-up period for the test.

EQUIPMENT AND SUPPLIES: Two-woods, mat with permanent tee, plastic golf balls, two standards, rope at least 20 feet long, and a ten pin or similar object such as a cone.

Accessories: Scoring and floor marking materials.

Facilities and Space: Indoor area such as a gymnasium or field house with a minimum space of 74 × 13 feet for each testing station. There should be no overhead obstructions.

SCORING METHOD AND NORMS: A numerical score from zero to three is assigned to each ball that passes under the rope on the fly and lands in the designated target area. The final score is the sum of the points accumulated for all fifteen trials. Two topped balls in succession count as only one trial with a zero score.

Scientific Authenticity

One hundred and ten university women students who had received fifteen lessons of group instruction served as subjects in this study.

VALIDITY: Validity coefficient of .71 reported.

RELIABILITY: Reliability coefficient of .90 was computed on odd-even sums and stepped up by the Spearman-Brown Formula.

CRITERION MEASURE: Judges' ratings of playing form.

Additional Comments

Besides measuring general golf ability, the Vanderhoof Test serves well as a practice device for students, and as a measure of student improvement. In addition, the test may be used to detect possible inconsistencies in the swing. Should the tester signify on the student's score card the spot where each ball lands, a pattern might possibly develop, and directional errors could then be corrected, accordingly.

Multiple test stations are suggested to reduce the time of test administration, but this may require an additional scorer for each.

Also, Davis[11] indicated that a rope is not needed for the test, since similar results were obtained without the use of a rope.

Furthermore, it is important that the tester use only one type of plastic golf ball per test group since a different type of ball may produce notably different results.

DAVIS FIVE-IRON TEST[11]

Also cited as Davis Outdoor Golf Test.

Date: 1960.

Purpose: To determine general golf ability and ability to hit a full-swinging 5-iron shot.

Description

Davis developed an outdoor golf skills test utilizing a full-swinging 5-iron golf shot that measures both distance and accuracy. A driving range or playfield area is marked off as a target zone. One target of 120 yards in width is divided into three equal sections. Another target of 150 yards in length is divided into fifteen intervals measuring 10 yards each. Each target section is assigned numerical value with the middle area (II) naturally having the higher scoring intervals. Refer to Figure 39 for clarification of the scoring areas.

EDUCATIONAL APPLICATION: College women.

Administrative Feasibility

TIME: Class of twenty students can easily be tested in one sixty-minute period.

PERSONNEL: One scorer-recorder.

TRAINING INVOLVED: Only two practice hits are permitted immediately prior to testing, but a reasonable number of practice swings is encouraged.

EQUIPMENT AND SUPPLIES: Five-irons, colored and plain balls.

Accessories: Scoring and field marking materials.

Facilities and Space: Outdoor driving range or similar hitting area with a minimum measurement of 150 × 120 yards.

Directions

To get ready for testing, four subjects (X) line up directly behind the hitting line (Fig. 39). Two trials of ten balls each are taken by each subject with a rest period between trials. Each subject hits five balls from each of the four test stations. Eight plain balls are needed for practice hits and four sets of different colored or coded balls for the test trials.

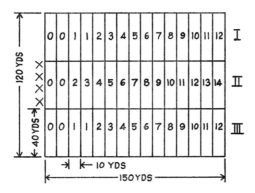

Figure 39. Field markings for Davis Five-Iron test.

SCORING METHOD: The final score is the point total obtained when multiplying the number of balls in each scoring zone by the numerical value assigned to the particular zone. It is important to remember that each ball is scored according to the spot at which it comes to rest, and not where it initially lands. After each ten-ball trial, the balls in each zone are gathered in the center and appropriately scored.

It is recommended that each scoring zone be labeled with a set of 4 × 8-inch signs placed on stakes.

Scientific Authenticity

VALIDITY: Face validity claimed.

RELIABILITY: In testing sixty-seven university women, a reliability coefficient of .80 was found when using the split-half procedure for obtaining reliability.

Additional Comments

The field size and marking requirement may create some concern for potential testers as the area called for in the test design is obviously larger than most playing fields. Construction of the forty-five target zones demands a good deal of marking time. Combine that with the signs and stakes that are to be placed in each scoring zone, and administrative time starts to become a prohibitive factor in the Davis Test.

In order to save on actual testing time, it is recommended that the scoring be conducted after all twenty shots are completed, instead of after the suggested ten.

REECE FIVE-IRON TEST[24]

Date: 1960.

Purpose: To measure ability to use a 5-iron.

Description

Reece studied the relationship of an indoor and outdoor golf skills test which measured ability to use a 5-iron.

Indoor: This item is designed to measure the angle of club impact or loft of the ball. Geometric computations, expert opinion, and results of a pilot study were sources of input regarding the placement of horizontal scoring lines on a wall target to measure the loft. The lines are made of cord or rope and were supported by four concrete posts in the above mentioned study. The use of standards might give more support to the rope or cord lines. More importantly, paint or tape lines may be placed directly on the wall in lieu of the rope or cord. It has been suggested that a 6-inch crepe paper apron be attached to each rope line to facilitate ease in scoring. Coding the crepe paper aprons with an assortment of colors may further assist the tester in scoring.

Whatever the structure of the wall target lines, they are placed at levels of 2, 3½, 5½, 8½, and 10 feet from the floor (Fig. 40). A mat line 15 feet, 10 inches from the wall marks the placement of the golf mats, making the actual hitting spot approximately 16 feet, 8 inches from the wall.

Outdoor: A hitting line and parallel target lines at 20, 40, and 60 yards are drawn. The lines may be made of chalk, paint, or some other suitable material, and colored flag markers should be placed on each side of the particular yard lines.

EDUCATIONAL APPLICATION: Designed for college women, but appropriate for high school girls.

Administrative Feasibility

TIME: Either test can be administered to twenty students in one hour.

PERSONNEL: Only the instructor and student scorers are needed to administer either test.

TRAINING INVOLVED: Plenty of pretest practice should be allowed for the indoor item. Three practice hits are permitted the student immediately prior to testing with one practice swing between hits. The practice procedure outlined above for the actual testing date also holds true for the outdoor test. It is recommended that the outdoor test be conducted after at least twelve hours of instruction have transpired.

EQUIPMENT AND SUPPLIES: Regulation and plastic golf balls, 5-irons, practice mats with brush inserts.

Accessories: Materials for scoring plus wall, floor, and field marking materials.

Facilities and Space: Indoor area with sufficient unobstructed wall and floor space and an outdoor area of 100 × 50 yards.

Directions

INDOOR: Each subject is assigned a partner, and one takes a 5-iron and assumes a hitting position. She proceeds to hit twenty consecutive shots with the plastic balls, then changes places with her partner. The test mat should be periodically checked to insure the front edge of the mat is even with the mat line on the floor.

OUTDOOR: One in a set of partners completes twenty trials using a 5-iron and regulation golf balls. Her partner or the scorer stands about 10 feet behind the hitter. Occasional checks should

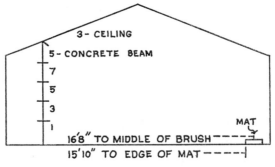

A. FRONT VIEW OF TARGET

WOOD CEILING	3 PTS	10′
CONCRETE BEAM	5 PTS	8′6″
ROPE	7 PTS	5′6″
ROPE	5 PTS	3′6″
ROPE	3 PTS	2′
FLOOR	1 PT	

B. SIDE VIEW OF TARGET AND TESTING AREA

3- CEILING
5- CONCRETE BEAM
7
5
3
1
MAT
16′8″ TO MIDDLE OF BRUSH
15′10″ TO EDGE OF MAT

Figure 40. Specifications of indoor test.

be made to insure that the hitter does not cross over the hitting line during one of the trials.

SCORING METHOD

Indoor: Each of the twenty shots receives a score based on the loft of the ball. No points are given if the ball is missed or touches the floor before reaching the target. Otherwise, points assigned follow the scoring scheme described in Figure 40. Maximum score is 140 points.

Outdoor: Each of the twenty shots is scored according to the following procedure:

a. 7 points–when ball hits beyond 60-yard markers or yellow flags.
b. 5 points–when ball hits between the 40- and 60-yard markers (red and yellow flags).
c. 3 points–when the ball hits between the 20- and 40-yard markers (green and red flags).
d. 1 point–when ball goes beyond the 20-yard markers or green flags but does not reach the minimum required height.
e. no points–when ball is missed completely or fails to hit beyond green flags.

Points awarded to a particular shot are determined by the location where the ball first touches the ground, not where it rolls.

There is one exception to the above scoring method. In order to receive either 3, 5, or 7 points, the ball must go at least as high as the subject's head during the initial flight of the ball.

Any ball hitting on a target line is given the score of higher value. Maximum score is 140 points.

Scientific Authenticity

The indoor test was administered to 142 college women from six beginning and two intermediate golf classes while 145 completed the outdoor test. Resulting data were used to compute the reliability coefficients of those tests.

VALIDITY: Face validity claimed for both tests.

RELIABILITY: A .92 coefficient for the indoor test and .89 for the outdoor version.

Additional Comments

Time required to set up the target for the indoor test is extensive. This shortcoming takes away from the overall good quality of the test.

Reece's study of the indoor and outdoor tests indicated that results on the outdoor test better reflect ability to use a 5-iron. Somewhat predictably, another conclusion confirmed that the two tests only moderately relate and measure essentially different types of skill. The indoor test basically reflects ball loft, and the outdoor item measures shot distance.

BENSON GOLF TEST[3]

Also cited as Benson Five-Iron Test and Benson Outdoor Golf Test.

Date: 1963.

Purpose: To determine overall golf playing ability.

Description

Benson developed an outdoor golf skills test in which skill with a 5-iron is measured. Flight distance and deviation from the intended flight of the golf ball are each considered in the test score.

The driving range or designated hitting area is dotted with distance signs placed at 25-yard intervals starting from the hitting line. Nine deviation signs are placed 5 yards apart on each side of a line that marks the middle of the hitting area. The deviation signs are 150 yards from and parallel to the hitting line and are numbered one to nine (Fig. 41).

EDUCATIONAL APPLICATION: Males and females from junior high through college.

Administrative Feasibility

TIME: One sixty-minute class period for twenty students.

PERSONNEL: One scorer-recorder.

Training Involved: Five practice shots are allowed for each student immediately prior to being tested.

Equipment and Supplies: Golf balls, 5-irons, marking flags or signs.

Accessories: Scoring materials.

Facilities and Space: Outdoor driving range or similar hitting area that has minimum measurements of 150 × 100 yards.

Directions

Assuming a proper position directly behind the hitting line, the subject proceeds to take twenty consecutive shots or test trials for score. The tester or scorer stands approximately 3 yards behind the hitting line and the test subject.

Scoring Method: The twenty distance and deviation scores are separately averaged, providing official results for distance and flight accuracy.

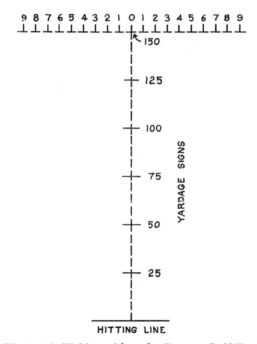

Figure 41. Field markings for Benson Golf Test.

Scientific Authenticity

VALIDITY: Correlation of actual golf scores with the distance and flight deviation scores produced a coefficient of .94.

RELIABILITY: Reliability coefficients of .90 and .70 were derived for the distance and deviation scores, respectively.

CRITERION MEASURE: Official score for round of golf.

Additional Comments

Preparation for the Benson Test is not as cumbersome as some of the other available outdoor tests. Marking the field should require no more than 30 minutes.

The low reliability value of the flight deviation item prohibits the use of its score alone in determining general golf ability. For that purpose, it should always be used along with the distance score.

NELSON GOLF PITCHING TEST[22]

Date: 1967.

Purpose: To measure the ability to use short irons in pitching.

Description

The outdoor golf test measures ability in hitting short iron shots to a flag 40 yards away. Either the 8-iron, 9-iron, or wedge is used to complete the test requirement.

Twenty yards away from the hitting line, a restraining line is located. A flag stick is positioned 20 yards from the restraining line or 40 yards from the hitting line (Fig. 42). The inner target circle is 6 feet in diameter with the flag stick located in the middle of this circle. From the center circle, each circle's radius is 5 feet wider than the radius of the previous one which means the circle diameters are 6, 16, 26, 36, 46, 56, and 66 feet. The target is divided into four equal quadrants.

EDUCATIONAL APPLICATION: High school and college males and females.

Administrative Feasibility

TIME: Twenty students can be tested in one sixty-minute period.

PERSONNEL: One scorer-recorder plus student assistants as spotters.

TRAINING INVOLVED: Three practice shots prior to testing for score.

EQUIPMENT AND SUPPLIES: Short irons (8- or 9-iron, or wedge), colored or coded balls, flag stick, flags or markers.

Accessories: Scoring and field marking materials.

Facilities and Space: Playing field area or driving range with minimum measurements of approximately 60 × 25 yards.

Directions

Two to four subjects stand behind the hitting line with their choice of the 8-iron, 9-iron, or wedge. Each is given thirteen golf balls, with three to be used as practice balls. Furthermore, each individual is assigned golf balls of a specific color or code. Ten test trials follow with the subject attempting to place each ball as close to the flag stick as possible. The subjects are to take turns hitting the ball, so as not to interfere with each other's concentration. Each swing counts as a test trial, even if the ball is missed or poor-

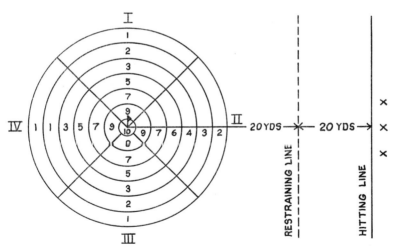

Figure 42. Field and target markings for Nelson Golf Pitching Test. From B. L. Johnson and J. K. Nelson: *Practical Measurements for Evaluation in Physical Education,* 1974. Courtesy of Burgess Publishing Company, Minneapolis.

ly hit. Any legal hit must be airborne until it passes the restraining line; thus, this eliminates as a scoring trial any ball that is "topped."

A fellow student is assigned to each test subject for spotting purposes. It is his job to assist the tester or recorder in the scoring process by calling out the subject's name and score after each shot. Both the spotter and recorder are positioned near the target.

SCORING METHOD: Total number of accumulated points for the ten test trials. Any ball resting on a line is assigned the higher point value.

Scientific Authenticity

VALIDITY: Utilizing college students enrolled in golf classes as subjects, a validity coefficient of .86 was determined.

RELIABILITY: Determined by odd-even trials and the Spearman-Brown Prophecy Formula, a reliability coefficient of .83 was obtained.

CRITERION MEASURE: Judges' ratings.

Additional Comments

The Nelson Test represents a unique contribution to golf skills measurement because previous tests excluded the testing of short iron ability, concentrating on either a wood or middle iron.

Adaptations to the original test may be considered by the potential tester. Reliability is little affected by requiring the best seven of ten shots when test time is short. Also, permanent target lines provide a very effective practice device for interested students. Third, the tester may wish to experiment with the hitting distance.

BROWN GOLF SKILLS TEST[5]

Also cited as Brown Revised Golf Skills Test.
Date: 1969.
Purpose: To determine golf ability.
EDUCATIONAL APPLICATION: College men and women.

Administrative Feasibility

TIME: Twenty students can be tested in two sixty-minute periods.

PERSONNEL: One scorer-recorder with student assistants.

TRAINING INVOLVED: Multiple trial items apparently negate the need for any appreciable amount of practice on the test date.

EQUIPMENT AND SUPPLIES: Woods, 7-, 8-, 9-irons, pitching wedge, putter and balls.

Accessories: Scoring and field marking materials, plus tees.

Facilities and Space: A large outdoor playing field or driving range; putting green.

Description and Directions

Brown's five-item test was initially used for motivation purposes but was later revised to measure overall golf ability.

CHIP: A 30 × 10-foot area is required, along with a ground target of three different sized trapezoids as shown in Fig. 43. The shooting line is 16 feet from the leading edge of the largest trapezoid. While standing behind this line, the subject hits fifteen consecutive chip shots at the target.

SHORT PITCH: A playing field or similar outdoor area is required with minimum measurements of 90 × 25 feet. A target, in the shape of three concentric circles, is placed on the ground. The circles have radii of 7½, 15, and 22½ feet for the inner, middle, and outer circles, respectively. The shooting arc or line is

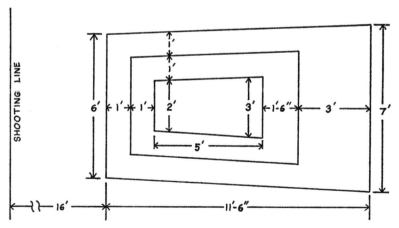

Figure 43. Target for chip test. From H. S. Brown: A test battery for evaluating golf skills, *TAHPER Journal,* 4-5, 28-29, May 1969. Courtesy of *TAHPER Journal.*

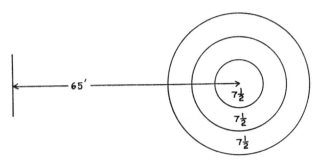

Figure 44. Target for short pitch test. From H. S. Brown: A test battery for evaluating golf skills, *TAHPER Journal,* 4-5, 28-29, May 1969. Courtesy of *TAHPER Journal.*

marked off 65 feet away from the center of the inner circle (Fig. 44).

Each subject stands behind the shooting line and hits fifteen consecutive short pitch shots at the target.

APPROACH: Field markings for the approach item are identical to the previously described short pitch test, except the measurements are in yards instead of feet (Fig. 44). The test is conducted in the same manner as the short pitch item.

DRIVING: Requirements include a driving range or similar playfield area with minimum measurements of 300 × 150 yards. Two tees are located in front of the target range and directly between the target lines. Two parallel longitudinal lines should be marked off on the driving area, 50 yards apart and 300 yards long. Four more lines are placed at right angles to the original two lines or parallel to the tee area. The first of the four lines is 100 yards from the tee area with each subsequent line only 50 yards apart. They all should measure the full width of the field. Field markings for female subjects are 50 yards shorter as indicated by the numbers in parentheses in Figure 45.

Two test subjects can be tested simultaneously. Each stands in the tee area and drives nine consecutive shots into the target area.

PUTTING: The test area is a putting green similar to the type normally found at golf courses. Ideally, the putting surface should be slightly rolling with six holes included, two of which are spaced 15 feet apart with the other four spaced 20 feet apart. One hole

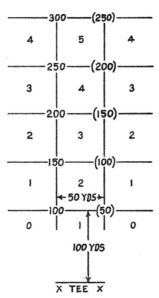

Figure 45. Field markings for drive test. From H. S. Brown: A test battery for evaluating golf skills, *TAHPER Journal,* 4-5, 28-29, May 1969. Courtesy of *TAHPER Journal.*

is downhill, one uphill, one breaks to the left, one to the right, and two holes are on a level putting surface.

The subjects are tested in pairs and move in a clockwise direction around the six holes. Each subject putts twelve holes or two rounds, sinking all putts.

SCORING METHOD AND NORMS

Chip: Each chip shot receives a numerical score ranging from zero to three based on the spot at which the ball initially lands. The points are assigned based on a three, two, and one value for the inner, middle, and outer trapezoids, respectively.

Whiff shots and balls that fail to land in the target area are given a score of zero. Any ball that strikes a line is given the score associated with the higher value zone.

Short Pitch: Same as the scoring procedure used for the chip item, except circles are used as a target area instead of trapezoids.

Approach: Identical to the short pitch test except that the score

TABLE LXX

CONVERSION SCALE FOR PUTTING TEST

Strokes	Score	Strokes	Score	Strokes	Score
21	45	29	29	37	13
22	43	30	27	38	11
23	41	31	25	39	9
24	39	32	23	40	7
25	37	33	21	41	5
26	35	34	19	42	3
27	33	35	17	43	1
28	31	36	15	44	0

From H. S. Brown: A test battery for evaluating golf skills, *TAHPER Journal,* 4-5, 28-29, May 1969. Courtesy of *TAHPER Journal.*

is based on the spot the ball comes to rest rather than where it first lands.

Driving: Each drive is assigned a numerical score ranging from zero to five based on the spot where the ball comes to rest. Whiff shots and balls that fail to land in the target area receive a score of zero. Any ball that ends up on a line is assigned the higher score.

Putting: The total number of strokes taken to putt all twelve holes is converted to a point score as shown by the norms found in Table LXX, so that the final putting score can be compared with the scores of the other tests in the battery.

T-scales for the whole battery are presented in Table LXXII.

TABLE LXXI

RELIABILITY AND VALIDITY COEFFICIENTS OF BROWN'S REVISED GOLF SKILLS TEST

Tests	Reliability		Validity	
	N	r	N	r
Chip Test	180	.74	86	.68
Short Pitch Test	148	.85	60	.76
Approach Test	155	.75	54	.65
Driving Test	104	.87	86	.73
Putting Test	58	.81	68	.71
Total Test Battery			134	.85

TABLE LXXII

T-SCALES FOR BROWN'S REVISED GOLF SKILLS TEST

Raw Score	Chip		Pitch		Approach		Driving		Putting	
	Men	Women	Men	Women	Men	Women	Men	Women	Men	Women
45	71	87	69	89	72	84	71	–	72	75
44	70	86	68	88	70	83	70	100	71	74
43	69	85	67	86	69	81	68	99	69	73
42	67	83	66	85	68	80	67	97	68	71
41	66	82	64	84	67	79	66	95	66	70
40	65	81	63	82	66	77	65	93	65	69
39	64	80	62	81	64	76	64	92	64	68
38	63	78	61	80	63	75	62	90	62	67
37	62	77	60	78	62	73	61	88	61	66
36	60	76	59	77	61	72	60	86	59	65
35	59	74	58	76	59	71	59	84	58	63
34	58	73	56	75	58	69	57	82	56	62
33	57	72	55	73	58	68	56	80	55	61
32	56	70	54	72	56	67	55	78	53	60
31	55	69	53	71	56	66	54	76	52	59
30	54	68	42	69	54	64	53	75	51	58
29	52	66	51	68	53	63	51	73	49	57
28	51	65	50	67	52	61	50	71	48	55
27	50	64	48	65	50	60	49	69	46	54
26	49	62	47	64	49	59	48	67	45	53
25	48	61	46	63	48	58	46	65	43	52
24	47	60	45	62	47	56	45	63	42	51
23	45	59	44	60	45	55	44	62	40	50
22	44	57	43	59	44	54	43	60	39	49
21	43	56	42	58	43	52	42	58	38	47
20	42	55	40	56	42	51	40	56	36	46
19	41	53	39	55	41	50	39	54	35	45
18	40	52	38	54	40	49	38	52	33	44
17	38	51	37	52	38	47	37	50	32	43
16	37	49	36	51	37	46	35	48	30	42
15	36	48	35	50	36	44	34	46	29	40
14	35	47	33	49	35	43	33	44	27	39
13	34	46	32	47	34	42	32	43	26	38
12	33	44	31	46	32	40	31	41	25	37
11	31	43	30	45	31	39	29	39	23	36
10	30	42	29	43	30	38	28	37	22	35
9	29	40	28	42	29	36	27	35	20	34
8	28	39	27	41	28	35	26	33	21	32
7	27	38	25	39	27	34	25	31	19	31
6	26	36	24	38	25	32	23	30	18	30
5	24	35	23	37	24	31	22	28	16	29
4	23	34	22	36	23	30	21	26	15	28
3	22	32	21	34	21	29	20	24	14	27
2	21	31	20	33	29	28	18	22	12	26

TABLE LXXII (continued)

Raw Score	Chip Men	Chip Women	Pitch Men	Pitch Women	Approach Men	Approach Women	Driving Men	Driving Women	Putting Men	Putting Women
1	20	30	19	32	19	27	17	20	11	24
Number	518	514	599	508	561	531	253	192	458	436
Mean	127.0	16.4	28.4	15.1	26.8	19.3	27.9	16.9	29.6	23.3
Standard Deviation	8.6	7.65	8.73	7.68	8.43	7.59	8.18	5.32	6.9	8.76

From H. S. Brown: A test battery for evaluating golf skills, *TAHPER Journal,* 4-5, 28-29, May 1969. Courtesy of *TAHPER Journal.*

Scientific Authenticity

Table LXXI presents the validity and reliability coefficients for each test item and the total battery, plus the number of participants for each.

CRITERION MEASURE: The score for nine best holes in a round of golf.

Additional Comments

The comprehensiveness feature of the Brown Test is its chief contribution to the literature on golf skills measurement. Reliability values of the chip and approach tests make those items questionable for use in grading purposes, but overall the strengths of the battery outweigh the weaknesses.

REFERENCES

1. Autrey, Elizabeth Parker: A Battery of Tests for Measuring Playing Ability in Golf. Master's thesis, Madison, University of Wisconsin, 1937.
2. Barrow, Harold M. and McGee, Rosemary: *A Practical Approach to Measurement in Physical Education,* 2nd ed. Philadelphia, Lea & Febiger, 1971.
3. Benson, David W.: Measuring Golf Ability Through Use of a Number Five-Iron Test. Read before the Research Section at the California Association for Health, Physical Education and Recreation Convention, April, 1963. In Clarke, H. Harrison: *Application of Measurement to Health and Physical Education,* 5th ed. Englewood Cliffs, P-H, 1976.

4. Bowen, Robert T.: Putting errors of beginning golfers using different points of aim. *Research Quarterly, 39:*31-35, 1968.

5. Brown, H. Steven: A test battery for evaluating golf skills. *TAHPER Journal,* pp. 4-5, 28-29, May, 1969.

6. Clarke, H. Harrison: *Application of Measurement to Health and Physical Education,* 5th ed. Englewood Cliffs, P-H, 1976.

7. Clevett, Melvin A.: An experiment in teaching methods of golf. *Research Quarterly, 2:*104-106, 1931.

8. Cochrane, June F.: The Construction of an Indoor Golf Skills Test as a Measure of Golfing Ability. Master's thesis, Minneapolis, University of Minnesota, 1960.

9. Coffey, Margaret: Achievement Tests in Golf. Master's thesis, Iowa City, University of Iowa, 1946.

10. Cotten, Doyice J.; Thomas, Jerry R.; and Plaster, Thomas: A Plastic Ball Test for Golf Iron Skill. Read at the AAHPER National Convention, Houston, Texas, March, 1972. In Johnson, Barry L. and Nelson, Jack K.: *Practical Measurements for Evaluation in Physical Education,* 2nd ed. Minneapolis, Burgess, 1974.

11. Davis, C. M.: The Use of the Golf Tee in Teaching Beginning Golf. Master's thesis, Ann Arbor, University of Michigan, 1960.

12. Edgren, Harry D. and Robinson, G. G.: *Individual Skill Tests in Physical Activities.* Chicago, the authors, 1937.

13. Green, Kenneth W.: The Development of a Battery of Golf Skill Tests for College Men. Doctoral dissertation, Fayetteville, University of Arkansas, 1974.

14. Haskins, Mary Jane: *Evaluation in Physical Education.* Dubuque, Iowa, Brown Bk, 1971.

15. Johnson, Barry L. and Nelson, Jack K.: *Practical Measurements for Evaluation in Physical Education.* 2nd ed. Minneapolis, Burgess, 1974.

16. McKee, Mary Ellen: A test for the full-swinging shot in golf. *Research Quarterly, 21:*40-46, 1950.

17. Meyers, Carlton R. and Blesh, T. Erwin: *Measurement In Physical Education.* New York, Ronald, 1962.

18. Meyers, Carlton R.: *Measurement in Physical Education,* 2nd ed. New York, Ronald, 1974.

19. Montoye, Henry J. (Ed.): *An Introduction to Measurement in Physical Education,* vol. III. Indianapolis, Phi Epsilon Kappa Fraternity, 1970.

20. Neal, Charlotte F.: The Value of Variations of Grip in Selected Sports for Women as Compensating Factors for Sex Differences in Strength. Master's thesis, Iowa City, State University of Iowa, 1951.

21. Neilson, N. P. and Jensen, Clayne R.: *Measurement and Statistics in Physical Education.* Belmont, Calif., Wadsworth Pub, 1972.

22. Nelson, Jack K.: An achievement test for golf. Unpublished study. In Johnson, Barry L. and Nelson, Jack K.: *Practical Measurements for Evaluation in Physical Education,* 2nd ed. Minneapolis, Burgess, 1974.

23. Olsen, Andrea C.: The Development of Objective Tests of the Ability of Freshmen and Sophomore College Women to Drive and to Pitch a Plastic Golf Ball in a Limited Indoor Area. Master's thesis, Boulder, University of Colorado, 1958.

24. Reece, Patsy Anne: A Comparison of the Scores Made on an Outdoor and the Scores Made on an Indoor Golf Test by College Women. Master's thesis, Boulder, University of Colorado, 1960.

25. Rehling, Conrad H.: Analysis of techniques of the golf drive. *Research Quarterly, 26:*80-81, 1955.

26. Scott, M. Gladys and French, Esther: *Measurement and Evaluation in Physical Education.* Dubuque, Iowa, Brown Bk, 1959.

27. Vanderhoof, Ellen R.: Beginning Golf Achievement Tests. Master's thesis, Iowa City, State University of Iowa, 1956.

28. Watts, Harriet: Construction and Evaluation of a Target on Testing the Approach Shot in Golf. Master's thesis, Madison, University of Wisconsin, 1942.

29. West, Charlotte and Thorpe, Jo Anne: Construction and validation of an eight-iron approach test. *Research Quarterly, 39:*1115-1120, 1968.

30. Wood, Janet Isabel: A Study for the Purpose of Setting up the Specifications of a Golf Driving Cage Target and Test for the Mid-Iron and the Brassie Clubs. Master's thesis, Madison, University of Wisconsin, 1933.

Chapter 15

Gymnastics

INTRODUCTION

THE WORD "GYMNASTICS" means different things to different people, depending upon such variables as sex, age, and geographical location. Whatever the interpretation, the scope of gymnastics entails the performance of movements on both light and heavy apparatus, as well as tumbling and free exercise skills.

The sport experiences a greater public interest in many foreign countries than the United States, but expanded television coverage of national and international competition has greatly influenced its popularity among Americans in the last decade. Perhaps the most solid testimonial to this country's increased interest in gymnastics is the definite improvement shown in caliber of competition and performance scores in recent years.

Gymnastics is one of the few physical education activities offered in educational institutions in which measurement of ability is almost entirely limited to subjective judgment. Therefore, the importance of the tester's skill in evaluating gymnastics performance cannot be overemphasized. The instructor automatically assumes a greater responsibility for measuring achievement than he does for those activities whereby the scoring systems are objective.

Several gymnastics organizations have their own version of competition and scoring system. Aside from utilizing skills tests such as those presented in this chapter, the tester may wish to modify a particular type of competition for his particular situation and evaluate accordingly. Some of these organizations are:

1. Amateur Athletic Union
2. National Association for Girls and Women in Sport
3. International Gymnastics Federation
4. National Collegiate Athletic Association
5. National Federation of State High School Associations
6. United States Gymnastics Federation

263

BOWERS GYMNASTICS SKILLS TEST[3]

Date: 1965.

Purpose: To evaluate beginning and low intermediate gymnastic skills.

Description

Bowers based her gymnastics test around the areas or events that reflect the official competitive schedule for women. Performance in tumbling, vaulting, and free standing floor exercise is measured along with ability demonstrated on the uneven parallel bars and balance beam.

Ordinarily, tumbling is included as part of the free standing floor exercise event in national women's competition but is a separate item in this test.

EDUCATIONAL APPLICATION: Females, junior high through college.

Administrative Feasibility

TIME: A class of twenty students can be tested in two sixty-minute periods.

PERSONNEL: One or two judges with student assistants as spotters.

TRAINING INVOLVED: Administration of the test should come at the end of a term of instruction to give the student full opportunity to master as many of the test items as possible.

EQUIPMENT AND SUPPLIES: Uneven parallel bars, balance beam, vaulting board, mats.

Accessories: Scoring and marking materials.

Facilities and Space: Gymnasium area.

Directions and Scoring Method

The number or numbers that follow each item represent the scoring scale for that particular item with the highest numerical value naturally representing a well-executed item. Subjects may repeat a particular event in an attempt to improve their score, but the second attempt is also recorded.

If a skill cannot be completed, a score of zero is given. The skills tested are scored from zero to a maximum number of points, and the highest score signifies perfect execution in body rhythm and form with both grace and poise.

It is to the subject's advantage to try each skill without the aid of spotters. Should the subject feel a spotter is needed at the lowest skill level, it is permissible, but no points are awarded.

1. *Event No. 1:* Tumbling
    A. Tumbling Items
        (1) Rolls
            a. forward–3, 2, 1
            b. backward–3, 2, 1
            c. backward extension–5
        (2) Cartwheels in Rhythm
            a. to the right side–3, 2, 1
            b. to the left side–3, 2, 1
        (3) Kip Progression (either movement a or b)
            a. from headspring off a rolled mat–4
            b. from shoulder-hand support–3, 2, 1
2. *Event No. 2:* Uneven Parallel Bars
    A. Uneven Parallel Bars Items
        (1) Bar Snap $\dfrac{\text{6-6-6-6-12-18 inches}}{\text{10-8-6-4- 2- 0 points}}$

   A line is drawn or taped on the landing mat 18 inches away from the bar, with another 12 inches from the first line, and then four more lines 6 inches apart. If the subject lands in the area between the bar and the first line, a score of zero points is awarded and successive scores are based on the above point and distance chart.
    B. Progressive Movement to the Kip
        (1) one leg swing up–1, 2, 4
        (2) walk out–4, 5, 6
        (3) glide–5, 6, 8
    C. Backward Hip Pullover–0, 2, 4

   If the subject is given only slight assistance during any portion of the pullover, only two points are awarded.
3. *Event No. 3:* Balance Beam
    A. Balance Beam Items

(1) three-step turn–1, 2, 4
(2) step, hops on both feet–1, 2, 4
(3) step, leap–1, 2, 4
(4) scale–1, 2, 4

The score is determined by adding the total points accumulated on the four movements. Sixteen points is the maximum score.

B. Arm Support–0, 1, 2, 4
C. Rolling
(1) backward shoulder roll–1, 2, 3, 4, 5, 6, 7

Total points accumulated without the aid of a spotter constitute the official score.

4. *Event No. 4:* Vaulting Event
   A. Vaulting Items
   (1) Floor items for body control of basic vault positions and flexibility.
      a. front support to straddle stand
      b. front support to stoop stand

```
     6  3   3 |   3        inches
  0   2   4   6 | 10   12  points
```

The scoring system is the same for each of the above items. A solid line is constructed on the gymnasium floor. On one side of the line are three parallel lines that are 12, 6, and 3 inches away. On the opposite side is another parallel line located 3 inches from the original line.

The subject places her hands on the solid line with the body extended in a front support over the line 12 inches away. Measurement of the landing is taken from the heel. Points are awarded on a 0, 2, 4, 6, 10, 12 basis as shown in the above point and distance chart.

(2) Approach test for the run, hurdle, and take-off.
   a. run, take-off–1, 2, 3, 4

A regulation reuther board that has a black stripe

on the front end is used. Lines are drawn on the board that are 5, 13, and 17 inches from the black stripe. The area where the ball of the foot hits is the scoring area.

No points are scored for hitting the area from the back of the board to the first line. Three, four, and two points are scored for the next three areas with no points given for the black part of the board. This score is added to the wall score minus the height score which is discussed below.

b. height measurement–0, 1, 2, 3, 4, 5, 6, 7

The take-off board is placed beside a wall that is marked off with 3-inch, alternating colored stripes of tape beginning at the 5-foot level. The stripes are numbered one through seven beginning with the bottom stripe. The score is the height of the subject's jump (in stripes) minus the height of the subject while standing.

5. *Event No. 5:* Free Standing Floor Exercise

TABLE LXXIII

SCORE SHEET FOR BOWERS GYMNASTICS TEST

I. Tumbling

   1. Rolls   2. Cartwheels   3. Kips

     <u>F</u>   <u>B</u>   <u>Ext.</u>   <u>R</u>   <u>L</u>

     <u>3</u> + <u>3</u> + <u>5</u>   +   <u>3</u> + <u>3</u>   +   <u>4</u>   =   <u>21</u>

II. Uneven Bars

   1. Bar Snap   2. Kip   3. Backward Hip Pullover

     <u>10</u>   +   <u>8</u>   +   <u>4</u>   =   <u>22</u>

III. Balance Beam

   1. Locomotor   2. Arm Support   3. Rolling

     <u>4</u> + <u>4</u> + <u>4</u> + <u>4</u> + <u>16</u>   <u>4</u>   +   <u>7</u>   =   <u>27</u>

IV. Vaulting

   A. Straddle   B. Stoop   2. Approach Test

                             Board + Wall Score - Height Score

     <u>12</u>   +   <u>12</u>   +   <u>4</u>   + (<u>5</u>   )   =   <u>33</u>

V. Free Standing Floor Exercise

   1. Tumbling Total   2. Continuity

     <u>21</u>   +   <u>10</u>   =   <u>31</u>

A. Free Standing Floor Exercise Items
   (1) Tumbling total (points from Event No. 1)–0–21
   (2) Continuity (routine)–0–10
      a. body wave
      b. leg leading turn
      c. scale
      d. concentric arm circles
      e. final pose
        One point is deducted for each stop in the flow of movement. The same is true for a break in form.

The score sheet depicted in Table LXXIII is used when scoring a student's performance on the Bowers Gymnastics Skills Test. The blanks reflect the maximum number of points that can be obtained for each item and event.

Equal weight value is given to the various events, even though they differ numerically. Since the numerical range of the five events is from 21 to 33 points, the event scores should be scaled or equated by the use of the standard scores.

Scientific Authenticity

VALIDITY: Face validity.

RELIABILITY: Tumbling, .98; uneven parallel bars, 1.00; balance beam, .98; vaulting, .99; free exercise, .97.

Additional Comments

The Bowers Test may be used effectively as a motivation and practice device as well as a tool for measuring progress in gymnastics achievement. Also, the comprehensiveness feature of the test makes it a valuable aid to those instructors who are developing gymnastics programs.

HARRIS TUMBLING AND APPARATUS PROFICIENCY TEST[9]

Date: 1966.

Purpose: To measure tumbling and apparatus skill proficiency.

Description

Harris' test originally included twenty-two items; four in tumbling and three each in the rings, parallel bars, high and low horizontal bars, side horse and the trampoline. Through a process of scientific assessment, all but six of the test items were eliminated. Although used for ability grouping purposes, the test was originally designated to serve as an alternative evaluation tool to the successful completion of a formal course of instruction.

EDUCATIONAL APPLICATION: College men.

Administrative Feasibility

TIME: Twenty students can be evaluated in one sixty-minute period.

PERSONNEL: One judge or scorer.

TRAINING INVOLVED: During the regular class periods preceding the test administration, it is recommended that a proper amount of instruction be given for the test items, so the student has a chance to adequately practice each. During the actual testing situation, each item should again be demonstrated and the steps in administration should be fully explained before the subjects attempt the first test item.

The tester should demonstrate a basic expertise in gymnastics judging. It is suggested that he refine his judging skill by occasionally assigning a mental score to the performance of students during instructional sessions.

EQUIPMENT AND SUPPLIES: Parallel bars, horizontal bar, and trampoline.

Accessories: Scoring materials.

Facilities and Space: Gymnasium area.

Directions

Each subject attempts to perform all six test items. Scoring proficiency of the instructor is enhanced if all students complete a particular test item before proceeding to the next. The test items and score values are shown in Table LXXIV.

SCORING METHOD: The test is scored by a judge or panel of judges with each item assigned a point total of seven to nine points. As shown on the score card, the point total for each item is divided into form and execution points. Forty-six points is the maximum score.

TABLE LXXIV

SCORE CARD FOR HARRIS TUMBLING AND APPARATUS PROFICIENCY TEST

Name: _____ Judge: _____ Class: _____ Date: _____

Directions: Circle the number which indicates the performer's score in areas of form and execution, respectively. Leave the totals until all testing has been completed.

Item. No.

1.	TUMBLING			
	Forward roll to head balance.	Form: 12		
		Execution: 12345		Total____
2.	PARALLEL BARS			
	Back uprise, shoulder balance, front or forward roll.	Form: 12		
		Execution: 12345		Total____
3.	Shoulder kip from arm support, swing, front dismount.	Form: 123		
		Execution: 123456		Total____
4.	HORIZONTAL OR HIGH BAR			
	Cast to kip up.	Form: 123		
		Execution: 123456		Total____
5.	Front pullover, cast, back hip circle.	Form: 12		
		Execution: 12345		Total____
6.	TRAMPOLINE			
	Back, front, seat, feet.	Form: 12		
		Execution: 12345		Total____

Total Points   _____

Mean scores associated with each test item are given below. Twenty-five male physical education majors completed the test in the Harris study and were ranked by groups according to mean score.

The first group was comprised of the four top subjects, and the second group was composed of the seventeen subjects that scored in the middle range. Four subjects who ranked at the bottom of the scale were in the third group. The mean scores were as follows:

Item No.	Group I	Group II	Group III
1	6.75	5.47	4.00
2	6.75	5.18	1.75
3	7.50	4.12	1.75
4	7.75	3.59	1.00
5	6.25	3.88	2.00
6	6.50	4.53	2.25

Scientific Authenticity

VALIDITY: Results of the Harris study revealed the test to be discriminatory in the determination of gymnastics ability.

RELIABILITY: Utilizing the test-retest method, each of the six test items met the acceptable reliability standards.

Additional Comments

The Harris Test rates high in time and ease of administration. Its chief limitation is that of most gymnastics skills tests; a lack of instructors with expertise in judging gymnastics performance restricts the test's use.

LARSON GYMNASTICS TEST[17]

Date: 1969.

Purpose: To measure general gymnastics skill.

Description

Larson felt that elementary school children, especially those in the upper elementary grades, would enjoy and benefit from a skills testing program similar to the competitive gymnastics found at higher levels of education. From his idea came a subjective scoring system that is simple, yet it is based on the more complicated scoring system utilized at the collegiate level.

Administrative Feasibility

TIME: A class of twenty students can be evaluated in one sixty-minute class.

PERSONNEL: One judge-recorder with student assistants.

TRAINING INVOLVED: Much practice is recommended for students on each item since elementary children need a lot of time to acquire basic gymnastics skills.

EQUIPMENT AND SUPPLIES: Basic gymnastics equipment including balance beam, trampoline, parallel bars, mats, etc.

Accessories: Scoring materials.

Facilities and Space: Gymnasium area.

Directions

The tester selects those items that the students are to practice. Each is given a point value commensurate with the item's level of difficulty. The determination of item difficulty values is relative to the student's level of skill.

On the test date, the student identifies a predetermined selection of stunts that he feels capable of performing. The subject executes the selected stunts, and the tester judges and assigns each a performance rating according to the scale in Table LXXV.

SCORING METHOD: The score for a particular stunt is derived by multiplying its difficulty point value by the performance rating of the judge or tester. If a subject performs a shoulder stand which is assigned a difficulty value of two points and he receives a score of three points, then his final score for that particular stunt is six $(2 \times 3 = 6)$.

Larson suggests a method of grading that challenges the stu-

TABLE LXXV

PERFORMANCE RATING SCALE FOR LARSON
GYMNASTICS TEST

Points	Performance Rating
3	Good performance, good form and knowledge of how to perform the stunt.
2	Fair form, but knowledge of how to perform the stunt.
1	Mere ability to perform the stunt with extremely poor form and knowledge of the stunt.
0	Inability to perform stunt.

From R. F. Larson: Skill testing in elementary school gymnastics, *Physical Educator, 26:*80-81, 1969. Courtesy of Phi Epsilon Kappa Fraternity.

dent, yet is easily administered. The student progresses at his own pace and is not compared to the rest of the class. He is given a percentage grade based on the number of points attained from a maximum amount. For example, fourteen points achieved out of a possible twenty results in a grade of seventy.

A grading scale should be developed by each tester which allows each subject to set and more easily attain positive and progressive goals. It should also be relative to the ability of the particular group which would not exclude the possibility of the highly skilled student receiving a high grade.

Scientific Authenticity

Not reported.

Additional Comments

Larson made a significant contribution to sports skills measurement by developing a test suitable for elementary school children. The test demonstrates diverse strengths as a motivation device, practice or self-testing tool, and grading instrument.

DIFFICULTY RATING SCALE FOR BEGINNER STUNTS OF WOMEN[12, 13]

Date: 1971.

Purpose: To measure individual stunt performance in gymnastics.

Description

This gymnastic skills test is a subjective rating scale that is applicable for beginning female gymnasts. Each subject selects two stunts to perform from each of five events: free exercise, vaulting, balance beam, uneven bars, and the trampoline. Each stunt is judged on a predetermined rating scale and assigned a numerical score. The maximum score for the ten-item test is 99.75.

EDUCATIONAL APPLICATION: Females, junior high through college.

Administrative Feasibility

TIME: A class of twenty students can easily be evaluated in two sixty-minute classes.

PERSONNEL: One judge-recorder with students serving as spotters.

TRAINING INVOLVED: Much instruction and practice time is recommended for the students prior to testing. Therefore, the test should be given for score toward the end of the instructional term.

EQUIPMENT AND SUPPLIES: Mats, vaulting horse and board, balance beam, uneven bars, and trampoline.

Accessories: Scoring materials.

Facilities and Space: Gymnasium area.

Directions

After each subject has been allowed adequate practice time and qualified instruction, she selects two stunts to perform from each of the five different events. Sample stunts from which the students make their selection are listed in Table LXXVI. For a complete listing of the stunts in the Difficulty Rating Scale, the reader is referred to the test source.[12]

SCORING METHOD: Each stunt has an average difficulty rating along with a suggested upper and lower limit which is based on a five-point scale.

Each stunt is assigned a numerical value which indicates the proficiency of execution. The maximum score on the ten-stunt test is 99.75.

Scientific Authenticity

Not reported.

Additional Comments

The rating scale shows value not only as an instrument for student evaluation but also for measuring skill progress during the course of instruction. It provides a logical, systematic approach to skills testing in gymnastics. The freedom and flexibility allowed the student in fulfilling the skill requirements is a plus for the test.

⟫→

Adapted from B. L. Johnson and P. D. Boudreaux: *Basic Gymnastics for Girls and Women.* New York, Appleton-Century-Crofts, 1971.

TABLE LXXVI

DIFFICULTY RATING SCALE FOR BEGINNER STUNTS OF WOMEN

	Lower Limit	Average Difficulty Rating	Upper Limit
Free Exercise			
Forward Roll	1.50	1.75	2.00
Shoulder Roll	2.25	2.50	2.75
Dive Roll	2.50	2.75	3.00
Tripod Balance	.75	1.00	1.25
Tip-up Balance	2.00	2.25	2.50
Backward Roll	3.25	3.50	3.75
Headstand	2.75	3.00	3.25
Head and Forearm Balance	3.25	3.50	3.75
Cartwheel	3.25	3.50	3.75
Handstand against Wall	1.75	2.00	2.25
Vaulting			
Front Vault	2.25	2.50	2.75
Flank Vault	2.25	2.50	2.75
Rear Vault	3.25	3.50	3.75
Squat Vault	3.00	3.25	3.75
Wolf Vault	3.25	3.50	3.75
Balance Beam			
Front Support Mount to "L" Position	2.00	2.25	2.50
Fence Vault Mount	2.75	3.00	3.25
Cast to Knee Scale and Return to Stand	2.75	3.00	3.25
Walk	1.00	1.25	1.50
Step Turn	2.00	2.25	2.50
Arabesque Turn	2.00	2.25	2.50
Squat Turn	2.25	2.50	2.75
Skip Step	2.00	2.25	2.50
Front Scale	2.75	3.00	3.25
Uneven Bars			
German Hang	2.25	2.50	2.75
Crotch Seat Mount	3.00	3.25	3.50
German Hang with Simple Turn	3.25	3.50	3.75
One-leg Squat Rise and Combination Movements	1.50	1.75	2.00
Back Pullover (Low Bar)	3.25	3.50	3.75
Swan Balance	2.75	3.00	3.25
Forward Roll to Knee Circle Dismount	3.00	3.25	3.50
Trampoline			
Tuck Bounce	1.25	1.50	1.75
Pike Bounce	1.50	1.75	2.00
Straddle Bounce	1.50	1.75	2.00
Seat Drop	1.00	1.25	1.50
Knee Drop	1.50	1.75	2.00
Hands and Knee Drop	2.25	2.50	2.75
Knee Drop--Front Drop	2.75	3.00	3.25
Front Drop	3.25	3.50	3.75
Back Drop	3.25	3.50	3.75

TABLE LXXVII

DIFFICULTY RATING SCALE FOR BEGINNER SKILLS

	Lower Limit	Average Difficulty Rating	Upper Limit
Horizontal Bar			
German Hang	1.25	1.50	1.75
German Hang-Full Turn	2.50	2.75	3.00
Back Pullover	3.00	3.25	3.50
Knee Kip-up	3.00	3.25	3.50
Underswing Dismount	3.25	3.50	3.75
Pick-up Swing and Simple Back Dismount	3.25	3.50	3.75
Parallel Bars			
Cross-Straddle Seat Travel	1.00	1.25	1.50
Front Dismount	3.00	3.25	3.50
Rear Dismount	3.00	3.25	3.50
Single Leg Cut and Catch	3.50	3.75	4.00
Forward Roll in Straddle Position	3.75	4.00	4.25
Hip-Kip Straddle	3.75	4.00	4.25
Still Rings			
German Hang	.75	1.00	1.25
Bird's Nest	.75	1.00	1.25
Inverted Hang	1.00	1.25	1.50
Single Leg Cut Dismount	3.00	3.25	3.50
Single Leg Straddle Dismount	3.00	3.50	4.00
"L" Position	4.00	4.25	4.50
Swinging To Tuck-Over Dismount	3.75	4.00	4.25
Side Horse			
Squat Mount to "L"	2.25	2.50	2.75
Feint Swings	2.00	2.25	2.50
Single Leg Half Circles	3.00	3.50	4.00
Single Leg Full Circle	3.25	3.75	4.25
Double Leg Half Circles	3.50	4.00	4.50
Single Rear Dismount	3.75	4.00	4.25

Adapted from B. L. Johnson and M. J. Garcia: *Gymnastics for the Beginner: A Coeducational Approach.* Manchaca, Texas, Sterling Swift, 1976.

Johnson and Garcia[13] later revised the original rating scale and added four new events (horizontal bar, parallel bars, still rings, and side horse). A fifth new division was also created by placing many of the original free exercise stunts into a new category labeled "balance and flexibility skills." The original difficulty rating was not changed.

The new rating scale was devised for both men and women and was renamed the *Difficulty Rating Scale for Beginner Skills*. Sample stunts with the accompanying rating scale for the four new events are presented in Table LXXVII. For a complete listing of the stunts in the Difficulty Rating Scale, the reader is again referred to the test source.[13]

REFERENCES

1. Amateur Athletic Union: *Gymnastics Guide.* New York, AAU, 1977 (periodically updated).
2. Barrow, Harold M. and McGee, Rosemary: *A Practical Approach to Measurement in Physical Education,* 2nd ed. Philadelphia, Lea & Febiger, 1971.
3. Bowers, Carolyn O.: Gymnastics Skill Test for Beginning to Low Intermediate Girls and Women. Master's thesis, Columbus, The Ohio State University, 1965.
4. Cotteral, Bonnie and Cotteral, Donnie: *The Scale for Judging Quality of Performance in Stunts and Tumbling.* New York, Ronald, 1936.
5. Edgren, Harry D. and Robinson, G. G.: *Individual Skill Tests in Physical Activities.* Chicago, the authors, 1937.
6. Edwards, V. M.: *Test Questions for Tumbling.* Philadelphia, Saunders, 1969.
7. Fagan, Clifford B. (Ed.): *Boys Gymnastics Rule Book.* Elgin, Illinois, National Federation of State High School Associations, 1975-76 (periodically updated).
8. Faulkner, John and Loken, Newt: Objectivity of judging at the NCAA gymnastics meet: a ten-year follow-up study. *Research Quarterly, 33:*485-486, 1962.
9. Harris, J. Patrick: A Design for a Proposed Skill Proficiency Test in Tumbling and Apparatus for Male Physical Education Majors at the University of North Dakota. Master's thesis, Grand Forks, University of North Dakota, 1966.
10. Hunsicker, Paul A. and Loken, Newt: The objectivity of judging at the National Collegiate Athletic Association gymnastics meet. *Research Quarterly, 22:*423, 1951.
11. Johnson, Barry L.: A screening test for pole vaulting and selected

gymnastic events. *Journal of Health, Physical Education and Recreation, 44*:71-72, 1973.

12. Johnson, Barry L. and Boudreaux, Patricia Duncan: *Basic Gymnastics for Girls and Women.* New York, Appleton, 1971.
13. Johnson, Barry L. and Garcia, Mary J.: *Gymnastics for the Beginner: A Coeducational Approach.* Manchaca, Texas, Sterling Swift, 1976.
14. Johnson, Barry L. and Nelson, Jack K.: *Practical Measurements for Evaluation in Physical Education,* 2nd ed. Minneapolis, Burgess, 1974.
15. Johnson, Marvin: Objectivity of judging at the National NCAA gymnastics meet: a twenty-year follow-up study. *Research Quarterly, 42*:454-455, 1971.
16. Landers, Daniel M.: A Comparison of Two Gymnastic Judging Methods. Master's thesis, Urbana, University of Illinois, 1965.
17. Larson, Robert F.: Skill testing in elementary school gymnastics. *Physical Educator, 26*:80-81, 1969.
18. Meyers, Carlton R.: *Measurement in Physical Education,* 2nd ed. New York, Ronald, 1974.
19. National Association for Girls and Women in Sport: *Gymnastic Guide.* Washington, AAHPER, 1976 (periodically updated).
20. National Collegiate Athletic Association: *Official Gymnastics Rules.* Shawnee Mission, Kansas, NCAA, 1976 (periodically updated).
21. Scheer, J.: Effect of placement in the order of competition on scores of Nebraska high school students. *Research Quarterly, 44*:79-85, 1973.
22. Schwarzkoph, Robert J.: The Iowa Brace Test as a Measuring Instrument for Predicting Gymnastic Ability. Master's thesis, Seattle, University of Washington, 1962.
23. United States Gymnastic Federation: *Age Group Workbook.* Tucson, USGF, 1976.
24. Wettstone, Eugene: Test for predicting potential ability in gymnastics and tumbling. *Research Quarterly, 9*:115, 1938.
25. Zwarg, Leopold F.: Judging and evaluation of competitive apparatus for gymnastic exercises. *Journal of Health and Physical Education, 6*:23, 1935.

Chapter 16

Handball

INTRODUCTION

HANDBALL COULD BE considered the oldest sport played with a ball since a similar game was reportedly played in the Egyptian and Greek cultures as early as the eleventh century BC. Several derivations preceded the modern American game which has its roots in the urban areas of the East Coast. Introduced to the United States around 1840, handball became a fixture in American sports culture by the early twentieth century.

Handball is commonly taught in college and university physical education programs today, especially in the larger ones. Moreover, the sport is well established in the Armed Forces and has solid popularity in several community and social organizations. The appeal of handball continues to spread beyond the eastern United States, a fact made evident by the large volume of courts being constructed annually.

Although the number of handball buffs has steadily increased through the years, its growth as a national sport has been slowed by some inherent limitations. For example, handball courts are rather expensive, and it is impractical to build only one. Therefore, schools are not able to build courts at a pace commensurate to the organizations mentioned above. Furthermore, spectator interest has been minimal due to the traditional design of the courts. However, this shortcoming might be alleviated when today's glass court trend becomes commonplace.

Of the dozen or so handball skills tests that have been developed, the first was completed in 1935 by Clevett,[2] and the initial tests devised by scientific procedures were done by Cornish[3] and McCachren[11] in 1949.

CORNISH HANDBALL TEST[3]

Date: 1949.
Purpose: To measure handball ability.
EDUCATIONAL APPLICATION: College men.

Administrative Feasibility

TIME: One sixty-minute period for a class of twenty students.

PERSONNEL: One person to serve as both scorer and timer plus student assistants as necessary.

TRAINING INVOLVED: Practice trials were not recommended by the developer but a uniform amount probably should be given.

EQUIPMENT AND SUPPLIES: Handballs, gloves, stop watch.

Accessories: Scoring and court marking materials.

Facilities and Space: Handball court or wall and floor space of similar design.

Description and Directions

Cornish investigated the value of five handball skill items, including the thirty-second volley, front wall placement, back wall placement, service placement, and power test. Only the thirty-second volley, service placement, and power test are presented in detail here, since multiple correlation results suggested that the three items comprehensively measure handball ability.

Thirty-Second Volley: Positioning himself behind the service line while holding a handball, the subject drops the ball to the

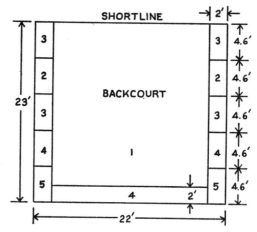

Figure 46. Court markings for service placement test. From C. Cornish: A study of measurement of ability in handball, *Research Quarterly, 20:*215-222, 1949. Courtesy of AAHPER.

floor and strokes it to the front wall continuously for thirty seconds. The ball must be stroked hard enough so the subject remains behind the serving line during the volley. If the ball fails to return to the service line, the subject is permitted to step into the front court to stroke the ball, but he must return to the service line for the next stroke. If the ball is completely missed, it is immediately replaced by the tester and play continues.

Service Placement: Standing in the service zone holding a handball, the subject proceeds to execute ten consecutive legal serves, any five of which must be cross-court serves. The preferred serving hand should be used.

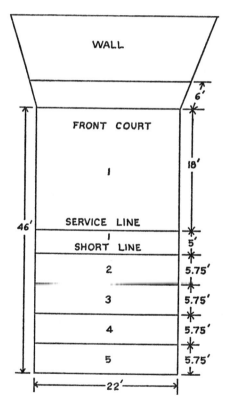

Figure 47. Court markings for power test. From C. Cornish: A study of measurement of ability in handball, *Research Quarterly, 20:*215-222, 1949. Courtesy of AAHPER.

Power: The floor of the court is divided into six scoring zones. A line that is 18 feet from and parallel to the base of the front wall marks the front court scoring zone. Five feet away, the scoring zone at the service area is located, with subsequent zones measuring 5.75 feet in depth. Numerical values are assigned to each of the six zones as shown in Figure 47.

Parallel to the base of the front wall, a 6-foot line is drawn.

The test begins with the subject standing in the service zone and tossing the ball to the front wall. The ball must be allowed to bounce after striking the front wall. After the ball bounces from the floor, the subject attempts to stroke the ball back to the front wall so that it hits below the 6-foot line. The test trial is repeated if the ball hits above the wall line or the subject steps into the front court. Ten total trials or strokes are given, five with each hand.

SCORING METHOD

Thirty-Second Volley: A point is recorded each time the ball strikes the front wall, and the final score is the total number of points accumulated during the thirty-second trial.

The mean score for the participants in the Cornish study was seventeen with a standard deviation of 2.9.

Service Placement: Points ranging from one to five are assigned to each of the ten serves, with the final score reflecting the total number of points accumulated up to a maximum of fifty points.

In the Cornish study, the mean score was fourteen, and a 2.1 standard deviation resulted.

Power: One to five points are given for trials with the final score determined by the total number of points accumulated up to a maximum of fifty points.

The mean score for the study was seventeen with a 2.9 standard deviation.

Scientific Authenticity

Subjects for the Cornish study were 134 college students enrolled in handball classes. The tests were administered in the second and tenth week of instruction.

VALIDITY: A correlation coefficient of .53 for the thirty-second volley and the service placement items, and .58 for the power test.

RELIABILITY: Not reported.

CRITERION MEASURE: Total number of points scored by a subject, minus those scored by his opponent, during four weeks of competition.

Additional Comments

When there is a time limitation or multiple courts are unavailable, the tester may wish to choose only one of the three items to administer. The power test would be the logical choice, but its reported validity coefficient in the Cornish study is low for grading purposes. As a practice device, however, the power item shows value because its performance requirement resembles the offensive and defensive strokes fundamental to handball.

The reputation of the timeless Cornish Test would be further enhanced if it were more fully authenticated by scientific procedures. Improvement in the test's validity and confirmation of an acceptable reliability value are obvious needs. Inclusion of practice trials preceding the test administration might promote a higher reliability coefficient for one or more of the items.

OREGON HANDBALL TEST[15]

Date: 1967.

Purpose: To measure general handball playing ability; to discriminate between good and poor handball performance.

Description

In correlating test scores of the seventeen items in the Oregon Test with game score averages in a round-robin tournament, the three-item battery showing the highest composite validity coefficient consisted of the service placement, total wall volley, and back wall placement items. These three items only were selected for detailed discussion because they collectively provide a comprehensive measure of handball ability.

Service Placement: The floor marking divides the court into target areas with each scoring zone assigned a point value ranging from two to five points (Fig. 48). Three side targets are 4 feet long with a fourth 5 feet in length. Each target area is 2 feet wide. The back target is 2 feet wide and 14 feet long.

Back Wall Placement: The front wall is divided into target areas with each assigned a numerical value ranging from one to five points. Four 3-foot squares are placed in both the lower right and left corners of the front wall (Fig. 49).

EDUCATIONAL APPLICATION: College men.

Administrative Feasibility

TIME: One sixty-minute period for a class of twenty students.

PERSONNEL: One person to time, score, and record the particular test items; student assistants.

TRAINING INVOLVED: Proper test familiarity should be insured prior to actual testing.

EQUIPMENT AND SUPPLIES: Handballs, gloves, stop watch.

Accessories: Scoring and court marking materials.

Facilities and Space: Regulation handball court or a facility with similar floor and wall space.

Directions

SERVICE PLACEMENT: The subject stands in the service zone holding a handball and serves ten consecutive legal serves in an attempt to place each serve into a target area of high point value. The preferred hand and any type of serve may be used.

TOTAL WALL VOLLEY: This particular test is divided into two parts. The first part is initiated with the subject assuming a position in the center of the court behind the short service line, holding a handball. The ball is then dropped to the floor and stroked to the front wall repeatedly for thirty seconds. Either hand may be used. The ball should be stroked hard enough to bounce back behind the short service line each time. Subjects are permitted to step in front of the line for only one return, but after that they must stay behind the line. If this rule is violated or control of the ball is lost, the subject must recover the ball and repeat the trial.

The second part of the test is identical to the first, except the subject may not strike the ball with the dominant hand.

BACK WALL PLACEMENT: The test begins with the subject

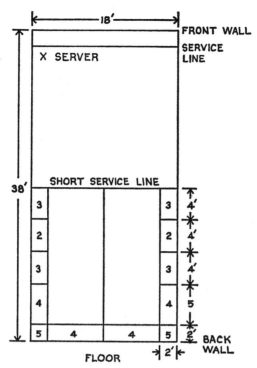

Figure 48. Floor markings for service placement test. From G. Pennington et al.: A measure of handball ability, *Research Quarterly, 38*:247-253, 1967. Courtesy of AAHPER.

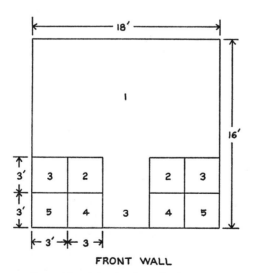

Figure 49. Front wall markings for back wall placement test. From G. Pennington et al.: A measure of handball ability, *Research Quarterly, 38*:247-253, 1967. Courtesy of AAHPER.

throwing the ball high and hard against the front wall. Allowing the rebounding ball to hit the floor and bounce off the back wall, the subject strokes it back to the front wall in an attempt to strike a target area of high point value. Each subject completes a total of ten trials, five with each hand.

SCORING METHOD

Service Placement: Each of the ten trials is worth two to five points. The final score is the total number of points accumulated up to a maximum of fifty points.

In the Oregon study, a mean of twenty was derived along with an 8.1 standard deviation.

Total Wall Volley: The final score is the total number of times the ball is legally stroked against the front wall for both of the thirty-second trials. The test mean and standard deviation were fourteen and 2.7, respectively, in the Oregon study.

Back Wall Placement: One to five points are allowed for each of the ten trials. The total number of points accumulated up to a maximum of fifty points equals the final score. A mean score of ten and standard deviation of 2.9 were reported by the investigators in the aforementioned study.

Scientific Authenticity

Thirty-seven male undergraduate students of diverse handball ability provided the data for test authentication.

VALIDITY: Correlation coefficients of .71, .66, and .38 were found for the respective items as presented above.

RELIABILITY: Not reported.

CRITERION MEASURE: Round-robin tournament results.

Additional Comments

The service placement item in the Oregon Test resembles the one included in the Cornish Handball Test (p. 280). However, the .71 validity coefficient for the Oregon Test item is far superior to the .53 validity finding in the Cornish Test. Perhaps the Oregon Test was better designed from the standpoint of target placement and assignment of target score values. Also, the cross-court serve requirement in the Cornish Test may be too advanced for the beginning handball player.

The total wall volley item is similar to the thirty-second volley item in the Cornish Test. Its reported validity value is also considerably higher than the thirty-second volley. An explanation for the disparity in validity coefficients is purely speculative because several differences exist in the test specifications of the two items.

The extremely low validity coefficient derived for the back wall placement test makes the item unacceptable for use as a single item, regardless of the purpose. It does seem to have some value as part of the three-item battery but, even then, should not be used for grading purposes.

Furthermore, the back wall shot is difficult to master and its use in measuring handball ability of beginners is questionable. Although not presented in this chapter, this item was also included in the Cornish Test and provided a very low validity coefficient.

The obvious shortcoming of the Oregon Handball Test is its unknown quality in the area of reliability. Until an acceptable reliability value is confirmed, the battery should not be considered very strongly for ability classification or grading purposes.

TYSON HANDBALL TEST[19]

Date: 1970.

Purpose: To measure the skills essential to succeed in handball.

Description

Study of seven handball skill items produced a rather impressive three-item battery, according to standards of scientific authenticity.

Front Wall Kill with Dominant Hand: See Figure 50 for description of the test layout.

Back Wall Kill with Dominant Hand: Court markings for this test are shown in Figure 51.

EDUCATIONAL APPLICATION: College men.

Administrative Feasibility

TIME: A class of twenty students can be tested in one sixty-minute period.

PERSONNEL: One scorer-timer-recorder with student assistants.

TRAINING INVOLVED: The instructor should be confident that each subject demonstrates complete familiarity with the test requirements prior to being tested.

EQUIPMENT AND SUPPLIES: Handballs, gloves, stop watch.

Accessories: Scoring and court marking materials.

Facilities and Space: Handball court or facility with similar wall and floor space.

Directions

THIRTY-SECOND VOLLEY: Standing behind the short line holding a handball, the subject, when designated to start, puts the ball into play with a toss to the front wall. He proceeds to volley the ball against the front wall as many times as possible within the thirty-second time period. The subject must hit each return from behind the short line. Hits do not count when the short line is violated or the ball has bounced more than once. If the subject loses control of the ball, another player in the court quickly tosses him another ball to be put back into play immediately. Either hand may be used.

FRONT WALL KILL WITH DOMINANT HAND: The subject assumes a position in the doubles service box against the left side wall if he is right-handed or the right side wall if left-handed. The tester or student assistant stands in the middle of the service zone and starts the trial by tossing the ball against the front wall so it rebounds to the right if the subject is right-handed and to the left if he is left-handed. As soon as the tester releases the ball, the subject is free to move, being sure to cross behind the tester to get into a better position for stroking the ball. Each subject is allowed five attempts to place the ball in a target area on the front wall.

BACK WALL KILL WITH DOMINANT HAND: The initial positioning of the subject is identical to the previously described front wall kill with dominant hand item. Positioning of the tester or student assistant is different since he is now stationed in the center of the court, 6 feet behind the short line.

The tester tosses the ball to the front wall so that it rebounds

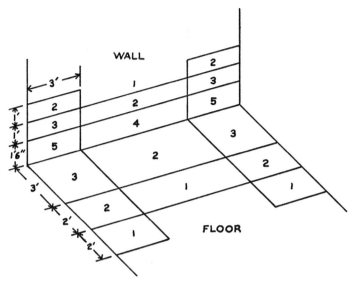

Figure 50. Markings for front wall kill test.

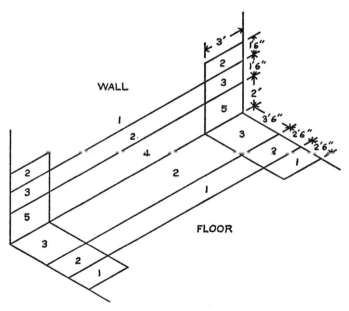

Figure 51. Markings for back wall kill test.

and bounces approximately 8 to 12 feet behind the short line and approximately 10 feet from the right side wall for a right-handed subject or 10 feet from the left side wall if the subject is left-handed. Experience has shown that the tester should aim for a spot between 15 and 18 feet high on the front wall for best results.

A bad toss does not have to be played by the test subject. As the tester tosses the ball, the subject may leave his starting position and move into a position that allows him to hit the ball with his dominant hand as the ball rebounds off the back wall. Each subject completes five trials.

SCORING METHOD

Thirty-Second Volley: Final score is the total number of legal hits made in the thirty-second trial.

Front Wall Kill with Dominant Hand: Total number of points accumulated on all five trials is the final score. The maximum number of points is twenty-five.

Back Wall Kill with Dominant Hand: Total number of points accumulated on all five trials with the maximum number of points being twenty-five.

Scientific Authenticity

Test data were derived from the skill item scores of sixty-four men enrolled in college handball classes. Each subject possessed at least one semester of handball experience.

VALIDITY: Coefficients of .87, .84, and .76 for the thirty-second volley, front wall kill with dominant hand, and back wall kill with dominant hand, respectively. The validity coefficient for the three-item battery was .92.

RELIABILITY: Coefficients of .82, .82, and .81 for the three items in their order of presentation above.

CRITERION MEASURE: Round-robin tournament results.

Additional Comments

The Tyson Test appears to be the most valuable handball skills test found in the literature today. Validity coefficients of the various test items show marked improvement upon those found for similar items in other handball skills tests. One might speculate that the higher validity coefficients resulted from the fact that participants in the Tyson study were experienced handball players.

Nevertheless, the Tyson Test rates highly in administrative feasibility in addition to the previously mentioned standards for scientific authentication. One area of possible improvement is that of test reliability. A structured practice drill for each subject immediately prior to testing may help to increase the reliability value. In reference to potential test reliability improvement, it is recommended that multiple trials on the thirty-second volley be given.

REFERENCES

1. Clarke, H. Harrison: *Application of Measurement to Health and Physical Education*, 5th ed. Englewood Cliffs, P-H, 1976.
2. Clevett, Melvin A.: All-round athletic championship. *Journal of Health and Physical Education*, 6:48, 1935.
3. Cornish, Clayton: A study of measurement of ability in handball. *Research Quarterly, 20:*215-222, 1949.
4. Edgren, Harry D. and Robinson, G. G.: *Individual Skill Tests in Physical Activities*. Chicago, the authors, 1937.
5. Friermood, Harold T.: A handball classification plan. *Journal of Health and Physical Education, 8:*106-107, 127, 1937.
6. Griffith, Malcolm A.: An Objective Method of Evaluating Ability in Handball Singles. Master's thesis, Columbus, The Ohio State University, 1960.
7. Leinbach, C. H.: The Development of Achievement Standards in Handball and Touch Football for Use in the Department of Physical Training for Men at the University of Texas. Master's thesis, Austin, The University of Texas, 1952.
8. Marsh, Jesse: A Study of Predictability of Ability in Handball. Master's thesis, Lubbock, Texas Tech University, 1972.
9. Mathews, Donald K.: *Measurement in Physical Education*, 4th ed. Philadelphia, Saunders, 1973.
10. McCachren, James R.: A Study of the University of Florida Handball Skill Test. Master's thesis, Chapel Hill, University of North Carolina, 1949.
11. Meyers, Carlton R.: *Measurement in Physical Education*, 2nd ed. New York, Ronald, 1974.
12. Millonzi, Frank: Development and Validation of a Handball Skill Test. Master's thesis, La Crosse, University of Wisconsin, 1972.
13. Montoye, Henry J. (Ed.): *An Introduction to Measurement in Physical Education*, vol. III. Indianapolis, Phi Epsilon Kappa Fraternity, 1970.

14. Montoye, Henry J. and Brotzman, J.: An investigation of the validity of using the results of a doubles tournament as a measure of handball ability. *Research Quarterly, 22:*214-218, 1951.
15. Pennington, G. Gary; Day, James A. P.; Drowatsky, John N.; and Hanson, John F.: A measure of handball ability. *Research Quarterly, 38:*247-253, 1967.
16. Phillips, Bernard E.: *Fundamental Handball.* New York, B&N, 1937.
17. Schiff, F. S.: A Test of Skills Performed in the Game Situation of Handball. Master's thesis, Columbus, The Ohio State University, 1938.
18. Simos, Thomas: A Handball Classification Test. Master's thesis, Springfield, Mass., Springfield College, 1952.
19. Tyson, Kenneth W.: A Handball Skill Test for College Men. Master's thesis, Austin, University of Texas, 1970.

Chapter 17

Ice Hockey

INTRODUCTION

THE FIRST ICE HOCKEY skills test was constructed in 1935,[2] but very little work has been done in this area since that time. Obviously, one reason for the lack of skills tests in ice hockey is the sport's limited offering in physical education programs on a nationwide basis. Ice hockey typifies a regional sport perhaps as much as any other sport included in the physical education curriculum.

The literature reveals only one skills test in ice hockey that meets the criteria of scientific authenticity. Consequently, instructors of skills classes in ice hockey have an excellent opportunity to make a contribution to sports skills measurement by devising authentic tests or subjecting existing ones to scientific analysis.

ITHACA ICE HOCKEY SKILL TESTS[7]

Also cited as Merrifield-Walford Ice Hockey Test.
Date: 1969.
Purpose: To measure the basic skills of ice hockey.

Description

The four-item battery includes the puck carry, forward skating speed test, backward skating speed test, and a skating agility item. The authors of the test concluded that the puck carry test was the best single-item test for general ice hockey playing ability. As implied by the item titles, the battery measures speed, agility, and puck control ability.

EDUCATIONAL APPLICATION: College men.

Administrative Feasibility

TIME: Two forty-minute class periods should be a realistic time allotment for testing a class of fifteen to twenty students.

PERSONNEL: The instructor and three trained student timers.

293

TRAINING INVOLVED: Single half-speed practice trials are suggested for each student in the puck carry and skating agility tests.

EQUIPMENT AND SUPPLIES: Adequate number of regulation ice hockey sticks and pucks, four stop watches, ten wooden obstacles, and one goal cage.

Accessories: Materials for construction of necessary ice markings in test battery; scoring materials.

Facilities and Space: An ice hockey rink.

Directions

FORWARD SKATING SPEED: The student faces the finish line with both feet behind the starting line. On the command *"Go,"* the subject skates the 120-foot distance as fast as possible (Fig. 52). Two trials are administered.

BACKWARD SKATING SPEED: Same as the forward skating speed test item except the student starts with his back to the starting line and skates backwards.

SKATING AGILITY: Figure 53 illustrates the ice markings and

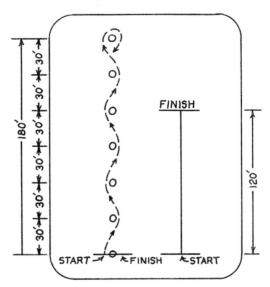

Figure 52. Ice markings for speed tests and puck carry. From H. H. Merrifield and G. A. Walford, Battery of ice hockey skill tests, *Research Quarterly, 40:*146-152, 1969. Courtesy of AAHPER.

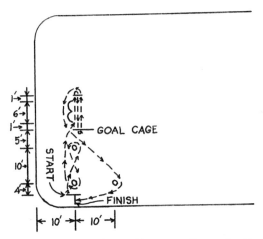

Figure 53. Ice markings for skating agility test. From H. H. Merrifield and G. A. Walford, Battery of ice hockey skill tests, *Research Quarterly, 40:* 146-152, 1969. Courtesy of AAHPER.

obstacle locations for the skating agility test. The wooden obstacles are the same size as those described for the puck carry test. On the starting signal, the subject skates to the left of the first obstacle and loops the second by passing it on the right, then returns to skate around the first obstacle on the way to the 4-foot line in front of the goal cage. The subject stops at the line and then continues on to the next 4-foot line. The stop-start action is repeated at the second 4-foot line. The subject completes the course by passing behind the goal cage and skating around the last obstacle while on the way performing a turn to skate backwards, skating backwards, and a turn to skate forward.

Each subject is allowed a half-speed trial prior to testing. Two test trials are permitted.

PUCK CARRY: The student assumes a position immediately behind the 4-foot start-finish line while the puck is placed on the line at the left of the first obstacle. On the starting signal, the subject passes to the right of the first obstacle and continues an alternating pattern until the test is completed.

As illustrated in Figure 52, seven wooden obstacles are placed on the ice in a straight line at 30-foot intervals. The obstacles are

30 inches high on a 2 × 4-inch base. The puck must be controlled by the subject during the test and the knockdown of two or more obstacles constitutes a violation; if either violation occurs, the test must be repeated.

A half-speed practice trial is permitted. Two test trials are administered.

Scoring Method

Forward Skating Speed: The better of two trial times to the nearest one-tenth of a second from the starting signal until the subject reaches the finish line.

Backward Skating Speed: Same as above except subject starts with back to finish line and skates backwards.

Skating Agility: Same as in forward skating speed test.

Puck Carry: Same as above.

Scientific Authenticity

VALIDITY: Validity coefficients of .83, .79, .75, and .96 were obtained for the respective test items. Fifteen members of the Ithaca College Hockey Club served as subjects.

RELIABILITY: The respective test item reliability coefficients were .74, .80, .94, and .93.

CRITERION MEASURE: A hockey coach's ranking of playing ability.

Additional Comments

A test item trial is repeated when a subject falls. Also, the hockey stick should be carried below shoulder level with both hands for all items.

The Ithaca Ice Hockey Skill Tests should be retested for validity and reliability values since only fifteen subjects participated in the original study to authenticate the test. The apparent value of the test would be more firmly substantiated if similar coefficients of correlation were obtained when using a significantly larger number of subjects.

Merrifield and Walford experimented with shooting and passing items in their study but eliminated them from the final battery because low reliability coefficients resulted. They indicated that the requirement of a large number of trials should produce an acceptable reliability value for a shooting test.

REFERENCES

1. Bovard, John F. and Cozens, Frederick W.: *Tests and Measurements in Physical Education,* 2nd ed. Philadelphia, Saunders, 1938.
2. Brown, Harriett M.: The game of ice hockey. *Journal of Health and Physical Education, 6:*28-30, 1935.
3. Clarke, H. Harrison: *Application of Measurement to Health and Physical Education,* 2nd ed. Englewood Cliffs, P-H, 1950.
4. Doroschuk, E. V. and Marcotte, G. E.: An Agility Test for Screening Ice Hockey Players. Sixteenth Biennial Convention Report of the Canadian Association for Health, Physical Education and Recreation, Toronto, 1965.
5. Glassow, Ruth B. and Broer, Marion R.: *Measuring Achievement in Physical Education.* Philadelphia, Saunders, 1938.
6. Hache, Roland E.: An Achievement Test in Ice Hockey. Master's thesis, Amherst, University of Massachusetts, 1967.
7. Merrifield, H. H. and Walford, Gerald A.: Battery of ice hockey skill tests. *Research Quarterly, 40:*146-152, 1969.
8. Meyers, Carlton R.: *Measurement in Physical Education,* 2nd ed. New York, Ronald, 1974.
9. Montoye, Henry J. (Ed.): *An Introduction to Measurement in Physical Education,* vol. III. Indianapolis, Phi Epsilon Kappa Fraternity, 1970.

Chapter 18

Lacrosse

INTRODUCTION

L ACROSSE IS NOT a new activity in the American sports scene since it was played by several of the American Indian tribes as early as the 1800s. Yet throughout the period of growth and development of physical education in the American educational system, the sport has never attained nationwide popularity. Even in those geographical regions where lacrosse is included in the physical education curriculum, its offering is limited primarily to the secondary school level.

The sport is also more popular among females than males. It has been included in the public and private secondary school physical education programs for girls in the northeastern United States for many years. In recent years, participation in lacrosse has started to spread slowly into the southern and mideastern states, with an increasing number of schools and colleges beginning to offer the activity in the physical education instructional program. There is also some evidence that males are starting to participate more widely in lacrosse.

Few skills tests for lacrosse appear in the literature, none of which more than marginally meets the feasibility criteria for scientific documentation. The most acceptable test thus far for measuring lacrosse playing ability was developed by Hodges.[3] A lacrosse skills tests study yet to be published is presently being conducted by the National Association for Girls and Women in Sports as part of the National Sports Skills Test Project of the American Alliance for Health, Physical Education and Recreation. The study includes eight lacrosse related test items with each reportedly measuring a specific skill.

HODGES LACROSSE TEST[3]

Date: 1967.

Purpose: To objectively measure selected lacrosse playing skills.

298

Description

Three lacrosse skills items were included in the original test, but only the wall volley and pickup-dodge-turn-run tests are presented here since the shooting accuracy item failed the test of scientific authenticity.

Wall Volley: The wall volley test is designed to specifically measure throwing and catching ability. A 15-foot line is drawn 6 feet above and parallel to the base of a wall. Another line of the same length is placed on the floor 10½ feet from the wall.

Pickup-Dodge-Turn-Run: This item measures ball control ability. An outdoor field is marked off with a 15-foot starting line (A) and a 15-foot turning line (B) that is 75 feet from and parallel to the starting line (Fig. 54). A ball is placed 30 feet away from the starting line between lines A and B. An obstacle, formed by placing one chair upon another, is placed 20 feet from the ball, closer to line B. Two more obstacles are placed 6½ feet from the first obstacle and each other, making a total of three obstacles. Line B is located 12 feet from the last obstacle.

EDUCATIONAL APPLICATION: College women.

Administrative Feasibility

TIME: Two sixty-minute class periods for a class of twenty students.

PERSONNEL: Scorer and timer with student assistants serving as line and turn judges.

TRAINING INVOLVED: To enhance the reliability value of the test, student practice prior to the test date is encouraged. Practice trials immediately preceding the test administration are not recommended by the test developer for either item.

EQUIPMENT AND SUPPLIES: Lacrosse sticks, balls, bucket, two stop watches, and six chairs.

Accessories: Line marking materials for wall and floor, plus scoring materials.

Facilities and Space: Wall and floor space of sufficient size to administer the wall volley item and an outdoor playing area slightly larger than 75 × 15 feet in size for the pickup-dodge-turn-run test.

Directions

WALL VOLLEY: The subject takes a position behind the restraining line with a ball in her crosse. On an audible signal, she throws the ball against the wall above the wall line and attempts to catch it on the return. This action is repeated for sixty seconds.

The ball must be thrown from behind the restraining line, but the subject may step over the line to catch the ball. If the ball is lost, the subject should quickly get another ball from the bucket and continue the test. The test consists of three trials, but not in consecutive order. No practice trials are given.

PICKUP-DODGE-TURN-RUN: Standing behind line A with a crosse in her hand, the student when signaled quickly runs forward, scoops up the ball, and proceeds toward the first obstacle. She then dodges the first obstacle on either side and continues dodging in and out among all three obstacles. After dodging the last obstacle, the subject runs to line B and either steps on or beyond it, then turns and runs back through the obstacles, continuing on to line A. The subject must be carrying the ball in the crosse when the finish line is crossed. If the ball is dropped at any point on the course, the subject should simply scoop it up and proceed on from that point.

Three trials are given, but they should not be consecutive. Should an obstacle be overturned, the subject should continue if possible; otherwise, the trial must be repeated. No practice trials are given.

SCORING METHOD

Wall Volley: The final score of the test is the sum of scores on

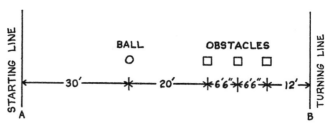

Figure 54. Field markings for pickup-dodge-turn-run test.

the three trials. Each trial score is the total number of hits made in sixty seconds. A hit counts one point only when the subject throws the ball from behind the restraining line and the ball hits the wall on or above the wall line.

The wall volley test scores in the Hodges study ranged from 107 to 15 with a mean score of 68 and a standard deviation of 19.

Pickup-Dodge-Turn-Run: The final score is the amount of time required for the subject to negotiate the course from the starting signal until the finish line is crossed. Only the better of three trials is counted. In the study by Hodges, the better time of three trials ranged from 12 to 19.3 seconds with a mean time of 14 seconds and a standard deviation of 1.1 seconds.

Scientific Authenticity

The wall volley item was administered to 135 college freshmen women enrolled in five beginning lacrosse classes while 133 students at that level completed the pickup-dodge-turn-run test.

VALIDITY: Validity coefficient of .40 for the wall volley item and .47 for the pickup-dodge-turn-run test.

RELIABILITY: Reliability coefficient of .88 for the wall volley item and .85 for the pickup-dodge-turn-run test.

CRITERION MEASURE: Judges' ratings.

Additional Comments

Both items in the Hodges Lacrosse Test show impressive reliability values, but the validity values leave something to be desired. From observation, however, it would appear that the wall volley test demonstrates face validity.

REFERENCES

1. Barrett, Kate A.: A lacrosse test for general ability. Unpublished study. In Montoye, Henry J. (Ed.): *An Introduction to Measurement in Physical Education,* vol. III. Indianapolis, Phi Epsilon Kappa Fraternity, 1970.
2. Barrow, Harold M. and McGee, Rosemary: *A Practical Approach to Measurement in Physical Education,* 2nd ed. Philadelphia, Lea & Febiger, 1971.
3. Hodges, Carolyn V.: Construction of an Objective Knowledge Test and

Skill Tests in Lacrosse for College Women. Master's thesis, Greensboro, University of North Carolina, 1967.

4. Lutze, Margaret C.: Achievement Tests in Beginning Lacrosse for Women. Master's thesis, Iowa City, State University of Iowa, 1963.

5. McGowan, Nancy: A skill test for the overarm pass. *Crosse Checks, 1:* 23-24, 1965.

6. Montoye, Henry J. (Ed.): *An Introduction to Measurement in Physical Education,* vol. III. Indianapolis, Phi Epsilon Kappa Fraternity, 1970.

7. Waglow, I. F. and Moore, Alan: A lacrosse skill test. *Athletic Journal, 34:*4, 1954.

8. Wilke, Barbara J.: Achievement Tests for Selected Lacrosse Skills of College Women. Master's thesis, Greensboro, University of North Carolina, 1967.

Chapter 19

Racquetball–Paddleball–Squash

INTRODUCTION

S PORTS SKILLS TESTS apparently do not exist for either racquetball, paddleball, or squash. This is especially noteworthy since racquetball and paddleball are obvious offshoots of handball, a sport for which several quality tests have been developed.

Instructors of these racquet sports have evidently made heavy use of round-robin tournaments in lieu of skills tests for input in the evaluation of skill performance. Skills tests should be developed for each of the sports because they are conducive to the construction of performance standards that have potential application to each class taught in a specific sport. A round-robin tournament ranking gives indication of a student's skill performance level only in relation to the performance of his classmates.

A discussion of the above mentioned racquet sports follows which includes the possible reasons why a skills tests void exists for each. The sports are presented in their order of chronological development.

SQUASH

Squash originated in England nearly 200 years ago and has become a very popular sport in several countries throughout the world. The sport has never generated widespread interest in America as evidenced by its limited offering in public school and college physical education programs. Squash courts in the United States are primarily limited to the larger universities and community organizations such as the Young Men's Christian Association. The facility limitation naturally contributes to the small amount of participation. Also, the uniqueness of the court design prohibits the play of a related wall sport, which is not true of handball, paddleball, and racquetball. The fast moving pace of squash requires a good deal of time for the learner to master the fundamental skills. As a result, it is played almost exclusively by males.

303

PADDLEBALL

Paddleball is classified as a racquet sport even though it is played with a paddle. Introduced in the United States in the 1930s, the sport reached its popularity height during the 1950s and the 1960s. It can be played on a regulation handball court, and the rules and regulations are very similar to handball. Paddleball is a slower moving game than either racquetball or squash and is played by both sexes of a wide age range. At the beginning skill level, the game is not as demanding as squash.

Despite all the positive features of paddleball, its popularity has waned considerably since the advent of racquetball. Nevertheless, the amount of participation in the sport still appears to be significant and has stabilized in recent years.

RACQUETBALL

Racquetball evolved as a spin-off of paddleball in the 1960s and its popularity growth in such a short period of time is perhaps unprecedented in the history of physical education. Unlike squash, the fast moving sport attracts the interest of females as well as males, although it is still considered to be predominantly a male's sport.

The absence of racquetball skills tests is surprising in consideration of its tremendous surge in popularity among American people. The situation provides one of the most lucrative and timely opportunities for the physical educator interested in contributing to sports skills tests literature. It seems to be only a matter of time until skills tests for the sport start to surface.

REFERENCES

1. Allsen, Philip E. and Witbeck, Alan: *Racquetball/Paddleball.* Dubuque, Iowa, Brown Bk, 1972.
2. Clarke, H. Harrison: *Application of Measurement to Health and Physical Education.* Englewood Cliffs, P-H, 1945.
3. Edgren, Harry D. and Robinson, G. G.: *Individual Skill Tests in Physical Activities.* Chicago, the authors, 1937.
4. Fleming, A. William and Bloom, Joel A.: *Paddleball and Racquetball.* Pacific Palisades, Calif., Goodyear, 1973.
5. Meyers, Carlton R. and Blesh, T. Erwin: *Measurement in Physical Education.* New York, Ronald, 1962.
6. Varner, Margaret and Bramall, Norman B.: *Squash Racquets.* Dubuque, Iowa, Brown Bk, 1967.

Chapter 20

Snow Skiing

INTRODUCTION

S NOW SKIING is a very popular activity in those regions of the country that are conducive to extreme cold weather and snow. It is enjoyed annually by millions of avid skiers, many of which have no exposure to formal instruction.

Snow skiing classes are restricted in number nationally due to the sport's limited geographic appeal. The usual correlation between number of classes offered and number of skills tests available holds true for snow skiing. Few tests had been constructed (with none of an objective nature) until the mid-1950s.

Minaert[3] conducted an earlier study to determine the value of dry-skiing when applying the learned skills to actual snow skiing. Results of the study definitely indicated that skiing skills classes need not be limited to the northern United States, and that a course in dry-skiing is advantageous to a beginning skier. Subjects completing dry-skiing classes before skiing on snow attained acceptable standards of achievement in less time than those enrolled only in the classes conducted on snow-covered slopes.

ROGERS SKIING TEST[4]

Date: 1954.

Purpose: To objectively measure selected skills of beginning skiers.

Description

Rogers concluded that beginning skiers find it necessary to climb hills of varying steepness, to change direction, to turn at various angles, and to slow speeds or to stop quickly. Based on this information, four tests were designed to measure the ability to execute climbing, sideslipping, turning, and stopping skills. The sideslipping test was never administered since it was discovered that most beginning skiers are unable to perform the skill. Test items for climbing, turning, and stopping were developed.

Climbing: The climbing test should be set up on a hill with a

305

convex curve that increases in steepness as the skier climbs. There should be a level space 25 feet in length at the base of the slope.

Turning: A slalom course consisting of six turns located at varying distances is set on a ski slope that is comparable to a beginners' slope at most public ski areas. A ski area approximately 130 feet in length and 45 feet in width is needed for this particular test. Open gates are set with a minimum distance of 10 feet and a maximum distance of 20 feet behind them.

Stopping: The ski slope for the snowplow stopping test should have the same steepness and contour as a typical slope for beginners.

EDUCATIONAL APPLICATION: Designed for high school boys and girls but is also applicable for college men and women.

Administrative Feasibility

TIME: The three-item battery can be administered to a class of twenty students in three sixty-minute periods.

PERSONNEL: Timer-recorder, finish judge, and point judges.

TRAINING INVOLVED: The battery should be administered late in the term for a beginners' class to assure that the students are thoroughly familiar with each item prior to testing.

EQUIPMENT AND SUPPLIES: Fourteen to sixteen ski slalom poles, stop watch, skis, and ski poles as needed.

Accessories: Scoring materials.

Facilities and Space: A ski area roughly the same size and showing a similar degree of difficulty as that normally associated with a beginning ski slope at a public ski facility.

Directions

CLIMBING: To start the test, each skier stands below the starting gate with his ski tips behind the first gate. On an audible signal, the subject proceeds to walk to the first gate, step turn to the right and half step to gate number two. Then he does a kick turn and half step to gate three; a herringbone to gate four; step turn to the left; side step to gate five; and completes a kick turn and side step with the left ski leading until he passes through the last gate.

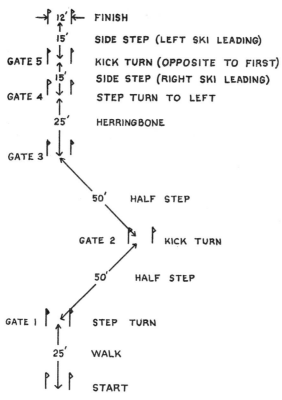

Figure 55. Specifications for climbing test.

Ski poles should be used with proper climbing techniques. If a skier fails to use the poles correctly while doing the herringbone, one point is deducted. Should the skier fall, he should quickly get up and continue the test. The only penalty for falling is the time lost. A subject is called back to the last gate passed and asked to repeat a particular skill when the original is incorrectly performed. Flags should be used to mark the distances between gates as indicated in Figure 55.

TURNING: The skier assumes a starting position with the ski tips behind the first gate. When an audible signal is given, the skier immediately heads for the first slalom gate located 30 feet

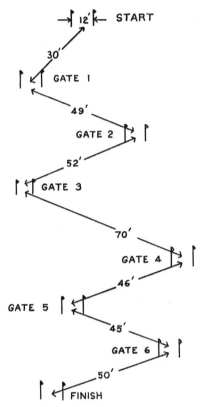

Figure 56. Slope markings for turning test.

away and proceeds to ski through all six gates as rapidly as possible (Fig. 56).

STOPPING: The subject positions his ski tips behind the starting gate. On the audible signal, the skier proceeds to ski straight down the fall line for 30 feet. When the tips of the skis reach the first 30-foot line, the skier immediately begins to execute a snowplow stop. He should come to a complete stop as quickly as possible.

Each skier is given three trials. If the subject falls or begins stopping before reaching the line, a repeat trial is given.

SCORING METHOD

Climbing: Two scoring devices are used with the climbing test. One method is the total time taken by the skier to climb the

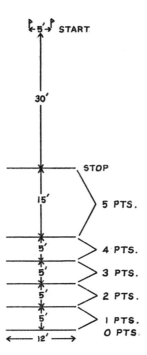

Figure 57. Specifications for stopping test.

course, starting with the audible starting signal and ending when the skier passes through the last gate. Each subject is given two trials, with only the best trial counted.

The other method is a point score. Each subject starts with ten points at the beginning of each trial, and one point is deducted each time the skier falls, slips, or does not use the technique required.

Since the time scores were found to be more reliable than the point scores in the Rogers study, the former method is considered the better scoring device for measuring the ability to climb.

Turning: Only one scoring method is used in this test. Each skier is awarded nine points at the beginning of each trial, with two trials given. Should the skier fall while making a turn through a gate, two points are deducted. If the subject should fall after completing a turn or during a traverse, one point is deducted. Both trials are counted.

Stopping: Two scoring devices may be used with the stopping test. Each skier is timed from the second his ski tips reach the first 30-foot line until he comes to a complete stop. Each trial may also be scored on a point basis, depending on the distance it takes the skier to stop. One point is lost for each 5-foot line crossed (see Fig. 57). The location of the ski tips determines the value of the stop. The point system is the recommended method of scoring as it proved more reliable than the time method.

Scientific Authenticity

VALIDITY: The test was given to fifty-three high school students who had completed seven hours of instruction in a beginning ski class. Face validity was claimed for each item.

RELIABILITY: For the climbing item, a coefficient of .80 was obtained. In administering multiple trials for each subject, the sums of the time scores of the first two trials were correlated with the time score sums of the last two trials.

Utilizing a correlation of the first and last two trial scores of the subjects, a .87 coefficient was found for the turning item. The first and last three trial scores were correlated for the stopping item, producing a .87 coefficient.

OBJECTIVITY: Consistency among judges in scoring the three test items was impressive. The coefficients ranged .94–1.0 on the climbing item, .99–1.0 for the turning test, and .84–1.0 for the stopping item.

Additional Comments

Each item is recommended for use as either a motivation or practice device. The climbing and stopping items may be used for grading purposes, but the turning item failed to satisfactorily discriminate the ability levels of participants in the study.

Instructors of snow skiing might find the item more discriminatory if the gate opening was narrowed somewhat or the gates were placed at various angles. Adding a time factor in the scoring method may improve the validity value of the item.

In ease of administration, the stopping test rates higher than the other two items. That item also produced a wider distribution of scores.

Overall, the battery seems satisfactory for measuring the skill of beginning skiers. In developing norms for the test items, snow conditions and slope difficulty are important factors to consider. Temperature, time of day, and equipment used should also be considered as norms are developed and, furthermore, when the scores of succeeding groups are compared to those norms.

STREET SKIING TEST[6]

Date: 1957.

Purpose: To measure general ability in downhill skiing.

Description

By interviewing eleven certified ski instructors and in utilizing numerous textbooks, Street surmised that the important basic motor elements in ski performance are balance, coordination, strength, power, reaction time, and endurance. These elements combined with the fundamental motor skills of jumping, climbing, rotating, ski-edge control, weight control, and pushing provided the basis of an objective ski performance test. The basic skiing skills selected for inclusion in the test were the kick turn, snowplow turn, stem turn, sideslip, and the parallel turn.

The skiing performance test was divided into two segments, the short course and the long course. Run at a 90-degree angle with the fall line directly across the base of the hill, the short course, or agility course, is only skied by the less competent skiers. The long course is for the better skiers; it involves a slalom around five poles and also includes the agility course across the bottom of the hill.

EDUCATIONAL APPLICATION: College men and women.

Administrative Feasibility

TIME: One class of twenty students can easily be tested in one sixty-minute period.

PERSONNEL: Two timer-recorders.

TRAINING INVOLVED: Before the course is skied for time, each participant must first ski an evaluative or subjective course so he can be properly evaluated and categorized according to level of ability. Any number of judges or evaluators may be used; Street initially used a panel of four, including himself, but later found that only one was needed. Each subject is classified into one of six ability groups.

The evaluation course should be the same slope used for the regular performance testing, except a wide open, six-gate slalom is utilized. Each subject is instructed to ski down the hill between the poles using his best form. Any turn may be used, but the more advanced the turn, the higher the rating. The measurement criterion for the evaluation course is form as opposed to speed.

Each subject receives a group classification based on the following criteria:

Group 1–Rank beginner; unable to ski the course.

Group 2–Demonstrates an uncontrolled snowplow; cannot complete the course standing up.

Group 3–Demonstrates controlled snowplow turns; able to complete the full course.

Group 4–Uses stem turns to ski the course.

Group 5–Uses stem christies, or poor, jerky unbalanced parallel christies.

Group 6–Uses linked parallel christies with rhythm, ease, and proficiency.

After the subjective tests are completed, all subjects with a score of three or higher are grouped at the start of the long course. Those receiving a rating of two or below are instructed to only ski the short course.

EQUIPMENT AND SUPPLIES: Seventeen slalom poles of 9 feet in length, marking flags (5 red, 4 blue, 6 yellow), two stop watches, a 50-foot measuring tape, and an inclinometer.

Accessories: Scoring materials.

Facilities and Space: Ski area of approximately 110 square feet with a slope of 25 to 30 percent grade. A flat terrain is necessary at the base of the ski slope.

Directions

Upon leaving the starting gate each subject follows the course illustrated in Figure 58. On the long course, the subject is required to ski to the left of the first pole and alternately right and left of poles two, three, four, and five. In skiing around pole five it is necessary to perform an uphill christianna turn in order to start across the lower portion of the course and stay to the uphill side of gate six. Continuing across the base of the hill, the subject is required to ski below pole seven, above pole eight, below pole nine, above pole ten, below pole eleven, then perform a kick turn or step turn and start back in the opposite direction above pole eleven and below pole ten.

From this point the skier follows the same course as in the other direction, ending through the finish gate.

The short course starts at pole five and follows the same course from that point to the finish gate. Skiers are allowed to use their poles at any time during the run.

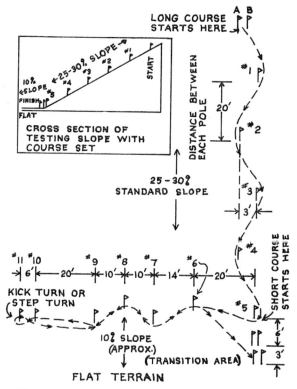

Figure 58. Slope markings for Street Skiing Test.

The poles for the long and short course should be measured and arranged according to the following placement:

1. Set the red flag pole five at the bottom right side of the hill in accordance with Figure 58.

2. Set the red flag poles three and one in direct line uphill with pole five and 40 feet apart.

3. Offset the blue flag poles two and four at 3 feet to the left and 20 feet between poles one and three. Then set the unmarked starting gate with pole B in direct line with poles two and four. Pole A should be inserted 2½ feet to the left of pole B.

4. Return to pole five and measure 6 feet downhill in direct line with poles one, three, and five. Insert two yellow flags beside each other at this spot and also insert two other yellow flags beside each other 3 feet farther directly downhill. These four yellow flags mark the finish gate and eliminate confusion when describing the course. Thus, poles one, three, five and the four yellow finish flags are in alignment directly on the fall line of the hill with poles two and four offset to the left.

5. Measuring from pole five, poles seven (red), nine (red), and ten and eleven (both yellow) are placed at the distances indicated in direct alignment across the base of the hill.

6. Blue pole eight is placed on a 2-foot offset from this alignment and blue pole six is inserted on a 3-foot offset from this same alignment. In looking across the hill, poles five, seven, nine, ten, and eleven are in a direct line with poles six and eight offset uphill.

7. Check the alignments from pole five both up the hill and across the hill.

Each subject stands at the starting gate with his feet positioned behind the starting line. The start is initiated on an audible signal of *"three, two, one, go,"* and each skier then proceeds to ski around the poles as previously described. Only one subject skis the course at a time.

It is suggested that one tester position himself at the starting gate of either the long or short course to start and time each subject. A second timer may be stationed at pole five to record the time the subject takes to go from this pole to the finish gate on the long course.

SCORING METHOD: The performance of each skier is measured to the nearest tenth-second. A subject is penalized five seconds for any turn not made or for crossing any pole on the wrong side.

In Street's study, the mean score achieved by the men that skied the long course was 50.8 seconds, and the mean for the short course was 40.1 seconds. For the women the mean score of the long course was 60.2 and 56.4 for the short course.

Scientific Authenticity

The test was administered to 102 male and eighty female skiers enrolled in college skiing classes.

VALIDITY: The validity was determined by correlating the objective score on the performance test and the subjective judgment of skiing skill. The resulting coefficients were as follows: .76–men's long course; .62–men's short course; .94–women's long course; .71–women's short course.

RELIABILITY: Reliability coefficients were derived over a period of one week for each skiing performance course and were as follows: .67–men's long course; .80–men's short course; .93–women's long course; .80–women's short course.

CRITERION MEASURE: Judges' ratings of skiing skill.

Additional Comments

Many variables could affect the student's score on the performance test. Factors such as the bumps in the skiing terrain, temperature, snow conditions, and the time of day should be maintained as constant as possible to insure a fair testing of subjects.

It is suggested that each tester carefully select a smooth 25- to 30-degree slope. Also, testing during the same time each day helps to stabilize the temperature; furthermore, a powdery consistency is preferred for the snow.

REFERENCES

1. Briggs, Laurence: The Boy Scout Skiing Merit Badge. Master's thesis, Amherst, University of Massachusetts, 1938.
2. Meyers, Carlton R.: *Measurement in Physical Education,* 2nd ed. New York, Ronald, 1974.
3. Minaert, Walter A.: An analysis of the value of dry-skiing in learning selected skiing skills. *Research Quarterly, 21:*47-52, 1950.
4. Rogers, Marilyn H.: Construction of Objectively Scored Skill Tests for

Beginning Skiers. Master's thesis, Seattle, University of Washington, 1954.
5. Safrit, Margaret J.: *Evaluation in Physical Education.* Englewood Cliffs, P-H, 1973.
6. Street, Richard H.: Measurement of Achievement in Skiing. Master's thesis, Salt Lake City, University of Utah, 1957.
7. Wolfe, J. E. and H. H. Merrifield: Predictability of Beginning Skiing Success from Basic Skill Tests in College Age Females. Paper read before the Annual Convention of the American Association for Health, Physical Education and Recreation, Detroit, April, 1971.

Chapter 21

Soccer

INTRODUCTION

SOCCER IS AN ESTABLISHED coeducational activity in many American public schools and colleges, yet in other educational institutions the sport is nonexistent. In the past its popularity was concentrated in certain areas of the country, but today the sport is becoming more national in scope as evidenced by the rapid increase of both amateur and professional teams. There is also a notable growth in number of soccer spectators.

The physical attributes required to play the game place a natural limitation on the number of participants it attracts. They include a high level of foot-eye coordination and cardiovascular endurance or stamina; the foot-eye coordination requirement especially creates a problem for American youth since they have been oriented toward activities that require mainly hand-eye coordination.

Soccer skills tests were among the earliest to be developed. Several were constructed as early as the 1920s, and the first scientifically devised soccer skills test was completed in 1932.[11] As customary, most of the early tests were in the form of multiple-item batteries and were not scientifically documented. More recent tests focus on the measurement of a single item which combines two or three basic soccer skills.

An exception to the recent trend toward construction of single item tests is the Crew Soccer Test.[9] It merits recognition because of its impressive validity value. Coefficients of .96, .95, .92, and .88 were derived for the ball control, aerial accuracy, dribbling, and wall volley items, respectively.

BONTZ SOCCER TEST[3]

Date: 1942.

Purpose: To determine general soccer ability.

Description

The Bontz Soccer Test is an extension of the Schaufele[28] study which was completed approximately two years earlier. A combination skill of dribbling, passing, and shooting the soccer ball is measured in the Bontz Test. This is repeated a total of eight times, four with each foot.

A 6-foot starting line is constructed parallel to the center of the 18-foot soccer goal and is located 55 yards away (Fig. 59). A 25-yard restraining line is marked from the left end of the starting line toward the goal line. Located 12 feet to the left of this restraining line is a permanent or temporary wall, 12 feet in length and 30 inches in height. The center of the wall area is situated directly opposite the end of the 25-yard line. Another restraining line is placed 6 yards from and parallel to the goal line. The field markings are needed for both the right and left foot, as indicated in Figure 59.

If a stationary wall is used, a new marking with the goal line as the starting point and the starting point as the goal line should be made. A temporary wall can easily be constructed. Three locker room benches placed on their sides and stacked on top of each other make a very functional wall, providing they are braced properly. The wall or benches may be outlined with paint or tape to provide a more visible target area for the students.

EDUCATIONAL APPLICATION: Fifth and sixth grade boys and girls.

Administrative Feasibility

TIME: A class of twenty students can be tested in two sixty-minute class periods.

PERSONNEL: One timer-recorder.

TRAINING INVOLVED: Two practice trials with each foot are allowed immediately prior to testing.

EQUIPMENT AND SUPPLIES: Soccer balls, two soccer goals, stop watch, and three benches (if permanent wall is not used).

Accessories: Scoring and field marking materials.

Facilities and Space: Outdoor playing field at least 60 yards in length and 20 yards wide.

Directions

On an audible starting signal, the subject dribbles the ball from the starting line to a point where it is kicked with the right foot diagonally against the wall while all the time staying to the right of the 25-yard restraining line. The kick is executed as though the subject is passing to a teammate. After recovering the rebounded ball, the subject continues the dribble while moving closer to the goal. The ball must be kicked for goal before the 6-yard restraining line is crossed. The sequence of dribble, kick, recovery, dribble, and kick is executed as quickly as possible without losing control of the ball. Four test trials with each foot are required for score. Test trials which include errors must be repeated.

SCORING METHOD: The amount of time that elapses between the starting signal and the instant the ball crosses the goal constitutes a trial. The final score is the total amount of time, recorded

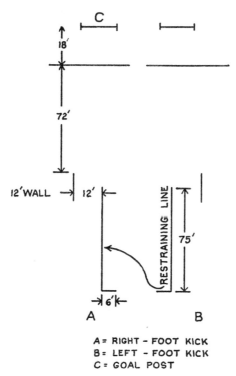

A = RIGHT - FOOT KICK
B = LEFT - FOOT KICK
C = GOAL POST

Figure 59. Field markings for Bontz Soccer Test.

to the nearest half-second, the subject requires to complete the eight trials. Each trial is timed separately.

The range of scores for the fifth grade students was 95.5 to 226.5 seconds with a median time of 139.2. The scores of the sixth grade students ranged from 90.0 to 191.0 seconds with a median time of 130.3 seconds. The range for girls only was 102.5 to 226.5 seconds with a median time of 143.4 while the same statistics for boys were 90.0, 198.0, and 126.7 seconds.

Scientific Authenticity

One hundred and twenty-four fifth and sixth grade students provided the test data in the study. Two separate groups, one containing ninety-two subjects and the other thirty-two, participated.

VALIDITY: Validity values of .92 and .53 were computed for the large and small groups, respectively.

RELIABILITY: Reliability coefficients of .93 and .96 were determined by use of the odd-even method and corrected by the Spearman-Brown Formula.

CRITERION MEASURE: Subjective rating.

Additional Comments

Although the Bontz Soccer Test receives high marks according to test feasibility criteria, it appears to have some limitations. Considerable time is required to prepare the testing area, and the potentially needed benches are not always readily accessible. Also, eight trials must be completed for score as a mistrial results in a retrial. Undue fatigue in some individuals could bias the test score results of a particular class.

MCDONALD SOCCER TEST[20]

Also cited as McDonald Volleying Soccer Test.

Date: 1951.

Purpose: To serve as an index of game performance and to be utilized as both a classification and prognostic tool.

Description

The McDonald Soccer Test is a result of the first effort to develop an objective means of measuring general soccer ability through a single skill item as opposed to a skills test battery as used in the past.

This test requires a subject to volley or kick a soccer ball from behind a 9-foot restraining line to a kickboard as many times as possible in a thirty-second time period. The kickboard is 30 feet wide and 11½ feet high. A restraining line is drawn 9 feet from and parallel to the kickboard.

EDUCATIONAL APPLICATION: College men.

Administrative Feasibility

TIME: A class of twenty students can be tested in one sixty-minute time period.

PERSONNEL: One scorer-recorder.

TRAINING INVOLVED: A brief warm-up should be allowed, but practice trials are unnecessary since the best three of four trials are counted for score.

EQUIPMENT AND SUPPLIES: Kickboard, soccer balls, stop watch.

Accessories: Scoring and field marking materials.

Facilities and Space: A flat, unobstructed outdoor area such as a soccer field.

Directions

The test begins on an audible signal with the subject proceeding to kick the soccer ball against the kickboard as many times as possible in a thirty-second time period. Any type kick or any body part may be used to control the ball on the rebound, including the hands. In order to be counted, each ball must be kicked from the ground while the supporting leg and the soccer ball are behind the restraining line.

Three soccer balls are used during the actual testing, each being inflated to 13 pounds. One ball is placed on the restraining line to be used initially. The other two balls are placed 9 feet behind the restraining line in the center of the test area. In the event of a wild kick or a lost ball, the subject may either retrieve the original ball or one of the remaining balls and put it in play as rapidly as possible with the only penalty being the kicking time lost during the recovery process.

SCORING METHOD: The test subject receives one point each time the ball hits the kickboard within the thirty-second time period, providing the kick is made from the ground while the supporting leg and the ball are located behind the restraining line. A total of four trials is given with the best three counted.

Scientific Authenticity

VALIDITY: Fifty-three college soccer players from three varsity levels participated in the study. A validity coefficient of .85 was obtained by correlating the subjective ratings of three coaches against the test scores.

RELIABILITY: Not reported.

CRITERION MEASURE: Subjective ratings of three coaches.

Additional Comments

This test may be given either indoors or outdoors, although outdoor testing is recommended. Instead of constructing a kickboard, a gymnasium wall area with the same dimensions could be marked off for testing.

It is recommended that each subject be given a rest between kicking trials so fatigue will not hinder test performance.

A vote of confidence in the value of the McDonald Test came from modifications by Mitchell[23] and Johnson.[14] Both tests show an improvement over the original one, according to scientific authenticity standards. The Mitchell Test presentation follows in this chapter. Since the Johnson study is so similar to the McDonald format, only a discussion of their differences is included:

1. Backboard size in the Johnson Test was changed to the same size as a regulation soccer goal, which is 8 feet high and 24 feet wide.
2. Restraining line was moved back to 15 feet.
3. Ball may be kicked on the fly as well as the ground.
4. Soccer balls used as extras were moved back to 15 feet behind the restraining line.
5. Only three trials are given with the sum reflecting the score.
6. Ball must be played according to soccer rules, which means the use of hands or arms is disallowed.

TABLE LXXVIII

GRADING SCALE FOR JOHNSON SOCCER TEST

Level	Number of Hits
Superior	42 & over
Good	37 - 41
Average	31 - 36
Below Average	25 - 30
Poor	24 & below

In a study involving physical education majors, varsity players, and students from physical education classes, the Johnson Test fared well in scientific authenticity as demonstrated by validity and reliability coefficients of .85 and .92, respectively. This particular test is definitely one of the more valuable soccer tests available today. The fact that it was developed by a former professional soccer player probably contributed to its success. Also, the test originated from one that was already well established, which always gives the developer an advantage.

MITCHELL SOCCER TEST[23]

Date: 1963.

Purpose: To determine general soccer ability.

Description

In an analysis of past studies, Mitchell selected the McDonald Soccer Test[20] as the most feasible test for evaluating soccer playing ability. Repetitive kicking by a single performer and the use of a wall target, restraining line, and short term trials were all features of the McDonald Test that convinced Mitchell to use it as a basis for his own study.

The Mitchell Test requires the subject to stand behind a 6-foot restraining line and for twenty seconds repeatedly kick a soccer ball to a rectangular backboard or rebound wall target.

Test dimensions include a rectangular wall target marked off on a smooth, unobstructed wall. The target is 4 feet high from the base of the wall and 8 feet long. It is placed in the middle of the forecourt or kicking area, which is 14 feet wide. This means that the forecourt area overlaps the wall target area by 3 feet on either side which naturally allows for some degree of deflection from angled kicks. The forecourt area is 12 feet in depth with a restraining line marked off 6 feet from and parallel to the wall. The forecourt area is split in half by the restraining line.

EDUCATIONAL APPLICATION: Upper elementary school boys; also seems suitable for girls in grades five and six, plus junior high students of both sexes.

Administrative Feasibility

TIME: Twenty students can be tested in one sixty-minute class period.

PERSONNEL: One scorer-recorder.

TRAINING INVOLVED: One practice trial immediately prior to testing.

EQUIPMENT AND SUPPLIES: Soccer balls, stop watch.

Accessories: Scoring, wall and floor marking materials.

Facilities and Space: Unobstructed, smooth wall space at least 8 feet long with a forecourt area measuring a minimum of 14 feet wide and 12 feet in depth.

Directions

The test begins with the subject standing behind the restraining line prepared to kick a soccer ball that is resting on or behind the restraining line. On an audible signal, the subject proceeds to kick the ball as many times as possible against the wall target in twenty seconds. Any kicking style or technique may be used with either foot or any other body part, except the hands or arms.

Students who act as ball retrievers are positioned around and a few feet back of the forecourt boundary lines to stop balls that come over the line. Should the test subject miskick or fail to block a ball, the retrievers stop the ball with their hands and place it back on the boundary line at the point where it rolled out. The test subject may retrieve the ball from that point and, after repositioning the ball, continue the test. A ball that is mishandled by the retrievers and results in an unnecessary time delay results in a

TABLE LXXIX

MITCHELL SOCCER TEST DATA*

| | Number of Cases | Total Scores of Three Initial Trials | | |
		Range High Low	Mean	Standard Deviation
Group I	28	50 – 18	34.4	6.83
Group II	25	50 – 19	33.0	6.61
Group III	31	54 – 14	34.8	10.74
Group IV	35	52 – 17	29.7	8.74
Group V	37	56 – 21	34.6	6.85
Group VI	36	52 – 18	30.8	7.27
Total	192	56 – 14	32.8	8.14

*Data based on scores of 192 fifth and sixth grade boys.

retrial. Subjects may go anywhere to retrieve the ball, but a legal kick must be made from behind the restraining line.

SCORING METHOD: A subject's score is determined by the number of times the ball strikes the wall target within the twenty-second time span, providing both the ball and the subject remain behind the restraining line during the kicking process. Use of the hands or arms at any time results in a one point reduction. The final score is the total number of legal hits made in the three trials. The trials are to be taken consecutively.

In the study, 192 test subjects were randomly divided into six test groups. The range, mean, and standard deviation of the scores for each group are shown in Table LXXIX.

Scientific Authenticity

VALIDITY: Fifth and sixth grade boys served as subjects in the Mitchell study. Validity coefficients of .84 and .76 were determined by the rank-difference and product-moment methods of correlation, respectively.

RELIABILITY: Reliability coefficients of .93 and .89 were found by use of the above correlation methods. They were determined by the test-retest method of obtaining reliability.

CRITERION MEASURE: Subjective ratings of teachers and coaches.

Additional Comments

Mitchell's modification of the McDonald Soccer Test is a highly acceptable tool for measuring general soccer ability of fifth and sixth grade boys. It has value for grading student achievement and serves well as a device to classify students by ability level.

The one characteristic of the test that could result in a shortcoming is the method of administering the three test trials in consecutive order. Fatigue might affect the test score results for some of the more poorly conditioned students.

REFERENCES

1. Andersen, Leonora: *An Athletic Program for Elementary Schools.* New York, B&N, 1927.
2. Bailey, C. I. and Teller, F. L.: *Test Questions for Soccer.* Philadelphia, Saunders, 1969.
3. Bontz, Jean: An Experiment in the Construction of a Test for Measuring Ability in Some of the Fundamental Skills Used by Fifth and Sixth Grade Children in Soccer. Master's thesis, Iowa City, State University of Iowa, 1942.
4. Brace, David K.: *Measuring Motor Ability.* New York, B&N, 1927.
5. Clarke, H. Harrison: *Application of Measurement to Health and Physical Education,* 5th ed. Englewood Cliffs, P-H, 1976.
6. Cozens, Frederick W. and Cubberley, Hazel J.: Achievement tests in soccer and speedball. *Spalding's Official Soccer and Speedball Guide.* New York, Am Sports, 1936.
7. Cozens, F. W., Cubberly, H. J., and Neilson, N. P.: *Achievement Scales in Physical Education Activities for Secondary School Girls and College Women.* New York, B&N, 1937.
8. Crawford, Elinor A.: The Development of Skill Test Batteries for Evaluating the Ability of Women Physical Education Major Students in Soccer and Speedball. Doctoral dissertation, Eugene, University of Oregon, 1958.
9. Crew, Vernon N.: A Skill Test Battery for Use in Service Program Soccer Classes at the University Level. Master's thesis, Eugene, University of Oregon, 1968.
10. Hartley, Grace: Motivating the physical education program for high school girls. *American Physical Education Review, 34:*284, 1929.
11. Heath, Marjorie L. and Rogers, Elizabeth G.: A study in the use of

knowledge and skill tests in soccer. *Research Quarterly, 3:*33-53, 1932.

12. Hillas, Marjorie and Knighton, Marian: *An Athletic Program for High School and College Women.* New York, B&N, 1929.
13. Holloway, T. F.: The Learning of the Big Muscle Skills in Soccer. Master's thesis, Springfield, Mass., Springfield College, 1929.
14. Johnson, Joseph R.: The Development of a Single-Item Test as a Measure of Soccer Skill. Master's thesis, Vancouver, University of British Columbia, 1963.
15. Knighton, Marian: Soccer questions. *Journal of Health and Physical Education, 1:*29, 1930.
16. Konstantinov, Kaum J.: The Development and Evaluation of a Battery of Soccer Skills as an Index of Ability in Soccer. Master's thesis, Springfield, Mass., Springfield College, 1939.
17. Lee, Harry C.: An Evaluation of Brock's Soccer Skill Test and a Rating Scale of Physical Endurance, Tackling, and Personality Traits on the Secondary School Level. Master's thesis, Springfield, Mass., Springfield College, 1941.
18. Mackenzie, John: The Evaluation of a Battery of Soccer Skill Tests as an Aid to Classification of General Soccer Ability. Master's thesis, Amherst, University of Massachusetts, 1968.
19. Mathews, Donald K.: *Measurement in Physical Education,* 4th ed. Philadelphia, Saunders, 1973.
20. McDonald, Lloyd G.: The Construction of a Kicking Skill Test as an Index of General Soccer Ability. Master's thesis, Springfield, Mass., Springfield College, 1951.
21. McElroy, H. N.: A report on some experiment with a skill test. *Research Quarterly, 9:*782-788, 1938.
22. Meyers, Carlton R.: *Measurement in Physical Education,* 2nd ed. New York, Ronald, 1974.
23. Mitchell, J. Reid: The Modification of the McDonald Soccer Skill Test for Upper Elementary School Boys. Master's thesis, Eugene, University of Oregon, 1963.
24. Munro, James B.: An Evaluation of Brock's Soccer Skill Test and a Rating Scale of Physical Endurance, Tackling, and Personality Traits in Soccer on the College Level. Master's thesis, Springfield, Mass., Springfield College, 1941.
25. Neilson, N. P. and Cozens, Frederick W.: *Achievement Scales in Physical Education Activities for Boys and Girls in Elementary and Junior High School.* New York, B&N, 1934.
26. Neilson, N. P. and Jensen, Clayne R.: *Measurement and Statistics in Physical Education.* Belmont, Calif., Wadsworth Pub, 1972.
27. New York State Physical Education Standards Project: *Standards Man-*

ual for Football, Soccer, and Softball Skills, Boys, Grades 7-12, Bulletin 3. Albany, New York State Education Department, 1951.

28. Schaufele, Evelyn F.: The Establishment of Objective Tests for Girls of the Ninth and Tenth Grades to Determine Soccer Ability. Master's thesis, Iowa City, State University of Iowa, 1940.

29. Scott, M. Gladys and French, Esther: *Measurement and Evaluation in Physical Education.* Dubuque, Iowa, Brown Bk, 1959.

30. Snell, Catherine: Physical education knowledge tests. *Research Quarterly, 7:*73, 1936.

31. Streck, Bonnie: An Analysis of the McDonald Soccer Skill Test as Applied to Junior High School Girls. Master's thesis, Fort Hays, Kansas, Fort Hays State College, 1961.

32. Tomlinson, Rebecca: Soccer skill test. *DGWS Soccer-Speedball Guide (1964-66).* Washington, AAHPER, 1964.

33. Vanderhoff, Mildred: Soccer skills test. *Journal of Health and Physical Education, 3:*42, 1932.

34. Warner, Floyd H.: The Development of Achievement Scales of Fundamental Soccer Skills for High School Boys. Master's thesis, Springfield, Mass., Springfield College, 1941.

35. Warner, Glenn F. H.: Warner soccer test. *Newsletter of the National Soccer Coaches Association of America, 6:*13-22, 1950.

36. Whitney, Alethea Helen and Chapin, Grace: Soccer skill testing for girls. *NSWA Soccer-Speedball Guide (1946-48).* Washington, AAHPER, 1946.

Chapter 22

Softball

INTRODUCTION

THE MAJORITY of softball tests that appear in the literature were constructed to measure the playing ability of high school girls and college women. Few have been developed for men and boys, but some of the tests designed for females have application for males. The main reason for the dearth of softball skills tests for males may be attributed to the sport's lack of recognition as a major offering for males in the physical education curriculum. The sport seems to be a more common offering for girls, especially at the levels whereby most of the present skills tests are directed, that of high school and college.

Team sports courses have declined in popularity in recent years, especially in the sport of softball; only one new scientifically authentic skills test has been developed in the last fifteen years.[37]

A notable softball skills test was developed in the early years of skills tests by Rodgers and Heath.[34] The five-item test battery for fifth and sixth grade boys demonstrated questionable reliability for use as a classifier of student ability or as a useful instrument for measurement of student progress. The authors of the test asserted that a study with greater control of test conditions would probably have demonstrated a higher reliability value. Nevertheless, the test did serve as a forerunner for sports skills tests developed by scientific procedures.

Softball is an example of a sport that requires the execution of varied and diverse skills; therefore, evaluation of softball playing ability should be conducted through the use of a battery as opposed to a single test. The throw for distance test seems to be the most valid single indicator of general playing ability, but when given alone its use should be limited to purposes of classification. For diagnostic purposes, a battery has the advantage as it often will reveal specific weaknesses in skill that may be hidden if a single test is administered to represent general playing ability. A comprehensive test battery would include test items from the major skill areas of fielding, throwing, hitting, and running.

In the literature of sports skills tests, softball is sometimes referred to as playground baseball. Tests in this textbook that fit in that category are presented in this chapter, not in the chapter on baseball.

UNDERKOFLER SOFTBALL SKILLS TEST[39]

Date: 1942.
Purpose: To measure softball playing ability.

Description

The distance throw and batting tests measure two of the basic skills in softball, one a defensive skill and another an offensive skill. Use of the 30-foot pitcher's box is necessary to insure consistency in test conditions for the batting test. The distance throw test could be administered on almost any type playing field if the particular school's softball playing field is not satisfactory. A proper amount of relatively flat throwing space would adequately satisfy the space needed.

EDUCATIONAL APPLICATION: Devised for seventh and eighth grade girls but appropriate for high school and college females.

Administrative Feasibility

TIME: Two forty-minute class periods for testing twenty students.

PERSONNEL: Two instructors with qualified assistants would be the ideal, especially in the administration of the batting test item. In situations where only one instructor is available to administer that item, he or she could ably serve as both pitcher and umpire.

TRAINING INVOLVED: A brief warm-up is necessary, especially for the distance throw test.

EQUIPMENT AND SUPPLIES: Several 14-inch softballs and regulation softball bats.

Accessories: Chalk for field markings; scoring materials.

Facilities and Space: A softball field with a 45-foot diamond and 30-foot pitcher's box. The distance throw test requires a throwing line of field markings set at 10-foot intervals for a suffi-cient distance.

Directions

DISTANCE THROW: Staying behind the throwing line and taking no more than one step, the subject releases the ball with any type of throw she desires. Three trials are allowed with three throws representing a trial. The best throw in each trial is recorded.

BATTING: The subject stands in the batter's box and attempts to hit ten legal pitches delivered by the pitcher. An umpire is utilized to call balls and strikes. A called strike counts as one of the ten trials while a "ball" is disregarded. Some control of the test conditions is achieved by employing the same umpire and pitcher throughout the administration of the test.

SCORING METHOD AND NORMS

Distance Throw: Of the nine throws in the three trials, the better of the three recorded constitutes the official score. The throw is measured to the nearest foot and represents the distance from the throwing line to the point where the ball first touches the ground.

Batting: A ball landing in the outfield counts five points with three points assigned to an infield hit. A foul ball gains the subject one point, and no points are counted for a ball that is swung at and missed or called a strike. The total number of points earned in the ten trials represents the final batting score.

Scientific Authenticity

VALIDITY: In the Underkofler study which involved 118 sev-enth and eighth grade girls, the distance throw produced a .81 coefficient. A .63 coefficient was derived for that skill in a study that utilized college girls as subjects.[35]

The validity coefficient for the batting test in the junior high group was .72.

RELIABILITY: A .95 coefficient of correlation on successive trials was obtained for the distance throw in the study utilizing junior high girls as subjects. The reliability coefficient for the bat-

TABLE LXXX

T-SCALES FOR UNDERKOFLER BATTING TEST

T-Score	Batting*	T-Score	Batting
76	42	53	23
75		52	22
74		51	
73		50	21
72	40	49	20
71		48	19
70		47	
69		46	18
68	38	45	17
67		44	16
66	36	43	
65	35	42	15
64		41	14
63		40	
62	34	39	13
61		38	12
60	32	37	11
59	30	36	9
58	29	35	8
57	28	34	
56	27	33	
55	26	32	6
54	24	31	
30		26	
29		25	
28	1	24	
27			

*Scale constructed from data collected on 118 seventh and eighth grade girls.

ting test was .65 by the odd-even method and raised to .79 with the Spearman-Brown correction.

CRITERION MEASURE: A subjective jury rating of player performance.

Additional Comments

The distance throw is said to be the best single test ever devised for softball playing ability as is the case for baseball (see Kelson, Chap. 4). Since the skill seems to correlate highly with other individual softball skills, especially speed of throwing, its inclusion into any softball test battery seems a must. Also, no softball test battery is complete without a batting test item since that skill comprises such a large share of offensive play.

The pitcher's tendency toward variance in speed and placement of pitches makes the batting test somewhat suspect, although a satisfactory validity coefficient resulted from the evaluation of the junior high school girls' batting skill. Use of a ball delivery machine should standardize the test to a greater degree, but a large number of schools do not possess equipment of that type of sophistication. Control of the factors that are conducive to standardization is the alternative when forced to administer the test with some person delivering the pitches. Official balls should be used, and an instructor probably should do the pitching in most cases. Also, adherence to the regulations of the 30-foot pitching distance and 45-foot diamond is imperative. The use of an umpire with some type of recognized qualifications would also add merit to the batting test.

O'DONNELL SOFTBALL SKILL TEST[32]

Also cited as O'Donnell Softball Test and O'Donnell Softball Test for High School Girls.

Date: 1950.

Purpose: To measure basic softball playing skills and to provide a classification measure.

Description

Speed Throw: This item measures the speed and distance of a throw. A 5-foot restraining line is drawn on the floor 65 feet from and parallel to the wall.

Fielding Fly Balls: This test item measures the ability to catch a fly ball and ball handling ability. The test requires a 15-foot line to be drawn on the wall at a height of 12 feet above the floor. A 15-foot line on the floor 6 feet from the wall and parallel to it is also drawn.

Throw and Catch: This item measures the combination defensive skill of throwing, running, and catching. A 50 × 20-foot rectangle is drawn on the floor with its length divided into ten equal areas by lines 5 feet apart. The jumping standards are placed so that the rope is stretched directly over the starting line which is at one end of the rectangle. The rope is located at a height of 8 feet from the floor.

Repeated Throws: The item measures primarily ball handling speed and to some extent catching and throwing ability. A 15-foot line is drawn on the wall 7½ feet high. A 15-foot line on the floor is placed 15 feet from the wall and parallel to it.

Fungo Batting: This is a test of batting ability, and a regulation softball diamond is used in the test administration.

Overhand Accuracy Throw: Throwing accuracy is measured by this test. A target is constructed on the wall with the center located 2 feet from the floor. The inner circle has a radius of 3 inches. The radii of the other circles are 11, 21, and 33 inches, respectively. A 5-foot restraining line is drawn on the floor parallel to the wall and 45 feet from the target.

EDUCATIONAL APPLICATION: Test was designed for high school girls; it seems appropriate for college men and women, and high school boys, provided pertinent modifications are made whenever feasible.

Administrative Feasibility

TIME: The test does not lend itself well to economy of time in test administration unless a mass testing arrangement is implemented. It has been estimated that in a forty-minute class period groups of 60, 50, 25, 50, 15, and 25 students can be tested respectively on the speed throw, fielding fly balls, throw and catch, repeated throws, fungo batting, and overhand accuracy throw items. Therefore, mass testing with multiple stations is necessary if the O'Donnell Test is to prove feasible in time of administration.

PERSONNEL: If the test items are administered separately, one instructor with student assistants assigned as needed should suffice for test personnel requirements. A number of trained and well-qualified student assistants could make a mass testing effort possible. The following assignment of duties has been suggested:

a. speed throw: one timer and one recorder.
b. fielding fly balls: one timer and one scorer.
c. throw and catch: one recorder and one assistant.
d. repeated throws: one timer and one scorer.
e. fungo batting: one to two ball retrievers, one scorer, a recorder; another assistant is necessary to hand balls to the batter.
f. overhand accuracy throw: same as fungo batting.

TRAINING INVOLVED: Since a learning condition appears to be a factor in the quality of performance in some of the test items, plenty of practice should be permitted for the test items, and an attempt should be made to make the amount of practice somewhat consistent from subject to subject. The normal amount of warm-up time should be permitted for those items conducive to that type of preparation.

A practice throw is performed immediately prior to taking the fielding fly balls test.

EQUIPMENT AND SUPPLIES: One stop watch and three regulation softballs are necessary equipment for the speed throw, fielding fly balls, and repeated throws tests. Two jumping standards, a 12-foot rope, one tape measure and softball should be available for the throw and catch test. Five to ten regulation softballs and one bat are required for the fungo batting test item. Five to ten regulation softballs are also needed for the overhand accuracy throw.

Accessories: Marking materials; determination of the tests that require the availability of marking materials may be made from the test item descriptions given earlier in this test presentation. Scoring materials also needed.

Facilities and Space: An unobstructed, flat wall surface for the speed throw, fielding fly balls, repeated throws, and overhand accuracy throw items. The fungo batting test should be given on a regulation softball diamond.

Directions

SPEED THROW: A ball is placed on the restraining line with the subject standing behind the line. On the starting signal, the ball is picked up and thrown against the wall as fast as possible.

The subject may step over the line after the throw but not before the release; otherwise, a trial is counted as zero. The time to the nearest tenth-second from the starting signal until the ball hits the wall is recorded. Three trials are administered.

FIELDING FLY BALLS: Standing behind the 15-foot line on the floor while holding a ball, the subject, on the starting signal, throws the ball repeatedly against the wall above the 12-foot line and catches the rebound. The line may be crossed to catch the ball, but the subject must return to a position behind the line for the next throw. Throwing continues for thirty seconds. One trial is given following a practice trial.

THROW AND CATCH: The subject stands behind the starting line with a ball in hand. The ball is then thrown over the rope, and the subject runs to catch it on the other side while trying to cover the maximum amount of distance in doing so. Any type of throw is permitted. The distance to the nearest foot from the starting line to the back of the subject's heel of the front foot is measured. Three trials are performed.

REPEATED THROWS: A ball is placed on the 15-foot line with the subject standing behind the line. On the starting signal, the student picks up the ball and throws it repeatedly against the wall above the 7½-foot line. The number of times the ball hits the wall in a thirty-second time period is recorded. One trial is given and the watch is not stopped for a fumbled or dropped ball.

FUNGO BATTING: The subject stands in the batter's box with a ball in hand. The ball is tossed into the air with the subject attempting to hit it on the downward flight. If no attempt is made to hit the ball, a trial is not counted. Ten trials are allowed.

OVERHAND ACCURACY THROW: The subject assumes a position behind the restraining line and throws the ball at the target, aiming at the center of the target. Stepping over the line results in the trial being counted with a score of zero given.

SCORING METHOD

Speed Throw: The time to the nearest tenth-second that elapses from the starting signal until the ball strikes the wall. The better of three trials is the final score.

Fielding Fly Balls: The number of legal catches in a thirty-second time period is recorded as the official score. Illegal catches include those situations where a ball hits the ground before being caught, is fumbled or dropped, or does not hit on or above the 12-foot line on the wall. Also, the subject's crossing of the line before making the throw is illegal.

Throw and Catch: The distance from the starting line to the point at which the ball is caught is recorded for three trials with the best trial counting as the final score. The distance is measured to the nearest foot from the starting line to the back of the heel of the subject's front foot. A ball not going over the rope or not caught constitutes a trial and is given a score of zero.

Repeated Throws: The number of legal wall hits during a thirty-second trial is the score. A subject may not cross the starting line prior to releasing the ball, and the throws must hit on or above the 7½-foot line on the wall.

Fungo Batting: The sum of points made on ten trials is the final score. A ball landing in the outfield counts five points; one landing in the infield counts three points; one point is given for a foul ball; and a ball swung at and missed counts zero points.

Overhand Accuracy Throw: The sum of points made on ten trials is the final score. The center target area counts four points, the next area three points, the next two points, and the outside area one point. A ball that misses the target is scored as zero. If the subject steps over the line prior to releasing the ball, that trial is scored as zero.

Six-Test Playing Ability Battery: The softball playing ability score = 0.6 (fielding fly balls) + 0.3 (throw and catch) + 0.6 (repeated throws) + 0.1 (fungo batting) + 0.4 (overhand accuracy) − 3 (speed throw).

Scientific Authenticity

VALIDITY: .91 coefficient for the six-test battery when administered to fifty high school girls.

RELIABILITY: Not reported.

CRITERION MEASURE: Although the O'Donnell Softball Test is commonly reported in the literature, no source identified the criterion used to validate the test battery.

Additional Comments

The O'Donnell Softball Test is one of the more comprehensive tests developed to measure softball playing ability. However, the test battery reveals some limitations.

The reliability of the individual test items was not reported. A test battery that demonstrates such a high validity value should be tested for its reliability value.

Secondly, the only apparent norms available were based on scores of only fifty subjects. Consequently, the development of local norms should prove more meaningful to the physical educator utilizing the O'Donnell Test.

FOX-YOUNG BATTING TEST[15]

Also cited as Fox and Young Bat for Distance Test.
Date: 1954.
Purpose: To measure batting distance skill in softball.

Description

The test was constructed as an attempt to standardize the measurement of batting skill. Use of the batting tee lends itself more to objective measurement than batting tests that depend upon the pitching consistency of some performer. However, the test still measures only one aspect of batting skill, i.e. ability to hit for distance.

Field markings for the test are as follows:

1. a baseline on which the batting tee is placed;
2. twenty lines 3 yards in length spaced 10 feet apart and parallel to the baseline;
3. twenty lines 1 yard in length midway between the 3-yard lines and parallel to them;
4. the distance from the baseline is marked at the end of each of the 3-yard lines.

EDUCATIONAL APPLICATION: College women.

Administrative Feasibility

TIME: One sixty-minute class period for class of twenty students.

PERSONNEL: Instructor with trained assistants to measure and record the distance of fly balls.

TRAINING INVOLVED: Much practice with the batting tee should be allowed prior to testing a class. The adjustment of hitting a ball off the batting tee requires considerable experience to enhance the test's validity and reliability.

EQUIPMENT AND SUPPLIES: A standard softball batting tee, five regulation softballs in good condition, and an assortment of softball bats.

Accessories: Field marking and scoring materials.

Facilities and Space: Regulation softball playing field or relatively flat area of sufficient size.

Directions

Three warm-up hits are permitted for each player with the tee adjusted at the height of the student's choice. Five trials are then completed without pause.

SCORING METHOD: The distance from the batting tee to the spot where each ball first touches the ground is recorded. The sum of the distance of each of the five trials reflects the official test score. A swing that strikes the tee or misses the ball completely counts as one trial.

Scientific Authenticity

VALIDITY: .64 when correlated with the sum of three judges' ratings. The scores of fifty-eight college women students provided the data for the validity computation.

RELIABILITY: A reliability coefficient of .87 was derived when the Spearman-Brown Prophecy Formula was applied to step up the split-half method for obtaining the test's reliability. The scores of sixty-two subjects from the collegiate group mentioned above were used to determine the reliability coefficient.

CRITERION MEASURE: Judges' ratings of the batter's grip, stance, swing, and hitting consistency.

Additional Comments

Although an impressive reliability coefficient was obtained for the test, a greater number of trials should provide an even greater consistency in individual test scores.

The test should only be used as part of a test battery since it is limited to the measurement of batting skill. To determine if skill in the bat for distance test really represents overall batting skill, test scores could be correlated with another criterion such as seasonal batting averages.

The development of this test was a definite contribution toward a more valid and objective measure of offensive softball skill.

KEHTEL SOFTBALL FIELDING AND THROWING ACCURACY TEST[23]

Date: 1958.

Purpose: To measure the ability to field ground balls and throw them accurately.

Description

The fielding and throwing accuracy test is administered on a floor layout as shown in Figure 60. The test is designed to measure a fundamental combination skill in defensive softball as the single test score reflects ability in both fielding and throwing accuracy skills.

The aforementioned layout includes two wall surfaces at right angles to each other. The starting line is placed 40 feet from wall A which has a 10-foot line located 4 feet above and parallel to the floor. Wall B is located 40 feet to the left of the center of the starting line.

As shown in Figure 60, the target is situated so that its center is 20 feet from wall A. It is circular and has a radius of 36 inches. The upper half of the target has a semicircle with a 12-inch radius. Two straight lines extend from each end of the semicircle to the bottom of the target. An incomplete circle, with a radius of 24 inches, is located around the oblong area.

EDUCATIONAL APPLICATION: College women.

Administrative Feasibility

TIME: One sixty-minute class period if two students are tested simultaneously; otherwise, two class periods of that length.

PERSONNEL: A timer, recorder, and three assistants to retrieve balls.

TRAINING INVOLVED: One practice trial immediately prior to the test; experience in throwing at the target prior to the test date is recommended.

EQUIPMENT AND SUPPLIES: Ten softballs in good condition and a stop watch.

Accessories: Marking materials such as masking tape and a box to hold the balls; scoring materials.

Facilities and Space: A gymnasium or other indoor facility of sufficient size and unobstructed wall space.

Directions

The subject stands behind the starting line while holding a 12-inch softball. On the starting signal the player throws the ball below the 4-foot line on wall A. She fields the rebound as quickly as possible and may cross the line for the recovery. Upon recovery, the ball is thrown at the target on the left wall. The action is immediately repeated and continues for the remainder of the two-minute allotment.

A step is allowed over the starting line as the subject throws. A ball that hits the floor before striking the wall is considered playable, but one that fails to reach the wall does not count. Another ball should be put into action immediately. One practice trial precedes two test trials.

The three student assistants have an important role in supplying the subject with balls ready for play. The helpers should take precautions not to interfere with the subject as she takes the test. Also, two assistants should roll the balls to the third helper who places them in the ball box near the starting line.

SCORING METHOD: Any ball that hits within the target area is scored according to the score value of the particular section it strikes. Five points are given for the center area, three for the middle, and one point for the outer area. A ball that strikes a line separating two sections is assigned the score of higher value.

The two methods of scoring the test are as follows:

1. The score value for each ball is totaled for the final score.
2. The number of balls striking the target in a two-minute period is the final test score.

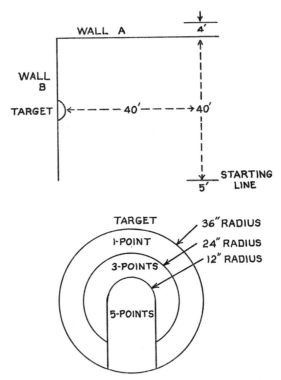

Figure 60. Floor and target markings for Kehtel Softball Test.

Either of these scoring methods may be used so long as the same method is used for each student in a particular group.

Scientific Authenticity

VALIDITY: .76 for the scoring method which reflects the total of point values and .79 for the method that indicates the number of times the target was struck. The test validity was computed from the scores of fifty-four college students.

RELIABILITY: The reliability coefficients were .90 and .91, respectively, for the two scoring methods. The coefficients were determined by the odd-even method and corrected by the Spearman-Brown Prophecy Formula.

CRITERION MEASURE: Three judges' subjective ratings of the subject's ability to field ground balls and throw them at a base.

Additional Comments

The test displays high validity and reliability values and should serve well as a test battery component. Kehtel suggests that the scoring method of recording target hits be used in beginning softball classes and the total score value method be utilized in advanced classes.

FRINGER SOFTBALL TEST[18]

Also cited as Fringer Softball Skill Tests and Fringer Softball Battery.

Date: 1961.

Purpose: To measure the important skill components of softball playing.

Description

The Fringer Softball Test is primarily used for measurement of student progress and for diagnostic purposes. A periodic check of student improvement is made easier with the use of a test so feasible in economy of time of administration. Results of the test also identify strengths and weaknesses of students' softball skills, allowing the instructor to concentrate to a large extent on correcting the weaknesses.

The fly ball test measures the ability to catch fly balls and throw quickly. The fielding grounders-agility-speed and accuracy test measures the ability to field grounders, to run quickly to a base, and to throw quickly and accurately to a target. The softball distance throw measures the ability to throw for long distances with some degree of accuracy (Figs. 61 and 62).

EDUCATIONAL APPLICATION: Designed for high school girls but appropriate for boys.

Administrative Feasibility

TIME: One sixty-minute class period for a class of fifteen to twenty students in a mass testing situation utilizing multiple stations.

PERSONNEL: One timer and scorer for the fly ball test while the fielding grounders-agility-speed and accuracy test requires the use of one scorer and timer plus a student at each base to check for foot faults. The softball throw for distance requires spotters who call out the distance, ball retrievers, and a scorer.

TRAINING INVOLVED: Practice prior to the test date and warm-up immediately before testing should be allowed for all items with more warm-up concentration on the preparation for the distance throw test item.

EQUIPMENT AND SUPPLIES: Several quality softballs and a stop watch for the fly ball test and the fielding grounders-agility-speed and accuracy test. An adequate supply of softballs for the distance throw item.

Accessories: Field markers for distance throw item and scoring materials.

Facilities and Space: A gymnasium with unobstructed wall space for the fly ball test, and a floor space of 30 × 40 feet with a 20 × 20-foot wall size needed for the fielding grounders-agility-speed and accuracy test. The throw for distance item requires a playing field of reasonable size.

Directions

FLY BALL TEST: Standing behind the 30-foot restraining line, the subject at a command to start throws a ball against the wall

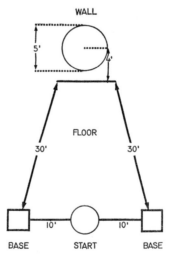

Figure 61. Specifications for fielding grounders-agility-speed and accuracy test.

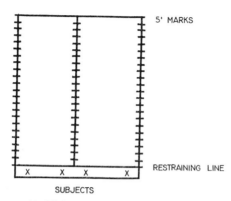

Figure 62. Field markings for distance throw test.

above a line 20 feet from the floor. The throwing motion used is at the subject's discretion. After the ball hits the wall, the student may retrieve the ball at any location on the floor. Three thirty-second trials are administered with intervals of rest given.

Fumbled balls and those that bounce before the catch do not count.

FIELDING GROUNDERS-AGILITY-SPEED AND ACCURACY TEST: When signaled to begin, the subject runs to a base while carrying a softball. While a foot is in contact with the base, the student throws the ball at the wall target (Fig. 61). The subject then rushes to retrieve the ball and quickly advances to the opposite base to make another throw at the target. The bases must be alternated for the throws and a foot must be in contact with a base on each throw. This action is repeated for forty-five seconds.

Two trials are permitted with an intervening rest period.

DISTANCE THROW: The subject throws from behind the restraining line and is allowed only one step prior to the throw. The restraining line may be crossed only after the ball has left the subject's hand. Three throws are allowed.

SCORING METHOD AND NORMS

Fly Ball Test: The cumulative total of catches made in the three trials is the final score.

Fielding Grounders-Agility-Speed and Accuracy Test: Balls

TABLE LXXXI

NORMS FOR FRINGER SOFTBALL TEST*

T-Score	Fielding Grounders Total of 2 trials	Fly Balls Total of 3 trials	Distance Throw Best trial	T-Score
75	25	31	150	75
70	24	30	115	70
65	21	28	105	65
60	18	25	95	60
55	15	21	83	55
50	12	17	71	50
45	10	11	61	45
40	7	7	55	40
35	5	2	47	35
30	2		41	30
25			37	25

*Based on scores of high school girls.

hitting on or with the target circle count. The final score is the total number of target hits made in the two trials.

Distance Throw: The better of the three allowed throws is measured to the nearest foot and constitutes the official score.

Scientific Authenticity

VALIDITY: Coefficients of .76, .70, and .72 resulted for the three tests in Fringer's study which utilized high school girls. One hundred and fifty-one girls participated in the fielding grounders-agility-speed and accuracy test while 136 were included in the distance throw test.

RELIABILITY: The test-retest correlation coefficients were .87, .72, and .90 for the respective test items as presented above.

CRITERION MEASURE: Scott and French Repeated Throws Test.[35]

Additional Comments

Although the Fringer Test is designed for measuring softball skill in high school girls, it is recommended for use in skill testing of boys at that school level. The instructor should remember that the available norms were based on the test scores of girls in grades ten to twelve; consequently, the norms are not appropriate for evaluating the test scores of boys. Development of performance norms for boys on the Fringer Test would be a worthy contribution to the literature pertaining to measurement of softball skills.

AAHPER SOFTBALL SKILL TEST[2, 3]

Date: 1966.

Purpose: To measure the fundamental softball skills of boys and girls.

EDUCATIONAL APPLICATION: Upper elementary and high school boys and girls, ages ten to eighteen.

Administrative Feasibility

TIME: A major limitation of the AAHPER Softball Skill Test is the large amount of time required for its administration. A mass testing setup with two or more instructors solves this problem. Apparently, the test's comprehensiveness is viewed as being of such importance that the time required for its administration is well spent.

PERSONNEL: One instructor with adequate number of trained assistants; two or more instructors preferred.

TRAINING INVOLVED: Prior to the testing date, the instructor should set aside some class time for students to practice each test item. The amount of practice time should be relatively uniform for each student.

EQUIPMENT AND SUPPLIES: Several softballs of good condition, a varied selection of bats, and at least one stop watch.

Accessories: Target and field marking materials, tape measure, rope, two 8-foot standards, and scoring materials.

Facilities and Space: Some tests are more conducive for administration outdoors while others are more easily given indoors. The catching fly balls item requires the use of a two-story building.

Description and Directions

The seven-item test covers all facets of softball play and is probably the most comprehensive softball test yet devised. Direc-

tions for administering and test specifications for the particular
items are as follows.

OVERHAND THROW FOR ACCURACY: The subject completes ten
throws from a distance of 65 feet for boys and 40 for girls at a
target with the following dimensions: three concentric circles with
1-inch lines, the center circle measuring 2 feet in diameter, the
next circle 4 feet, and the outer circle is located 3 feet from the
floor. The target may be marked on a wall or canvas against a mat
hung on the wall (Fig. 63).

One to two practice throws are allowed prior to ten trials that
are counted.

UNDERHAND PITCHING: The rectangular target represents the
strike zone, and its bottom is located 18 inches from the floor.
The outer lines are 42 inches long and 29 inches wide. An inner
rectangle dimension is 30 × 17 inches. A 24-inch pitching line is
placed 46 feet from the target for boys and 38 feet for girls (Fig. 64).

One practice pitch precedes fifteen underhand trials. One foot
must remain intact with the pitching line while delivering the ball,
but one step forward may be taken. Only legal pitches are scored.

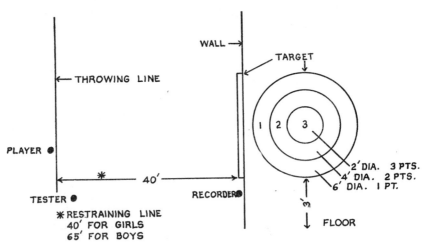

Figure 63. Floor markings and wall target for overhand throw for accuracy
test. From AAHPER: *Skills Test Manuals: Softball for Boys and Girls,*
D. K. Brace, test consultant, 1966. Courtesy of AAHPER, Washington,
D. C.

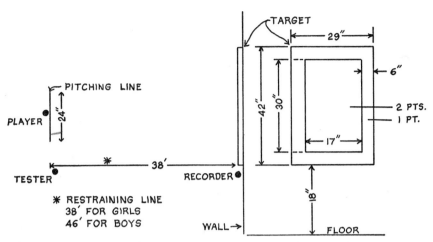

Figure 64. Specifications for underhand pitching test. From AAHPER: *Skills Test Manuals: Softball for Boys and Girls,* D. K. Brace, test consultant, 1966. Courtesy of AAHPER, Washington, D. C.

SPEED THROW: The subject stands holding a softball behind a line located 9 feet from a smooth unobstructed wall. On the starting signal, he or she throws the ball against the wall and catches the rebound as rapidly as possible for fifteen trials. Balls falling between the wall and the 9-foot line may be retrieved, but the subject must be back of the line upon continuing. One new trial is given if the ball gets away completely.

Two trials are performed for time after one practice throw.

FUNGO HITTING: The subject selects a bat and stands behind home plate with a ball in hand. The ball is then tossed in the air, and the subject attempts to hit the ball to right field. The next ball is hit to left field; this action is repeated until ten balls have been hit in each direction.

Anytime the ball hits the bat, it constitutes a trial. Wherever the ball is hit, the next ball should be hit to the opposite field. Hits to specific sides must cross the baseline between second and third base or first and second base. Practice trials are permitted.

BASE RUNNING: Subjects stand in the right hand batter's box. On the starting signal, the subject swings at an imaginary ball,

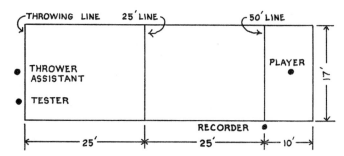

Figure 65. Layout for fielding ground balls test. From AAHPER: *Skills Test Manuals: Softball for Boys and Girls,* D. K. Brace, test consultant, 1966. Courtesy of AAHPER, Washington, D. C.

drops the bat and circles the bases. The bat cannot be thrown or carried, and a complete swing must be taken before running. Bases must be touched in sequence.

One practice and two timed trials are given.

FIELDING GROUND BALLS: Figure 65 illustrates the 17 × 60-foot rectangular area. Two lines, 25 and 50 feet, run parallel to the throwing line. The 17 × 10-foot area at the end of the rectangle contains the subject with a basket of ten balls. A ground ball is thrown every five seconds into the 17 × 25-foot zone. An overarm throw with speed is used. Each throw must hit the ground for at least one bounce. The thrower should not try to make the subject miss the ball, although a variation in direction of throws

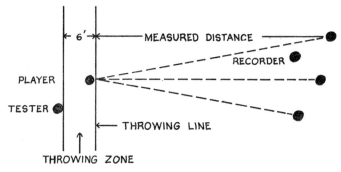

Figure 66. Layout for distance throw test. From AAHPER: *Skills Test Manuals: Softball for Boys and Girls,* D. K. Brace, test consultant, 1966. Courtesy of AAHPER, Washington, D. C.

is desirable. A ball not landing where specifically aimed should be thrown again. The subject attempts to field each ball cleanly, then toss it aside. Starting back of the 50-foot line, the subject may field the ball anywhere in back of the 25-foot line.

A practice trial and twenty trials for score are administered.

THROW FOR DISTANCE: The subject throws from within a 6-foot restraining area which is drawn parallel to a number of lines denoting 5-yard field intervals. Three trials are given for the best distance.

CATCHING FLY BALLS (GIRLS): The subject stands at second base in the center of a 60-foot square. Another person throws fly balls to the subject as directed while standing in a restraining zone 5 feet behind home plate. The ball must be thrown over an 8-foot high rope which is attached to standards located 5 feet in front of home plate. Consistent speed should be placed on the throws by the thrower. An instructor instructs the thrower to throw left, right, or straight into the catching zone. The subject should receive a fairly equal amount from each of the three directions. The subject catches the ball, throws it aside, and prepares for the next throw.

One practice trial precedes two trials of ten balls each.

CATCHING FLY BALLS (BOYS): The tester assumes a position 6 feet from an open second-story window. On a signal a second

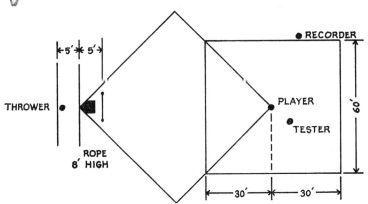

Figure 67. Specifications for catching fly balls test (girls). From AAHPER: *Skills Test Manual: Softball for Girls,* D. K. Brace, test consultant, 1966. Courtesy of AAHPER, Washington, D. C.

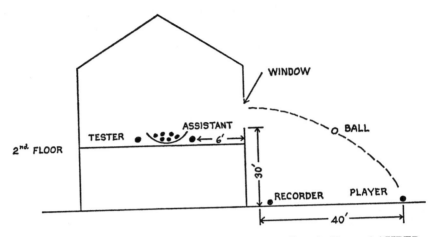

Figure 68. Specifications for catching fly balls test (boys). From AAHPER: *Skills Test Manual: Softball for Boys,* D. K. Brace, test consultant, 1966. Courtesy of AAHPER, Washington, D. C.

tester tosses a ball with good speed underhand through the window for the subject to catch. The subject is standing on the ground about 30 to 40 feet from the side of the building. Balls are tossed at 10-second intervals until ten are tossed.

The player catches a ball, tosses it aside, and gets ready for the next toss. The tester in the building should remain out of sight of the subject and not pay attention to the quality of the subject's performance. The tester should vary the direction of his throws but keep the speed constant. A trial may be started over one time if an interruption of the timing of the throws occurs.

A practice trial precedes two trials of ten throws each.

Scoring Method and Norms

Overhand Throw for Accuracy: Point values of three, two, and one are given for the center, middle, and outer circles, respectively. A ball hitting on a line is given the higher value. The score is the sum of points made on ten throws. The maximum score is thirty points.

Underhand Pitching: Point values of two and one are assigned to the center and outer areas of the target in that order. The score is the sum of all points made on fifteen pitches. The maximum score is thirty points.

Speed Throw: The score is reflected in seconds and tenths of seconds for the time required to complete fifteen consecutive hits. This is timed from the instant the first ball hits the wall and ends the instant the fifteenth throw hits the wall. The better time of two trials is the final score.

Fungo Hitting: The sum of points made on twenty hits is the score. These hits are alternated right and left in directions with ten hits taken to each side. Fly balls clearing the baseline on the intended side count two points, and ground balls passing the baseline on the intended side count one point. Balls hit to the wrong side do not count. The maximum score is forty points.

Base Running: Trials are recorded in seconds and tenths of seconds. The score reflects the elapsed time from the starting signal to the instant the subject touches home plate after running the bases. The better time of two trials is the official score.

Fielding Ground Balls: The score is derived on a pass or fail basis. Each throw scores one or zero points. The maximum score is twenty points.

Throw for Distance: The distance to the nearest foot in the better of three trials is the official score. The measurement is made at right angles from the spot where the farthest throw landed to the restraining line.

Catching Fly Balls (Girls): The number of successful catches from a total of twenty balls or two trials of ten each. One point is scored for each successful catch. The maximum score is twenty points.

Catching Fly Balls (Boys): same as catching fly balls test for girls.

Scientific Authenticity

VALIDITY: Face validity is apparently accepted.
RELIABILITY: Not reported.

Additional Comments

A major criticism of the AAHPER Sports Skills Tests is the absence of scientific authenticity in their development. Some of the

Tables LXXXII through XCVII are percentile scores for AAHPER Softball Test, based on scores of over 600 students for each sex and age group (10 to 18). From AAHPER: *Skills Test Manual: Softball for Boys,* 1966 and *Skills Test Manual: Softball for Girls,* 1966, D. K. Brace, test consultant. Courtesy of AAHPER, Washington, D.C.

TABLE LXXXII

OVERHAND THROW FOR ACCURACY (BOYS)
Test Scores in Points

Percentile	10-11	12	13	14	15	16	17-18	Percentile
100th	22	22	23	25	25	27	25	100th
95th	14	17	18	19	20	20	21	95th
90th	12	15	16	17	17	18	19	90th
85th	11	13	15	16	16	17	18	85th
80th	9	12	13	15	15	16	17	80th
75th	8	11	12	14	14	15	16	75th
70th	8	11	12	13	13	14	15	70th
65th	7	10	11	12	12	14	15	65th
60th	6	9	10	11	11	13	14	60th
55th	5	9	10	11	11	12	13	55th
50th	5	8	9	10	10	11	13	50th
45th	4	7	8	10	10	11	12	45th
40th	4	6	7	9	9	10	11	40th
35th	3	6	7	8	9	9	11	35th
30th	3	5	6	8	8	8	10	30th
25th	2	4	5	7	7	8	9	25th
20th	1	3	4	6	7	7	8	20th
15th	1	3	3	6	6	6	7	15th
10th	0	2	2	5	5	5	6	10th
5th	0	0	1	3	3	4	4	5th
0	0	0	0	0	0	1	0	0

TABLE LXXXIII

OVERHAND THROW FOR ACCURACY (GIRLS)
Test Scores in Points

Percentile	Age							Percentile
	10-11	12	13	14	15	16	17-18	
100th	24	26	26	26	30	30	26	100th
95th	17	17	18	19	19	22	20	95th
90th	14	16	16	17	18	20	18	90th
85th	13	14	15	15	16	18	17	85th
80th	12	13	14	14	15	17	16	80th
75th	11	12	13	13	14	16	15	75th
70th	10	11	12	12	13	15	14	70th
65th	9	10	11	11	12	13	13	65th
60th	8	9	10	11	11	12	12	60th
55th	7	9	9	10	11	12	11	55th
50th	6	8	9	9	10	11	10	50th
45th	5	7	8	9	9	10	9	45th
40th	4	6	7	8	8	9	8	40th
35th	4	5	6	7	8	8	7	35th
30th	3	4	6	6	7	7	6	30th
25th	2	4	5	5	6	6	5	25th
20th	1	3	4	4	5	5	4	20th
15th	1	2	3	3	3	4	3	15th
10th	0	1	1	2	2	2	2	10th
5th	0	0	0	1	1	1	1	5th
0	0	0	0	0	0	0	0	0

TABLE LXXXIV

UNDERHAND PITCH (BOYS)
Test Scores in Points

Percentile	10-11	12	13	Age 14	15	16	17-18	Percentile
100th	18	23	21	22	24	25	25	100th
95th	12	14	15	16	18	19	19	95th
90th	10	12	13	15	16	17	17	90th
85th	9	11	11	14	15	15	16	85th
80th	8	9	10	12	14	14	15	80th
75th	7	9	10	12	13	13	14	75th
70th	7	8	9	11	12	12	13	70th
65th	6	7	8	10	11	12	12	65th
60th	6	7	8	9	10	11	12	60th
55th	5	6	7	9	10	10	11	55th
50th	4	6	7	8	9	9	10	50th
45th	4	5	6	7	8	9	10	45th
40th	3	4	5	7	7	8	9	40th
35th	3	4	5	6	7	8	8	35th
30th	2	3	4	6	6	7	8	30th
25th	2	3	4	5	5	6	7	25th
20th	1	2	3	4	4	5	6	20th
15th	1	2	3	4	4	4	5	15th
10th	1	1	2	3	3	3	4	10th
5th	0	0	1	2	2	2	3	5th
0	0	0	0	0	0	0	0	0

TABLE LXXXV

UNDERHAND PITCH (GIRLS)
Test Scores in Points

Percentile	10-11	12	13	Age 14	15	16	17-18	Percentile
100th	23	22	24	24	26	27	26	100th
95th	12	14	16	17	16	19	21	95th
90th	10	13	14	15	15	16	18	90th
85th	8	11	12	14	13	14	17	85th
80th	7	10	11	13	12	12	15	80th
75th	6	9	10	12	11	12	14	75th
70th	6	8	9	11	10	11	13	70th
65th	5	7	9	10	9	10	12	65th
60th	5	6	8	9	8	10	11	60th
55th	4	6	7	8	7	9	10	55th
50th	4	5	7	8	6	8	9	50th
45th	3	5	6	7	6	8	9	45th
40th	3	4	6	6	5	7	8	40th
35th	2	4	5	5	4	6	7	35th
30th	2	3	4	5	4	5	6	30th
25th	1	2	4	4	3	5	5	25th
20th	1	2	3	3	2	4	5	20th
15th	0	1	2	3	2	3	4	15th
10th	0	0	2	2	1	2	3	10th
5th	0	0	1	1	0	0	2	5th
0	0	0	0	0	0	0	0	0

TABLE LXXXVI

SPEED THROW (BOYS)
Test Scores in Seconds and Tenths

Percentile	Age							Percentile
	10-11	12	13	14	15	16	17-18	
100th	13.1	11.0	10.0	9.0	13.0	10.0	10.0	100th
95th	16.1	15.3	14.9	13.0	13.5	12.5	12.1	95th
90th	17.1	16.1	14.9	14.0	13.8	13.2	12.8	90th
85th	17.6	16.8	15.7	14.6	14.2	13.7	13.2	85th
80th	18.0	17.3	16.2	15.1	14.5	14.1	13.3	80th
75th	18.6	17.6	16.8	15.6	14.9	14.5	13.9	75th
70th	19.1	18.0	16.9	15.9	15.6	14.8	14.2	70th
65th	19.7	18.4	17.3	16.3	15.9	15.1	14.5	65th
60th	20.2	18.9	17.6	16.6	16.0	15.5	14.8	60th
55th	20.8	19.5	17.9	17.1	16.4	15.8	14.9	55th
50th	21.3	19.8	18.4	17.3	16.7	16.4	15.3	50th
45th	21.8	20.4	19.1	17.7	17.1	16.6	15.6	45th
40th	22.6	21.0	19.3	18.1	17.5	17.1	16.2	40th
35th	23.6	21.5	19.8	18.5	17.9	17.4	16.7	35th
30th	24.6	22.2	20.6	19.0	18.3	18.2	17.2	30th
25th	25.7	23.1	12.2	19.5	18.9	18.8	17.6	25th
20th	26.7	23.9	21.9	20.2	19.5	19.4	18.3	20th
15th	28.2	25.4	23.0	21.3	20.2	19.9	18.9	15th
10th	30.1	27.8	24.2	22.5	20.9	20.9	19.9	10th
5th	34.7	29.5	26.4	25.1	22.2	23.0	21.2	5th
0	43.1	36.0	29.3	28.2	24.9	25.5	26.1	0

TABLE LXXXVII

SPEED THROW (GIRLS)
Test Scores in Seconds and Tenths

				Age				
Percentile	10-11	12	13	14	15	16	17-18	Percentile
100th	10.0	12.0	12.0	12.0	12.0	14.0	14.0	100th
95th	20.1	13.8	13.0	13.0	15.6	15.8	15.0	95th
90th	21.4	15.8	16.3	13.9	16.6	16.9	15.0	90th
85th	22.8	17.7	17.8	15.3	17.6	17.6	15.6	85th
80th	24.1	18.8	18.6	16.5	18.1	18.1	16.1	80th
75th	25.2	19.8	19.4	17.6	18.6	18.5	17.6	75th
70th	26.0	20.8	20.0	18.2	19.1	18.9	18.0	70th
65th	27.0	21.6	20.6	18.7	19.6	19.4	18.5	65th
60th	27.4	22.3	21.3	19.3	20.1	20.0	18.9	60th
55th	28.8	23.1	21.9	19.9	20.6	20.7	19.3	55th
50th	29.8	24.1	22.7	20.7	21.1	21.4	19.8	50th
45th	30.9	25.2	23.4	21.1	21.7	22.2	20.3	45th
40th	31.9	26.2	24.3	21.8	22.6	22.9	20.8	40th
35th	33.0	27.5	25.4	22.5	23.3	23.7	21.4	35th
30th	34.1	28.6	26.4	23.5	24.3	24.8	22.3	30th
25th	35.9	29.8	27.5	24.6	25.4	26.1	23.3	25th
20th	38.0	31.3	28.9	25.8	26.9	27.8	24.1	20th
15th	41.0	33.1	30.9	27.4	28.7	30.4	25.0	15th
10th	46.1	36.7	33.0	30.2	31.5	33.0	26.1	10th
5th	55.2	40.8	38.5	33.5	37.4	36.9	28.9	5th
0	105.0	66.0	52.0	50.0	50.0	52.0	40.0	0

TABLE LXXXVIII

FUNGO HITTING (BOYS)
Test Scores in Points

Percentile	10–11	12	13	Age 14	15	16	17–18	Percentile
100th	40	40	39	36	40	40	40	100th
95th	35	36	38	35	39	38	39	95th
90th	32	33	34	35	37	36	37	90th
85th	29	31	33	33	34	34	36	85th
80th	27	30	31	31	33	33	35	80th
75th	26	29	30	30	31	33	34	75th
70th	24	28	29	29	30	32	32	70th
65th	22	27	28	28	29	30	31	65th
60th	21	26	27	27	28	29	30	60th
55th	20	25	25	26	26	28	29	55th
50th	19	23	24	24	24	26	28	50th
45th	17	22	23	23	23	25	26	45th
40th	16	20	21	21	21	23	25	40th
35th	14	19	19	19	19	21	23	35th
30th	13	17	18	18	17	19	21	30th
25th	11	15	16	16	16	17	19	25th
20th	10	13	15	15	14	15	17	20th
15th	8	11	14	13	12	13	15	15th
10th	6	10	12	12	11	11	13	10th
5th	3	7	9	11	9	9	11	5th
0	0	0	1	9	1	0	3	0

TABLE LXXXIX

FUNGO HITTING (GIRLS)
Test Scores in Points

Percentile	10-11	12	13	Age 14	15	16	17-18	Percentile
100th	30	38	38	38	38	38	38	100th
95th	21	28	30	31	30	30	31	95th
90th	18	24	26	30	27	27	28	90th
85th	15	22	23	26	25	25	26	85th
80th	14	20	22	23	23	24	25	80th
75th	13	18	20	21	22	22	23	75th
70th	12	17	19	20	20	21	22	70th
65th	12	16	18	19	19	19	20	65th
60th	11	15	17	18	18	18	19	60th
55th	9	14	16	17	17	17	18	55th
50th	9	13	14	15	16	16	17	50th
45th	8	12	13	14	15	15	16	45th
40th	7	11	13	13	14	14	15	40th
35th	6	10	12	12	13	13	14	35th
30th	6	9	11	11	12	12	14	30th
25th	5	8	10	10	11	11	13	25th
20th	4	7	8	9	10	10	12	20th
15th	3	5	7	8	8	9	10	15th
10th	2	4	6	6	7	8	8	10th
5th	0	2	4	3	4	5	6	5th
0	0	0	0	0	0	0	0	0

TABLE XC

BASE RUNNING (BOYS)
Test Scores in Seconds and Tenths

Percentile	10-11	12	13	14	15	16	17-18	Percentile
100th	10.1	9.6	9.4	9.7	10.0	10.0	10.0	100th
95th	12.9	12.4	11.7	11.5	11.6	11.3	11.1	95th
90th	13.5	12.5	12.2	11.9	11.9	11.6	11.4	90th
85th	13.9	13.3	12.7	12.2	12.2	11.8	11.6	85th
80th	14.1	13.5	12.9	12.5	12.4	12.0	11.8	80th
75th	14.3	13.7	13.2	12.7	12.5	12.1	11.9	75th
70th	14.5	13.9	13.4	12.9	12.7	12.3	12.0	70th
65th	14.8	14.1	13.6	13.0	12.8	12.4	12.2	65th
60th	14.9	14.3	13.8	13.1	13.0	12.5	12.3	60th
55th	15.1	14.5	13.9	13.3	13.1	12.6	12.4	55th
50th	15.2	14.7	14.1	13.4	13.2	12.8	12.6	50th
45th	15.4	14.8	14.3	13.5	13.3	12.9	12.7	45th
40th	15.6	15.0	14.5	13.7	13.5	13.0	12.8	40th
35th	15.8	15.2	14.7	13.9	13.6	13.2	12.9	35th
30th	16.0	15.4	14.9	14.1	13.7	13.3	13.0	30th
25th	16.2	15.7	15.1	14.2	13.9	13.6	13.2	25th
20th	16.5	15.9	15.4	14.5	14.0	13.8	13.4	20th
15th	17.0	16.2	15.7	14.8	14.3	14.1	13.6	15th
10th	17.4	16.5	15.9	15.2	14.5	14.4	13.9	10th
5th	18.2	17.4	16.7	15.8	15.0	15.3	14.9	5th
0	23.0	20.6	17.2	17.2	15.8	18.0	17.8	0

TABLE XCI

BASE RUNNING (GIRLS)
Test Scores in Seconds and Tenths

			Age					
Percentile	10-11	12	13	14	15	16	17-18	Percentile
100th	11.0	11.0	12.0	12.0	12.0	12.0	12.0	100th
95th	13.1	13.4	12.6	12.7	12.9	13.2	13.6	95th
90th	13.8	13.7	13.1	13.1	13.5	13.7	13.9	90th
85th	14.3	14.0	13.5	13.5	13.7	14.0	14.3	85th
80th	14.7	14.3	13.7	13.7	13.9	14.4	14.6	80th
75th	14.9	14.5	13.9	13.8	14.1	14.6	14.8	75th
70th	15.2	14.7	14.1	14.0	14.3	14.8	14.9	70th
65th	15.4	14.9	14.3	14.2	14.5	14.9	15.1	65th
60th	15.6	15.0	14.5	14.4	14.7	15.1	15.3	60th
55th	15.8	15.2	14.7	14.5	14.9	15.3	15.5	55th
50th	16.0	15.3	14.8	14.8	15.0	15.5	15.7	50th
45th	16.2	15.5	15.0	14.9	15.2	15.6	15.9	45th
40th	16.4	15.7	15.2	15.1	15.4	15.8	16.1	40th
35th	16.7	15.8	15.4	15.3	15.5	15.9	16.3	35th
30th	17.0	16.0	15.6	15.5	15.8	16.0	16.5	30th
25th	17.3	16.2	16.0	15.7	16.1	16.2	16.9	25th
20th	17.7	16.5	16.3	16.0	16.3	16.3	17.1	20th
15th	18.2	16.9	16.6	16.4	16.7	16.4	17.6	15th
10th	18.8	17.4	17.2	16.9	17.3	17.8	18.2	10th
5th	19.9	18.2	18.0	17.8	18.1	18.4	19.2	5th
0	27.0	20.0	22.0	23.0	28.0	31.0	32.0	0

TABLE XCII

FIELDING GROUND BALLS (BOYS)
Test Scores in Points

Percentile	10-11	12	13	Age 14	15	16	17-18	Percentile
100th	20	20	20	20	20	20	20	100th
95th	19	20	20	20	20	20	20	95th
90th	18	19	19	19	19	20	20	90th
85th	18	19	19	19	19	20	20	85th
80th	17	18	18	18	18	19	19	80th
75th	17	18	18	18	18	19	19	75th
70th	16	17	17	17	18	19	19	70th
65th	16	17	17	17	17	18	18	65th
60th	15	16	16	16	16	18	18	60th
55th	15	16	16	16	16	17	17	55th
50th	14	15	15	15	15	17	17	50th
45th	13	15	14	14	15	16	17	45th
40th	13	14	14	14	14	16	16	40th
35th	12	14	13	13	13	15	16	35th
30th	11	13	13	12	12	14	15	30th
25th	10	12	12	10	11	13	14	25th
20th	9	11	11	10	10	10	12	20th
15th	8	9	10	9	9	9	10	15th
10th	6	8	8	8	8	9	9	10th
5th	4	6	6	6	7	8	9	5th
0	0	0	1	1	1	5	6	0

TABLE XCIII

FIELDING GROUND BALLS (GIRLS)
Test Scores in Points

| Percentile | Age | | | | | | | Percentile |
	10-11	12	13	14	15	16	17-18	
100th	20	20	20	20	20	20	20	100th
95th	18	20	20	20	20	20	20	95th
90th	17	19	19	19	20	20	20	90th
85th	16	19	19	19	19	19	19	85th
80th	15	18	19	19	19	19	19	80th
75th	15	18	18	18	18	19	19	75th
70th	14	17	18	18	18	18	18	70th
65th	13	16	17	17	18	18	18	65th
70th	13	15	17	17	17	18	18	60th
55th	12	15	16	17	17	17	17	55th
50th	11	14	16	16	16	17	17	50th
45th	10	13	15	15	16	17	17	45th
40th	10	12	15	15	15	16	16	40th
35th	9	10	14	14	15	16	16	35th
30th	8	10	13	13	14	15	15	30th
25th	8	9	12	12	13	14	14	25th
20th	7	9	11	10	12	13	14	20th
15th	6	8	10	10	11	12	13	15th
10th	5	7	9	9	10	10	11	10th
5th	3	5	8	8	9	8	9	5th
0	0	0	0	0	0	0	0	0

TABLE XCIV

SOFTBALL THROW FOR DISTANCE (BOYS)
Test Scores in Feet

Percentile	10-11	12	13	Age 14	15	16	17-18	Percentile
100th	200	208	200	230	242	247	255	100th
95th	154	163	185	208	231	229	229	95th
90th	144	152	175	203	205	219	222	90th
85th	127	146	167	191	198	213	216	85th
80th	121	140	160	184	192	208	213	80th
75th	118	135	154	178	187	202	207	75th
70th	114	132	150	173	182	196	204	70th
65th	111	129	145	168	178	193	199	65th
60th	109	125	142	163	174	190	196	60th
55th	106	122	138	159	170	186	192	55th
50th	103	118	135	154	167	183	188	50th
45th	100	115	131	152	165	180	185	45th
40th	98	113	128	148	161	174	182	40th
35th	95	109	125	144	157	171	178	35th
30th	92	106	122	140	154	167	173	30th
25th	91	102	117	137	148	164	169	25th
20th	85	98	113	133	143	159	163	20th
15th	80	93	107	129	138	152	153	15th
10th	72	85	101	123	133	146	147	10th
5th	62	76	97	113	119	140	140	5th
0	24	31	60	105	93	135	90	0

TABLE XCV

SOFTBALL THROW FOR DISTANCE (GIRLS)
Test Scores in Feet

Percentile	10-11	12	13	Age 14	15	16	17-18	Percentile
100th	120	160	160	160	200	200	200	100th
95th	99	113	133	126	127	121	120	95th
90th	84	104	112	117	116	109	109	90th
85th	76	98	105	109	108	103	102	85th
80th	71	94	98	104	103	98	97	80th
75th	68	89	94	99	97	94	93	75th
70th	66	85	90	95	93	91	89	70th
65th	62	81	86	92	88	87	87	65th
60th	60	77	83	88	85	84	84	60th
55th	57	74	81	85	80	81	82	55th
50th	55	70	76	82	77	79	80	50th
45th	53	67	73	79	75	76	77	45th
40th	50	64	70	76	72	73	74	40th
35th	48	61	68	73	70	70	72	35th
30th	45	58	64	69	67	67	69	30th
25th	43	55	62	66	64	63	66	25th
20th	41	51	60	61	61	60	63	20th
15th	38	48	56	57	58	56	60	15th
10th	34	43	51	52	54	51	55	10th
5th	31	37	43	43	49	45	50	5th
0	20	20	20	20	20	10	10	0

TABLE XCVI

CATCHING FLY BALLS (BOYS)
Test Scores in Points

Percentile	10-11	12	13	Age 14	15	16	17-18	Percentile
100th	20	20	20	20	20	20	20	100th
95th	20	20	20	20	20	20	20	95th
90th	20	20	20	20	20	20	20	90th
85th	19	19	19	19	20	20	20	85th
80th	19	19	19	19	19	19	19	80th
75th	19	19	19	19	19	19	19	75th
70th	18	19	18	19	19	19	19	70th
65th	18	18	18	18	18	19	19	65th
60th	17	18	17	18	18	18	18	60th
55th	17	17	17	18	17	18	18	55th
50th	16	17	16	16	17	17	18	50th
45th	15	16	16	16	16	16	17	45th
40th	14	15	15	15	15	15	16	40th
35th	12	14	14	13	14	13	15	35th
30th	10	12	13	12	12	10	14	30th
25th	9	10	11	10	11	10	11	25th
20th	8	10	10	10	10	10	10	20th
15th	7	8	9	9	9	9	10	15th
10th	6	7	8	8	8	9	9	10th
5th	3	5	6	7	7	8	9	5th
0	0	0	0	0	0	0	0	0

TABLE XCVII

CATCHING FLY BALLS (GIRLS)
Test Scores in Points

Percentile	Age							Percentile
	10-11	12	13	14	15	16	17-18	
100th	15	17	19	19	20	20	20	100th
95th	13	15	17	17	19	19	19	95th
90th	10	13	15	16	18	19	19	90th
85th	9	11	13	15	18	18	18	85th
80th	9	10	12	14	17	17	17	80th
75th	8	9	11	13	16	16	16	75th
70th	7	8	10	12	15	15	16	70th
65th	7	7	9	11	14	14	15	65th
60th	6	7	8	10	13	13	15	60th
55th	6	6	7	9	12	13	14	55th
50th	5	6	6	9	11	12	13	50th
45th	4	5	5	8	10	11	12	45th
40th	4	5	5	8	9	10	11	40th
35th	3	4	4	7	8	9	10	35th
30th	3	3	3	6	7	8	9	30th
25th	2	3	3	5	6	7	8	25th
20th	2	2	2	4	5	6	7	20th
15th	1	2	2	3	4	5	6	15th
10th	1	1	1	2	3	4	5	10th
5th	0	0	0	1	2	3	4	5th
0	0	0	0	0	0	0	0	0

softball skills test items have been validated and included in other tests. However, some of the items have not been validated; therefore, their value for grading purposes is questionable. The main value of the AAHPER Softball Skill Test is its comprehensiveness in number of test items, providing a variety of skill items that are conducive to self-testing as an indicator of improvement.

The catching fly balls test for boys receives low marks in feasibility of administration. A two-story facility is not always readily available. Moreover, an adequate substitute for this item should not prove too difficult to develop.

SHICK SOFTBALL TEST BATTERY[37]
Date: 1970.
Purpose: To measure defensive softball skills in college women.

Description

Repeated Throws: An item to measure the student's ability to align herself with an aerial ball, and to throw the ball rapidly after fielding it from the air or floor. A line is drawn on the wall 10 feet from and parallel to the floor. A line 23 feet from the wall is drawn on the floor and lies parallel to the wall.

Fielding Test: Designed to measure the student's ability to align herself with a ground ball, and to throw the ball rapidly after fielding it on the bounce or from the floor. This test calls for a line to be drawn on the wall 4 feet from the floor and one on the floor 15 feet from the wall. Both lines are parallel to the wall.

Target Test: The target test measures accuracy and power in the student's throw. The target values and dimensions for both the floor and wall targets are shown in Figure 69. Target value areas should be color coded as follows: 5–red; 4–medium blue; 3–bright yellow; 2–pale aqua; and 1–black. The wall target is 66 inches square with the center located 36 inches from the floor. The restraining line lies parallel to the wall and 40 feet away.

EDUCATIONAL APPLICATION: College women.

Administrative Feasibility

TIME: Two forty-minute class periods when a mass testing procedure is utilized.

PERSONNEL: An instructor and at least two trained assistants.

TRAINING INVOLVED: One practice throw is allowed prior to each of the four trials for the repeated throws test item. Two practice throws are permitted prior to the throw trials in the target test item.

EQUIPMENT AND SUPPLIES: Adequate supply of softballs; stop watch.

Accessories: Tape and chalk for floor markings; scoring materials.

Facilities and Space: A regulation size gymnasium with unobstructed wall space.

Directions

REPEATED THROWS: The student stands behind the restraining

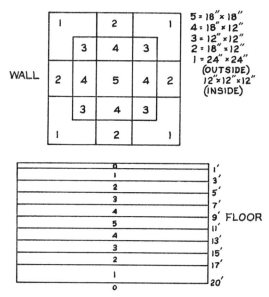

Figure 69. Target test layout. From J. Shick: Battery of defensive softball skills tests for college women, *Research Quarterly, 41*:82-87, 1970. Courtesy of AAHPER.

line and holds a softball. On the starting signal, she throws at the wall with an overhand or sidearm motion, attempting to hit the wall above the 10-foot line. She attempts to catch the rebound in the air or field it from the floor. This action is taken as often as possible in thirty seconds. Four trials are given. Failure to field a ball cleanly does not constitute a penalty other than loss of time.

FIELDING TEST: The test directions follow those for the repeated throws, including the four thirty-second trials with two exceptions:

a. Any type throw may be used.

b. The student attempts to hit the wall below the drawn line.

TARGET TEST: Two trials of ten throws each are permitted. Each throw is made behind the restraining line.

For the repeated throws and fielding tests, the student completes a trial, then waits until each class member finishes her trial before proceeding to the next.

SCORING METHOD

Repeated Throws: A ball striking below the wall line or one thrown with the student stepping on or crossing the restraining line does not count. The total number of legal hits for the four trials are summed for the official score.

Fielding Test: Identical to the repeated throws scoring method except a legal hit is recorded for a ball that hits below the wall line.

Target Test: Two separate scores are given for each throw, one for the wall hit and the other for the hit of the first bounce. Hits outside either scoring area do not count. The highest possible score for the test is 200 points (fifty per target per trial).

Scientific Authenticity

VALIDITY: The validity coefficients for the three tests as previously presented were .69, .48, and .63, respectively. The coefficient for the battery was .75. The coefficients were obtained from the scores of fifty-nine college female students enrolled in two general softball classes.

RELIABILITY: The reliability coefficients were .86, .89, and .88 for the three tests in the order presented above. The coefficient for the battery was .88.

CRITERION MEASURE: Judges' ratings of individual performance in game situations. Each student was observed twice a week.

Additional Comments

Administration of this test in a reasonable amount of time could require more trained manpower than is sometimes available. Also, the test is limited to the measurement of softball defensive skills; therefore, it could never serve as a comprehensive skills test for softball.

The reliability coefficients computed for the three test items are impressive. Perhaps the most important feature of Shick's test is its improvement in the area of scientific authenticity over previous tests of similar design. The reliability and validity coefficients for the repeated throws and the reliability coefficient for the fielding item in this test was notably superior to the coefficients obtained for those items in previous studies.

REFERENCES

1. American Association for Health, Physical Education and Recreation: *Measurement and Evaluation of Materials in Health, Physical Education and Recreation*. Washington, AAHPER, 1950.
2. ————: *Skills Test Manual: Softball for Boys*. Brace, David K. (Test Consultant). Washington, AAHPER, 1966.
3. ————: *Skills Test Manual: Softball for Girls*. Brace, David K. (Test Consultant). Washington, AAHPER, 1966.
4. Barrow, Harold M. and McGee, Rosemary: *A Practical Approach to Measurement in Physical Education*. Philadelphia, Lea & Febiger, 1964.
5. ————: *A Practical Approach to Measurement in Physical Education*, 2nd ed. Philadelphia, Lea & Febiger, 1971.
6. Bliss, James G.: A study of progression based on age, sex, and individual differences in strength and skill. *American Physical Education Review, 32:*21, 1927.
7. Brace, David K.: *Measuring Motor Ability*. New York, B&N, 1927.
8. Brophy, Kathleen: *Spalding's Athletic Library*. New York, Am Sports, 1934.
9. Cale, Audrey A.: The Investigation and Analysis of Softball Skill Tests for College Women. Master's thesis, College Park, University of Maryland, 1962.
10. Campbell, W. R. and Tucker, N. M.: *An Introduction to Tests and Measurements in Physical Education*. London, Bell & Sons, 1967.
11. Clarke, H. Harrison: *Application of Measurement to Health and Physical Education*, 4th ed. Englewood Cliffs, P-H, 1967.
12. Davis, Rosemary: The Development of an Objective Softball Batting Test for College Women. Master's thesis, Normal, Illinois State University, 1951.
13. Eckert, Helen M.: *Practical Measurement of Physical Performance*. Philadelphia, Lea & Febiger, 1974.
14. Elrod, Joe M.: Construction of a Softball Skill Test Battery for High School Boys. Master's thesis, Baton Rouge, Louisiana State University, 1969.
15. Fox, Margaret G. and Young, Olive G.: A test of softball batting ability. *Research Quarterly, 25:*26-27, 1954.
16. Franks, B. Don and Deutsch, Helga: *Evaluating Performance in Physical Education*. New York, Acad Pr, 1973.
17. Friermood, Harold T. (Ed.): *Athletic Achievement Program for Boys and Girls*. New York, Assn Pr, 1960.

18. Fringer, Margaret Neal: A Battery of Softball Skill Tests for Senior High School Girls. Master's thesis, Ann Arbor, University of Michigan, 1961.
19. Glassow, Ruth B. and Broer, Marion R.: *Measuring Achievement in Physical Education*. Philadelphia, Saunders, 1938.
20. Hardin, Donald H. and Ramirez, John: Elementary school performance norms. *TAHPER Journal*, 1:8-9, 1972.
21. Johnson, Barry L. and Nelson, Jack K.: *Practical Measurements for Evaluation in Physical Education*. Minneapolis, Burgess, 1969.
22. ———: *Practical Measurements for Evaluation in Physical Education*, 2nd ed. Minneapolis, Burgess, 1974.
23. Kehtel, Carmen H.: The Development of a Test to Measure the Ability of a Softball Player to Field a Ground Ball and Successfully Throw It at a Target. Master's thesis, Boulder, University of Colorado, 1958.
24. Larson, Leonard A. and Yocom, Rachael Dunaven: *Measurement and Evaluation in Physical, Health and Recreation Education*. St. Louis, Mosby, 1951.
25. McCloy, Charles Harold and Young, Norma Dorothy: *Tests and Measurements in Health and Physical Education*, 3rd ed. New York, Appleton, 1954.
26. Meyers, Carlton R. and Blesh, T. Erwin: *Measurement in Physical Education*. New York, Ronald, 1962.
27. Montoye, Henry J. (Ed.): *An Introduction to Measurement in Physical Education*, vol. III. Indianapolis, Phi Epsilon Kappa Fraternity, 1970.
28. ———: *An Introduction to Measurement in Physical Education*, vol V. Indianapolis, Phi Epsilon Kappa Fraternity, 1970.
29. Mosbek, Ellen: *Spalding's Athletic Library*. New York, Am Sports, 1937.
30. Neilson, N. P. and Jensen, Clayne R.: *Measurement and Statistics in Physical Education*. Belmont, Calif., Wadsworth Pub, 1972.
31. New York State Physical Education Standards Project: *Standards Manual for Football, Soccer, and Softball Skills, Boys, Grades 7-12*, Bulletin 3. Albany, New York State Education Department, 1951.
32. O'Donnell, Doris J.: Validation of Softball Skill Tests for High School Girls. Master's thesis, Bloomington, Indiana University, 1950.
33. Palmer, Gladys E.: *Baseball for Girls and Women*. New York, B&N, 1929.
34. Rodgers, Elizabeth G. and Heath, Marjorie L.: An experiment in the use of knowledge and skill tests in playground baseball. *Research Quarterly*, 2:113, 1931.
35. Scott, M. Gladys and French, Esther: *Better Teaching Through Testing*. New York, B&N, 1945.

36. ————: *Measurement and Evaluation in Physical Education.* Dubuque, Iowa, Brown Bk, 1959.

37. Shick, Jacqueline: Battery of defensive softball skills tests for college women. *Research Quarterly, 41:*82-87, 1970.

38. Sopa, Adeline: Construction of an Indoor Batting Skills Test for Junior High School Girls. Master's thesis, Madison, University of Wisconsin, 1967.

39. Underkofler, Audrey: A Study of Skill Tests for Evaluating the Ability of Junior High School Girls in Softball. Master's thesis, Iowa City, University of Iowa, 1942.

40. Weiss, Raymond A. and Phillips, Marjorie: *Administration of Tests in Physical Education.* St. Louis, Mosby, 1954.

41. Willgoose, Carl E.: *Evaluation in Health Education and Physical Education.* New York, McGraw, 1961.

Chapter 23

Speedball

INTRODUCTION

S PEEDBALL IS A RATHER unique activity since it relates so closely to soccer and contains some features of basketball and
football. A study by Crawford,[4] in which soccer skills tests were
adequately used for determining general speedball ability, confirmed the close similarity of the two sports. Only the skills that
involved the conversion of a ground ball to an aerial ball are exclusively common to speedball and are measured by the kick-up
or lift-to-self type tests.

The sport is played primarily by females at both the secondary
and college levels, and though not an extremely popular activity,
its inclusion in the physical education curriculum at those educational levels is not uncommon.

Of the very few skills tests developed for speedball, the two that
follow merit presentation.

BUCHANAN SPEEDBALL TEST[2]

Date: 1942.

Purpose: To measure fundamental skills in speedball and predict playing ability.

Description

The Buchanan Test may be used as either a six-item or two-
item battery, depending on the time allowed for testing. Included
in the two-item battery are the throwing and catching, and passing
items. Its relationship with the test criterion reflected a correlation
coefficient of .93.

When using the two-item battery, the following equation applies
for score determination:

1.0 throwing and catching + 3.0 passing = playing ability score

Lift to Others: A net 2½ feet high and at least 30 feet long is
stretched between two standards. Six feet from the net and on
each side is located a parallel line the length of the net. All along

both sides of the net are placed 3-foot squares at 3-foot intervals (Fig. 70).

The primary test objective is to lift the stationary ball and pass it for accuracy.

Throwing and Catching While Standing: A restraining line is drawn 6 feet away and parallel to an unobstructed wall. The length of the line depends upon the available wall surface and the number of students that need to be tested simultaneously.

Kick-up: The sideline markings of any playing field may be used as part of the field markings. A 2-foot square is drawn with its inner side located three feet from the sideline mark. A starting line, located 4 feet from the corner of the square, is drawn perpendicular to an imaginary extension of the diagonal of the square (Fig. 71). More than one square may be constructed to economize in test administration time.

Dribbling and Passing: A starting line is drawn 60 yards away from and parallel to the end line of the playing field. Two or four goal areas, depending on the number of subjects to be tested simultaneously, are marked off on the end line. The goal areas are marked with 12-inch perpendicular lines and each is 6 yards wide. Obstacles such as Indian clubs, cones, etc., are placed at 10-yard intervals in a straight line between the end line and the starting line. The obstacle lines are placed 3 yards to the right and left of the particular goal areas with a 10-yard space located between goal areas (Fig. 72).

Passing: Identical in description to dribbling and passing item.
Dribbling: Description identical to dribbling and passing item.
EDUCATIONAL APPLICATION: High school girls.

Administrative Feasibility

TIME: Two or three sixty-minute class periods for administering the six-item battery to twenty students and one to two periods for the two-item battery, depending upon how extensive mass testing is employed.

PERSONNEL: A person to score or time each item, whichever the case, then record the result. Student assistants are needed for the administration of some items.

TRAINING INVOLVED: Plenty of practice time on the lift to oth-

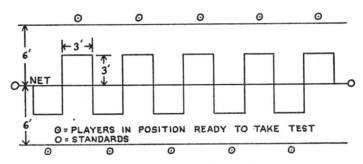

Figure 70. Markings for lift to others test.

ers item is recommended for the students. Five practice trials are allowed each subject on the kick-up item immediately before being tested. Familiarity in dribbling around obstacles should be instilled in each student before testing them on the items requiring that skill.

EQUIPMENT AND SUPPLIES: Soccer balls, net, standards, stop watch, obstacles such as Indian clubs or cones, regulation soccer goals if available.

Accessories: Materials for scoring and marking the field and court.

Facilities and Space: Playing field and gymnasium with unobstructed wall space.

Directions

LIFT TO OTHERS: Ten subjects can be tested simultaneously when utilizing the test station layout described earlier. Five subjects line up behind the 6-foot restraining line on either side of the net. Each subject takes a position directly behind a 3-foot square and each set of partners has a single ball which is placed on the line. The test begins with a subject lifting the ball with either foot and passing it over the net in an attempt to hit the square diagonally across the net and to the right. The partner recovers the ball and then becomes the test subject by proceeding to lift the ball back over the net diagonally to her right and across the net. Alternate turns are taken until each partner has taken ten trials, five to the right and five to the left.

THROWING AND CATCHING WHILE STANDING: The test begins

with the subject positioning herself immediately behind the restraining line with a soccer ball in her hands. When an audible signal is given, the subject proceeds to throw the ball against the wall and catch it on the rebound. This is done as many times as possible during each of five thirty-second trials. Should the subject lose control of the ball, it should be recovered as quickly as possible and again put back into play from behind the restraining line.

The five trials are not taken in consecutive order. Also, the partner system is again used, meaning that after the test subject completes each thirty-second trial, she will change places with her partner. The partner not being tested stands behind and to the side of the test subject. It is the duty of the partner not being tested to count the number of successful completions in each trial.

KICK-UP: Once again the subjects work as partners in the testing procedure. To get ready for testing, the subject assumes a standing position behind the starting line while the thrower or partner stands behind the sideline. The test begins with the thrower executing an overhead toss with a soccer ball so that it

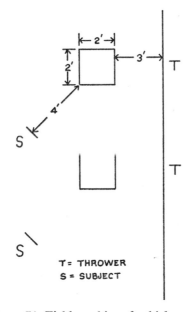

Figure 71. Field markings for kick-up test.

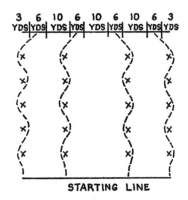

Figure 72. Field markings for dribbling and passing test.

lands in the 2-foot square. As soon as the thrower releases the ball, the subject runs toward the ball and proceeds to execute a kick-up. The kick-up requires a player to control a moving ball accurately with the foot and kick it up to herself. If the thrown ball does not land in the 2-foot square, the trial should be repeated.

DRIBBLING AND PASSING: The subject stands behind the starting line with the soccer ball resting on the line directly in line with the obstacles. On an audible signal, she starts to dribble toward the first obstacle. The first obstacle is passed on the right, the second on the left, and so on down the field. After passing the last obstacle on the right, the subject passes the ball to the left in an attempt to send it into the appropriate goal area.

Ten trials are required with five trials coming from the left and five from the right. A systematic testing order should be followed to insure an adequate rest period for the subjects between trials.

PASSING: Directions same as dribbling and passing item.

DRIBBLING: Administration identical to dribbling and passing item except that the passing requirement is deleted.

SCORING METHOD AND NORMS

Lift to Others: Partners score for each other. The final score is the total number of accurate and correct lifts out of ten trials, with each successful lift counting one point. Lifts are considered successful if the ball clears the net and falls within the appropriate 3-foot square. Should the ball touch the net and land in the designated area, it still counts. Balls hitting the square lines also count.

Throwing and Catching While Standing: The final score is the average number of complete throws and catches made in each of the five thirty-second trials. One point is scored for each completion. Partners score for each other.

Kick-up: The total number of successfully executed and caught kick-ups for the ten trials constitutes the final score. Again the subject's score is kept by her partner.

Dribbling and Passing: The final score is the sum of the time scores (dribbling 50 yards) on all ten trials minus ten times the total number of accurate passes on all ten trials. The time score is measured to the nearest second.

Passing: The total number of accurate passes out of ten test trials is the final score.

Dribbling: The total time it takes to dribble the 50-yard distance as described in the dribbling and passing item.

TABLE XCVIII

ACHIEVEMENT SCALES FOR SELECTED ITEMS
IN BUCHANAN SPEEDBALL TEST*

Rating	Lift to Others	Throwing and Catching	Passing	Kick-Ups
Superior	10 & up	18.8 & up	10	9 & up
Good	8-9	16.3-18.7	7-9	7-8
Average	5-7	14.3-16.2	4-6	4-6
Poor	2-4	11.3-14.2	2-3	2-3
Inferior	1 & below	11.2 & below	1 & below	1 & below

N = 72, number of trials as specified in directions.

Rating	Lift to Others	Throwing and Catching	Passing	Kick-ups
Superior	10 & up	27.8 & up		10
Good	8-9	23.8-27.7	5	8-9
Average	6-7	17.8-23.7	3-4	4-7
Poor	3-5	11.8-17.7	2	2-3
Inferior	2 & below	11.7 & below	1 & below	1 & below
	N = 262	N = 159	N = 190	N = 262
	10 trials	M of 2 trials	5 trials	10 trials

*Based on scores of high school girls.

TABLE XCIX

T-SCALES FOR SELECTED ITEMS IN BUCHANAN SPEEDBALL TEST

T-Score	Lift To Others*	Throwing And Catching Standing†	Throwing And Catching Standing‡	Kick-Ups§	Passing‖	Passing¶	T-Score
75		19.8-20.2					75
74							74
73							73
72		19.3-19.7	27.8-29.7	10			72
71	10					10	71
70							70
69		18.8-19.2					69
68					5		68
67		18.3-18.7					67
66				9		9	66
65		17.8-18.2	25.8-27.7				65
64							64
63	9						63
62		17.3-17.7				8	62
61							61
60		16.8-17.2					60
59				8		7	59
58		16.3-16.7					58
57	8		23.8-25.7			6	57
56		15.8-16.2					56
55							55
54		15.3-15.7		7			54
53	7						53
52			21.8-23.7				52
51		14.8-15.2			4	5	51
50				6			50
49							49
48			19.3-21.7				48
47	6			5			47
46		14.3-14.7				4	46
45			17.8-19.7				45
44							44
43	5	13.8-13.2		4	3		43
42		13.3-13.7					42
41		12.8-13.2	15.8-17.7				41
40		12.3-12.7				3	40
39	4	11.8-11.2					39
38				3			38
37			13.8-15.7				37
36		11.3-11.7					36
35					2	2	35
34	3			2			34

TABLE XCIX (continued)

T-Score	Lift To Others*	Throwing And Catching Standing†	Throwing And Catching Standing‡	Kick-Ups§	Passing‖	Passing⁋	T-Score
33			11.8-13.7				33
32							32
31							31
30	2						30
29				1			29
28					1		28
27							27
26			9.8-11.7				26
25	1					1	25

*Ten trials, 262 cases.
†Mean of five trials, 72 cases.
‡Mean of two trials, 159 cases.
§Ten trials, 262 cases.
‖Five trials, 190 cases.
⁋Ten trials, 72 cases.

Scientific Authenticity

Seventy-two high school girls served as test subjects in the Buchanan study.

Item	Validity	Reliability
a. Lift to Others	.88	.93
b. Throwing and Catching While Standing	.79	.92
c. Kick-up	.85	.93
d. Dribbling and Passing	.69	.98
e. Passing	.86	.91
f. Dribbling	.57	.98

Reliability coefficients were determined by correlating the odd and even trials and corrected by the Spearman-Brown Prophecy Formula.

CRITERION MEASURE: Subjective ratings of three instructors.

Additional Comments

As alluded to earlier, the lift to others item should be given extra attention in practice since it is so difficult to master and, furthermore, used so often in speedball. The same is true for the kick-up item.

The throwing and catching while standing test is a part of the previously mentioned two-item battery. A rest period should be given to each student between test trials to avoid fatigue. An advantage of the item is the short amount of time required for its administration.

Buchanan's study of the dribbling and passing items produced an interesting finding. According to the validity coefficients obtained, the dribbling item when given by itself or the dribbling and passing item combined do not simulate gamelike skills quite as much as the passing item does.

Obviously, the main shortcoming of the Buchanan Test is the considerable amount of time required to administer the whole battery. Instructors may wish to select only certain items for administration.

SMITH SPEEDBALL TESTS[11]

Date: 1947.

Purpose: To measure general speedball ability.

Description

Smith developed a three-item test battery for use in an indoor setting. The test items include a kick-up to self, wall pass, and foot pass to wall test. The first two tests were devised specifically for speedball, while the other is equally applicable to soccer, as are some other speedball tests. Since the validity and reliability values of the foot pass to wall item are below the minimum acceptable level, that test is not presented here.

The kick-up to self test requires each subject to throw a soccer ball against a wall while standing behind a restraining line and then control its rebound by executing either a one- or two-foot kick-up to self. In the wall pass test, the subject repeatedly throws the ball against the wall and catches it while standing behind a restraining line.

For the kick-up to self item, an unobstructed wall space is required that is at least 6 feet wide and 8 to 10 feet high. An equally wide floor space is needed that measures 10 feet long. A restraining line is drawn on the floor that is 7 feet from and parallel to the base of the wall.

The wall space and floor markings for the wall pass test are identical to those required for the kick-up to self test.

EDUCATIONAL APPLICATION: Designed for college women, but also appropriate for junior and senior high school boys and girls.

Administrative Feasibility

TIME: Twenty students can be tested in two sixty-minute class periods.

PERSONNEL: One timer-recorder.

TRAINING INVOLVED: Only a brief warm-up is necessary to get the "feel" of the skill requirement.

EQUIPMENT AND SUPPLIES: Soccer balls, stop watches.

Accessories: Scoring and floor marking materials.

Facilities and Space: Unobstructed wall and floor space at least 6 feet wide and 10 feet long, respectively.

Directions

KICK-UP TO SELF: While standing behind the restraining line holding a soccer ball and upon hearing an audible signal, the subject throws the ball against the wall at any desired height; however, 2 to 3 feet is recommended. The subject is to control the rebound by executing a kick-up to self and immediately throw the ball against the wall again, continually repeating the process for six separate thirty-second trials. If the ball does not rebound back to the restraining line, the subject is permitted to recover the ball regardless of its location, but it must be put back into play from behind the restraining line. It is recommended that three subjects be assigned to each testing station. This allows them to keep a running score for each other, and prevents fatigue from becoming a factor in their performance, since each receives a one-minute rest interval between trials.

WALL PASS: The directions are very similar to the kick-up to self item with the exception that the ball is caught directly on the rebound and not kicked up. The ball is thrown, then caught; this action is repeated as many times as possible during each of four fifteen-second trials.

SCORING METHOD

Kick-up to Self: Each legal kick-up counts as one point. A legal kick-up is defined as one which goes directly off the subject's foot or instep to the hands, but does not roll up the shins or touch any part of the body except the hands. The final score is the total number of legal kick-ups for all six thirty-second trials.

Wall Pass: The final score is the total number of legal throws made during all four trials. Each counts one point.

Scientific Authenticity

The subjects were sixty-three freshmen women physical education majors who completed the test at the end of eighteen forty-five-minute periods of instruction, extending over a nine-week period.

VALIDITY: Validity coefficients of .54 and .51 for the kick-up to self and wall pass items, respectively.

RELIABILITY: Reliability coefficients of .90 and .86 for the tests in the order presented above.

CRITERION MEASURE: General playing ability ratings by three judges.

Additional Comments

The kick-up to self item is very similar to the kick-up item in the previously discussed Buchanan Speedball Test. Also, the wall pass item closely resembles the throwing and catching while standing item of the Buchanan Test.

The chief strength of the Smith Test is its obvious ease of administration. On the other hand, the validity values appear questionable in view of the lengthy instructional period the students had in preparation for the test.

REFERENCES

1. Barrow, Harold M. and McGee, Rosemary: *A Practical Approach to Measurement in Physical Education,* 2nd ed. Philadelphia, Lea & Febiger, 1971.
2. Buchanan, Ruth E.: A Study of Achievement Tests in Speedball for High School Girls. Master's thesis, Iowa City, State University of Iowa, 1942.
3. Colvin, Valerie: Achievement tests for speedball. *Spalding's Official Soccer and Speedball Guide.* New York, Am Sports, 1936.
4. Crawford, Elinor A.: The Development of Skill Test Batteries for Evaluating the Ability of Women Physical Education Major Students in Soccer and Speedball. Doctoral dissertation, Eugene, University of Oregon, 1958.

5. Hillas, Marjorie and Knighton, Marian: *An Athletic Program for High School and College Women.* New York, B&N, 1929.
6. Meyers, Carlton R.: *Measurement in Physical Education,* 2nd ed. New York, Ronald, 1974.
7. Miller, S. B.: A Battery of Speedball Skill Tests for College Women. Master's thesis, Lincoln, University of Nebraska, 1959.
8. Scott, M. Gladys and French, Esther: *Better Teaching Through Testing.* New York, B&N, 1945.
9. ——— and ———: *Evaluation in Physical Education.* St. Louis, Mosby, 1950.
10. ——— and ———: *Measurement and Evaluation in Physical Education.* Dubuque, Iowa, Brown Bk, 1959.
11. Smith, Gwen: Speedball Skill Tests for College Women. Master's thesis, Normal, Illinois State University, 1947.
12. Stephyns, Opal Ruff: Achievement Tests in Speed-A-Way for High School Girls. Master's thesis, Normal, Illinois State University, 1965.
13. Weiss, Raymond A. and Phillips, Marjorie: *Administration of Tests in Physical Education.* St. Louis, Mosby, 1954.

Chapter 24

Swimming

INTRODUCTION

SWIMMING IS ONE of man's oldest sports and today has international popularity. This is natural since the activity has always served the fundamental purposes of transportation and survival, especially during the earlier years of mankind. The sport was also a forerunner in skills tests development. Starting in the 1920s, over fifty tests have been constructed with well over half introduced before 1950. The number of scientifically documented skills tests remains meager, perhaps because swimming is another example of a sport whereby the actual skills required in competition can be measured as opposed to simulated skills.

Several organizations promote swimming and in turn have influenced the rapid development of the numerous tests. Organizations such as the American National Red Cross, Young Men's Christian Association, Young Women's Christian Association, Boy Scouts of America, Girl Scouts of America, National Recreation Association, and the Armed Forces have contributed to the advancement of swimming. The American Alliance for Health, Physical Education and Recreation plus educationally related organizations, such as the National Collegiate Athletic Association and the National Federation of State High School Associations, have also played important roles in the promotion of swimming. Availability of tests, achievement scales, and information on instructional techniques by these groups supports the implication of genuine interest.

Even so, only one skills test pertaining to synchronized swimming was located. Durrant's[25] subjective test consists of seven swimming stunts. High correlation coefficients were obtained, and a comprehensive rating scale appears in the original source.

HEWITT ACHIEVEMENT SCALES FOR COLLEGE MEN[34]

Date: 1948.

Purpose: To measure performance and improvement in swimming skills.

Description

Hewitt is considered to be one of the leaders in the development of swimming skills tests due to his construction of swimming achievement scales for the armed forces, college men, and high school boys and girls. Each of these achievement scales represents a major contribution to a particular constituency, but only the two that apply to an educational situation are presented in this chapter.

The Wartime Swimming Test,[33] designed for men in the Armed Forces, measures the time utilized for the 20- and 25-yard underwater swims, distance covered during the fifteen-minute swim for endurance, and number of strokes used to cover 50 yards in the elementary back, side, and breast strokes. The Hewitt Achievement Scales for College Men includes the same tests found in the Wartime scales with the addition of the 25- and 50-yard sprints.

EDUCATIONAL APPLICATION: College men.

Administrative Feasibility

TIME: Three sixty-minute class periods for twenty students.

PERSONNEL: One timer-recorder-scorer with student assistants.

TRAINING INVOLVED: Before being tested for evaluation purposes, the student should demonstrate at least a minimum degree of proficiency in the test items. Immediately prior to testing, a uniform warm-up period should be allowed for the students.

EQUIPMENT AND SUPPLIES: Stop watch.

Accessories: Scoring materials.

Facilities and Space: Regulation pool.

Directions, Scoring Method and Norms

20- OR 25-YARD UNDERWATER SWIM: The subject executes a regulation start from the pool deck and swims the entire distance under water. Any swimming style is acceptable. The final score is represented by the time taken, recorded to the nearest tenth-second, to swim the particular distance. No score is given if any part of the body breaks water, which means the finish also must be under water.

FIFTEEN-MINUTE ENDURANCE SWIM: Using a regulation start, each subject attempts to swim continuously for fifteen minutes, trying to cover as much distance as possible. The type of stroke used or the turning method employed is left to the discretion of each swimmer. The final score is the number of yards covered in the fifteen-minute trial period. It is suggested that each swimmer count his own lengths, which are converted into yards for scoring purposes. If more than a half-length has been completed when the time expires, the subject is given credit for a full length; otherwise, the extra distance is disregarded. No score is given to a subject who fails to swim continuously for the full fifteen minutes.

25- OR 50-YARD SPRINT SWIM WITH THE CRAWL, BREAST, AND BACK STROKES: Using a regulation diving start, each subject swims the preselected distance as fast as possible for each of the different strokes. A sufficient rest period should naturally be allowed between each of the three trials. The final score is the time, measured to the nearest tenth-second, taken to swim the required distance for each of the three strokes.

50-YARD GLIDE RELAXATION WITH THE ELEMENTARY BACK, SIDE, AND BREAST STROKES: Starting from the water and using both a regulation push-off and turn, each subject swims the 50-

TABLE C

HEWITT SWIMMING ACHIEVEMENT SCALES FOR COLLEGE MEN

Rating	Underwater Swim 20 yds.	Underwater Swim 25 yds.	15-Minute Endurance Swim	Crawl	25-yd. Sprint Swim Breast	Back
Superior	14.6 & below	19.7 & below	784 & up	13.5 & below	18.7 & below	19.3 & below
Good	14.7-16.0	19.8-21.2	694-783	13.6-14.1	18.8-20.1	19.4-21.1
Average	16.1-17.6	21.3-22.8	612-693	14.2-15.0	20.2-21.7	21.2-22.7
Poor	17.7-19.0	22.9-24.7	525-611	15.1-15.8	21.8-23.2	22.8-24.5
Inferior	19.1 & up	24.8 & up	424 & below	15.9 & up	23.3 & up	24.6 & up

Rating	50-Yd. Sprint Swim Crawl	50-Yd. Sprint Swim Breast	50-Yd. Sprint Swim Back	50-yd. Glide and Relaxation Elem. Back	50-yd. Glide and Relaxation Side	50-yd. Glide and Relaxation Breast
Superior	32.9 & below	45 & below	40 & below	19 & below	19 & below	18 & below
Good	33.0-36.1	46-48	41-44	20-23	20-23	19-21
Average	36.2-39.8	49-54	45-49	24-29	24-29	22-26
Poor	39.9-42.8	55-58	50-53	30-33	30-33	27-30
Inferior	42.9 & up	59 & up	54 & up	34 & up	34 & up	31 & up

From J. E. Hewitt: Swimming achievement scales for college men, *Research Quarterly, 19:*282-289, 1948. Courtesy of AAHPER.

yard distance with as few strokes as possible. No arm or leg action is allowed on the push-off. Regulation strokes must be used, otherwise the trial is not recorded. The final score for each swimming style is the number of strokes plus the number of push-offs.

Scientific Authenticity

VALIDITY: Validity coefficients ranging from .54 to .93 were determined by correlating each individual test item with the total score of all test items.

RELIABILITY: Reliability coefficients of .89 to .95 were determined by use of the test-retest method for obtaining reliability with 200 students participating.

CRITERION MEASURE: Individual's total test score on the Hewitt Swimming Achievement Scales for College Men.

Additional Comments

When time is limited, the tester may wish to administer the shorter version of the test items allowing an option. Furthermore, additional experimentation with the test is warranted since an individual's total score is not considered to be a reliable test criterion.

HEWITT ACHIEVEMENT SCALES FOR HIGH SCHOOL SWIMMING[32]

Date: 1949.

Purpose: To measure performance and improvement in swimming skills.

Description

Hewitt also constructed achievement scales for high school boys and girls. The test includes the 50-yard crawl stroke for time, the 25-yard flutter kick for time with a polo ball, and the 25-yard glide relaxation with the elementary back, side, and breast strokes.

EDUCATIONAL APPLICATION: High school boys and girls.

Administrative Feasibility

TIME: Twenty students can be tested in two sixty-minute periods.

PERSONNEL: One timer-recorder-scorer with student assistants.

TRAINING INVOLVED: Proper warm-up time should be permitted immediately prior to testing.

EQUIPMENT AND SUPPLIES: Stop watch, polo ball.

Accessories: Scoring materials.

Facilities and Space: Regulation pool.

Directions, Scoring Method and Norms

50-YARD CRAWL STROKE FOR TIME: Using a regulation racing dive, the subject swims the 50-yard crawl stroke as fast as possible. The time required, measured to the nearest tenth-second, constitutes the final score.

25-YARD FLUTTER KICK FOR TIME WITH A POLO BALL: Stationed in the water, the subject holds on to the gutter with one hand and the ball with the other. When the audible signal *"Go"* is given, the subject uses a regulation push-off, grasps the ball with both hands, and swims the 25 yards as fast as possible using only the flutter kick. The final score is the time utilized, measured to the nearest tenth-second.

25-YARD GLIDE RELAXATION WITH THE ELEMENTARY BACK,

TABLE CI

HEWITT SWIMMING ACHIEVEMENT SCALES FOR
HIGH SCHOOL BOYS AND GIRLS

Rating	25 yd. Flutter Kick, Polo Ball	50 yd. Crawl	Elementary Back	Glide Relaxation Side	Breast
		High School Boys			
Superior	15 & below	27 & below	6 & below	6 & below	6 & below
Good	16–27	28–34	7–10	7–11	7–10
Average	28–42	35–45	11–18	12–17	11–17
Poor	43–65	46–59	19–30	18–28	18–28
Inferior	66 & up	60 & up	31 & up	29 & up	29 & up
		High School Girls			
Superior	24 & below	36 & below	6 & below	6 & below	6 & below
Good	25–31	37–45	7–10	7–10	7– 9
Average	32–47	46–60	11–18	11–17	10–17
Poor	48–52	61–80	19–30	18–28	18–28
Inferior	53 & up	81 & up	31 & up	29 & up	29 & up

From J. E. Hewitt: Achievement scales for high school swimming, *Research Quarterly, 20:*170-179, 1949. Courtesy of AAHPER.

TABLE CII

HEWITT PERCENTILE NORMS FOR HIGH SCHOOL BOYS AND GIRLS*

Percentile	Boys				Girls				Percentile
	Seconds 25-yd. Flutter Kick	Strokes			Seconds 25-yd. Flutter Kick	Strokes			
		Elem. Back Stroke	Side Stroke	Breast Stroke		Elem. Back Stroke	Side Stroke	Breast Stroke	
95	17	7	8	6	26	7	8	7	95
90	22	8	9	8	27			8	90
85	23	9	10	9	29	8	9	9	85
80	25	10		10	30		10		80
75	27	11	11		31				75
70	28			11	32	9	11	10	70
65	30	12	12	12	34	10			65
60	32				35	11	12	11	60
55	33	13	13	13	37	12			55
50	34	14		14	39		13		50
45	35	15	14		40	13		12	45
40	36	16	15	15	42	15	14	13	40
35	38	17	16	16	44	16	15		35
30	40	18	17	17	46	17	16	14	30
25	43	19	18	18	48	19	17	15	25
20	46	20	19	19	52	20	18	16	20
15	50	23	21	21	57	22	19	18	15
10	54	26	23	23	65	24	21	20	10
5	60	30	27	27	83	28	24	24	5

*Push-off permitted on each item and counted as one stroke on last three items.

The Hewitt norms are adjusted slightly to fit the 5-step intervals in the percentile scale.

From J. E. Hewitt: Achievement scales for high school swimming, *Research Quarterly, 20:*170-179, 1949. Courtesy of AAHPER.

SIDE, AND BREAST STROKES: This test is performed and scored the same as the one previously described in Hewitt's Achievement Scales for College Men. The only difference is in the distance.

Hewitt devised both achievement scales and percentile norms for this particular test (Tables CI and CII).

Scientific Authenticity

VALIDITY: Validity coefficients ranging from .60 to .94 were determined by correlating each individual test item with the total score of all items.

RELIABILITY: Coefficients of .89 to .96 were computed with the data obtained by the test-retest method.

CRITERION MEASURE: Individual's total score on this test.

Additional Comments

When time is a factor in the evaluation process, consideration may be given to using the 25-yard glide relaxation side stroke item to fulfill the purpose of the battery in view of the .94 correlation it showed with the total test scores. However, the tester is reminded that the value of the total test score criterion is questionable.

FOX SWIMMING POWER TEST[28]

Date: 1957.

Purpose: To measure swimming power.

Description

Fox developed an objective test of swimming power for both the front crawl and side stroke. Test layout conditions include the stretching of a rope, twenty feet longer than the width of the pool, across the pool at a distance of 2 feet from one end. One end of the rope is firmly attached to the side of the pool while the other end across the pool remains free and unattached. A weight is attached to the rope in the middle of the pool. It should be heavy enough so that when the free end of the rope is released, the weight causes the rope to immediately drop to the bottom of the pool.

Starting 2 feet from the end of the pool, or where the rope crosses the pool, the pool deck is marked off in 5-foot intervals continuously for at least 60 feet with adhesive or masking tape. It is recommended that the interval markings be coded by color to facilitate scoring ease.

EDUCATIONAL APPLICATION: Initially constructed for college women, the test is reportedly appropriate for college men and high school students.[48]

Administrative Feasibility

TIME: One sixty-minute period for twenty students.

PERSONNEL: One scorer-recorder with student assistants.

TRAINING INVOLVED: It is recommended that the test subjects be given several practice starts from the rope so they can become accustomed to the motionless starting position.

EQUIPMENT AND SUPPLIES: 50-foot rope, marking tape, weight.

Accessories: Scoring materials.

Facilities and Space: Pool.

Directions

To begin the test, the rope is stretched so that it is 1 foot under the water surface. The rope acts as the starting line and is used to give the starting signal. The subject or swimmer assumes the appropriate motionless floating position (depending on the stroke to be used) with the ankles resting on the rope. For the front crawl the start is from a prone float position, and a side float position is used for the side stroke.

When the rope is dropped, the subject immediately proceeds to take six complete powerful strokes, emphasizing the glide to obtain distance. Each is tested for both the side stroke and front crawl. It is important that the rope be held steady so the subject does not drift from the starting position.

SCORING METHOD AND NORMS: The final score is the total distance, measured to the nearest foot, covered by each subject for five complete strokes. The score for the side stroke is the distance from the starting line to the position of the ankles at the beginning of the recovery of the legs for the sixth stroke. For the crawl stroke, the distance is measured from the rope to where the ankles are at the moment the fingers enter the water to begin the sixth arm cycle. Accuracy on the crawl stroke scoring is improved if each arm stroke is counted because the distance is scored at the beginning of the eleventh arm entry.

Scores are recorded only on strokes performed with correct arm and leg action, and any kick taken before starting the arms or during a glide counts as a stroke. The scorer should be parallel with the subject's feet at the finish.

TABLE CIII

T-SCORES FOR FOX SWIMMING POWER TEST*

T-Score	Crawl (Feet)	Side Stroke (Feet)	T-Score	Crawl (Feet)	Side Stroke (Feet)
76	50	52	51	27	28
73	47–49	51	49	26	26–27
72	46	50	48	25	25
70		48–49	47		24
69	45	46–47	46	24	
68	44	45	45		23
67	43	44	44	23	22
66	40–42	43	43		21
65		42	42	22	
64	39		41	21	19–20
63		40–41	40	20	18
62	38	37–39	39 ·		17
61	36–37	36	38	19	16
60	35	35	37		15
59	34	34	36	18	
57	33	33	35	17	14
56	32		34		9–13
55	31	32	33	16	8
54	30	31	32		7
53	28–29	30	30	15	6
52		29	27	9–14	
			24	8	5

*Based on scores of 50 college women.

From M. G. Fox: Swimming power test, *Research Quarterly, 28:*233-237, 1957. Courtesy of AAHPER.

Scientific Authenticity

Fifty college women ranging in ability from beginning to advanced swimmers served as subjects.

VALIDITY: Coefficients determined were .83 for the side stroke and .66 for the crawl stroke.

RELIABILITY: Resulting coefficients were .97 for the side stroke and .95 for the crawl stroke. The reliability coefficients were determined by each subject taking three trials for each stroke.

CRITERION MEASURE: Expert ratings of swimming form.

Additional Comments

This particular test made a valuable contribution to the area of swimming skills measurement, but it has some limitations. Difficulty in the ability to accurately judge the exact time to take a distance reading presents a potential problem for the tester. The subject's ability to start correctly is another important factor in the test administration. A problem with either could affect test reliability.

ROSENTSWEIG POWER SWIMMING TEST[52]

Date: 1968.
Purpose: To measure form and power on five basic swimming strokes.

Description

Rosentsweig revised the previously discussed Fox Swimming Power Test by changing the starting procedure, increasing the number of test strokes and trials, adding a form rating, testing five different strokes instead of two, and altering the measuring point. The five strokes include the front crawl, side crawl, elementary back stroke, back crawl, and breast stroke. For test administration, the length of the pool deck is marked off in 1-foot intervals beginning 8 feet from the shallow end. The first marker represents the starting line, or point zero.

EDUCATIONAL APPLICATION: The test was initially developed using college women but is reportedly appropriate for both sexes from junior high school through college.[36]

Administrative Feasibility

TIME: Twenty students can be tested in two or three sixty-minute periods.

PERSONNEL: One person to judge, score, and record with student assistants needed for the starting procedure.

TRAINING INVOLVED: Proper warm-up time should be permitted the students before testing.

EQUIPMENT AND SUPPLIES: Marking tape.

Accessories: Scoring materials.
Facilities and Space: Pool.

Directions

Test subjects are assigned partners since two individuals are needed for the starting procedure. The subject assumes the appropriate floating position in the water, depending on the stroke that is being tested, with his or her shoulders even with and parallel to the starting line. Standing to the side of the swimmer, the partner forms a cradle with the forearms to hold the legs of the subject to the surface of the water. The subject is allowed to scull or float in the starting position until ready to start the test.

When the subject is ready, he swims away from his partner by using an arm stroke first. If a kick is made prior to the first arm stroke, the trial is immediately stopped. Twelve arm strokes or six cycles are allowed, depending on the stroke, and two trials are given.

SCORING METHOD: The final score includes two measures, one each for distance and form. The first score represents the distance covered in the twelve strokes or six cycles using the subject's shoulders as a reference point. Also, a subjective rating of the swimming form is made during the actual test trial with the use of a five-point scale.

Scientific Authenticity

A total of 184 college women served as subjects.

VALIDITY: Although face validity was claimed for the test, co-

TABLE CIV

RELIABILITY AND VALIDITY COEFFICIENTS FOR
ROSENTSWEIG POWER SWIMMING TEST*

Stroke	Reliability	Validity
Front Crawl	.89	.72
Side Crawl	.91	.81
Elementary Back Stroke	.96	.83
Back Crawl	.91	.63
Breast Stroke	.95	.74

*Based on performance of 184 college women.

efficients were also determined by correlating the better power scores against the ratings of judges. These correlation coefficients were not originally intended as a validity measure (Table CIV).

RELIABILITY: Coefficients were based on two trials or a test-retest situation (Table CIV).

CRITERION MEASURE: Judges' ratings.

Additional Comments

The Rosentsweig Power Swimming Test shows value not only for measuring achievement but also as a motivating instrument and practice device for students.

Administering two trials of five separate test items can be time-consuming. Additional use of student assistants for testing a greater number of subjects per class period is one suggestion for coping with the problem. On the other hand, ease of test administration would be enhanced if performance measurement of the various strokes was spread out over a longer period of time as opposed to the recommended two or three class periods.

CONNOR SWIMMING TEST[16]

Date: 1962.

Purpose: To determine swimming ability.

Description

Connor developed two swimming skill test items for elementary school children, ages five to twelve. No special pool markings are required.

EDUCATIONAL APPLICATION: Elementary school boys and girls.

Administrative Feasibility

TIME: A class of twenty students can be tested in one sixty-minute period.

PERSONNEL: One person to time, score, and record results.

TRAINING INVOLVED: Uniform warm-up period prior to testing suggested.

EQUIPMENT AND SUPPLIES: Stop watch.

Accessories: Scoring materials.

Facilities and Space: Pool.

Directions

50-YARD PRONE SWIM: Starting while in the water, the subject executes a simple push-off and swims 50 yards in a prone position without stopping.

50-YARD COMBINED SWIM: Again assuming a position in the water, the subject executes a push-off and swims continuously in a prone position for 25 yards. Any turn may be executed with the subject turning over and swimming the next 25 yards on his back.

SCORING METHOD: The 50-yard swim is scored based on the time taken to swim the designated distance. Final score of the combined swim equals the total number of strokes used to cover the 50-yard distance.

Scientific Authenticity

Not reported.

Additional Comments

Connor made a unique contribution to the swimming skills measurement area by developing a test for elementary school children. It was the only test located by the authors that was designated exclusively for that particular age group.

By scientifically documenting the test's value and constructing norms for children in the 5 to 12 age range, the interested investigator could make a significant contribution to sports skills measurement.

BURRIS SPEED-STROKE TEST OF THE CRAWL[10]

Date: 1964.
Purpose: To measure crawl stroking ability.

Description

Burris developed a skills test to measure stroke proficiency by keeping the distance constant, with the time and number of strokes varying with each swimmer. Each subject swims 25 yards using a regular crawl stroke with a flutter kick and rhythmical breathing.

Chapman[13] conducted a study soon thereafter that seemed to confirm the value of Burris' method of evaluation. She compared the three following methods of measuring stroke proficiency:

1. number of strokes constant, time and distance vary.
2. time constant, number of strokes and distance vary.
3. distance constant, time and number of strokes vary.

The third method proved to be the most satisfactory.

EDUCATIONAL APPLICATION: Men and women swimmers at the intermediate level and above.

Administrative Feasibility

TIME: A class of twenty students can easily take the test in one sixty-minute period.

PERSONNEL: One timer-scorer-recorder with student assistants.

TRAINING INVOLVED: Test subjects should demonstrate at least an intermediate level of swimming proficiency. Preceding the test, a proper warm-up period should be provided.

EQUIPMENT AND SUPPLIES: Stop watch.

Accessories: Scoring materials.

Facilities and Space: Pool.

Directions

Assuming a position in deep water with one hand grasping the gutter and his body and legs in a vertical position away from the wall, the subject begins swimming on an audible signal, without pushing off the wall. Subjects swim as fast as possible, yet at the same time use as few strokes as possible. The idea is to get the maximum amount of power from both the kick and arm pull. The regular crawl stroke, utilizing a flutter kick and rhythmical breathing, is required during the 25-yard swim.

SCORING METHOD AND NORMS: The final scores are based on both speed and stroke count.

Speed: The watch is started when the audible signal is given and stopped when any part of the subject's body touches the wall at the 25-yard distance; the time is recorded to the nearest tenth-second.

Stroke: One stroke is counted each time either hand enters the water for a pull. The first stroke is counted when the hand that

TABLE CV

T-SCORES FOR MEN FROM BURRIS SPEED-STROKE TEST OF THE CRAWL*

Seconds

10	11	12	13	14	15	16	17	18	19	20	21	22	23	24	25	26	27	28	29	30	31	32	33	34
90	85	80	75	70	65	61	58	55	52	50	47	45	42	40	38	36	35	33	31	29	28	27	26	25

T-Scores

Strokes

Strokes	T-Score
10	92
11	89
12	85
13	83
14	80
15	77
16	75
17	72
18	70
19	68
20	66
21	64
22	62
23	60
24	58
25	56
26	54
27	52
28	50
29	48
30	46
31	44
32	42
33	40
34	38
35	36
36	34
37	32
38	31
39	30
40	28
41	27
42	25

DIRECTIONS
Place the corner of the score sheet in the angle between the two sets of conversion scores. Round the time score to the nearest second and look for the appropriate number along the top row of figures marked seconds. Immediately below the score in seconds is the T-score equivalent of that score. Look up the raw score in strokes in the left hand column marked strokes. Just to the right of the stroke score is the T-score equivalent for strokes. Add the T-score for strokes to the T-score for seconds for the combined speed-stroke score.

*Based on scores of 89 college men.

TABLE CVI

T-SCORES FOR WOMEN FROM BURRIS SPEED-STROKE TEST OF THE CRAWL*

Seconds

16	17	18	19	20	21	22	23	24	25	26	27	28	29	30	31	32	33	34	35	36	37	38	39	40	41
91	85	80	75	70	66	62	58	55	53	51	49	48	46	44	43	42	40	39	38	36	34	33	31	30	27

T-Scores

Strokes

Strokes	T-Score
14	89
15	85
16	82
17	80
18	78
19	75
20	73
21	71
22	68
23	66
24	64
25	62
26	60
27	57
28	55
29	53
30	51
31	49
32	47
33	45
34	44
35	42
36	41
37	40
38	39
39	37
40	36
41	35
42	34
43	33
44	31
45	30
46	28
47	26
48	25

DIRECTIONS
Place the corner of the score sheet in the angle between the two sets of conversion scores. Round the time score to the nearest second and look for the appropriate number along the top row of figures marked seconds. Immediately below the score in seconds is the T-score equivalent of that score. Look up the raw score in strokes in the left hand column marked strokes. Just to the right of the stroke score is the T-score equivalent for strokes. Add the T-score for strokes to the T-score for seconds for the combined speed-stroke score.

*Based on scores of 143 college women.

has been grasping the gutter enters the water. The touch to the wall is counted as a stroke if part of the arm pull has occurred.

Norms were developed from the scores of eighty-nine men and 143 women swimmers at the college level but are not available. T-scores for time and strokes of both men and women are given in Tables CV and CVI. The tester is reminded that the speed-stroke scores represent two T-scores combined; therefore, the average score is one hundred instead of fifty.

Scientific Authenticity

The Burris Test was administered to sixty-nine college men and women.

VALIDITY: Coefficients of .89 and .86 for men and women, respectively.

RELIABILITY: Coefficients of .91 for men and .90 for women, utilizing the test-retest method for obtaining reliability.

OBJECTIVITY: Coefficients of .99 for men and .99 for women were derived.

Additional Comments

If a 25-yard pool is not available to the tester, it is recommended that a rope be used as the 25-yard marker. The rope should be stretched tight and positioned level with the water surface.

REFERENCES

1. *American Association for Health, Physical Education, and Recreation Youth Fitness Test Manual.* Washington, AAHPER, 1958.
2. American National Red Cross: *Lifesaving Rescue and Water Safety.* Garden City, New York, Doubleday, 1968.
3. ———: *Lifesaving and Water Safety Course.* Washington, American National Red Cross, 1968.
4. ———: *Swimming and Water Safety.* Washington, American National Red Cross, 1968.
5. Anderson, Charlotte W.: Achievement records in swimming. *Journal of Health and Physical Education, 1:*40, 1930.
6. Arrasmith, Jean L.: Swimming Classification Test for College Women. Doctoral dissertation, Eugene, University of Oregon, 1967.
7. Barrow, Harold M. and McGee, Rosemary: *A Practical Approach to Measurement in Physical Education.* Philadelphia, Lea & Febiger, 1964.

8. ————: *A Practical Approach to Measurement in Physical Education,* 2nd ed. Philadelphia, Lea & Febiger, 1971.

9. *Boy Scouts of America—Handbook for Boys,* 5th ed. Albany, New York, Boy Scouts of America, 1948.

10. Burris, Barbara J.: A Study of the Speed-Stroke Test of Crawl Stroking Ability and Its Relationship to Other Selected Tests of Crawl Stroking Ability. Master's thesis, Philadelphia, Temple University, 1964.

11. *Camp Fire Girls Book of Aquatics.* New York, Camp Fire Outfitting Co., 1925.

12. *Camp Fire Girl's Manual.* New York, Girl Scouts, Inc., 1948.

13. Chapman, Peggy: A Comparison of Three Methods of Measuring Swimming Stroke Proficiency. Master's thesis, Madison, University of Wisconsin, 1965.

14. Clarke, H. Harrison: *Application of Measurement to Health and Physical Education,* 4th ed. Englewood Cliffs, P-H, 1967.

15. ————: *Application of Measurement to Health and Physical Education,* 5th ed. Englewood Cliffs, P-H, 1976.

16. Connor, Donald J.: A Comparison of Objective and Subjective Testing Methods in Selected Swimming Skills for Elementary School Children. Master's thesis, Pullman, Washington State University, 1962.

17. Cozens, Frederick W.; Cubberley, Hazel J.; and Neilson, N. P.: *Achievement Scales in Physical Education Activities for Secondary School Girls and College Women.* New York, B&N, 1937.

18. Cureton, Thomas K., Jr.: *Beginning and Intermediate National YMCA Progressive Aquatic Tests.* New York, Assn Pr, 1938.

19. ————: *How to Teach Swimming and Diving,* vol I. New York, Assn Pr, 1934.

20. ————: *Objective Scales for Rating Swimming Performance and Diagnosing Fault.* Springfield, Mass., Springfield College, 1935.

21. ————: Standards for testing beginning swimming. *Research Quarterly, 10:*54-59, 1939.

22. ————: *The Teaching and Practice of Intermediate Aquatics.* Springfield, Mass., Springfield College, 1935.

23. ————: A test for endurance in speed swimming. *Research Quarterly, 6:*106-112, 1935.

24. Daviess, Grace B.: *Swimming.* Philadelphia, Lea & Febiger, 1932.

25. Durrant, Sue M.: An analytical method of rating synchronized swimming stunts. *Research Quarterly, 35:*126-134, 1964.

26. Evans, Dorothy: Swimming to physical fitness. *Journal of Health and Physical Education, 15:*193, 1944.

27. Fagan, Clifford B. (Ed.): *Swimming and Diving Rules.* Elgin, Illinois, National Federation Publications, 1976 (periodically updated).

28. Fox, Margaret G.: Swimming power test. *Research Quarterly, 28:*233-237, 1957.

29. *Girl Scout Handbook*. New York, Girl Scouts, Inc., 1947.
30. Hartley, Grace: Motivating the physical education program for high school girls. *American Physical Education Review, 34:*284, 1929.
31. Haskins, Mary Jane: *Evaluation in Physical Education*. Dubuque, Iowa, Brown Bk, 1971.
32. Hewitt, Jack E.: Achievement scales for high school swimming. *Research Quarterly, 20:*170-179, 1949.
33. ————: Achievement scales for wartime swimming. *Research Quarterly, 14:*391, 1943.
34. ————: Swimming achievement scales for college men. *Research Quarterly, 19:*282-289, 1948.
35. Jackson, Andrew S. and Pettinger, John: The Development and Discriminant Analysis of Swimming Profiles of College Men. Paper read at the 72nd Annual Meeting of the National College Physical Education Association for Men, 1969.
36. Johnson, Barry L. and Nelson, Jack K.: *Practical Measurements for Evaluation in Physical Education,* 2nd ed. Minneapolis, Burgess, 1974.
37. Karpovich, Peter V.: Analysis of the propelling force in the crawl stroke. *Research Quarterly, 6:*49, 1935.
38. ————: Prediction of time in swimming breast stroke based on O_2 consumption. *Research Quarterly, 11:*40-44, 1940.
39. Kilby, Emelia-Louise J.: An Objective Method of Evaluating Three Swimming Strokes. Doctoral dissertation, Seattle, University of Washington, 1956.
40. Kiphuth, Robert J. H.: *Swimming*. New York, B&N, 1942.
41. Manchee, Marie: From tadpole to seal. *Journal of Health and Physical Education, 3:*29, 1932.
42. Meyers, Carlton R. and Blesh, T. Erwin: *Measurement in Physical Education*. New York, Ronald, 1962.
43. Meyers, Carlton R.: *Measurement in Physical Education,* 2nd ed. New York, Ronald, 1974.
44. Midtlyng, Joanna (Ed.): *DGWS Aquatics Guide* Washington, D. C., AAHPER, 1973.
45. Munt, Marilynn R.: Development of an Objective Test to Measure the Efficiency of the Front Crawl for College Women. Master's thesis, Ann Arbor, University of Michigan, 1964.
46. National Collegiate Athletic Association: *Official Collegiate—Scholastic Swimming Guide*. Shawnee Mission, Kansas, NCAA, 1976 (periodically updated).
47. *Naval Aviation Physical Training Manuals: Swimming*. Annapolis, US Naval Institute, 1944.
48. Neilson, N. P. and Jensen, Clayne R.: *Measurement and Statistics in Physical Education*. Belmont, Calif., Wadsworth Pub, 1972.

49. Parkhurst, Mary G.: Achievement tests in swimming. *Journal of Health and Physical Education, 5:*34-36, 58, 1934.
50. Popularizing the swimming badge tests. *Recreation, 27:*183, 205, 1933.
51. Reichart, Natalie and Brauns, Jeanette: *The Swimming Workbook.* New York, B&N, 1937.
52. Rosentsweig, Joel: A revision of the power swimming test. *Research Quarterly, 39:*818-819, 1968.
53. Scott, M. Gladys and French, Esther: *Measurement and Evaluation in Physical Education.* Dubuque, Iowa, Brown Bk, 1959.
54. Sheffield, Lyba and Sheffield, Nita: *Swimming Simplified.* New York, B&N, 1931.
55. Smith, Ann A.: Aids to efficient swimming instruction for girls and women. *Journal of Health and Physical Education, 2:*32-33, 45-46, 1931.
56. ————: *Swimming and Plain Diving.* New York, Scribner, 1930.
57. Spindler, Evelyn: Do you grade or guess? *Journal of Health and Physical Education, 2:*26-28, 48, 1931.
58. Swimming badge tests for boys and girls. *American Physical Education Review, 34:*298-304, 1929.
59. Troemel, Ernestine A.: Swimming—on an efficient grading basis. *American Physical Education Review 33:*414-418, 1928.
60. Wayman, Agnes R.: *Education Through Physical Education,* 2nd ed. Philadelphia, Lea & Febiger, 1934.
61. Weiss, Raymond A. and Phillips, Marjorie: *Administration of Tests in Physical Education.* St. Louis, Mosby, 1954.
62. Willgoose, Carl: *Evaluation in Health Education and Physical Education.* New York, McGraw, 1961.
63. Wilson, Calvin T.: Coordination tests in swimming. *Research Quarterly, 5:*81-88, 1934.
64. Wilson, Marcia Ruth: A Relationship Between General Motor Ability and Objective Measurement of Achievement in Swimming at the Intermediate Level for College Women. Master's thesis, Greensboro, Women's College of the University of North Carolina, 1962.
65. Young Men's Christian Association: *Beginning and Intermediate National YMCA Progressive Aquatics Test.* New York, Assn Pr, 1948.
66. ————: *Swimming and Life Saving Manual.* New York, YMCA, 1972.

Chapter 25

Table Tennis

INTRODUCTION

TABLE TENNIS is not a common offering in secondary school and college physical education programs, but it is commonly found in intramural sports programs at both levels. For the schools that do include table tennis as one of their physical education activities, the instructors of the sport might consider the one objective test found in the literature that is designed to measure table tennis skill.[6]

MOTT-LOCKHART TABLE TENNIS TEST[6]

Also cited as Mott-Lockhart Table Tennis Backboard Test.
Date: 1946.
Purpose: To measure skill in table tennis.

Description

The one-item test is designed to measure table tennis skill or achievement but is also useful to classify and motivate students in the learning situation. The ability to rally the ball against a perpendicular surface for thirty seconds is measured.

A simulated net line is drawn on the perpendicular half of a propped tennis table, 6 inches above the horizontal half.

Administrative Feasibility

TIME: If two or more table tennis tables are available, the test could easily be administered to a class of twenty students in one forty-minute class period.

PERSONNEL: The instructor and a trained student assistant to serve as scorer and timer, respectively.

TRAINING INVOLVED: A practice session is recommended prior to the testing date, plus one practice trial should be permitted immediately before the three test trials are administered.

EQUIPMENT AND SUPPLIES: One stop watch, a minimum of

three table tennis balls in good condition, one table tennis racket, and at least one official table tennis table.

Accessories: A kitchen match box approximately 5 × 2¾ inches, some thumbtacks to attach match box to edge of table, a piece of chalk for line marking, and scoring materials.

Facilities and Space: An area of sufficient size to allow for a table tennis table to be hinged at the center with half of it propped against a wall or post perpendicular to the floor while the other half sits in a horizontal manner, plus the additional space required for player maneuverability.

Directions

The subject stands with a racket and one ball in hand with two extra balls placed in a match box which is tacked to the edge of

TABLE CVII

T-SCALES FOR MOTT-LOCKHART TABLE TENNIS TEST*

T-Score	Raw Score	T-Score	Raw Score	T-Score	Raw Score
77	60	59	45	41	29
76		58		40	
75		57	44	39	28
74		56		38	27
73	58	55	43	37	26
72		54	42	36	
71	55	53	41	35	25
70		52	40	34	24
69	54	51		33	23
68	52	50	39	32	22
67	51	49	38	31	
66	50	48	37	30	
65	49	47	36	29	21
64	48	46	34–35	28	
63		45	33	27	
62	47	44	32	26	20
61		43	31	25	
60	46	42	30	24	16

*Based on scores of 162 college women.

From J. A. Mott and A. Lockhart: Table tennis backboard test, *Journal of Health and Physical Education,* 17:550-552, 1946. Courtesy of AAHPER.

the table. On the starting signal, the subject drops a ball to the table and rallies it against the perpendicular surface as often as possible in a period of thirty seconds. There is no restriction on the number of bounces taken. A ball kept in the match box may be used if control of the original ball is lost; the ball is put into play the same as the original. Hits below the 6-inch chalk line do not count; neither do any volleyed balls nor those whereby the subject places a free hand on the table during or immediately preceding the hits. Three trials are given with intervening rest periods.

SCORING METHOD AND NORMS: The number of legal hits is recorded for each trial with the best of the three trials being the official score.

T-scales resulting from the scores of 162 college women are presented in Table CVII.

Scientific Authenticity

VALIDITY: A coefficient of .84 was reported for the relationship between the test scores and subjective ratings of judges while viewing each subject for three games in a round-robin tournament.

RELIABILITY: Seventy-nine subjects were tested by the odd-even method, and a reliability coefficient of .90 was obtained.

CRITERION MEASURE: Judges' ratings of player performance in tournament action.

Additional Comments

The Mott-Lockhart Table Tennis Test receives high marks as an excellent measuring instrument for table tennis playing skill. It more than adequately meets most of the common criteria for a well-constructed test. However, the test is not designed to measure skill in specific table tennis strokes; therefore, the test used in combination with round-robin tournament rankings should provide the most adequate measure of table tennis skill.

REFERENCES

1. American Association for Health, Physical Education and Recreation: *Measurement and Evaluation of Materials in Health, Physical Education and Recreation.* Washington, AAHPER, 1950.
2. Barrow, Harold M. and McGee, Rosemary: *A Practical Approach to*

Measurement in Physical Education. Philadelphia, Lea & Febiger, 1964.

3. Campbell, W. R. and Tucker, N. M.: *An Introduction to Tests and Measurements in Physical Education.* London, Bell & Sons, 1967.

4. Clarke, H. Harrison: *Application of Measurement to Health and Physical Education,* 5th ed. Englewood Cliffs, P-H, 1976.

5. Meyers, Carlton R. and Blesh, T. Erwin: *Measurement in Physical Education.* New York, Ronald, 1962.

6. Mott, Jane A. and Lockhart, Aileen: Table tennis backboard test. *Journal of Health and Physical Education, 17:*550-552, 1946.

7. Scott, M. Gladys and French, Esther: *Measurement and Evaluation in Physical Education.* Dubuque, Iowa, Brown Bk, 1959.

8. Stroup, Francis: *Measurement in Physical Education.* New York, Ronald, 1957.

9. Willgoose, Carl E.: *Evaluation in Health Education and Physical Education.* New York, McGraw, 1961.

Chapter 26

Tennis

INTRODUCTION

THE INSTRUCTIONAL environment in tennis often simulates actual game conditions. Therefore, the instructor has a greater opportunity to evaluate student performance in a game situation than is possible for some of the other common activities taught in the physical education curriculum. Perhaps the best indicator of a student's general playing ability at a particular skill level is his ranking with classmates in a round-robin tournament. Unfortunately, that type of tournament is not always practical in time and ease of administration. A viable alternative for measurement of progress and achievement in tennis is the development of reliable, valid, administratively feasible skills tests.

The tests presented here include some that measure general playing ability and others that assess an evaluatee's skill level in the performance of specific strokes. Tests for each sex at all grade levels are presented.

One of the more popular and widely recognized sports skills tests of all time is the Dyer Backboard Test of Tennis Ability.[13] The 1935 test was the first tennis skills test to be subjected to scientific analysis and led the way to development of a number of useful tests in the sport of tennis. The availability of these tests serves the physical education profession well at a time when the popularity of tennis appears to be soaring at all grade levels.

DYER BACKBOARD TEST OF TENNIS ABILITY[13, 14]

Also cited as Dyer Backboard Test and Dyer Tennis Test.
Date: 1935, revised in 1938.
Purpose: To measure general tennis playing ability.

Description

The test was developed for use as a classification device. It has shown merit as a practice tool for tennis players and has been

411

used extensively to measure the progress of developing tennis performers.

A net line is drawn on the wall or backboard 3 inches wide, with the top edge 3 feet from the floor. A 5-foot restraining line is drawn parallel to the wall hitting area.

EDUCATIONAL APPLICATION: Originally designed for college women but has value for testing the tennis ability of both sexes at the high school and college levels.

Administrative Feasibility

TIME: One forty-minute class period for a class of twenty students with a proportional increase in number tested to number of available walls or backboards.

PERSONNEL: It is recommended that the class be divided into groups of three with one person designated as the subject and the other two as timer and scorer. The instructor of the class probably should serve as the timer when only one wall or backboard is available to a class.

TRAINING INVOLVED: Subjects should be thoroughly familiar with the test conditions prior to being tested for score.

EQUIPMENT AND SUPPLIES: A proper selection of tennis racquets, one dozen quality tennis balls, and a stop watch per testing station.

Accessories: A cardboard box or wire basket per testing station along with floor and wall marking materials; scoring materials.

Facilities and Space: A flat wall or backboard (at least 10 feet high and 15 feet wide) with at least 15 to 20 feet of cleared space facing the wall or backboard.

Directions

The student stands behind the 5-foot restraining line while holding a racquet and two tennis balls. On the starting signal, the subject bounces one of the balls on the floor and hits it above the net line on the wall. This action is repeated for thirty seconds.

The restraining line may be crossed to retrieve a ball, and volleying is permitted once the ball is put into play. Balls hit in front of the restraining line do not count. For use when balls get out of control, a box of extra balls should be stationed near the subject, preferably on the right side for right-handed players, and vice versa for left-handers. There is no limit on the number of balls that may be used during the testing period. New balls are put into play in the same manner as the original one.

SCORING METHOD AND NORMS: A point is counted each time the ball hits on or above the net line during the thirty-second time span. The sum of points made in the three trials is the final score. A table (Table CVIII) for the revised method of scoring the Dyer Test appears below. An ability rating scale based on scores of 672

TABLE CVIII

T-SCALE FOR NEW METHOD SCORING IN DYER TEST

T-Scale	Test Score	T-Scale	Test Score	T-Scale	Test Score	T-Scale	Test Score
100	67	75	50	50	33	25	16
99	66	74	49	49	32	24	15
98		73		48		23	
97	65	72	48	47	31	22	14
96	64	71	47	46	30	21	13
95		70		45		20	
94	63	69	46	44	29	19	12
93	62	68	45	43	28	18	11
92		67	44	42	27	17	10
91	61	66		41		16	
90	60	65	43	40	26	15	9
89	59	64	42	39	25	14	8
88		63		38		13	
87	58	62	41	37	24	12	7
86	57	61	40	36	23	11	6
85		60		35		10	
84	56	59	38	34	22	9	5
83	55	58	39	33	21	8	4
82		57		32		7	
81	54	56	37	31	20	6	3
80	53	55	36	30	19	5	2
79		54		29		4	
78	52	53	35	28	18	3	1
77	51	52	24	27	17	2	
76		51		26		1	

From J. T. Dyer: Revision of backboard test of tennis ability, *Research Quarterly*, 9:25-31, 1938. Courtesy of AAHPER.

TABLE CIX

ABILITY RATINGS FOR DYER TENNIS TEST

Rating*	College Women	Women Majors Physical Education
Superior	46 & up	79 & up
Good	38-45	58-78
Average	29-37	35-57
Poor	21-28	13-34
Inferior	20 & below	12 & below

*Based on scores of 672 women students and physical education majors.

From Miller, Wilma K.: Achievement Levels in Tennis Knowledge and Skill for Women Physical Education Students. Doctoral dissertation, Bloomington, Indiana University, 1952.

college women students and physical education majors is shown in Table CIX.

Scientific Authenticity

VALIDITY: A study of the original Dyer Test yielded correlation coefficients of .85 and .90 with judges' ratings. A validity study of the revised test utilizing round-robin tournament rankings as the criterion produced coefficients ranging from .85 to .92.

RELIABILITY: Utilizing the test-retest method with samples of fourteen to thirty-seven women, reliability coefficients of .86, .87, and .92 were derived for the Dyer Revision. A coefficient of .90 was computed for the original test.

CRITERION MEASURE: Judges' ratings and round-robin tournament rankings.

Additional Comments

A reference in the literature to the Dyer Tennis Test usually refers to the 1938 revision. The 1935 original test did not utilize a restraining line; this was standardized at 5 feet in the 1938 revision. In the revision, the scoring method was also altered somewhat and the method of supplying extra balls to the subject was changed to reduce the degree of variability.

The Dyer Test was certainly a forerunner to tests devised by scientific procedure and has demonstrated vast popularity through the years as evidenced by the many studies and revisions that have resulted from its existence. Interestingly enough, the revisions for the most part have never achieved the status of the 1938 version due to lesser validity and reliability values.

Fox[19] derived a correlation coefficient of .53 between Dyer Test scores of college women beginners and ability ratings on the forehand drive, the backhand drive, and the serve. Koski[30] used a 28-foot restraining line and college men as subjects in obtaining correlation coefficients that ranged from .51 to .68 between tests results and tournament rankings.

Changes of the Dyer Test have basically dealt with the distance of the restraining line and the time length for rallying. It is purported that the Dyer Test better discriminates tennis ability at the advanced level. As a result, the revisions have instituted an increase in the restraining line distance, providing a more adequate test for beginning players.

Two successful revisions of the Dyer Test include those by Hewitt[22] and Ronning.[51] These tests are presented elsewhere in this chapter.

Based on the results of the studies made of the Dyer Test, it appears that a distance in the 20-foot range would be more suitable for beginners, and a distance of 30 feet or so would be more useful for measuring tennis ability of intermediate and advanced players. A problem with the 5-foot restraining line recommended in the 1938 revision is its promotion of a poor stroking technique. The short distance does not lend itself to the use of proper stroking form.

RONNING REVISION OF DYER BACKBOARD TENNIS TEST[51]

Also cited as Ronning Wall Test.

Date: 1959.

Purpose: To measure tennis playing ability.

Description

The test layout dimensions call for an unobstructed wall space at least 10 feet in height and 15 feet in width plus 35 feet of clear floor space perpendicular to the designed wall area. A simulated net line (3 inches in width) is drawn along the wall or backboard space so that the top of the line is 3 feet from the floor.

EDUCATIONAL APPLICATION: Designed for college men but could be used for measuring tennis ability of college women.

Administrative Feasibility

TIME: One forty-minute class period for a class of fifteen to twenty students, provided two or more unobstructed walls are available.

PERSONNEL: A scorer, timer, and ball retriever for each test station.

TRAINING INVOLVED: Familiarization of test conditions should be permitted for each student prior to testing.

EQUIPMENT AND SUPPLIES: An assortment of tennis racquets, a stop watch per test station, and at least two dozen quality tennis balls.

Accessories: Wall marking and scoring materials.

Facilities and Space: Indoor or outdoor tennis facility with sufficient ground surface area and unobstructed wall space to properly conduct the Ronning Revision of the Dyer Tennis Test.

Directions

Two balls and a racquet are required to complete the test. On the starting signal, the subject, while standing behind a 35-foot restraining line, drops one ball and puts it in play against the wall. This action continues for sixty seconds.

There is no limit to the number of times the ball may bounce before playing it, and volleying is allowed. The ball must touch the floor at the beginning of the test and when a new ball is put into play. Any type of stroke is permitted, and all balls must be played behind the restraining line. The line may be crossed to retrieve balls; any balls hit in front of the restraining line do not count. The same is true if the subject steps on or crosses the restraining line during a hit. A ball that gets away should not be retrieved because the purpose of holding a second ball is to use it when this occurs. If both get away, two more balls should be taken from a box containing extras and the test proceeds as before.

TABLE CX

TEST SCORES FOR RONNING REVISION OF
DYER TENNIS TEST*

Final Criterion Rank†	Distance and Time							
	5 feet		15 feet		25 feet		35 feet	
	30 sec.	60 sec.	30 sec.	60 sec.	30 sec.	60 sec.	30 sec.	60 sec.
1	88	179	74	150	61	108	48	88
2	108	210	72	142	48	94	40	80
3	76	155	49	105	49	95	38	71
4	100	205	59	124	54	108	40	77
5	88	178	57	115	40	78	35	58
6	95	185	65	123	47	93	39	69
7	74	155	54	104	41	84	30	61
8	105	221	58	117	39	77	28	55
9	105	216	57	109	45	96	27	53
10	86	168	56	109	47	90	28	56
11	109	212	58	121	43	82	29	52
12	110	212	67	127	49	95	33	69
13	72	135	43	85	39	67	27	55
14	82	178	60	121	44	82	27	49
15	93	172	58	107	36	74	35	65
16	133	256	62	124	43	85	26	51
17	66	139	51	108	39	80	26	48
18	85	166	55	109	44	93	28	57
19	106	213	61	122	46	83	25	55
20	77	168	60	116	35	78	31	56
21	86	178	53	99	38	82	22	50
22	88	173	51	103	41	79	25	51
23	79	163	51	95	25	57	30	50
24	101	234	52	107	44	89	30	45
25	63	107	46	81	43	81	31	54
26	61	118	41	83	37	76	24	49
27	97	197	49	100	42	84	24	42
28	70	137	40	80	36	60	21	43
29	63	123	49	98	33	66	21	43
30	86	171	47	88	40	67	20	44
31	78	154	49	102	37	66	26	48
32	81	175	51	98	39	74	25	44
33	70	144	50	103	33	69	21	46
34	51	109	44	97	34	59	22	40
35	76	151	55	98	41	73	25	47
36	71	155	43	92	30	55	13	31
37	72	151	50	99	37	76	19	41
38	64	115	33	76	33	61	22	46
39	52	111	39	75	33	62	18	44
40	58	121	46	86	35	63	19	43
41	44	92	44	78	25	47	15	29
42	58	111	24	59	21	45	17	35

*Based on scores of 42 college men.

†Represents final rank-order standings derived from round-robin tournament results.

TABLE CXI

VARSITY SQUAD TEST SCORES ON RONNING REVISION*

Final Criterion Rank	Distance and Time							
	5 feet		15 feet		25 feet		35 feet	
	30 sec.	60 sec.	30 sec.	60 sec.	30 sec.	60 sec.	30 sec.	60 sec.
1	115	222	89	144	88	150	46	102
2	105	212	85	158	60	115	56	98
3	93	178	73	123	42	85	46	86
4	124	230	79	142	54	102	43	86
5	76	144	85	140	51	92	40	81
6	66	140	65	116	54	93	56	80
7	63	107	47	92	52	82	39	66
8	95	182	69	136	52	97	40	69

*Based on scores of 8 varsity tennis players.

Three trials are given. A demonstration by the instructor is recommended prior to testing the subjects.

SCORING METHOD AND NORMS: Each ball that hits the wall on or above the net line and within the 15-foot target area counts as one point. The final score is the sum of the three trials.

Scientific Authenticity

VALIDITY: Forty-two college men enrolled in activity classes provided part of the data for the validation. A correlation coefficient of .90 was derived from relating the test scores to a round-robin tournament ranking criterion. A validity coefficient of .97 was computed from varsity tennis squad scores.

RELIABILITY: .92 for the group enrolled in tennis classes.

CRITERION MEASURE: Round-robin tournament rankings.

Additional Comments

In his study of the Dyer Test, Ronning experimented with 5-, 15-, 25-, and 35-foot restraining line distances plus test time periods of thirty and sixty seconds. It was concluded that the 35-foot restraining line and sixty-second test period was the best combination for testing beginning tennis players.

The validity and reliability coefficients cited for the Ronning

Revision attest to its value as an instrument to test the playing ability of beginning tennis players at the collegiate level.

HEWITT REVISION OF DYER BACKBOARD TENNIS TEST[22]

Also cited as Hewitt Revision of the Dyer Test.
Date: 1965.
Purpose: To classify beginning and advanced tennis players by measuring rallying and service ability.

Description

The test measures the ability to serve and rally. The rally may consist of any type stroke.

A gymnasium wall serves well in the administration of the wall test. A line is marked 20 feet from the wall, and a parallel 20-foot line is marked at a height of 3 feet on the wall. The wall should be 20 feet high and 20 feet wide.

EDUCATIONAL APPLICATION: High school and college males and females.

Administrative Feasibility

TIME: The test is notably feasible regarding time of administration. This is especially true in situations where two or more walls are utilized simultaneously. Each student spends two minutes in practice and ninety seconds in testing (three trials of thirty seconds each).

PERSONNEL: An instructor and a trained assistant for scoring and timing. In tests utilizing multiple test areas, a trained assistant could serve as scorer if an additional instructor is not available.

TRAINING INVOLVED: Two-minute wall rally warm-up immediately prior to the testing period.

EQUIPMENT AND SUPPLIES: A basket of one to two dozen quality tennis balls, tennis racquet, and a stop watch measured in $\frac{1}{10}$ seconds.

Accessories: Marking materials for wall and floor (or particular surface of outdoor facility); scoring materials.

Facilities and Space: At least one smooth wall 20 feet high and

20 feet wide. Twenty feet of unobstructed space directly in front of the wall must also be available.

Directions

With two new tennis balls ready for play, the subject serves a ball against the wall while stationed behind the restraining line. Any type of serve is permitted. The stop watch is started when the served ball hits above the net line on the wall. The student then initiates a rally using any type of ground or volley stroke. When a ball gets away from the subject, another may be taken from the ball container but must be served from behind the restraining line. The rally continues for thirty seconds. Three trials are administered.

SCORING METHOD: One point is counted each time the ball hits on or above the 3-foot net line on the wall. Stepping over the restraining line and hitting the ball below the net line are test violations and result in no points counted. The final score is the average point value of the three trials.

Scientific Authenticity

VALIDITY: Validity coefficients of .68, .71, .72, and .73 were derived for four beginner classes and .84 and .89 for advanced classes when their test scores and round-robin tournament rankings were correlated. Rank order coefficients of correlation were originally computed and then converted to r's.

College classes ranging from twenty-one to twenty-five in size participated in the beginner group, and class sizes of seventeen and fourteen were represented in the advanced group.

RELIABILITY: Reliability coefficients of .93 and .82 were computed for the advanced and beginner groups, respectively. The test-retest method was used.

CRITERION MEASURE: Rankings in a round-robin tennis tournament.

Additional Comments

Hewitt's Revision of the Dyer Test resulted in a significant contribution to the literature on sports skills tests in tennis because of its demonstrated capacity to discriminate playing ability sufficiently at the beginner level. The restraining line was extended to 20 feet from the wall as opposed to 5 feet on the Dyer Test. This revision logically explains the reason that the Dyer Test ably discriminates at the advanced player level since volleying is an advanced tennis skill and not used as often by beginners. The 20-foot line forced the beginners to use other strokes such as the forehand, backhand, etc. The change resulted in a valid test for both beginning and advanced levels. In fact, an improvement was shown over the Dyer Test in the validity coefficients of the advanced groups.

The revision is also more comprehensive than the original test because the serve was added. Also, it shows simplicity and is easy to administer because outdoor courts are not necessary; therefore, the negative effects of weather and test preparation time for marking the courts, etc., are eliminated.

SCOTT-FRENCH REVISION OF DYER WALLBOARD TEST[54]

Date: Not known.
Purpose: To measure tennis playing ability.

Description

A 3-inch wide line is drawn on the wall to represent the net. The top of the line is exactly 3 feet from the floor. A restraining line is drawn 27½ feet away from and parallel to the wall.

EDUCATIONAL APPLICATION: High school and college males and females.

Administrative Feasibility

TIME: Two testing stations would assure completion of testing in one forty-minute class period for a class of thirty students or less.

PERSONNEL: One scorer and one timer per testing station.

TRAINING INVOLVED: A sufficient amount of practice time for each student to become adequately familiar with test conditions.

EQUIPMENT AND SUPPLIES: A stop watch and two quality tennis balls per testing station, plus an assortment of tennis racquets.

Accessories: A box for extra balls per testing station, wall marking materials, and scoring materials.

Facilities and Space: Backboard or unobstructed wall space, approximately 10 feet in height and 15 to 20 feet in width plus 40 feet of clear floor or ground space in front of the wall target.

Directions

On the starting signal, the subject drops the ball to the floor and begins to rally against the wall while standing behind the restraining line. Rallying is continued for thirty seconds with three trials given.

The ball may bounce more than once and may be volleyed. All strokes must be made behind the restraining line with any type of stroke used. The subject may cross the restraining line to retrieve a ball but must return to the starting line for the hit to be considered legal. When a ball gets out of control, another may be taken from the extra ball box. Also, the ball must be bounced at least once at the start of the test or whenever another ball is put into play.

SCORING METHOD: The trial score is determined by the number of legal hits accumulated during the thirty-second period. The higher tally of the three trials is recorded as the final score.

Scientific Authenticity

VALIDITY: .61 in relating test scores and judges' ratings of stroke, form, and footwork of 468 college students.

RELIABILITY: .80 when stepped up by the Spearman-Brown Formula.

CRITERION MEASURE: Judges' ratings.

Additional Comments

The test represents one of the several useful revisions of the Dyer Tennis Test. Experimentation with the 27½-foot restraining line proved conducive to testing students of both sexes at the high school and college levels.

BROER-MILLER TENNIS TEST[5]

Also cited as Broer-Miller Tennis Forehand-Backhand Drive Test.

Date: 1950.

Purpose: To evaluate tennis playing ability as measured by performance on forehand and backhand drive placement.

Description

The test was designed for use as a classification device and grading instrument. Figure 73 indicates the necessary court markings for scoring purposes. A rope is stretched 4 feet above the top of the net.

EDUCATIONAL APPLICATION: College women and high school girls.

Administrative Feasibility

TIME: One forty-minute period for testing of twenty students.

PERSONNEL: Instructor to serve as scorer and student helpers for retrieving balls, etc.

TRAINING INVOLVED: Uniform test familiarity session for each student prior to taking test.

EQUIPMENT AND SUPPLIES: A selection of tennis racquets, a rope of sufficient length to stretch above the net, and two dozen quality tennis balls.

Accessories: Court marking materials and poles for holding ropes, plus scoring materials.

Facilities and Space: At least one regulation tennis court.

Directions

The subject takes a racquet and assumes a position behind the baseline, then bounces the ball and hits it into the opposite court. The ball must go between the top of the net and the rope to receive maximum score; clearing the rope is given one-half the value of the scoring area in which it lands. A trial is counted if the ball is missed, and "let" balls are taken again.

Every student completes fourteen trials each for the forehand and backhand drives.

SCORING METHOD: The final score is the sum of points made on the twenty-eight trials (fourteen for each drive).

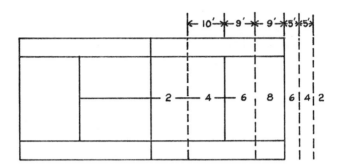

Figure 73. Court markings for Broer-Miller Tennis Test. From M. R. Broer and D. M. Miller: Achievement tests for beginning and intermediate tennis, *Research Quarterly, 21*:303-321, 1950. Courtesy of AAHPER.

Scientific Authenticity

VALIDITY: .85 for intermediate players and .61 for a beginning group when test scores and judges' ratings were correlated.

RELIABILITY: A coefficient of .80 was reported for both the intermediate and beginning groups.

CRITERION MEASURE: Judges' ratings.

Additional Comments

A unique feature of this test is that the coefficient of validity is higher than the reliability value. Broer and Miller concluded that the test appears to be more valid for testing intermediate players as opposed to beginners because of the higher validity value computed for the intermediates.

A study by Fox[19] indicated that the Dyer and Broer-Miller Tennis Tests do not measure the same thing due to a relatively low correlation between them. It was further suggested that a test for serving ability would enhance the scientific authenticity of the Broer-Miller Test. On the basis of a .79 coefficient of correlation, Fox concluded that the Broer-Miller Test could be used as a measure of beginners' tennis ability with some degree of confidence. When a ball throwing machine was used instead of the subject dropping the ball by hand, a .79 coefficient was produced.[38]

TIMMER TENNIS SKILL TEST[58]

Date: 1965.

Purpose: To assess tennis playing ability as measured by accuracy of forehand and backhand drive strokes.

Description

Placement of the forehand and backhand strokes was selected in this test to represent general playing ability. The ball-boy machine used is an electrical device that projects a tennis ball at a given speed with a definite degree of accuracy based on the uniformity in resilience of the balls used. The test should ideally be offered indoors because of the wind factor but for practical purposes may be given outdoors if adherence to the ease of administration criterion is evidenced.

The machine is set up in the center of the court, 8 feet in from the baseline. This position allows the balls to land in the 5-foot squares as shown in Figure 74. The machine is set at "high" speed and projects one ball every five seconds. Furthermore, the machine is aimed at the forehand side of the court for the first trial, assuming the subject is right-handed. Adjustments are made accordingly for left-handed subjects. Twelve to fifteen balls are placed in the machine to allow for balls that do not land in the aforementioned 5-foot areas.

A rope is suspended above the net 51 inches in height. The test layout, including the subject's position area, designated areas for projected balls to bounce, and scoring value areas are shown in Figure 74.

EDUCATIONAL APPLICATION: High school and college males and females.

Administrative Feasibility

TIME: Approximately fifteen minutes per subject, including a warm-up period.

PERSONNEL: An instructor with one assistant to serve as scorer if one court is used. The instructor should prepare the ball-boy machine for testing. It is also recommended that the instructor stand behind the baseline and point to the side of the court which the subject should be aiming for to prevent any confusion that may arise as to which side is properly the next one in sequence.

The use of multiple courts would necessitate a training session for each student assistant who is faced with the task of preparing his assigned ball-boy machine for testing.

TRAINING INVOLVED: A five-minute warm-up period is permitted prior to taking the test. Previous experience for each student at hitting balls projected from the ball-boy machine should also be assured.

EQUIPMENT AND SUPPLIES

a. One ball-boy machine per court.
b. Fifteen tennis balls of similar resiliency per testing.
c. Assortment of tennis racquets.
d. A 38-foot rope.
e. For holding a rope taut, some poles, ladders, or other alternatives at the sides of the net for each court used.

Accessories: Materials for court markings and scoring.

Facilities and Space: A regulation singles tennis court.

Directions

The subject takes a position within the designated 3-foot square area located behind the baseline as shown in Figure 74. At the release of the first ball, the subject assumes a position to hit the ball into the opposite court in the designated area. The first and all odd-numbered balls should be returned down the alley to maximize the chance of obtaining the greatest number of points possible. The second and all even-numbered balls should be returned across court. The subject returns to the starting position for each stroke.

The subject is given ten trials to the forehand and the same number for the backhand with an intervening rest period of one minute.

Each ball must clear the net, go under the rope, and land within the court boundaries to score. The subject must use the forehand stroke for all balls designated for that side. The same is true for the backhand. The one-minute rest period allows time to re-

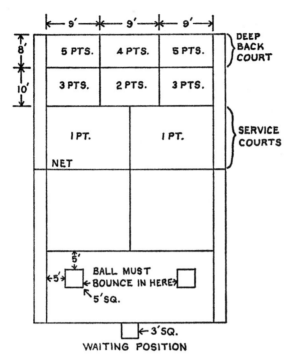

Figure 74. Court markings and scoring areas for Timmer Tennis Skill Test.

adjust the machine and remind the student of the adjustment in court area selection for hitting the balls.

The test (ten trials for the forehand and backhand) is administered twice in succession.

SCORING METHOD: The scoring values of the respective court areas are shown in Figure 74. In addition, a ball returned to the wrong side of the court and beyond the service lines but within the boundaries is counted as two points.

The maximum score for the forty strokes or two complete tests is 200 points.

Scientific Authenticity

VALIDITY: The rank-difference coefficient of correlation *(Rho)* was .86 for a college tennis team composed of freshmen men and

.75 for a women's extramural tennis team at the college level. The scores of nine women and seven men provided the test data.

RELIABILITY: Not reported.

CRITERION MEASURE: Round-robin tournament rankings.

Additional Comments

A limitation of this test is its questionable validation process. A larger number of students to determine the test's validity would have better substantiated the worth of the test as a reported valid measure of tennis ability.

The financial commitment in purchasing a ball-boy machine may be too much to bear for some school systems or colleges. The diverse features of the machine, however, seem to justify its relatively reasonable cost.

Perhaps the most notable void in the presentation of the Timmer Test was the absence of established reliability values. This is a must before the test could ever gain popularity as a scientifically authenticated test.

WISCONSIN WALL TEST FOR SERVE[17]

Date: 1965.

Purpose: To measure serving ability, utilizing the criteria of force and height.

Description

The Wisconsin Test measures improvement and achievement, provides a partial basis for a grade, and serves as a diagnostic tool for tennis ability.

The wall target is 42½ feet in distance from the serving line. Lines that are drawn at intervals of 1 foot reach from the floor to 12 feet in height. The 3-foot line which represents the height of the net is drawn somewhat thicker. There is no limit set on the width of the target.

EDUCATIONAL APPLICATION: Constructed for testing of college women but appropriate also for secondary school girls.

Administrative Feasibility

TIME: One sixty-minute class period for class of fifteen to twenty students.

PERSONNEL: The instructor should serve as timer, and participants serve well as scorers.

TRAINING INVOLVED: When measuring sports skills, any modification of a game situation mandates sufficient practice time for the skill required under the modified test conditions. This type of attention to practice is particularly applicable to the Wisconsin Wall Test for Serve. Three practice trials immediately precede the administration of the test for score.

EQUIPMENT AND SUPPLIES: Two new tennis balls per student and a variety of tennis racquets for student selection; stop watch.

Accessories: Marking materials for wall target lines; scoring materials.

Facilities and Space: The test may be administered either indoors or outdoors so long as a smooth wall surface or suitable alternative is available.

Directions

The subject assumes a position behind the restraining line with two balls in the tossing hand. Ten serves are completed at a point of aim above the line representing the net height. Serves not reaching the wall in flight are repeated. The value of the area where the ball lands is recorded on each serve along with the time the ball takes to travel from the racquet face to the target.

SCORING METHOD AND NORMS: The placement and time values are converted into point values which are then combined to provide an official score for the serve test.

The scorer and timer stand to the left and approximately 6 feet behind the server for recording the proper wall area number and the time for each serve. The score is the total number of point values for velocity and vertical placement that result from a performance of ten serves. The velocity measures for the ten serves are added and then converted to the point values in Table CXII. The placement conversions are also found in Table CXII. They too are added.

Scientific Authenticity

VALIDITY: The test reportedly validates well with subjective ratings. Content or face validity should be accepted for the test.

TABLE CXII

WISCONSIN WALL TEST CONVERSION TABLES

Vertical Placement		Velocity*	
Wall Area	Point Values	Time	Point Values
11'	1	4.00	300
10'	2	4.25	290
9'	4	4.50	280
8'	6	4.75	270
7'	7	5.00	260
6'	8	5.25	250
5'	9	5.50	240
4' Net	10	5.75	230
3'	6	6.00	220
2'	4	6.25	210
1'	2	6.50	200
		6.75	190
		7.00	180
		7.25	170
		7.50	160
		7.75	150
		8.00	140
		8.25	130
		8.50	120
		8.75	110
		9.00	100
		9.50	90
		10.00	80
		10.50	70
		11.00	60
		11.50	50
		12.00	40
		12.50	30
		13.00	20
		13.50	10
		13.51+	0

*Velocity scores treated in terms of 10 serves, not in terms of individual serves.

From A. C. Farrow: *Skill and Knowledge Proficiencies for Selected Activities in the Required Program at Memphis State University.* Doctoral dissertation, Greensboro, University of North Carolina, 1971.

It closely approximates the tennis serve used in competition. The Wisconsin Wall Test for Serve also correlated .62 with tournament rankings of 229 college students in nine tennis classes.

RELIABILITY: Separate time and placement scores showed respective reliability coefficients of .98 and .94. The combined speed and placement values (final scores) showed a reliability coefficient of .96 when twenty trials were given during a two-day period. A .91 coefficient was obtained as ten trials on one day were administered.

CRITERION MEASURE: Subjective ratings and tournament rankings.

Additional Comments

The test demonstrates an impressive reliability value as reflected in the above mentioned correlation coefficients. The validity value was less substantial perhaps because tournament rankings are a result of many skills, with the serve representing only one component of general tennis ability.

The test shows merit as a supplement to a more comprehensive tennis skills test. Caution should be taken in attaching too much importance to the test results due to the fact that some excellent tennis players possess only an average or less than average serve for their particular ability level.

HEWITT TENNIS ACHIEVEMENT TEST[23]

Date: 1966.

Purpose: To measure achievement in the basic tennis skills of the service, forehand, and backhand drives.

Description

The test battery is designed to evaluate three basic tennis skills: the forehand drive, backhand drive, and service. The specific test items include the forehand drive placement, backhand drive placement, service placement, and speed of service.

The court markings for the test items are shown in Figures 75 and 76. In each of the tests, a quarter-inch rope is stretched above the net at a height of 7 feet.

EDUCATIONAL APPLICATION: College men and women at the

beginner, advanced, and varsity levels; also appropriate for high school boys and girls.

Administrative Feasibility

TIME: Depends largely on number of courts available; accessibility to three courts would promote the test's administration in one sixty-minute class period for a class of fifteen to twenty students.

PERSONNEL: An instructor to serve as scorer for the service placement and speed of service test items plus trained assistants wherever deemed necessary.

TRAINING INVOLVED: A student in the advanced group should have completed at least one academic term of tennis instruction or its equivalent as determined by the instructor.

Prior to testing, each subject is given ten minutes of practice time on the three skills to be measured. The forehand and backhand drive test is immediately preceded by five practice strokes.

EQUIPMENT AND SUPPLIES: A box or basket to serve as a ball container, three dozen new heavy-duty tennis balls, and a number and variety of tennis racquets dependent upon the administrative structure of the test and individual differences in racquet requirements.

Accessories: Scoring materials and those for the court markings as shown in Figures 75 and 76.

Two poles, ladders, or some suitable alternative is needed to hold the rope taut in the service placement test.

Facilities and Space: At least two regulation tennis courts should be available to allow testing to be conducted on each court simultaneously.

Directions

SERVICE PLACEMENT: The subject serves ten balls into the service courts as shown in Figure 75. The ball must be served between the net and the rope. Balls served into the net (hit in service court) are repeated.

SPEED OF SERVICE: Ten good serve placements are scored according to the distance each serve bounces. This test item may be scored at the same time the service placement item is scored.

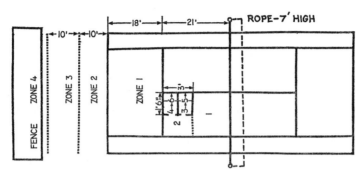

Figure 75. Court markings for service placement and speed of service tests. From J. E. Hewitt: Hewitt's Tennis Achievement Test, *Research Quarterly,* 37:231-240, 1966. Courtesy of AAHPER.

FOREHAND AND BACKHAND DRIVES: The subject takes a position at the center mark of the baseline. The instructor is stationed with a box or basket of balls on the other side of the net at the intersection of the center line and the service line. The instructor hits the five practice strokes to the subject prior to the ten test trials that are given for both the forehand and backhand strokes. The student chooses which ten balls to hit with the backhand and forehand.

The student should attempt to hit the ball under the rope to maximize his score potential. The same instructor should hit to all

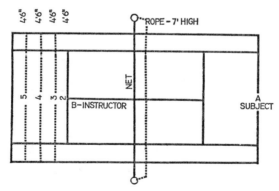

Figure 76. Court markings for forehand and backhand drive test. From J. E. Hewitt: Hewitt's Tennis Achievement Test, *Research Quarterly,* 37:231-240, 1966. Courtesy of AAHPER.

students for the purpose of test standardization. Net balls and those hit long and wide are repeated.

Scoring Method and Norms

Service Placement: The point value for the zone (Fig. 75) in which each ball lands is totaled for the ten trials and serves as the official score. Balls served long, wide, and over the restraining line (rope) are not scored.

Speed of Service: For each of the ten legal service placements, the appropriate value is assigned according to the zone values shown in Figure 75.

Backhand and Forehand Drives: Ten backhand and forehand drives that clear the net and go under the restraining rope are

TABLE CXIII

HEWITT TENNIS ACHIEVEMENT SCALES

Grade	Service Placements	Service Speed	Forehand Placements	Backhand Placements
	Junior Varsity and Varsity Tennis (16 cases--5 S.D.)			
F	20-24	20-22	25-28	20-23
D	25-29	23-25	29-32	24-27
C	30-39	26-32	33-39	28-34
B	40-45	33-36	40-45	35-40
A	46-50	37-40	46-50	41-47
	Advanced Tennis (36 cases--5 S.D.)			
F	11-14	8- 9	24-25	22-26
D	15-19	11-13	26-29	27-30
C	20-30	14-21	30-39	31-37
B	31-37	22-25	40-44	38-42
A	38-44	26-30	45-48	43-46
	Beginning Tennis (91 cases--5 S.D.)			
F	1- 2	1- 3	1- 3	1- 2
D	3- 6	4- 7	4- 8	3- 7
C	7-16	8-13	9-21	8-19
B	17-21	14-17	22-28	20-26
A	22-26	18-21	29-36	27-34

From J. E. Hewitt: Hewitt's tennis achievement test. *Research Quarterly,* *37:*231-240, 1966. Courtesy of AAHPER.

TABLE CXIV

SCORING SCALE FOR HEWITT'S SERVICE PLACEMENT TEST*

College Men	Performance Level	College Women
20-60	Excellent	14-60
16-19	Good	10-13
7-15	Average	4- 9
3- 6	Poor	1- 3
0- 2	Very Poor	0

*Based on scores of a limited number of beginning students in tennis as reported by Stan Johnson, NLU, Monroe, La., 1973.

From B. L. Johnson and J. K. Nelson: *Practical Measurements for Evaluation in Physical Education,* 1974. Courtesy of Burgess Publishing Company, Minneapolis.

TABLE CXV

RANK ORDER PLAY ABILITY IN TENNIS VS. HEWITT
TENNIS ACHIEVEMENT TEST SCORES

Hewitt Achievement Tennis Tests	Varsity/ Jr. Varsity		Advanced		Beginners	
	No. Cases	Rho	No. Cases	Rho	No. Cases	Rho
Forehand drive placements	16	.57	22	.618	91	.67
Backhand drive placements	16	.52	22	.613	91	.62
Service placements	16	.93	22	.625	91	.72
Speed of service or the distance the serve bounces	16	.86	22	.723	91	.89
Dyer wall test with 20' restraining line	16	.87	22	.84	91	.73

From J. E. Hewitt: Hewitt's tennis achievement test. *Research Quarterly, 37:*231-240, 1966. Courtesy of AAHPER.

scored. Balls that hit over the restraining rope and land in a scoring zone receive one-half the regular values. Balls that are wide, long, or hit the net are not scored.

Scientific Authenticity

VALIDITY: The coefficients *(Rho)* shown in Table CXV reflect the validity values of the test items. The number of subjects for each skill level is also shown in Table CXV.

RELIABILITY: The reliability values as determined by the test-retest method were as follows:

Forehand Drive Placement	.75
Backhand Drive Placement	.78
Service Placement	.94
Speed of Service	.84

CRITERION MEASURE: Round-robin tournament rankings for all ability levels.

Additional Comments

The backhand and forehand drive tests could be improved with the use of a ball-throwing machine, inasmuch as the reliability coefficients do not quite meet the acceptability level.

The test is fairly comprehensive in measurement of overall tennis ability and lends itself to mass testing if appropriate facilities and personnel are available.

An interesting contribution of the Hewitt Achievement Test to tennis skills testing is its confirmation of the assumption that the bounce distance of a served ball is a valid indicator of its speed. This discovery greatly simplifies the test for speed of service.

In comparing this test with his revision of the Dyer Tennis Test (see p. 419), Hewitt recommends the latter because of its simplicity and ease of administration. In addition, a high validity value was found for Hewitt's Revision of the Dyer Test when testing varsity players as well as beginners and students at the advanced level. Of course, the Hewitt Achievement Test becomes necessary in a situation where no wall is available.

HEWITT CLASSIFICATION TESTS[24]

Date: 1968.

Purpose: To classify students into homogeneous ability groups for instruction and play.

Description

The two-item test requires a demonstration of skill in bouncing a tennis ball on the court and hitting a tennis ball above the shoulder level.

EDUCATIONAL APPLICATION: College men and women; also appropriate for high school boys and girls.

Administrative Feasibility

TIME: One sixty-minute class period when test items are administered simultaneously for a class of fifteen to twenty students.

PERSONNEL: Following Hewitt's recommendation to divide the class on each test so half would serve as scorers, the instructor could be utilized to demonstrate and oversee the overall test administration.

TRAINING INVOLVED: The subject is allowed a fifteen-second warm-up immediately prior to taking each test. Since the skills required in the test are not specific tennis skills but merely indicators of tennis ability, each student should practice the test items a sufficient amount of time to gain proper familiarity with them.

EQUIPMENT AND SUPPLIES: A new tennis ball per student, a variety of tennis racquets according to student needs, and a stop watch per court utilized.

Accessories: Scoring materials.

Facilities and Space: A tennis court facility.

Directions

THIRTY-SECOND BOUNCE: The instructor first demonstrates the test item. The student then assumes a ready position by taking a forehand grip on a racquet. A ball is bounced on the court to a height of hip level or above by hitting it out of the hand with the racquet. The subject continues to bounce the ball for thirty seconds. Three trials are given.

THIRTY-SECOND FOREHAND AND BACKHAND HIT ABOVE THE SHOULDERS: The instructor again demonstrates the test item. The subject takes a backhand grip and hits a tennis ball out of the hand to above the shoulder level. Succeeding hits are alternated from forehand to backhand with rotation during the thirty-second time period. The racquet must be kept below shoulder level and the ball is not bounced on the court. Three trials are allowed.

TABLE CXVI

ABILITY LEVEL SCALE FOR HEWITT
CLASSIFICATION TEST*

Ability Level	30-sec. Tennis Bounce	30-sec. Forehand-Backhand Hit Above Shoulders
High–Good	77–98	53–72
Middle–Average	51–76	31–52
Low–Poor	26–50	10–30

*Based on scores of 114 college students.

From J. E. Hewitt: Classification tests in tennis, *Research Quarterly, 39:*552-555, 1968. Courtesy of AAHPER.

SCORING METHOD AND NORMS

Thirty-Second Bounce: The best score for the three trials constitutes the official score. The ball must be bounced to hip level or above to score.

Thirty-Second Forehand and Backhand Hit Above the Shoulders: The best score on three trials is recorded as the final score. No point is given if the balls fail to reach the shoulder level or

TABLE CXVII

RANK ORDER TENNIS PLAY ABILITY VS. HEWITT
TENNIS CLASSIFICATION TEST ITEM PERFORMANCE

N in Class	Range	Correlation Coefficient 30-sec. Tennis Bounce	Correlation Coefficient 30-sec. Forehand-Backhand Hit Above Shoulders
9	64–98	.78	.23
12	45–71	.88	.72
12	71–87	.57	.61
13	60–93	.88	.71
13	71–88	.59	.56
13	51–76	.72	.52
16	68–78	.58	.35
11	51–80	.56	.61
15	26–77	.82	.88

From J. E. Hewitt: Classification tests in tennis, *Research Quarterly, 39:*552-555, 1968. Courtesy of AAHPER.

above at contact or if the subject does not follow the proper sequence in the forehand-backhand alternation.

Scientific Authenticity

VALIDITY: As shown in Table CXVII, the validity coefficients for the thirty-second bounce ranged from .56 to .88 for 114 college students in nine tennis classes. The range for the thirty-second forehand and backhand hit above the shoulders was from .23 to .88 for those classes.

RELIABILITY: The test-retest method revealed coefficients of .88 and .83 for the respective bounce and shoulder test items. The same 114 college students were utilized to gather the data.

CRITERION MEASURE: Tournament ranking.

Additional Comments

Hewitt devised this test as an alternative to his revision of the Dyer Test for use in schools not having access to backboards and walls suitable for required test conditions. The test serves its intended use well, that of a rough classifier of tennis ability. The test should not be used for grading purposes.

In any instance where a wall or backboard is available, Hewitt rightfully suggests that the Dyer revision be used instead of the items in his classification test.

KEMP-VINCENT RALLY TEST[29]

Date: 1968.

Purpose: To measure achievement in tennis skill and to classify students according to rally ability in a simulated tennis game.

EDUCATIONAL APPLICATION: Designed for college men and women but is also appropriate for secondary school boys and girls.

Administrative Feasibility

TIME: Very feasible in time of administration: Two students are tested every three minutes.

PERSONNEL: Three scorers are recommended: one to count the total hits of each subject and the other two to score the errors.

The instructor would probably be the logical choice to serve as the scorer assigned to count total hits.

TRAINING INVOLVED: One practice trial per subject in an earlier class period and a one-minute warm-up immediately prior to testing.

EQUIPMENT AND SUPPLIES: One stop watch, four quality tennis balls per court, and an assortment of racquets.

Accessories: Scoring materials.

Facilities and Space: A regulation tennis court.

Directions

Two subjects of similar ability assume opposing positions on a singles court. On the starting signal, one of the subjects bounces a ball from behind the baseline and puts it in play with a courtesy stroke. The students then proceed to keep the ball in play for three minutes. A ball hit into the net or out of bounds temporarily halts play until one of the subjects puts another ball into play. It is put into play in the same manner as the one starting the rally test. The use of any tennis stroke is permissible.

Four balls are ready for use at the outset of the test. When these balls are used, the subjects must retrieve their own balls for the remainder of the test.

An error by a subject refers to (1) failure to put ball into play with courtesy stroke; (2) failure to hit the ball over the net on rally; (3) failure to put a new ball in play from behind the baseline; (4) failure to keep ball within singles court area; and (5) failure to hit ball before second bounce.

As in singles tennis, balls hitting the boundary lines are in play, and those that strike the top of the net and land over the net and in bounds are also playable. Balls landing out of bounds may be played at the discretion of the subjects for time-saving purposes.

SCORING METHOD: Initially the total number of hits for the two students are counted including those in which errors are committed. A courtesy stroke constitutes a hit. From the combined total hits of the two subjects, each subtracts his number of errors to determine the final rally score.

Scientific Authenticity

VALIDITY: Coefficients of correlation *(Rho)* by the Spearman-Brown Formula were .84 and .93 for twenty-four college men and women in a beginners' instructional class and thirty students in an intermediate level class. The skills test scores of 362 men and women students of varied ability levels were related to scores on the Iowa Modification of the Dyer Tennis Test, producing a validity coefficient of .80.

RELIABILITY: Sixty-two beginners and forty-eight intermediate performers served as subjects to determine the reliability of the Kemp-Vincent Rally Test. A test-retest approach produced coefficients of .90 and .86 for the beginning and intermediate groups, respectively.

CRITERION MEASURE: In the study involving the fifty-four college men and women, round-robin tournament rankings served as the criterion. For the second study conducted by Kemp and Vincent, the criterion used was the Iowa Modification of the Dyer Tennis Test.

Additional Comments

The Kemp-Vincent Rally Test has a number of pluses not found in some of the other tennis skills tests. First, the test closely approximates game conditions, especially when the subject pairing is virtually equal. Second, the time involved in administering the test is relatively small for a test that measures general playing ability. Third, no special equipment or court markings are required which contributes to ease of administration. Furthermore, the test eliminates the problem of inconsistency in force, direction, and accuracy of balls thrown or hit to the test subject as is common in other tests.

A possible liability of the test is the difficulty in pairing students by playing ability. A student capable of placing the ball so that it might easily be returned could contribute to an inflated score of the opponent and gross exaggeration of his true ability. However, one cannot deny the impressive reliability and validity values that the test demonstrates. The test truly has definite advantages over most of the other available tennis skills tests.

OVERHEAD SMASH TEST[48]

Date: 1972.

Purpose: To measure the effectiveness of the overhead smash stroke.

EDUCATIONAL APPLICATION: Both sexes from junior high through college.

Administrative Feasibility

TIME: One sixty-minute class period for a class of fifteen to twenty students.

PERSONNEL: The instructor and student assistants to serve as judges, scorers, and ball retrievers.

TRAINING INVOLVED: Some practice on the Tennis Set-up Machine's* method of dropping the ball should be permitted for each student to get the "feel" of its mode of operation. Three practice smashes are allowed for each subject immediately prior to taking the test.

EQUIPMENT AND SUPPLIES: The tennis and badminton machine (Tennis Set-up Machine), several tennis balls, and a racquet conducive to each student's needs.

Accessories: Scoring materials.

Facilities and Space: A regulation tennis court either indoors or outdoors.

Directions

The Tennis Set-up Machine is situated to allow the ball to drop at the junction of the center service line and the service line. The subject assumes the proper position for the smash and strikes the ball as it drops from the top pulley of the machine. Three practice trials precede the ten trials that are performed for score. The student attempts to smash each ball across the net and into the singles playing court. Trials should not be counted when the subjects fail to execute satisfactory form and force for a smash.

SCORING METHOD AND NORMS: One point is given for each

---

* The Tennis Set-up Machine, Model M4, Patent Pending—1972 by Barry L. Johnson, Texas A&I University at Corpus Christi, Corpus Christi, Texas 78411.

TABLE CXVIII

NORMS FOR OVERHEAD SMASH TEST*

College Men	Performance Level
9-10	Excellent
7- 8	Good
5- 6	Average
3- 4	Poor
0- 2	Very Poor

*Based on scores of a limited number of college men as
reported by Mike Recio and Charles Prestidge, NLU, Monroe,
La., 1972.

From B. J. Johnson and J. K. Nelson: *Practical Measurements for Evaluation in Physical Education,* 1974. Courtesy of Burgess Publishing Company, Minneapolis.

successful smash. An incorrect repeated trial is scored as a zero. Ten points is the maximum score.

Scientific Authenticity

VALIDITY: Face validity is accepted because the measured skill closely approximates the skill required under game conditions, plus the overhead smash is one of the common and important tennis strokes.

RELIABILITY: A .96 coefficient of correlation was obtained in a 1973 study.[27]

Additional Comments

An alternate form of the test may be administered on a backboard with the net line drawn. This is especially useful for individual practice during class sessions.

The tennis and badminton machine utilized in this test is an inexpensive testing and training device for the sport of tennis. Both automatic and manual machines are available.

REFERENCES

1. American Association for Health, Physical Education and Recreation: *Measurement and Evaluation of Materials in Health, Physical Education and Recreation.* Washington, AAHPER, 1950.

2. Barrow, Harold M. and McGee, Rosemary: *A Practical Approach to Measurement in Physical Education,* 2nd ed. Philadelphia, Lea & Febiger, 1971.

3. Beall, Elizabeth: Essential qualities in certain aspects of physical education with ways of measuring and developing the same. *American Physical Education Review, 33:*648, 1928.

4. Bovard, John F. and Cozens, Frederick W.: *Tests and Measurements in Physical Education,* 2nd ed. Philadelphia, Saunders, 1938.

5. Broer, Marion R. and Miller, Donna Mae: Achievement tests for beginning and intermediate tennis. *Research Quarterly, 21:*303-321, 1950.

6. Campbell, W. R. and Tucker, N. M.: *An Introduction to Tests and Measurements in Physical Education.* London, Bell & Sons, 1967.

7. Clarke, H. Harrison: *Application of Measurement to Health and Physical Education,* 3rd ed. Englewood Cliffs, P-H, 1959.

8. ———: *Application of Measurement to Health and Physical Education,* 4th ed. Englewoods Cliffs, P-H, 1967.

9. Condon, Carlton J.: The Development and Evaluation of a Battery of Tennis Skills as an Index to Ability in Tennis. Master's thesis, Springfield, Mass., Springfield College, 1941.

10. Cutts, Jeanette: A practice board test of the fundamental strokes in tennis. *Research Quarterly, 9:*75, 1938.

11. DiGennaro, Joseph: Construction of forehand drive, backhand drive, and serve tennis tests. *Research Quarterly, 40:*496-501, 1969.

12. Driver, Helen Irene: *Tennis for Teachers.* Philadelphia, Saunders, 1936.

13. Dyer, Joanna T.: The backboard test of tennis ability. *Research Quarterly, 6:*63-74, 1935.

14. ———: Revision of backboard test of tennis ability. *Research Quarterly, 9:*25-31, 1938.

15. Eckert, Helen M.: *Practical Measurement of Physical Performance.* Philadelphia, Lea & Febiger, 1974.

16. Edgren, Harry D.: Tennis technique. *Journal of Health and Physical Education, 5:*30-31, 1934.

17. Edwards, Janet: A Study of Three Measures of the Tennis Serve. Master's thesis, Madison, University of Wisconsin, 1965.

18. Farrow, Andrea C.: Skill and Knowledge Proficiencies for Selected Activities in the Required Program at Memphis State University. Doctoral dissertation, Greensboro, University of North Carolina, 1971.

19. Fox, Katharine: A study of the validity of the Dyer Backboard Test and the Miller Forehand-Backhand Test for beginning tennis players. *Research Quarterly, 24:*1-7, 1953.

20. Glassow, Ruth B. and Broer, Marion R.: *Measuring Achievement in Physical Education.* Philadelphia, Saunders, 1938.

21. Haskins, Mary Jane: *Evaluation in Physical Education.* Dubuque, Iowa, Brown Bk, 1971.

22. Hewitt, Jack E.: Revision of the Dyer Backboard Tennis Test. *Research Quarterly, 36:*153-157, 1965.

23. ⸻: Hewitt's Tennis Achievement Test. *Research Quarterly, 37:* 231-240, 1966.

24. ⸻: Classification tests in tennis. *Research Quarterly, 39:*552-555, 1968.

25. Hulac, Georgia May: The Construction of an Objective Indoor Test for Measuring Effective Tennis Serves. Master's thesis, Greensboro, Woman's College of the University of North Carolina, 1958.

26. Hunsicker, Paul A. and Montoye, Henry J.: *Applied Tests and Measurements in Physical Education.* Englewood Cliffs, P-H, 1953.

27. Johnson, Barry L. and Nelson, Jack K.: *Practical Measurements for Evaluation in Physical Education,* 2nd ed. Minneapolis, Burgess, 1974.

28. Jones, Shirley K.: A Measurement of Tennis Serving Ability. Master's thesis, Los Angeles, University of California, 1967.

29. Kemp, Joann and Vincent, Marilyn F.: Kemp-Vincent Rally Test of Tennis Skill. *Research Quarterly, 39:*1000-1004, 1968.

30. Koski, W. Arthur: A tennis wall rally test for college men. In Clarke, H. Harrison: *Application of Measurement to Health and Physical Education,* 3rd ed. Englewood Cliffs, P-H, 1959.

31. Larson, Leonard A. and Yocom, Rachael Dunaven: *Measurement and Evaluation in Physical, Health and Recreation Education.* St. Louis, Mosby, 1951.

32. Leighton, Harry: Leighton tests for accuracy. *NSWA Tennis and Badminton Guide (1952-54).* Washington, AAHPER, 1952.

33. Lockhart, Aileene: A survey of testing in tennis. *Journal of Health and Physical Education, 9:*433, 462-463, 1938.

34. Malinak, Nina R.: The Construction of an Objective Measure of Accuracy in the Performance of the Tennis Serve. Master's thesis, Urbana, University of Illinois, 1961.

35. Mathews, Donald K.: *Measurement in Physical Education,* 4th ed. Philadelphia, Saunders, 1973.

36. McAdams, Linda Butler: The Use of Rebound Nets as a Means of Determining Tennis Skill. Master's thesis, Pullman, Washington State University, 1964.

37. McCloy, Charles Harold and Young, Norma Dorothy: *Tests and Measurements in Health and Physical Education,* 3rd ed. New York, Appleton, 1954.

38. McDonald, Kaye: A Comparison of the Broer-Miller Forehand Drive Test in Which a Ball-Boy Is Employed to Deliver the Ball. Master's thesis, Boulder, University of Colorado, 1960.

39. Meyers, Carlton R. and Blesh, T. Erwin: *Measurement in Physical Education.* New York, Ronald, 1962.
40. Meyers, Carlton R.: *Measurement in Physical Education,* 2nd ed. New York, Ronald, 1974.
41. Miller, Wilma K.: Achievement Levels in Tennis Knowledge and Skill for Women Physical Education Students. Doctoral dissertation, Bloomington, Indiana University, 1952.
42. ————: Achievement levels in tennis knowledge and skill for women physical education major students. *Research Quarterly, 24:*81-90, 1953.
43. Montoye, Henry J. (Ed.): *An Introduction to Measurement in Physical Education,* vol. III. Indianapolis, Phi Epsilon Kappa Fraternity, 1970.
44. Murphy, William E.: The Measurement of Some Skills Necessary to Success in Tennis. Master's thesis, Chicago, George Williams College, 1941.
45. Mynard, Virginia: A Preliminary Analysis of the Game of Tennis, the Reliability of Certain Tennis Skill Tests, and the Determination of Practice Board Areas for Serve and Drive. Master's thesis, Wellesley, Mass., Wellesley College, 1938.
46. Neilson, N. P. and Jensen, Clayne R.: *Measurement and Statistics in Physical Education.* Belmont, Calif., Wadsworth Pub, 1972.
47. Newport, Margaret F.: Tennis skill tests. *NSWA Tennis and Badminton Guide (1938-40).* Washington, AAHPER, 1938.
48. Recio, Michael and Prestidge, Charles: The Overhead Smash Test utilizing the Johnson tennis and badminton machine. In Johnson, Barry L. and Nelson, Jack K.: *Practical Measurements for Evaluation in Physical Education,* 2nd ed. Minneapolis, Burgess, 1974.
49. Reid, Ruth: A tennis skills test. *DGWS Guide for Tennis and Badminton (1960-62).* Washington, AAHPER, 1960.
50. Reilly, F. J.: *New Rational Athletics for Boys and Girls.* Boston, Heath, 1917.
51. Ronning, Hilding E.: Wall Tests for Evaluating Tennis Ability. Master's thesis, Pullman, Washington State University, 1959.
52. Scott, M. Gladys: Achievement examinations for elementary and intermediate tennis classes. *Research Quarterly, 12:*40-49, 1941.
53. Scott, M. Gladys and French, Esther: *Better Teaching Through Testing.* New York, B&N, 1945.
54. Scott, M. Gladys and French, Esther: *Measurement and Evaluation in Physical Education.* Dubuque, Iowa, Brown Bk, 1959.
55. Shay, Clayton T.: An application of the Dyer Test. *Journal of Health and Physical Education, 29:*273, 1949.
56. Sherman, Patricia: A Selected Battery of Tennis Skill Tests. Doctoral dissertation, Iowa City, University of Iowa, 1972.

57. Swift, Betty M.: A Skill Test and Norms for the Speed of the Tennis Serve. Doctoral dissertation, Fayetteville, University of Arkansas, 1969.

58. Timmer, Karen L.: A Tennis Skill Test to Determine Accuracy in Playing Ability. Master's thesis, Springfield, Mass., Springfield College, 1965.

59. Wagner, Miriam M.: An objective method of grading beginners in tennis. *Journal of Health and Physical Education, 6*:24-25, 79, 1935.

60. Weiss, Raymond A. and Phillips, Marjorie: *Administration of Tests in Physical Education.* St. Louis, Mosby, 1954.

61. Willgoose, Carl E.: *Evaluation in Health Education and Physical Education.* New York, McGraw, 1961.

62. Varner, Margaret: A Skill Test for College Women Enrolled in Beginners' Tennis Classes. Master's thesis, Denton, Texas State College for Women, 1950.

Chapter 27

Track and Field

INTRODUCTION

TRACK AND FIELD EVENTS date back to early Greece and played a prominent role in the first recorded Olympic Games of 776 BC. In 1896, the first modern Olympic Games introduced one of the all-time great sport attractions. Through the years, track and field has reached a lofty level in popularity during the periodic playing of the Games. This international competition has done much to promote track and field as today most colleges and schools field athletic teams in the sport. As a matter of fact, a 1976 survey by the National Federation of State High School Associations revealed that outdoor track is now the most popular interscholastic sport for girls and third in popularity for boys.[17]

Instruction in track and field is another matter, however. Its inclusion in course schedules is not uncommon at the public school or college level, yet a significant percentage of educational institutions still do not offer the sport as part of the physical education activity curriculum.

Skills tests in the traditional sense are not emphasized nor really necessary for track and field. It is one of the few sports in which actual skills required in competiton are measured instead of those that have been validated as authentic approximations. Thus, measurement of track and field ability has something in common with archery and bowling in that test requirements inherently demonstrate face validity.

Some reference sources are recommended to assist the tester in locating necessary field specifications and dimensions for particular events. They include the *National Collegiate Athletic Association Track and Field Guide*,[15] and the *Track and Field Rules and Record Book of the National Federation of State High School Athletic Associations*.[16] One other useful source is the *Track and Field Guide* by the National Association for Girls and Women in

448

Sport, a subgroup of the American Alliance for Health, Physical Education and Recreation.[14]

AVAILABLE TESTS FOR MEASUREMENT OF TRACK AND FIELD SKILLS

Traditionally, track and field events have been included as part of physical or motor fitness test batteries. Few tests are limited specifically to track and field events, so the discussion of available tests which follows makes reference to a number of tests in the former category.

Mitchell[11] is credited with developing the first skills test that included track and field items. Norms were constructed for the 50-yard dash and running broad jump, with the basketball throw also included.

A few years later, Cozens[5] developed a decathlon type skills test complete with a scoring system for each event. The purpose of this test was to stimulate an expansion of competition and evaluate scientifically the individual abilities of a college track squad. Ten events were developed and may be administered over a three-day period in the following suggested order:

1. first day–75-yard dash, 12 pound shot-put, standing hop, step and jump, and 330-yard run.
2. second day–120-yard low hurdles, running high jump, and 660-yard run.
3. third day–running broad jump, discus throw, and 1,320-yard run.

The scoring scheme is based on a 1,000 point maximum.

Conger[4] developed a percentile scale for boys, based on age only, in seven events including basketball foul shooting, 50-yard dash, pull-ups, push-ups, running high jump, running broad jump, 8 pound shot-put, and 12 pound shot-put. The elaborate study utilized the performance record of over 44,000 subjects, but unfortunately, height and weight were not considered.

Another skills test that could be used to determine general track and field ability is the Sigma Delta Psi Test.[13] The national honorary athletic fraternity devised a fifteen-item test for college students with six having direct relation to the sport of track and field. The six track and field items are the 100-yard dash, 120-yard low hurdles, running high jump, running broad jump, 16 pound shot-put, and the one-mile run. Non-track and field requirements include the football punt, 100-yard swim, front handspring, bar vault, posture, scholarship, an option of either a handstand or bowling performance, a 20-foot rope climb or performance in golf, and baseball performance or the javelin throw. An elaborate scoring system has been developed for each to evaluate student performance.

The national collegiate rules are used as the accepted standards for the various activities in the Sigma Delta Psi Test. It may be used to measure either individual or team performance. Ten students who have the highest total points, as determined by the scoring tables on the basis of individual performances for each test, comprise a team for competition with other local, state, or national teams. Individual records indicating the best times, distances, and most points earned may be maintained and used in a self-examining program. Additional information may be obtained from almost any college or university intramural sports department as those institutions administer the test upon request.

The AAHPER Youth Fitness Test[1] is designed to measure general motor fitness; however, several of its test items can be used to determine track and field ability. In 1957, a committee appointed by the American Association for Health, Physical Education and Recreation (under the leadership of Paul A. Hunsicker) developed a seven-item test battery to measure different components of fitness for boys and girls in grades five through twelve. Three or possibly four of the test items relate to track and field skills. The original test items include: pull-ups (boys), flexed-arm hang (girls), sit-ups, shuttle-run, standing broad jump, 50-yard dash, softball throw, and the 600-yard run-walk. Percentile norms, based on both age and the Neilson-Cozens (California) Classification Index, were developed for the original seven-item test battery.

A revision of several test items was completed in 1965, along with a new set of norms developed from the scores of 9,200 children from age ten to seventeen. In 1975, a second revision was proposed jointly by the AAHPER and the President's Council on Physical Fitness and Sports and implemented. The softball distance throw was eliminated and the bent-knee sit-ups for one minute item replaced the unlimited straight-knee sit-ups test. The 600-yard run-walk was retained, but two optional runs were added: the one mile or nine-minute run for ages ten to twelve, and 1½ miles or twelve-minute run for ages thirteen and over. Percentile norms were developed for college men and women, plus boys and girls from ten through eighteen years of age.

POTENTIAL MEASUREMENT PROBLEMS IN TRACK AND FIELD

As alluded to earlier, perhaps the most effective way to evaluate students in a track and field skills class is to simply measure their performance in the common events unless viable alternatives are available. Even with the use of this valid approach in measurement, there are some potential pitfalls which the tester should be aware of when measuring student performance.

For example, lack of facilities and equipment places a limitation on those instructors who desire to use a scientific approach in skills measurement. Almost as important as the competence of the tester is a testing environment that enhances the scientific value of the particular test being administered. The inevitable differences found in the various test settings dictate the need for construction of local norms and illustrate the potential danger of relying too heavily on norms collected on a national level.

In administering track and field events for score, a significant challenge to the tester is to assure satisfactory reliability in item performance. Ways to improve the reliability of these items should receive the constant attention of the tester. However, an event's practical value in administrative feasibility should not be compromised. The ideal is to decrease the time of administration and number of trials given while at the same time retaining or increasing the reliability value.

Findings of a study by Jackson and Baumgartner[7] illustrate this point, as a possible improvement for measuring performance reliability in the 50-yard dash was indicated. Only two trials were found necessary for obtaining a reliable criterion score when the first 20 yards were excluded in the measurement. Greater consistency was shown among runners during the last 30 yards of the dash, which suggests that administration of multiple trials for the 50-yard dash may not be necessary to determine a student's ability level in running short dashes.

REFERENCES

1. American Association for Health, Physical Education and Recreation: *Youth Fitness Test Manual.* Washington, AAHPER, 1962.
2. Bovard, John F.; Cozens, Frederick W.; and Hagman, E. Patricia: *Tests and Measurements in Physical Education,* 3rd ed. Philadelphia, Saunders, 1949.
3. Clarke, H. Harrison: *Application of Measurement to Health and Physical Education,* 5th ed. Englewood Cliffs, P-H, 1976.
4. Conger, Ralph G.: Percentile scales of seven physical activity tests for boys from 12-19. In Bovard, John F. and Cozens, Frederick W.: *Tests and Measurements in Physical Education,* 3rd ed. Philadelphia, Saunders, 1949.
5. Cozens, Frederick W.: A fall decathlon for track squads. *Research Quarterly, 9:*3-14, 1938.
6. Foreman, Ken and Husted, Virginia: *Track and Field.* Dubuque, Iowa, Brown Bk, 1966.
7. Jackson, Andrew S. and Baumgartner, Ted A.: A measurement schedule of sprint running. *Research Quarterly, 40:*708-711, 1969.
8. Johnson, Barry L. and Nelson, Jack K.: *Practical Measurements for Evaluation in Physical Education,* 2nd ed. Minneapolis, Burgess, 1974.
9. Kennedy, Robert E.: *Track and Field for College Men.* Philadelphia, Saunders, 1970.
10. Meyers, Carlton R.: *Measurement in Physical Education,* 2nd ed. New York, Ronald, 1974.
11. Mitchell, A. Viola: A scoring table for college women in the fifty-yard dash, the running broad jump, and the basketball throw. *Research Quarterly, 5:*86-91, 1934.
12. Montoye, Henry J. (Ed.): *An Introduction to Measurement in Physical Education,* vol. III. Indianapolis, Phi Epsilon Kappa Fraternity, 1970.
13. Mueller, Pat and Mitchell, Elmer D.: *Intramural Sports,* 3rd ed. New York, Ronald, 1963.
14. National Association for Girls and Women in Sport: *Track and Field Guide for Girls and Women.* Washington, AAHPER, 1976.

15. National Collegiate Athletic Association: *Track and Field Guide.* Shawnee Mission, Kansas, NCAA, 1977.

16. National Federation of State High School Associations: *Track and Field Rules and Records.* Elgin, Illinois, National Federation Publications, 1977 (periodically updated).

17. Sports survey shows increases in participants. *The First Aider, 46:*1, 11, 1977.

18. United States Office of Education, Federal Security Agency: *Handbook on Physical Fitness for Colleges and Universities.* Washington, U. S. Government Printing Office, 1943.

Chapter 28

Volleyball

INTRODUCTION

WITH THE EXCEPTION of softball, the sport of volleyball perhaps demonstrates more carry-over value for later life than any other team sport. Opportunity for participation in the post-school years is prevalent as the recreation programs of traditional social and community service organizations commonly include the sport for both sexes, and more increasingly on a coeducational basis. The popularity of volleyball seems to be expanding as a greater awareness of the sport is being promoted through media coverage of national and international competition.

One of only a few American-born sports, volleyball seems to attract more women than men, especially at the interscholastic level. The 1976 Sports Participation Survey, compiled by the National Federation of State High School Associations,[60] showed volleyball as the third leading sport for girls in number of participants while it failed to make the top ten on the list of sports for males. Yet in the leagues that play volleyball on a more informal basis, men are well represented. And, of course, it is included in the Olympic Games competition for both men and women.

Alterations of skills tests requirements as a result of changes in the rules or style of play in particular sports are probably evidenced in volleyball as much or more than any other sport. When the girls' rules were changed to restrict the number of hits to one, the influence was soon shown in the format of skills tests. An even more profound effect on the game has resulted from the introduction of what is commonly known as "power volleyball," which accents the offensive aspect of the game. The transition from a slow, deliberate type offensive strategy to a fast-paced, quick tempo style has revolutionized the sport, and the trend is discernible today at all levels of organized volleyball. Much of this is due to the emphasis and importance that present-day volleyball instructors are placing on the power game. Low and fast serves, high and accurate passes, in addition to strong, decisive spikes are starting to dominate the sport even at the levels of lowest organization. Variations in skills tests pertaining to the number and length of trials, plus restraining and wall line locations, depict an attempt to keep pace with the new emphasis.

Investigators for skills tests in volleyball have made a genuine contribution toward scientific measurement of the sport through a prolific number of developed tests. Highlighted by the timeless Brady Test of 1945,[6] exceptional quality has been displayed in the overall production of volleyball skills tests. Many of the better ones are presented in this chapter.

WISCONSIN VOLLEYBALL TEST[4]

Date: 1937.

Purpose: To measure volleyball ability of college women.

Description

The Wisconsin Test was one of the forerunner tests in volley-ball and includes the most common item found in skills tests for that sport, the repeated volley. Also included in the two-item battery is a serving test.

Volley: A 6-foot restraining line is placed parallel to the wall. A line, 2 inches wide and 12 feet long, is placed on the wall, with the lower edge 7½ feet from the floor.

Serve: A target consisting of four concentric squares, 16, 12, 8, and 4 feet in size, is placed in the far left corner of the service court so that two sides of the 8-foot square coincide with the end line and sideline of the court. A wire may be placed 3½ feet above the net.

EDUCATIONAL APPLICATION: College women.

Administrative Feasibility

TIME: Two sixty-minute class periods for fifteen to twenty students.

PERSONNEL: One timer and scorer.

TRAINING INVOLVED: Students should be thoroughly familiar

with the volley item requirements before testing. A brief warm-up on this item is warranted for the student immediately prior to testing.

EQUIPMENT AND SUPPLIES: Volleyballs, stop watch.

Accessories: Wall and floor marking materials, materials for scoring, and a wire the length of a volleyball net (optional) with appropriate standards.

Facilities and Space: Gymnasium or indoor space conducive to construction of a regulation volleyball court.

Directions

VOLLEY: Standing behind the restraining line, the subject when signaled tosses the ball against the wall, then completes as many legal wall hits as possible in thirty seconds. After the initial toss, the subject is not required to remain behind the restraining line. Three trials are administered.

SERVE: When ready, the subject proceeds to serve fifteen balls to the previously mentioned target placed in the far left corner of the service court.

SCORING METHOD

Volley: Number of legal wall hits in three thirty-second trials.

Serve: The four target zones are valued at 7, 6, 5, and 4 points according to degree of difficulty; two points are awarded for in-bound serves not hitting the target and one point for an out-of-bounds serve. If the wire is used, balls passing between it and the net score an additional point.

Scientific Authenticity

VALIDITY: Coefficients of .51 and .79 for the volley and serve items, respectively.

RELIABILITY: Coefficients of .89 and .84 for the items in the above order.

CRITERION MEASURE: Composite ability ratings of three judges.

Additional Comments

The Wisconsin Test was the first recognized volleyball test for college women. Overall, the test appears satisfactory for use, but its validity coefficient for the repeated volley is considerably less than those derived for similar items found in later tests at varying levels of educational application.

RUSSELL-LANGE VOLLEYBALL TEST[52]

Date: 1940.

Purpose: To measure volleyball playing ability of junior and senior high girls.

Description

In adapting the French-Cooper Test[20] to junior high girls, Russell and Lange improved upon the reliability of the items, making the battery more valuable for use in testing volleyball ability of junior and senior high girls, as the test is also appropriate for the latter age level.

Volley: Marked on a wall at net height or 7½ feet from the floor is a line 10 feet in length. A parallel line of the same length is marked on the floor, 3 feet from the wall.

Serve: Figure 77 reflects the necessary court markings for the serve item.

EDUCATIONAL APPLICATION: Junior and senior high school girls.

Administrative Feasibility

TIME: Two sixty-minute periods for twenty students.

PERSONNEL: One timer and scorer.

TRAINING INVOLVED: Students should become thoroughly familiar with the volley item requirement prior to testing.

EQUIPMENT AND SUPPLIES: Volleyballs, stop watch.

Accessories: Scoring, wall, and floor marking materials.

Facilities and Space: Gymnasium or indoor area of sufficient size to serve as a regulation volleyball court.

Directions

VOLLEY: On an audible signal, the subject, while standing behind the restraining line, starts the test by using an underhand movement to toss the ball against the wall. It is repeatedly volleyed for thirty seconds. The action may be restarted as many

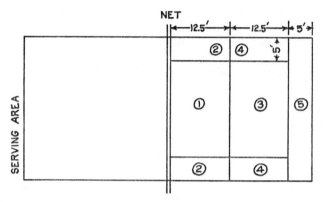

Figure 77. Court markings for Russell-Lange Volleyball Test. From N. Russell and E. Lange: Achievement tests in volleyball for junior high school girls, *Research Quarterly, 11*:33-41, 1940. Courtesy of AAHPER.

times as desired, but the ball must be tossed from behind the restraining line each time.

SERVE: From the serving area behind the end line, the subject completes two trials of ten legal serves. "Let" balls are reserved.

SCORING METHOD AND NORMS

Volley: The number of legal volleys that hit on or above the wall line with the subject remaining behind the restraining line. The top score of the three trials is recorded.

Serve: Points accumulated (Fig. 77) in the best trial are recorded as the final score. Serves in which foot faults occur are given a score of zero, and balls landing on a line are given the score of higher value.

Scientific Authenticity

VALIDITY: Coefficients of .80 and .68 for the volley and serve items, respectively.

RELIABILITY: Reliability coefficients ranged from .87 to .92.

CRITERION MEASURE: Subjective ability ratings of seven judges.

Additional Comments

As indicated earlier, the Russell-Lange Test is a derivative of the French-Cooper Test but was designed for junior high girls.

TABLE CXIX

NORMS FOR RUSSELL-LANGE VOLLEYBALL
TEST FOR GIRLS*

Sigma Scale	Serve	Repeated Volleys	Sigma Scale	Serve	Repeated Volleys
100		51	50		22
99	45	50	49	16	
98	44		48		21
97		49	47		
96	43		46	15	20
95		48	45		
94	42		44		19
93	41	47	43	14	
92		46	42		
91	40		41		18
90		45	40	13	
89	39		39		17
88		44	38		
87	38	43	37	12	16
86	37		36		
85		42	35		15
84	36		34	11	
83		41	33		
82	35		32		14
81		40	31	10	
80	34	39	30		13
79	33		29		
78		38	28	9	12
77	32		27		
76		37	26		
75	31	36	25	8	11
74	30		24		
73		35	23		10
72	29		22	7	
71		34	21		9
70	28		20		
69		33	19	6	8
68	27	32	18		
67	26		17		
66		31	16		7
65	25		15		
64		30	14		6
63	24		13		
62	23	29	12		5
61		28	11		
60	22		10	3	4
59		27	9		
58	21		8		
57		26	7	2	3

TABLE CXIX (continued)

Sigma Scale	Serve	Test Scores Repeated Volleys	Sigma Scale	Serve	Test Scores Repeated Volleys
56	20	25	6		
55	19		5		2
54		24	4	1	
53	18		3		1
52		23	2		
51	17		1		

*Based on scores of junior and senior high school girls.

From N. Russell and E. Lange: Achievement tests in volleyball for junior high school girls, *Research Quarterly, 11:*33-41, 1940. Courtesy of AAHPER.

The test is an improvement upon the original and does have application for high school females. The two tests are virtually the same except the volley item in the French-Cooper Test is fifteen seconds in length and ten trials are given. The score is the total of the five best trials. Validity coefficients were .72 and .63 for the volley and serve items in that order while reliability estimates of .78 and .81 were determined for the respective items. Results of other studies suggest that the test shows greater reliability when administered to college women.[56]

In administering the Russell-Lange Test to classes of women over a period of years, Mohr and Haverstick[46] found that the students tended to bat or volley the ball more frequently than setting it up and then volleying. To encourage use of the set-up skill, they experimented with restraining lines of 5 and 7 feet. The elimination of height as a factor in the test conditions was also an objective of the study since taller players seemed to have an advantage at the 3-foot restraining line.

Utilizing the same test layout dimensions as the Russell-Lange Test except that the two additional restraining lines were added, three thirty-second trials were administered to 110 college women, one at 3, 5, and 7 feet, respectively. Reliability estimates for the restraining lines as listed above were .81, .81, and .83. Validity coefficients obtained for the same distances were .64, .67, and .75. Results of their study led Mohr and Haverstick to eliminate the distances of 3 and 5 feet and retain the 7-foot restraining line for administration of all three trials. The sum of legal volleys was retained as the final score.

BRADY VOLLEYBALL TEST[6]

Also cited as Brady Wall Volley Test, and Brady Volleying Test for College Men.

Date: 1945.

Purpose: To measure general volleyball playing ability of college men.

Description

In experimenting with several skill items as possible indicators of general volleyball playing ability, Brady developed a rather simple and practical test that has proven to be a forerunner for scientifically authentic volleyball tests.

The test layout plan is formulated by utilizing a smooth wall on which a target is drawn that consists of a horizontal chalk line 5 feet in length and 11½ feet from the floor. Vertical lines extend upward at the ends of the horizontal line toward the ceiling.

EDUCATIONAL APPLICATION: College men.

Administrative Feasibility

TIME: One sixty-minute period for a class of twenty to thirty students. Considerably more could be tested if multiple test stations are utilized.

PERSONNEL: A person to score and record results.

TRAINING INVOLVED: As an example of a single-item skills test whereby the requirement only approximates an actual game skill, it is strongly recommended that an extensive amount of uniform practice time be allowed each student in class periods that precede the day of testing. Also suggested as a pretest requirement for the students on the day of testing is that a brief uniform period of time be allowed for practice.

EQUIPMENT AND SUPPLIES: Volleyball, stop watch.

Accessories: Scoring and test layout marking materials.

Facilities and Space: An unobstructed, smooth wall space at least 15 feet high and 15 feet wide.

Directions

Standing at a position of his choice, the subject, when signaled, initiates the test by throwing the ball against the wall. On the first return and those thereafter, he attempts to volley the ball within the boundaries of the chalk lines. As many as possible are completed in a sixty-second time period. Catching or loss of control of the ball requires the subject to resume the test with a throw as at the beginning of the test. Only one trial is permitted.

SCORING METHOD: The number of legal volleys hitting in the target area in the required time allotment constitutes the score. Thrown balls are not counted.

Scientific Authenticity

VALIDITY: A coefficient of .86 was reported for the correlation between test scores and the criterion.

RELIABILITY: With 282 subjects participating in a test-retest situation on the same day, a coefficient of .93 resulted.

CRITERION MEASURE: Subjective ratings of four qualified judges.

Additional Comments

All variables considered, the Brady Test merits its reputation as one of the most valuable skills tests ever constructed. Insofar as fulfilling the purpose for which it was developed, few tests can match the test's overall quality rating in the major areas of scientific authenticity and administrative feasibility. It is reportedly useful as an instrument for classifying ability levels, measuring student skill improvement, assessing teaching effectiveness, plus grading and practice.

In an attempt to inject the improvement factor into the method of grading the test, Brady suggests that the difference between scores made on the first and last tests be added to the last test score. This provides due credit to the unskilled beginner who progresses rapidly, yet does not penalize the student who demonstrates some degree of skill at the beginning of the class and improves at a lesser rate.

The only notable shortcoming of the Brady Volleyball Test is its limited adaptation with regard to age groups. Brady states that the test is less valuable when given to students below college level or to those in the unskilled category. That potential problem has been solved through revisions of the original Brady Test.

Cummisky's[18] adaptation of the Brady Test was designed for boys aged eleven to fourteen years. The wall line remained at 5 feet, but its height was lowered to 8 feet above the floor. Four-foot vertical lines were placed at the ends of the 5-foot horizontal wall line as in the Brady Test.

Cummisky added a fifteen-second practice trial to the test procedure. Furthermore, two volleying sessions were utilized, one for thirty seconds and the other for forty-five seconds. Reliability for the test was computed at .86, somewhat less than that derived for the Brady Test.

Another revision of the Brady Test was completed by Kronqvist and Brumbach[32] and was designed for testing high school boys. Deviations from the Brady Test include the location of the wall line at 11 feet in height instead of 11½, and three twenty-second trials are administered as opposed to one sixty-second trial. The validity coefficient was .77 with judges' ratings used as the criterion, and a reliability of .82 was derived by use of the test-retest method. The score is the total number of legal volleys made in the three trials.

CLIFTON SINGLE-HIT VOLLEY TEST[15]
Date: 1962.

Purpose: To evaluate volleying ability of college women.

Description

In response to the introduction of the single-hit rule in 1957 for women's volleyball, Clifton constructed a test with application for testing volleyball skill achievement of females at the collegiate level.

The horizontal wall line for this test is 10 feet long and is located 7½ feet from the floor. A 10-foot restraining line is drawn on the floor 7 feet away from the wall.

EDUCATIONAL APPLICATION: College women.

Administrative Feasibility

TIME: One sixty-minute period for a class of twenty students.

PERSONNEL: One timer and scorer.

TRAINING INVOLVED: Students should be given ample practice time on the test requirement in class sessions prior to the day of testing and a uniform amount of practice volleys immediately before the test.

EQUIPMENT AND SUPPLIES: Stop watch, properly inflated volleyball.

Accessories: Scoring, floor and wall marking materials.

Facilities and Space: An unobstructed wall and floor space commensurate to proper maneuverability within the test layout dimensions.

Directions

Standing behind the restraining line with a volleyball, the subject on an audible command makes an underhand toss against the wall. For thirty seconds, she performs as many legal volleys as possible above the 7½-foot wall line while remaining behind the restraining line. If control of the ball is lost, the subject recovers it and proceeds with an underhand toss in the same manner as the original. Two thirty-second trials are administered with an intervening rest period of two minutes.

SCORING METHOD: The number of legal volleys touching on or above the wall line in the thirty-second time period constitutes the trial score. Volleys made while the subject is standing on or over the restraining line do not count. The two trial scores are added for the final score.

Scientific Authenticity

VALIDITY: Correlation coefficient of .70.

RELIABILITY: A coefficient of .83, using the test-retest method.

CRITERION MEASURE: Ratings of volleying ability by five experienced judges.

Additional Comments

In a study designed to better approximate game conditions in single-hit volleyball, Cunningham and Garrison[19] deviated from the Clifton Test by eliminating the restraining line, raising the wall line to 10 feet, and reducing the wall line length to only 3 feet. With 111 college women participating, validity and reliability co-efficients obtained were .72 and .83, respectively. The better of two thirty-second trials is recorded for score.

Cunningham and Garrison claim that the test minimizes but does not eliminate the height factor in girl's volleyball and that the test promotes good footwork and judgment in playing oncoming balls. It is further indicated that the small target area emphasizes the importance of accurate volley placement, and that the test requires the subject to use a high volley which is used by the more highly skilled player in the single-hit game.

LIBA-STAUFF VOLLEYBALL PASS TEST[37]

Also cited as Liba and Stauff Volleyball Test.
Date: 1963.
Purpose: To measure the ability to execute a volleyball chest pass.

Description

In developing a test for the chest pass in volleyball, Liba and Stauff produced an instrument that has application for either sex from junior high through college. The adaptability feature was made possible through the investigators' study of desired pass trajectories for particular educational groups.

The resulting desired trajectory for college women was 15 feet for the vertical height and 20 feet for the horizontal distance. With this information, the velocity and direction of the projected ball was determined. Figure 78 depicts the desired trajectory when utilizing the above dimensions. Thus, to administer the test, ropes are located at heights of 13 and 11 feet and are placed 10½ feet from the restraining line. The top rope insures that adequate clearance is made. A 2 × 30-foot target is placed on the floor to determine the distance the ball travels. Each zone measures 2-foot square with the number eight zone the desired area for the subject to hit.

The desired vertical height determined for junior high girls was 13 feet, and the horizontal distance was marked at 15 feet. Placing the ropes at 12 and 10 feet from the floor with a restraining line of 6½ feet provides the proper dimensions for the junior high age level. The target for this group should be 2 × 28 feet with target area number seven the preferred landing site.

EDUCATIONAL APPLICATION: Suitable for both sexes from junior high through college.

Administrative Feasibility

TIME: The test is highly feasible in time of administration. Total test time depends upon the number of trials an instructor wishes to require.

PERSONNEL: One scorer.

TRAINING INVOLVED: Two practice trials immediately before testing for score and prior practice on the item to develop proper familiarity with the skill required.

EQUIPMENT AND SUPPLIES: Properly inflated volleyballs, two ropes at least 10 feet in length, and standards to hold them.

Accessories: Floor marking and scoring materials.

Facilities and Space: A facility with a smooth floor area at least 40 feet long and 10 feet wide with the ceiling height a minimum of 20 feet.

Directions

Beginning with a self-toss to initiate the pass, the subject attempts to clear the top rope with the ball and place it on the target zone of higher value. Passes interfered with by a rope are repeated. All passes should be performed from behind the restraining line, but no penalty is assessed for stepping over the line.

SCORING METHOD: Only legal volleyball hits count for score with three points assigned to balls clearing the top rope and two points given for those going between the two ropes. One point is given for a ball that goes under the low rope, and zero points are scored if the ball fails to reach the ropes. Balls landing within 5 or 6 feet of the target are given a distance score since a pass of that nature could easily be handled by a teammate.

In scoring the horizontal distance achieved on the passes, the particular zone where the ball hits is simply recorded. The passing

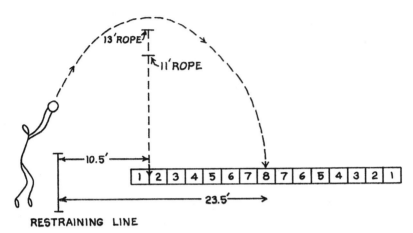

Figure 78. Floor markings for Liba-Stauff Volleyball Pass Test. From M. R. Liba and M. R. Stauff: A test for the volleyball pass, *Research Quarterly, 34:*56-63, 1963. Courtesy of AAHPER.

test score is the sum of the vertical height score multiplied by the horizontal distance score for each trial. For example, the maximum trial score for a college subject is twenty-four ($3 \times 8 = 24$).

Scientific Authenticity

VALIDITY: Face validity claimed since the test skill is required in volleyball performance.

RELIABILITY: Coefficients of .90 and .88 were obtained for two college groups; coefficients of .84 and .90 were derived from the scores of seventh and eighth grade students, respectively. The test's reliability was studied through the use of analysis of variance procedures.

Additional Comments

Although alleged to contain face validity, the extent to which it measures general volleyball playing ability has not been determined. Thus, the test's validity value should be substantiated. In selecting the number of test trials to administer, the tester should be aware that fifteen to twenty trials performed at one time reportedly yield satisfactory reliability.

The Liba-Stauff Test should serve well as one component of a comprehensive volleyball test battery.

BRUMBACH VOLLEYBALL SERVICE TEST[8]

Date: 1967.

Purpose: To measure the ability to serve the volleyball low and deep into the opponent's court.

Description

Either tall standards or regular ones with extensions are used to stretch a rope 4 feet above and parallel to the net. Floor markings are shown in Figure 79.

EDUCATIONAL APPLICATION: College men.

Administrative Feasibility

TIME: One sixty-minute period for twenty students when only one court is available.

PERSONNEL: The tester to score and students assisting where needed.

TRAINING INVOLVED: No practice trials are permitted on the day of testing, but prior practice to provide the student some experience at serving the ball between the top of the net and the rope 4 feet above is imperative.

EQUIPMENT AND SUPPLIES: Rope, tall standards, and some properly inflated volleyballs.

Accessories: Scoring and floor marking materials.

Facilities and Space: Regulation volleyball court.

Directions

Standing behind the rear boundary line, the subject tries to serve the ball between the top of the net and the rope so that it lands as close as possible to the rear boundary line of the opposite side. Six trials are administered on two separate occasions for a total of twelve. The ten most successful serves count for score.

SCORING METHOD: A serve that passes between the net and rope is given the score of higher value for the particular zone in which it lands. The lesser score is assigned to those going over the

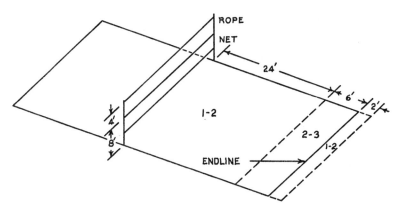

Figure 79. Brumbach Service Test floor plan.

rope. Balls hitting the rope are repeated, and those that hit the net or go out-of-bounds, except for the 2-foot extension zone at the end of the court, are given a zero score. A service in which a foot fault occurs is also scored zero. The total points accumulated in the ten best trials represent the final score, with thirty points the maximum.

Scientific Authenticity

Not reported.

Additional Comments

The Brumbach Service Test is especially fitting for the modern style of volleyball which emphasizes the strong, low serve. Obviously, the test demonstrates face validity, but the reliability estimate should be formulated to determine the number of serves actually needed to adequately reflect the type of serving skill required in the power game. Furthermore, allowing practice trials might permit a reduction in the number of test trials without sacrificing reliability.

Student assistants can be helpful to the tester in administering the Brumbach Test by retrieving balls, watching the flight of the serve to determine whether it goes over or under the rope, checking for foot faults, and recording the scores if desired by the tester.

PETRY VOLLEYBALL SERVE TEST[50]

Date: 1967.

Purpose: To measure ability in performing the underhand, sidearm, and overhand volleyball serves.

Description

On the opposite side of the court from the server, four lines which are parallel to the net are drawn across the court. From the net to the end line, the lines are located at 6-foot intervals. Another line is placed 6 feet from the end line along with sideline extensions to complete the construction of six scoring zones of equal size. A rope is stretched taut at 3 feet above the net.

EDUCATIONAL APPLICATION: Designed for high school girls but also appropriate for boys at that level.

Administrative Feasibility

TIME: Assuming only one court is available, two sixty-minute class periods would be necessary to test twenty students.

PERSONNEL: Instructor to serve as scorer with student assistants used for ball retrieving, checking of foot faults, observing ball flight to determine serve placement, and for recording scores as the tester confirms them.

TRAINING INVOLVED: Ample time should be given for the students to master the three basic serves utilized in the test. A practice trial on each should be permitted the student immediately prior to testing.

EQUIPMENT AND SUPPLIES: Rope, standards, and properly inflated volleyballs.

Accessories: Scoring and floor marking materials.

Facilities and Space: Regulation volleyball court.

Directions

Utilizing a rotational plan, the student completes ten underhand serves, then waits until each classmate finishes that portion of the test. The same procedure is followed for the remaining sidearm and overhand serve items. The objective for each serve is to pass between the net and rope, then land in the boundary zone bordering the end line.

SCORING METHOD: The rear boundary zone on the regulation court has a score value of ten with the adjacent extension zone and the next one in toward the net yielding eight points for each ball hitting in them. The three remaining zones are worth two, four, and six points in that order, starting with the zone nearest the net and moving toward the end line.

Balls passing between the rope and net receive the full value of the particular zone in which they land, and those going over the rope are scored at half value. An illegal serve, net ball, or foot fault leads to a trial score of zero. The sum of the thirty trials constitutes the final score.

Scientific Authenticity

VALIDITY: Discriminatory validity was established.

RELIABILITY: Coefficients of .64, .54, .78, and .82 were derived for the underhand serve, sidearm serve, overhand serve, and the thirty-trial total, respectively.

Additional Comments

The low reliability estimates for the underhand and sidearm serve items could possibly be elevated through an increase in the number of required trials. However, the time of administration criterion should not be overly compromised to achieve the increase in reliability. Moreover, the reliability estimate for the complete battery is acceptable.

CHAMBERLAIN FOREARM BOUNCE PASS TEST[10]

Date: 1969.

Purpose: To measure ability to perform the volleyball bounce pass.

EDUCATIONAL APPLICATION: College women.

Administrative Feasibility

TIME: Conducive to a multistation testing procedure, the test can be administered to twenty students at each station in sixty minutes.

Personnel: One scorer per station.

Training Involved: Little practice is needed on the day of testing since the test requires fourteen trials. However, students should be given the opportunity to become thoroughly familiar with the test requirement prior to the day of testing.

Equipment and Supplies: Three ropes the width of the court, standards to hold the ropes, and three volleyballs comprise the necessary equipment needs at each testing station.

Accessories: Scoring and floor marking materials.

Facilities and Space: Regulation size volleyball court.

Description and Directions

As depicted in Figure 80, a set-up person tosses the ball under-hand between the 5- and 7-foot high ropes to the test subject. The

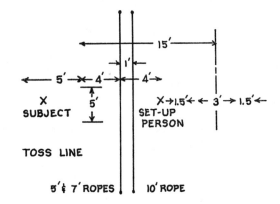

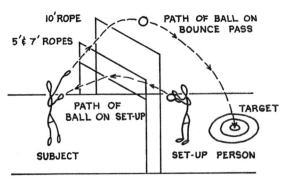

Figure 80. Top and side views of floor plan for Chamberlain Forearm Bounce Pass Test.

subject attempts to place a bounce pass over the 10-foot rope and into a floor target area with dimensions as shown in Figure 80. Subjects may move forward beyond the toss line to complete the bounce passes. Fourteen trials are performed. When the ball hits a rope, the trial is repeated.

SCORING METHOD: Two points are awarded for each ball that clears the 10-foot rope. A ball landing in one of the concentric circles of the target yields either four, three, or two points with the inner circle having the highest value. Balls striking one of the lines separating two circles are given the scores of higher value. No points are scored if a ball fails to go over the 10-foot rope. Six points is the maximum score per trial.

Scientific Authenticity

VALIDITY: Fisher's test of significance was used to determine the differences in performance of extreme ability groups. A significant 12.4 validity rating resulted, confirming that the test demonstrates discriminatory validity.

RELIABILITY: By use of the odd-even method, a reliability coefficient of .78 was obtained.

Additional Comments

A worthy contribution to volleyball skills testing resulted from the development of the Chamberlain Test since it is the lone forearm bounce pass test found in the literature. The test serves well as part of a comprehensive battery, but its scores should not be used to exclusively represent general volleyball playing ability.

To enhance the reliability of the test, the set-up performers should demonstrate an acceptable skill level in that particular aspect of the game of volleyball. Accurate and consistent tosses by the set-up person are vital to proper test administration.

AAHPER VOLLEYBALL SKILLS TEST[1]

Date: 1969.

Purpose: To measure general volleyball ability as indicated by performance in four fundamental skills.

Description

Volley: Closely resembling the Brady Wall Volley Test, the test layout includes a 5-foot horizontal line placed 11 feet above the floor, and vertical lines that extend 3 or 4 feet upward at the end of the horizontal line.

Serve, Pass, and Set-up: Figures 81, 82, and 83 portray the test setting for the respective test items.

EDUCATIONAL APPLICATION: Boys and girls in the ten to eighteen age group.

Administrative Feasibility

TIME: Time of administration depends upon the number of available volleyball courts; each item can be administered to twenty students in a sixty-minute class period.

PERSONNEL: A scorer for each test, a timer for the volley item, and student assistants wherever necessary. The instructor should probably act as thrower in the passing and set-up tests.

TRAINING INVOLVED: Plenty of practice should be permitted for each item with less emphasis on the serve since it is the only item that fully satisfies the criterion of face validity. Allowing practice items immediately prior to testing is prudent, but this approach makes the lengthy test even more time-consuming.

EQUIPMENT AND SUPPLIES: Plenty of properly inflated volleyballs, ropes with standards for the passing and set-up items.

Accessories: Scoring materials, wall and floor marking materials.

Facilities and Space: Regulation volleyball court.

Directions

VOLLEY: In sixty seconds, the subject performs as many legal

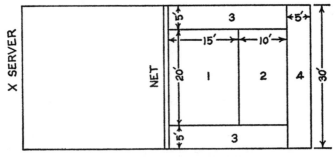

Figure 81. Specifications for serve test. From AAHPER: *Skills Test Manual: Volleyball for Boys and Girls,* C. T. Shay, test consultant, 1969. Courtesy of AAHPER, Washington, D. C.

volleys as possible. The test begins with the subject tossing the ball into the target area, then starting the continuous volleys. On a missed or caught ball, the subject again tosses the ball against the wall and volleys for the remaining amount of time. Incidentally, the test is identical to the Kronqvist-Brumbach modification of the Brady Test.

SERVE: Ten trials are completed by the subject. For children under twelve years of age, the serving line is located at 20 feet as opposed to 30.

PASS: The subject passes a ball tossed by the tester (T) over an 8-foot high rope into the 4 × 6-foot area (Fig. 82). Twenty trials are performed alternately to the right and left target area.

SET-UP: Receiving a high toss from the tester (T), the subject executes a set-up in such a manner that enables the ball to clear a rope suspended 10 feet above the floor and land in the 4 × 6-

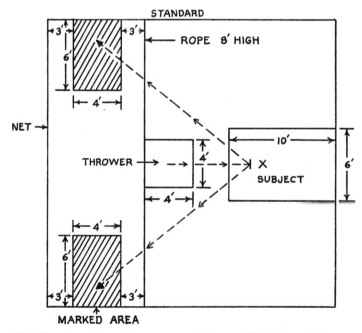

Figure 82. Court markings for pass test. From AAHPER: *Skills Test Manual: Volleyball for Boys and Girls,* C. T. Shay, test consultant, 1969. Courtesy of AAHPER, Washington, D. C.

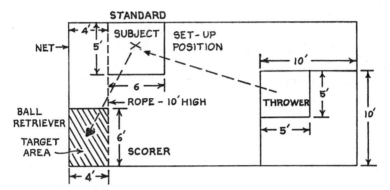

Figure 83. Court markings for set-up test. From AAHPER: *Skills Test Manual: Volleyball for Boys and Girls,* C. T. Shay, test consultant, AAHPER, 1969. Courtesy of AAHPER, Washington, D. C.

foot target area. Twenty trials are completed, ten to the right and ten to the left.

SCORING METHOD AND NORMS

Volley: The number of legal volleys completed in one minute. Scores over fifty are not recorded.

Serving: Total points made in performing the ten trials as determined by the value of the zones in which balls land.

Passing: One point is awarded for each ball that lands in the target area. With twenty trials required, a perfect score is twenty. A ball hitting the rope or net or one which falls outside the target area counts as a trial completed with no points awarded.

Set-up: As in the passing item, one point is given for each successful set-up, yielding a maximum score of twenty points. Balls touching the net or rope, plus those hitting outside the target area, receive a zero score for those trials. Inaccurate throws by the tester are repeated.

Scientific Authenticity

VALIDITY: Face validity implied.
RELIABILITY: Not reported.

Additional Comments

Some of the criticisms directed toward the AAHPER Volleyball Skills Test are obvious ones. Much floor and wall marking is

Tables CXX through CXXVII are percentile scores for AAHPER Volleyball Test, based on scores of over 600 students of each sex and age group (10 to 18). From AAHPER: *Skills Test Manual: Volleyball for Boys and Girls,* 1969, C. T. Shay, test consultant. Courtesy of AAHPER, Washington, D.C.

TABLE CXX

VOLLEYING TEST (BOYS)
Test Scores in Points

Percentile	10-11	12	13	Age 14	15	16	17-18	Percentile
100th	40	42	44	50	50	50	50	100th
95th	24	31	35	39	42	44	45	95th
90th	19	28	30	36	40	41	42	90th
85th	17	24	28	33	36	38	42	85th
80th	15	22	26	31	34	36	41	80th
75th	13	19	24	29	32	34	40	75th
70th	12	18	22	27	30	33	39	70th
65th	11	17	21	26	29	32	37	65th
60th	9	16	19	24	28	30	36	60th
55th	8	15	18	23	27	28	34	55th
50th	7	13	17	21	25	26	32	50th
45th	6	12	15	19	24	25	29	45th
40th	5	11	14	18	22	23	27	40th
35th	4	9	12	17	20	21	24	35th
30th	3	8	11	15	18	19	23	30th
25th	3	7	9	13	17	18	20	25th
20th	2	6	8	11	15	16	19	20th
15th	1	4	7	9	13	15	17	15th
10th	0	3	5	7	10	12	14	10th
5th	0	2	3	5	6	11	11	5th
0	0	0	0	0	0	0	0	0

TABLE CXXI

VOLLEYING TEST (GIRLS)
Test Scores in Points

Percentile	10-11	12	13	14	15	16	17-18	Percentile
100th	47	49	49	50	50	50	50	100th
95th	21	29	31	32	37	40	40	95th
90th	13	24	25	26	31	36	38	90th
85th	10	19	20	21	24	28	31	85th
80th	8	16	17	19	21	25	27	80th
75th	6	13	15	17	18	22	23	75th
70th	5	11	13	14	16	20	20	70th
65th	4	10	11	13	15	18	18	65th
60th	3	8	10	12	13	16	16	60th
55th	3	7	9	11	12	14	14	55th
50th	2	6	8	10	11	12	12	50th
45th	2	5	7	9	10	11	11	45th
40th	1	4	6	8	9	9	9	40th
35th	1	3	5	7	8	8	8	35th
30th	1	2	4	6	7	7	7	30th
25th	0	2	3	5	6	6	6	25th
20th	0	1	1	4	5	5	5	20th
15th	0	1	1	3	4	4	4	15th
10th	0	0	0	1	2	3	3	10th
5th	0	0	0	0	1	2	2	5th
0	0	0	0	0	0	0	0	0

TABLE CXXII

SERVING TEST (BOYS)
Test Scores in Points

				Age				
Percentile	10-11	12	13	14	15	16	17-18	Percentile
100th	39	40	40	40	40	40	40	100th
95th	29	31	32	34	36	37	37	95th
90th	27	28	29	31	33	33	33	90th
85th	25	26	27	29	32	32	32	85th
80th	23	24	26	27	30	30	31	80th
75th	22	23	24	25	28	29	30	75th
70th	21	21	23	24	28	29	30	70th
65th	20	20	22	23	27	28	29	65th
60th	18	19	21	22	25	27	27	60th
55th	17	18	20	21	24	25	26	55th
50th	16	16	19	20	22	23	24	50th
45th	15	15	18	19	21	22	22	45th
40th	14	14	17	18	20	21	21	40th
35th	13	13	16	17	19	19	20	35th
30th	12	12	15	16	18	19	19	30th
25th	11	11	13	15	16	17	17	25th
20th	9	10	12	14	15	15	16	20th
15th	8	9	10	12	12	13	14	15th
10th	7	8	8	10	11	12	12	10th
5th	4	5	5	8	9	10	11	5th
0	0	3	3	5	6	6	7	0

TABLE CXXIII

SERVING TEST (GIRLS)
Test Scores in Points

Percentile	10-11	12	13	Age 14	15	16	17-18	Percentile
100th	36	38	40	40	40	40	40	100th
95th	24	26	26	28	30	31	32	95th
90th	20	22	23	26	26	26	26	90th
85th	18	20	20	23	23	24	24	85th
80th	16	18	18	21	21	22	23	80th
75th	15	16	17	20	20	21	21	75th
70th	14	15	15	18	19	20	20	70th
65th	13	14	14	17	17	19	19	65th
60th	12	13	13	15	16	18	18	60th
55th	11	12	12	14	15	17	17	55th
50th	10	11	11	13	14	16	16	50th
45th	9	10	10	11	13	15	15	45th
40th	8	9	9	10	12	14	14	40th
35th	7	8	8	9	11	13	14	35th
30th	6	6	7	8	10	13	13	30th
25th	5	5	5	7	9	11	11	25th
20th	4	4	4	6	8	10	10	20th
15th	2	3	3	5	6	8	9	15th
10th	1	1	1	3	4	7	7	10th
5th	0	0	0	1	2	4	4	5th
0	0	0	0	0	0	0	0	0

TABLE CXXIV

PASSING TEST (BOYS)
Test Scores in Points

Percentile	Age							Percentile
	10-11	12	13	14	15	16	17-18	
100th	19	19	19	20	20	20	20	100th
95th	12	14	16	17	17	17	17	95th
90th	10	13	14	16	16	16	16	90th
85th	9	12	13	15	15	15	15	85th
80th	8	11	12	14	14	14	14	80th
75th	7	10	12	13	13	13	13	75th
70th	6	9	11	12	12	12	13	70th
65th	5	8	10	12	12	12	13	65th
60th	4	8	9	11	11	12	12	60th
55th	4	7	9	10	10	12	12	55th
50th	3	6	8	10	10	11	11	50th
45th	3	5	7	9	9	10	10	45th
40th	2	4	7	8	8	9	9	40th
35th	2	4	6	8	8	9	9	35th
30th	1	3	5	7	7	8	8	30th
25th	1	2	4	6	6	7	8	25th
20th	0	2	4	5	5	6	7	20th
15th	0	1	3	4	4	5	6	15th
10th	0	0	2	3	3	4	4	10th
5th	0	0	1	2	2	2	2	5th
0	0	0	0	0	0	0	0	0

TABLE CXXV

PASSING TEST (GIRLS)
Test Scores in Points

Percentile	10-11	12	13	14	15	16	17-18	Percentile
100th	19	19	20	20	20	20	20	100th
95th	10	12	12	13	13	14	15	95th
90th	8	10	10	11	11	12	13	90th
85th	7	8	9	10	10	11	12	85th
80th	6	7	8	9	9	10	11	80th
75th	5	6	7	8	8	8	9	75th
70th	4	6	6	7	7	8	9	70th
65th	3	5	5	6	6	8	8	65th
60th	3	4	4	6	6	7	8	60th
55th	2	4	4	5	5	6	7	55th
50th	2	3	4	5	5	6	6	50th
45th	1	3	3	4	4	5	6	45th
40th	1	2	3	4	4	4	5	40th
35th	0	2	2	3	3	4	4	35th
30th	0	1	2	3	3	3	4	30th
25th	0	1	1	2	2	3	3	25th
20th	0	0	1	1	2	2	3	20th
15th	0	0	0	1	1	2	2	15th
10th	0	0	0	0	1	1	1	10th
5th	0	0	0	0	0	0	0	5th
0	0	0	0	0	0	0	0	0

TABLE CXXVI

SET-UP TEST (BOYS)
Test Scores in Points

Percentile	10-11	12	13	Age 14	15	16	17-18	Percentile
100th	16	18	20	20	20	20	20	100th
95th	10	14	16	16	16	17	17	95th
90th	9	12	14	15	15	15	15	90th
85th	8	11	13	13	13	14	15	85th
80th	7	10	12	12	12	13	14	80th
75th	6	9	11	11	11	12	13	75th
70th	6	8	10	10	10	10	11	70th
65th	5	8	9	9	9	9	11	65th
60th	5	7	8	8	8	9	10	60th
55th	4	7	7	8	8	8	10	55th
50th	4	6	7	7	7	7	9	50th
45th	3	6	6	6	6	6	9	45th
40th	3	5	6	6	6	6	8	40th
35th	3	5	5	5	5	5	7	35th
30th	2	4	4	5	5	5	7	30th
25th	2	4	4	4	4	4	6	25th
20th	2	3	3	4	4	4	6	20th
15th	1	3	3	3	3	3	5	15th
10th	0	1	1	2	2	2	2	10th
5th	0	1	1	1	1	1	2	5th
0	0	0	0	0	0	0	1	0

TABLE CXXVII

SET-UP TEST (GIRLS)
Test Scores in Points

Percentile	10-11	12	13	14	15	16	17-18	Percentile
100th	19	20	20	20	20	20	20	100th
95th	11	13	14	14	14	15	15	95th
90th	9	11	11	12	12	12	14	90th
85th	7	9	10	10	11	11	12	85th
80th	6	8	9	10	10	10	11	80th
75th	5	7	8	9	9	9	10	75th
70th	5	6	7	8	8	8	8	70th
65th	4	6	7	7	7	7	7	65th
60th	4	5	6	6	6	7	7	60th
55th	3	5	5	6	6	6	6	55th
50th	3	4	5	5	5	6	6	50th
45th	2	4	4	4	4	5	5	45th
40th	2	3	4	4	4	5	5	40th
35th	2	3	3	3	3	4	4	35th
30th	1	2	3	3	3	3	4	30th
25th	1	2	2	2	2	3	3	25th
20th	1	2	2	2	2	2	3	20th
15th	0	1	1	1	1	2	2	15th
10th	0	0	1	1	1	1	1	10th
5th	0	0	0	0	0	1	1	5th
0	0	0	0	0	0	0	0	0

necessary, and administration of the complete battery can be rather time-consuming. More importantly, the widely publicized test naturally is given strong consideration by the potential user, yet the test has not been scientifically documented to support its alleged value.

One of the significant areas of scientific authenticity, of course, is reliability. The reliability value of two items, the passing and set-up tests, are suspect since a consistent performance by the tester or thrower is vital to the test's successful administration.

REFERENCES

1. American Association for Health, Physical Education and Recreation: *Skills Test Manual: Volleyball for Boys and Girls.* Shay, Clayton T. (Test Consultant). Washington, AAHPER, 1969.
2. Barrow, Harold M. and McGee, Rosemary: *A Practical Approach to Measurement in Physical Education.* Philadelphia, Lea & Febiger, 1964.
3. ——— and ———: *A Practical Approach to Measurement in Physical Education,* 2nd ed. Philadelphia, Lea & Febiger, 1971.
4. Bassett, Gladys; Glassow, Ruth B.; and Locke, Mabel: Studies in testing volleyball skills. *Research Quarterly, 8:*60-72, 1937.
5. Blackman, Claudia J.: The Development of a Volleyball Test for the Spike. Master's thesis, Carbondale, Southern Illinois University, 1968.
6. Brady, George F.: Preliminary investigations of volleyball playing ability. *Research Quarterly, 16:*14-17, 1945.
7. Broer, Marion R.: Reliability of certain skill tests for junior high school girls. *Research Quarterly, 29:*139-145, 1958.
8. Brumbach, Wayne B.: *Beginning Volleyball, A Syllabus for Teachers,* revised ed. Eugene, Oregon, the author, 1967.
9. Camp, Billie Ann: The Reliability and Validity of a Single-Hit Repeated Volleys Test in Volleyball and the Relationship of Height to Performance on the Test. Master's thesis, Boulder, University of Colorado, 1963.
10. Chamberlain, Diane: Determination of Validity and Reliability of a Skill Test for the Bounce Pass in Volleyball. Master's thesis, Provo, Utah, Brigham Young University, 1969.
11. Chaney, Dawn S.: The Development of a Test of Volleyball Ability for College Women. Master's thesis, Denton, Texas Woman's University, 1967.
12. Chun, Donna M.: Construction of an Overhead Volley-Pass Test for

College Women. Master's thesis, Pullman, Washington State University, 1969.

13. Clarke, H. Harrison: *Application of Measurement to Health and Physical Education*. 4th ed. Englewood Cliffs, P-H, 1967.

14. ———: *Application of Measurement to Health and Physical Education*. 5th ed. Englewood Cliffs, P-H, 1976.

15. Clifton, Marquerite A.: Single hit volley test for women's volleyball. *Research Quarterly, 33:*208-211, 1962.

16. Cozens, Frederick W. et al.: *Achievement Scales in Physical Education Activities for Secondary School Girls and College Women*. New York, B&N, 1937.

17. Crogan, Corrinne: A simple volleyball classification test for high school girls. *Physical Educator, 4:*34-37, 1943.

18. Cummisky, Joseph K.: The Effects of Motivation and Verbal Reinforcement upon Performance and Complex Perceptual-Motor Tasks. Doctoral dissertation, Palo Alto, Calif., Stanford University, 1962.

19. Cunningham, Phyllis and Garrison, Joan: High wall volley test for women's volleyball. *Research Quarterly, 39:*480-490, 1968.

20. French, Esther and Cooper, Bernice I.: Achievement tests in volleyball for high school girls. *Research Quarterly, 8:*150-157, 1937.

21. Glassow, Ruth B. and Broer, Marion R.: *Measuring Achievement in Physical Education*. Philadelphia, Saunders, 1938.

22. Hartley, Grace: Motivating the physical education program for high school girls. *American Physical Education Review, 34:*284, 1929.

23. Haskins, Mary Jane: *Evaluation in Physical Education*. Dubuque, Iowa, Brown BK, 1971.

24. Helmen, R. M.: Development of Power Volleyball Skill Tests for College Women. Read before the Research Section at the Annual Convention of the American Association for Health, Physical Education and Recreation, Detroit, 1971.

25. Hupprich, Florence L.: Volleyball practice tests. *Spalding Athletic Handbook for Women (1929-30)*. New York, Am Sports, 1929.

26. Jackson, Patricia: A Rating Scale for Discriminating Relative Performance of Skilled Female Volleyball Players. Master's thesis, Edmonton, University of Alberta, 1967.

27. Johnson, Judith A.: The Development of a Volleyball Skill Test for High School Girls. Master's thesis, Normal, Illinois State University, 1967.

28. Johnson, Barry L. and Nelson, Jack K.: *Practical Measurements for Evaluation in Physical Education*, Minneapolis, Burgess, 1969.

29. ———: *Practical Measurements for Evaluation in Physical Education*, 2nd ed. Minneapolis, Burgess, 1974.

30. Jones, Richard N.: The Development of a Volleyball Skills Test for Adult Males. Master's thesis, Springfield, Mass., Springfield College, 1964.

31. Kessler, Adrian A.: The Validity and Reliability of the Sandefur Volleyball Spiking Test. Master's thesis, Long Beach, California State College, 1968.

32. Kronqvist, Robert A. and Brumbach, Wayne B.: A modification of the Brady volleyball skill test for high school boys. *Research Quarterly, 39:*116-120, 1968.

33. Ladner, Jane: Volleyball Wall Volley Skill Test. Paper read at the Annual AAHPER/Southern District Convention, Biloxi, Mississippi, 1954.

34. Lamp, Nancy A.: Volleyball skills for junior high school students as a function of physical size and maturity. *Research Quarterly, 25:* 189-197, 1954.

35. Latchaw, M.: Measuring selected motor skills in fourth, fifth and sixth grades. *Research Quarterly, 25:*439-449, 1954.

36. Laveaga, Robert C.: *Volleyball,* 2nd ed. New York, Ronald, 1960.

37. Liba, Marie R. and Stauff, Marilyn R.: A test for the volleyball pass. *Research Quarterly, 34:*56-63, 1963.

38. Locke, Mabel: A Survey of Volleyball Skills Tests and Studies on the Reliability and Validity of a Proposed Test. Master's thesis, Madison, University of Wisconsin, 1936.

39. Londeree, B. R. and Eicholtz, E. C.: Reliabilities of Selected Volleyball Skill Tests. Paper read before the Research Section at the Annual Convention of the American Association for Health, Physical Education and Recreation, Seattle, 1970.

40. Lopez, Delfina: Serve test. *DGWS Volleyball Guide (1957-59).* Washington, AAHPER, 1957.

41. Mathews, Donald K.: *Measurement in Physical Education,* 3rd ed. Philadelphia, Saunders, 1968.

42. McCloy, Charles Harold and Young, Norma Dorothy: *Tests and Measurements in Health and Physical Education,* 3rd ed. New York, Appleton, 1954.

43. Meyers, Carlton R. and Blesh, T. Erwin: *Measurement in Physical Education.* New York, Ronald, 1962.

44. Meyers, Carlton R.: *Measurement in Physical Education,* 2nd ed. New York, Ronald, 1974.

45. Michalski, Rosalie A.: Construction of an Objective Skill Test for the Underhand Volleyball Serve. Master's thesis, Iowa City, University of Iowa, 1963.

46. Mohr, Dorothy R. and Haverstick, Martha V.: Repeated volleys test for women's volleyball. *Research Quarterly, 26:*179-184, 1955.

47. Montoye, Henry J. (Ed.): *An Introduction to Measurement in Physical Education,* vol. III. Indianapolis, Phi Epsilon Kappa Fraternity, 1970.

48. Morris, Harold H.: A Critique of the AAHPER Skill Test Series. Paper read before the Measurement and Evaluation Council at the An-

nual Convention of the American Alliance for Health, Physical Education and Recreation, Seattle, March 25, 1977.

49. Neilson, N. P. and Jensen, Clayne R.: *Measurement and Statistics in Physical Education.* Belmont, Calif., Wadsworth Pub, 1972.

50. Petry, Kathryn: Evaluation of a Volleyball Serve Test. Master's thesis, Los Angeles, Los Angeles State College, 1967.

51. Reynolds, Herbert J.: Volleyball tests. *Journal of Health and Physical Education, 42:*44, 1930.

52. Russell, Naomi and Lange, Elizabeth: Achievement tests in volleyball for junior high school girls. *Research Quarterly, 11:*33-41, 1940.

53. Ryan, Mary F.: A Study of Tests for the Volleyball Serve. Master's thesis, Madison, University of Wisconsin, 1969.

54. Safrit, Margaret J.: *Evaluation in Physical Education.* Englewood Cliffs, P-H, 1973.

55. Scott, M. Gladys and French, Esther: *Better Teaching Through Testing.* New York, B&N, 1945.

56. ———— and ————: *Measurement and Evaluation in Physical Education.* Dubuque, Iowa, Brown BK, 1959.

57. Shavely, Marie: Volleyball skill tests for girls. *DGWS Selected Volleyball Articles.* Washington, AAHPER, 1960.

58. Shaw, John H.: A Preliminary Investigation of a Volleyball Skill Test. Master's thesis, Knoxville, University of Tennessee, 1967.

59. Slaymaker, T. and Brown, V. H.: *Test Questions for Power Volleyball.* Philadelphia, Saunders, 1969.

60. Sports survey shows increases in participants. *The First Aider, 46:*1, 11, 1977.

61. Suttinger, Joan: A Proposal Predictive Index of Volleyball Playing Ability for College Women. Unpublished study, Berkeley, University of California, 1957.

62. Thomas, Jesselene: Skill tests. *Official Softball-Volleyball Guide.* New York, B&N, 1943.

63. Thorpe, Jo Anne and West, Charlotte: A volleyball skills chart with attainment levels for selected skills. *DGWS Volleyball Guide (1967-69).* Washington, AAHPER, 1967.

64. Watkins, A.: Skill testing for large groups. *DGWS Selected Volleyball Articles.* Washington, AAHPER, 1960.

65. Weiss, Raymond A. and Phillips, Marjorie: *Administration of Tests in Physical Education.* St. Louis, Mosby, 1954.

66. West, Charlotte: A Comparative Study Between Height and Wall Volley Test Scores as Related to Volleyball Playing Ability of Girls and Women. Master's thesis, Greensboro, University of North Carolina, 1957.

67. Willgoose, Carl E.: *Evaluation in Health Education and Physical Education.* New York, McGraw, 1961.

Chapter 29

Wrestling

V ERY LITTLE IS REPORTED in the literature about measurement of wrestling ability. This is chiefly due to the limited interest shown in course development for this activity as opposed to some of the more traditional physical education offerings. An illustration of the limited interest shown is the dearth of physical educators trained to teach wrestling. Methods courses are not common in this area. Consequently, the vast majority of activity courses in wrestling are found at the college level where the volume of physical education instructors assures some expertise in wrestling instruction. The resulting void is mostly found at the public school level.

The fact that the sport has been traditionally limited to one sex also has an effect on the amount of work done in the measurement of wrestling ability. The immense social change taking place in sports today does not include any significant interest in wrestling on the part of girls, so the activity is due to remain in the foreseeable future a male's sport.

If interest should increase among physical educators in regard to the expansion of instruction in wrestling at one or all educational levels, the development of objective instruments for measuring wrestling ability should be commensurate to the growth of course offerings. Growth of popularity in the sport would provide a lucrative opportunity for the physical educator interested in wrestling and scientific measurement of performance in the sport.

The few tests developed for measuring wrestling ability do not fully satisfy the major criteria for scientifically constructed tests. The physical educator who plans to develop a skills test in wrestling would be wise to study and use these tests as bases for further exploration. The bibliography below cites the references for the aforementioned forerunner tests in wrestling.

REFERENCES

1. Barrow, Harold M. and McGee, Rosemary: *A Practical Approach to*

Measurement in Physical Education, 2nd ed. Philadelphia, Lea & Febiger, 1971.

2. McCloy, Charles Harold and Young, Norma Dorothy: *Tests and Measurements in Health and Physical Education,* 3rd ed. New York, Appleton, 1954.

3. Sickels, W. L.: A Rating Test of Amateur Wrestling Ability. Master's thesis, San Jose, Calif., San Jose State College, 1967.

4. Sievers, Harry L.: The Measurement of Potential Wrestling Ability. Master's thesis, Iowa City, State University of Iowa, 1934.

5. Yetter, Henry: A Test of Wrestling Aptitude: A Preliminary Exploration. Master's thesis, Madison, University of Wisconsin, 1963.